Victor Walker, born in Lincoln in 1930, has worked as a journalist in Greece for more than thirty years. He is the Athens correspondent of *The Journal of Commerce* (New York), an editor in the English-language department of the Athens News Agency, and a contributor to specialist publications dealing mainly with the economy, shipping, tourism and industrial relations.

Other Harper Independent Traveller guidebooks include:

Mainland Greece
Spain
Portugal
Turkey
Soviet Union
South-west France
Southern Italy

The Harper INDEPENDENT TRAVELLER

GREEK ISLANDS

VICTOR WALKER

Series Editor Robin Dewhurst

PERENNIAL LIBRARY

Harper & Row, Publishers, New York
Grand Rapids, Philadelphia, St. Louis, San Francisco
London, Singapore, Sydney, Tokyo, Toronto

Note
While every effort has been made to ensure that prices, hotel and restaurant recommendations, opening hours and similar factual information in this book are accurate at the time of going to press, the Publishers cannot be held responsible for any changes found by readers using this guide.

Much of the history and introductory information about Greece Today in this book is taken from that in The Harper Independent Traveller: Mainland Greece by the same author.

This work is published in Great Britain by William Collins Sons & Company Ltd.

THE HARPER INDEPENDENT TRAVELLER: GREEK ISLANDS. Copyright © 1989 by Victor Walker. All rights reserved. Printed in the United States of America. No part of this book may be used or reproduced in any manner whatsoever without written permission except in the case of brief quotations embodied in critical articles and reviews. For information address Harper & Row, Publishers, Inc., 10 East 53rd Street, New York, NY 10022.

First PERENNIAL LIBRARY edition published 1990

Series Commissioning Editor: Louise Haines
Maps by Maltings Partnership

Library of Congress Cataloging-in-Publication Data
Walker, Victor.
    Greek islands / Victor Walker.
      p.   cm. — (The Harper independent traveller)
    Includes bibliographical references.
    ISBN 0-06-273184-X
    1. Aegean Islands (Greece and Turkey)—Description and travel—1981–   —Guide-books. I. Title. II. Series.
DF895.W35 1990
914.9504′76′09142—dc20   89-45728

92 93 94 95 MB 10 9 8 7 6 5 4 3 2 1

Contents

Introduction	7
The Land and the People	11
History	15
The Greeks and the Sea	27
Greece Today	42
The Weather and When to Go	81
Travelling Around	84
Where to Stay	95
Eating and Drinking	103
Entertainment	116
Shopping	120
General Basics	123

GAZETTEER

Introduction	134
The Resort Islands: Corfu, Rhodes and Crete	136
The Cyclades Islands	178
The Dodecanese Islands	234
The East Aegean Islands	266
Euboia	292
The Ionian Islands	296
The North Aegean Islands	316
The North Sporades Islands	322
The Saronic Islands	337
Useful Reading	345
Index	346

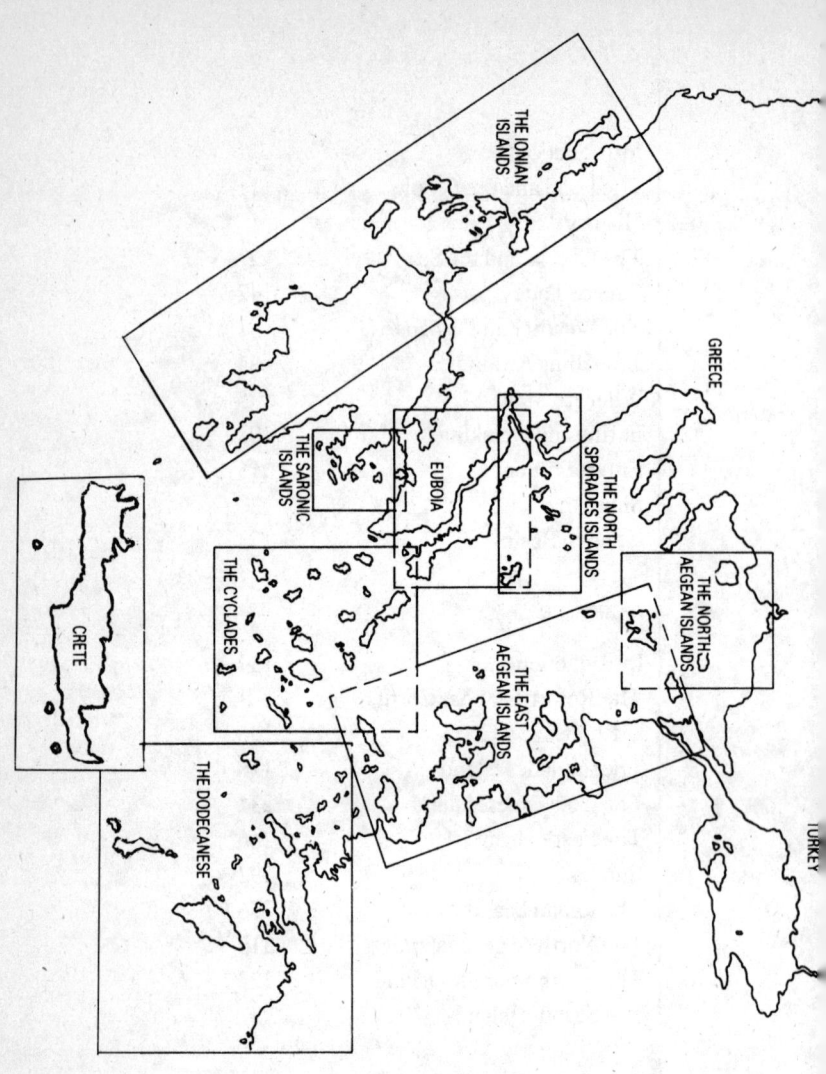

Introduction

You cannot live for more than a few years in Athens without acquiring Greek friends who look at you pityingly, or in wonder, and ask how you can stand 'it': the heat, dust, pollution, traffic and household noises, the myriad insufficiencies of a capital that was never planned but simply happened, and the outmoded pressures that derive from lack of foresight – still and always the real national failing.

A stock response that you like to be 'a long way from head office' will meet with understanding even if recognised as evasive, but will scarcely answer the two questions that the Greeks, for all their renowned curiosity, would not venture to pose in so many words: are you an exile by choice or of necessity and, by extension, could you go back to where you came from if you wanted to?

After a time, you conclude that there is no real purpose in trying to explain that what makes the Greek cities endurable is the existence of the Greek islands, no matter how infrequently you may have the opportunity to slip away nor how often an intended escape may have to be postponed. For the Greeks have a different view of their islands; they neither know them intimately nor, outside the geopolitical context of an assumed Turkish threat, hold them in anything like the same high regard as those who came to them after experience of industrialised Europe and, in particular, of the British climate.

With the exception of Athens and Thessaloniki, Greece has no heavily industrialised cities. To the extent that a slum can be conceived at all, it is likely to be envisaged in terms of a village without paved roads or flush toilets. On an island, this becomes a village made more remote, and therefore more neglected, by the intervening water. You have only to take a bus to Lefkimi, close to the southern tip of Corfu, if you wish to understand why, for a third of the three and a quarter million inhabitants of Athens and as large a proportion of those who make up the Greek communities abroad, islands are places from which they or their parents were spurred to escape by youthful ambition and a determination that primitive and squalid poverty should not extend into another generation. In the last two decades, and in particular since Greece's 1981 accession to the European Community, there has been a levelling-out in standards of living as between cities and countryside and mainland and islands, but this has not yet had time to affect traditional attitudes. There is still a world of difference between the ways in which a Greek and a tourist view, experience and remember a Greek island.

For this reason, it is the leisured foreign businessman, the pastured diplomat and the retired executive who is likely to have a holiday home on an island, with some kind of boat trestled in the garage. The moneyed Greek's dream of gentility embraces a villa in the hills outside Athens, a couple of cars and the means and leisure to holiday abroad at least twice a year; to retire to an island would be somehow to remove himself from the 'centre', to abandon entrenchments occupied and consolidated during a lifetime of toil, craft or intrigue. No matter how understandable this concept may be from a Greek standpoint, it can only seem the damnedest thing to those who first encountered an island with money in their pockets and relaxation as their only goal, and to whom island life is associated with comfortable accommodation in a setting of incomparable beauty made up of sights and sounds in exquisite harmony: curving beaches and misty green hills, crickets applauding in pale grey olive groves, the distant throb of a caique engine in the silent dawn, and the rippling colours that flit across a chameleon sea – soft light, soft times and totally unhellenic soft bargains.

In these circumstances, it should not seem altogether strange that the islands in their majority, despite their loveliness and their accessibility, still comprise the little known and little visited part of Greece.

Little known? Little visited? When at least half of the 8 million tourists who arrive in Greece every year spend at least a few days on an island? Quite so! But on which of the islands?

On the authority of the National Statistics Service, Greece is a country with 169 inhabited islands. For the purposes of package tourism, there are between a dozen and eighteen. For the independent traveller, there are at least sixty on which the basic essentials of rented accommodation and cooked food can be obtained. But with a small boat, a tent, a frying pan and no fear of loneliness, your choice theoretically lies among as many as 2,000, often smaller than a football field, where it is easy to believe that only the occasional pirate, shipwrecked mariner or hydrographic surveyor can have been before you through all the millennia.

However, at some point it is necessary to become practical. You are unlikely – as yet – to envisage a Greek island as your final resting-place; rather, you are wondering where to spend a week or ten days. The type of island you choose will inevitably influence, but need not wholly determine, the pattern of your holiday.

The resort islands . . .

Corfu, Rhodes and Crete are Greece's three fully-developed resort islands, the easiest to reach by direct charter flight from almost any European country, and the ones for which the most and usually the cheapest package tours are available. They are by no means to be disdained as an introduction to Greece.

When you have arrived, the pattern into which you will be tempted to fall is a simple and undemanding one: days beneath an umbrella by the sea, varied by excursions to the main towns, archaeological sites, beauty spots and offshore islands; one meal in your hotel because it's included in the package, and the other on the beach in the afternoon or a nearby restaurant at night.

You will find your 'full English breakfast' if you want it in Greek temperatures, no licensing hours to regulate your consumption of alcohol, not much of a language barrier and the opportunity to converse in English with the Greeks who attend to your needs. Cars are available for hire, though the moped business tends to be brisker. On Corfu and Rhodes, and probably on Crete too by 1989, you can enjoy a flutter in a casino provided that both your wardrobe and your wallet are sufficient. You will not feel extended or challenged in any way, and need make no provision for the unexpected.

Though you will probably have travelled to the island as members of a group, nothing prevents you from getting away by yourselves if you wish; either way, you will scarcely feel that you are thrust upon your own devices.

. . . And the rest

The in-between islands, not yet full resorts but obvious contenders, include Zakynthos (Zante) among the Ionians, Kos and Patmos in the Dodecanese, Thera (Santorini), Myconos and Ios in the Cyclades, Skiathos in the North Sporades and, not yet so familiar to the non-Greek holiday-maker, Chios, Samos and Lesbos in the East Aegean.

You can spend a week on these islands, or allow them a couple of days. You will feel a little closer to nature and to Greece as it used to be, without deprivation of creature comforts. You will need to be just a little more adventurous if you are to make the most of them.

The unbeaten tracks lead in two general directions:
- To the workaday islands, which welcome but in no way rely on tourism. These include Euboia off the east coast of mainland Greece, Naxos, Syros, Paros, Milos, Tinos and Andros in the Cyclades, Kalymnos in the Dodecanese, Cephalonia and Lefkas in the Ionians,

Skopelos and Skyros in the North Sporades, and Thassos and Lemnos in the North and East Aegean. You will find the people observably engaged in pursuits that have no relation to your needs, and will certainly be less protected by numbers from exposure to the everyday, non-holiday world.

● And to those islands, some of them quite populous but most of them tiny, that lie at the end of tedious journeys and that offer an assurance of astonishment and delight provided only that your requirements are modest and your pleasures simple. For example, Anafi, Sikinos and Folegandros in the Cyclades, Astipalaia, Simi and Kastellorizon in the Dodecanese, the Oinousses islands in the East Aegean, or Paxi in the Ionians. On these, you will begin to appreciate the infinite variety of the Greek islands; you will become aware that, no matter how often you have been to Greece, and how widely you have travelled, there is always something new to return for, some revelation waiting to be experienced.

Greek islands are lovely in their variety, and above all for their pastel colours and incomparable light – the two attributes the Greek misses most and longest when forced by circumstances to leave his homeland.

They are not places in which you will ever feel threatened by excessive unfamiliarity; to the contrary, you will feel at home, among likable people.

At the same time, Greece is the easiest of all archipelago countries to reach, and far and away the cheapest for a simple holiday.

The rosebuds are still there for the gathering ...

The Land and the People

The National Tourist Organisation of Greece (NTOG, or EOT in Greek), likes to proclaim in its international advertising that 'there is no place like Greece'. Perhaps! But the explanation lies in the people, not the geography. It is possible, of course, to visit the Greek islands for the sea and sunshine and to divide an enjoyable holiday between the public rooms of a hotel and its stretch of private beach. But even then, only the practising misanthropist will fail to establish a personal relationship with the Greeks who cater to his needs.

This is as true today, when the visitor is one among eight million, as it was a quarter of a century ago when he was one among eighty thousand. The Greeks are a perverse people: they seem unable to appreciate that the tourist is no more than a single strand in a golden fleece, insist on regarding him as an individual, and retain the curiosity that has always been their most engaging characteristic. For the visitor, this implies an obligation to respond.

The discovery waiting to be made is that obstacles to communication exist only in the mind; that there is a world to explore, requiring only a readiness to converse. And this readiness is not a matter of language, but of attitude. The Greeks are not chauvinistic about their language. They do not expect the foreigner to learn Greek, no matter how long he stays or how often he visits. They appreciate that it is spoken only in a tiny corner of the world and, if born and brought up in the communities abroad, they often will not bother to learn it properly themselves. This turns them into linguists.

Though the Greeks learn English more intensively than in the past, because of membership of the European Community, tourism and the number of jobs for which English is a prerequisite, they still want to use their facility for the simple pleasure of communication. And the mere fact that you are a foreigner makes you interesting. If you do not fall at the hurdle of the opening questions – your name, where you live, do you have children and, directly or by inference, how much do you earn – you are on the way towards an instant friendship.

You then arrive at the waterjump. If you expect your new acquaintance to talk to you of England or America, London or New York, let alone sheep farming in the Mendip hills, the conversation will fade into awkward silences and you will politely be left to your own devices. Reasonably and inevitably, your potential friend expects to be met in the middle, to receive something in exchange for his knowledge of your language. He needs from you intelligent questions and a degree of informed comment on his own country, its characteristics and quirks, and at least the broader political, economic and social issues around which mealtime talk will revolve in his own home.

Make the effort (this book will help you), and you have turned the key to understanding Greece and the islands without even leaving your hotel. To open the door and slip through, you have to move about a little in the country itself. Do not just see Athens and the main town of your chosen island but, at least in passing, visit the bustling little provincial cities and the villages behind the mountains; observe the industries as well as the antiquities, and go to where the grapes grow, as well as where the wine is drunk.

You will find a country that is undergoing rapid, but superficial, change. The main effect, at one level, is to help you see it more easily: new or improved roads lead into the interior, and there are hotels where only a few years ago you had to rely on family hospitality or unfold a tent. Greece is making a determined attempt to turn itself into a European country, to modernise its structures and institutions and to de-Balkanise itself socially and politically. The challenge has been accepted, but the process is not altogether painless.

The immediate result has been the emergence of tensions in society that were not present before, or were not obvious. Where *avrio* ('tomorrow') was once a way of life, the Greeks are now looking for tangible results as of yesterday. Freed from the pressures of a day-to-day struggle for mere survival, they have subjected themselves to ambitions that can be unnerving in their imprecision. Not so long ago, contentment was a regular income sufficient to ensure food, clothing and shelter, an occasional night out and a few gold sovereigns under the mattress in case of illness. Now, the Greek family wants at least one car and a country cottage to escape to at weekends; it wants an assurance of affluence and the leisure to enjoy it, today and indefinitely.

The Greeks were told, and most of them believed, that this would be the effortless reward of membership of the European Community. Eight years later, they are learning better. They are also discovering, from the broken promises of successive governments, that it is more painful to have to retreat from uplands prematurely occupied than it was to gaze at them from the valleys as unattainably utopian. You will not need to be particularly acute to observe the symptoms of discontent. The Greeks in the main retain their politeness towards the foreigner, but they surprise themselves by their rudeness towards one another since losing the contentment of modest aspirations.

Greece as a country and a society is in a state of transition: for the independent traveller, this can only add to its fascination.

The Greece you visit

Greece is an archipelago country that, since its final enlargement with incorporation of the Dodecanese islands, has a surface area of 131,944 sq km. In south-east Europe at the southern tip of the Balkan peninsula, it is the only member of the European Community without a land frontier with another member; its closest Community neighbour, Italy, can be reached by ferry across the Adriatic or by land through Yugoslavia. To the north and east, Greece has land borders with Albania (247 km), Yugoslavia (246 km), Bulgaria (474 km) and Turkey (203 km).

Though roughly four-fifths of Greece is mountainous, no part of mainland Greece is more than 100 km from the sea; in central Greece the maximum is 60 km and in the Peloponnese 50 km. Of the twenty-eight mountains above 2,000 metres, the best-known are Olympos (2,917 m), Parnassos (2,457 m), Taygettus (2,407 m) and Athos (2,033 m).

The Peloponnese, which is not regarded as an island although it is severed from the mainland by the Corinth Canal, has an area of 21,439 sq km. The 169 inhabited islands, of which the largest are Crete and Euboia, together total 24,909 sq km, and uninhabited islets another 257 sq km. There is no exact tally of these islets, some of which are little more than dangers to shipping, but the generally accepted figure is around 2,000. Total length of mainland and island coasts is put by the National Statistics Service at 15,020 km.

Two of the larger islands are almost as close to the mainland as the Peloponnese itself: the width of the Corinth Canal is 24.6 m, while the bridge across the Evripos straits to Euboia at Halkis spans a waterline of only 40 m and that joining the mainland to Lefkas in the Ionian islands a canal of a mere 25 m.

Though obviously every inhabited island has at least one harbour, and there are several dozen along the mainland coasts, Greece has seven main ports: Piraeus, Thessaloniki, Patras, Volos, Igoumenitsa, Kavala and, on the islands, Irakleion in Crete.

Greece is not well provided with rivers – it has none that are navigable – but makes maximum use of those it has both for irrigation and hydro-electricity production.

The 1981 census established a Greek population of 9.71 million, compared with 8.76 million in 1971, 8.38 million in 1961 and 7.63 million in 1951. The growth by almost a million in the ten years to 1981 was the result mainly of a decline in post-war emigration and the beginning of a move back by temporary migrants to western Europe. The present population is assumed to be around or slightly above 10 million.

During the thirty years from 1951 to 1981 in which the population of Greece rose by 2.08 million, that of Greater Athens alone (Athens, Piraeus and the suburbs of both cities) rose by 1.64 million, from 1.37 million in 1951 to 3.02 million in 1981. The urban population in its entirety rose by more than the total population increase, as a result of migration from villages and islands. It is the causes and effects of this, along with a relatively low birth-rate, which constitute Greece's 'demographic problem'.

History

Through the ages

If there is one single achievement that makes the Greeks unique, it is their retention of a sense of identity through successive 'dark ages'; this is, perhaps, the only consistency to which they can lay an unchallenged claim. As the modern Greek will sometimes permit himself to observe when pushed into an objectionable defensiveness, there were Greeks in Greece, attending theatres, at a time when the tribes of the island that would become Britain were painting themselves with woad, and those in Germany, if not actually swinging from the trees, were at least huddling beneath them clad in animal skins.

The Greeks identify themselves with their precursors to a greater degree than other peoples might choose. But though they remember that they invented democracy, they do not remember that they combined it with the practice of slavery; they recall that they bequeathed to the west the seeds of the Renaissance, but not that they simultaneously persecuted thought under the dictate of political expediency. Whereas they defeated great empires in the name of freedom, they look differently on the establishment of their own ancient colonies and the exploits of Alexander the Great. What the modern visitor sees is some of the physical evidence both of the continuity and the inconsistency: much of it he has to infer, or imagine.

Minoans and earlier

Travelling along the motorway from Athens to Thessaloniki, or visiting the Cyclades islands, you are in countryside where, as much as 9,000 years ago, Neolithic man was already farming the land and rearing livestock. Your Aegean ferry takes you through waters where, in the same general period, according to theories put to the test in 1987, there was already a kind of merchant marine to ship obsidian from outcrops on the island of Milos to settlements in the Peloponnese.

As many years before the birth of Christ as have passed since, the Minoan civilisation was developing on the island of Crete. The palaces of Knossos, Phaestos, Mallia and Kato Zakros are silent reminders of the legendary King Minos and the decidedly unpleasant Minotaur that Theseus slew, of Cretan dominance of the Aegean, and of the earliest known examples of flush toilets and toplessness in high fashion. In their spare time the Minoans played a kind of backgammon, distant ancestor of the *tavli* in Greek coffee-shops today and of the love of dice among the Romans.

Sometime in the fifteenth century BC, the volcano on the island of Thera (known also as Santorini) blew up, creating the most spectacular of the Aegean islands as well as (possibly) the legend of the Lost Continent of Atlantis. The accompanying earthquakes, tidal waves and dust clouds coincided with, and probably caused, the collapse of Minoan power.

A Minoan city at a site now called Acrotiri was discovered on Thera a little more than twenty years ago by the late Professor Spyridon Marinatos and has since been partly excavated and roofed over. You enter what appears to be a giant aircraft hangar, and find yourself walking along narrow streets that were populous more than 3,000 years ago, and peering into tiny rooms where families once gathered for dinner. Though by modern standards the houses were mean and poky, frescoes discovered there (now on display in the Athens Archaeological Museum) give a vivid impression of the power of Minoan Crete and the luxury to which the wealthy could aspire.

Professor Marinatos was fatally injured in a fall during the excavations: if Acrotiri was indeed a village of 'Atlantis', a belief based in part on the writings of Plato, his was the last death in the Lost Continent (see also pp. 224–8).

And so to Mycenae

With the Minoans on the way out, the opportunity came for the Mycenaeans: Agamemnon, in whose time brave men lived; Helen 'of Troy', who launched the thousand ships; Clytemnestra, Elektra, Orestes and the rest of the ill-fated Atreus family. They are remembered today because the Greeks were already tellers of stories that have inspired playwrights from Aeschylus to Eugene O'Neill.

The gold death masks, portions of armour, gold and silver utensils and tomb furnishings that were discovered in 1876 by Heinrich Schliemann are now in the Athens Archaeological Museum. The beehive tombs themselves, the Lion Gate and the remains of the city are included on every coach tour of the Peloponnese.

From Mycenae came the first form of written Greek, the Linear B script deciphered in 1952 by the late Michael Ventris. Later the Greeks adopted a 24-letter modified version of the Phoenician alphabet, which is essentially the alphabet still in use today. Unlike Linear

B, which was of as little help to the creative writer as the Egyptian hieroglyphics, this had seven letters representing vowels. Without it, neither the *Odyssey* and *Iliad* nor the works of the ancient dramatists would have survived. But even in the times of Linear B, it is now known that more than a hundred recognised occupations were represented among the people who used it, inviting speculation whether they might have been organised into some form of trade unions.

This great civilisation was obliterated by the Dorian invasions of the twelfth century BC, and the result was a 450-year so-called 'dark age'. But the term is to some extent a misnomer: the era saw the adoption of the alphabetic writing, Homer as man or firm lived and worked during it, cities sprang up, refugees founded the first Greek colonies on the Asia Minor coast, and the gods set up home on Mount Olympos. In art this was the so-called Geometric period: its curiously modernistic forms may be seen most concentratedly in the Goulandris Museum in Athens. And out of this relative darkness came Sparta and Athens.

The real Ancient Greece

Together, the Archaic, Classical and Hellenistic periods carry the story of Ancient Greece from the end of the 'dark age' up to the Roman conquest – from around 700 to 146 BC. These years contain almost everything that makes up the popular concept of Ancient Greece, and need to be signposted:

Archaic (700 to 500 BC): saw the development of city states and of uniform social, religious and political life; the demise of monarchy, except in Sparta, and early experiments with forms of government that included aristocracy, tyranny and degrees of democracy. A sense of Greekness came to be acquired, as seen in the panhellenic athletic contests and the first Olympic Games.

Classical (500 to 323 BC): saw the three Persian invasions, and the battles of Marathon, Thermopylae and Salamis; the Golden Age of Pericles, of the dramatists and the philosophers; the Peloponnesian War and the defeat of Athens by Sparta. Philip II of Macedonia and his son, Alexander the Great, were among the dominant figures.

Hellenistic (323 to 146 BC): the decline of Athens and Sparta was accompanied by the development of Greek civilisation overseas. The Romans moved in and took over.

Nothing would have been quite the way it was, and probably would not be quite the way it is today, if there had never been city states in Ancient Greece. They were the product initially of geography. Then as now, or at least until the fever of road construction that began in the early 1950s, Greece was a land divided by mountains and united by the sea. So the city state, consisting of the town and its surrounding countryside up to the next natural barrier, had to be large enough to be defensible but not so populous as to be either ungovernable or too frequently subject to famine.

When the city states outgrew their possibilities, the Greeks went out to colonise: on the coast of what is now Turkey, along the Sea of Marmara and the Black Sea all the way to the Crimea, and westward to Sicily, Italy and the South of France – Marseilles, Nice, Monaco and Naples were all founded by the Greeks. (In the same way, after the Second World War, comparable pressures drove modern Greeks to communities in the United States and Australia and to the factories of West Germany.)

The word for the city state, *polis*, has come down to us as politics, matters concerning the state. Periodic clashes between the ruling class and the common people provided not just experimentation in governmental systems but also the first written codes of law: in Athens in 621 BC one Drakos gave his name to the Draconian code that stipulated death even for minor theft, much as in eighteenth-century England. The Greeks are still experimenting: in the past twenty years they have twice deposed a monarchy (once at the point of a gun and once voluntarily), experienced a dictatorship and instituted two republics, one military and the other civilian.

The Ancient Greeks had the custom of ostracism, despatching into temporary exile even their most distinguished governors if they sniffed a tyranny in the offing. Exile was not then and is not now considered a sentence of political death; rather, it was intended to be a chastening experience and an invitation to acquire circumspection. Though too close a parallel would be misleading, the present century has seen the exile or self-exile of three ruling monarchs and Greece's two greatest modern statesmen, Eleftherios Venizelos and Constantine Karamanlis.

The Ancient Greek demanded and exercised the right to realise his full potential and speak his mind. These same freedoms are enshrined in the 1975 Constitution, clearly if perhaps not quite so forthrightly as when Pericles declared: 'We do not say of a man who takes no interest in politics that he is minding his own business; we say he has no business to be here at all.' Deprivation of these rights was the chief misery of the 1967–74 dictatorship, and explains the ongoing demand that Greeks living abroad should be able to vote, in consulates or by post, in general elections in Greece.

Tucked away in the Classical period is the thirty-year Golden Age of Pericles, from 460 to 429 BC. An incomparable minister of public works before the title was coined, Pericles commissioned the great works of architecture, including the Parthenon, that modern Greece is still living on.

In 27 BC Greece formally became a province of Rome, with Corinth the administrative capital and Athens the principal artistic centre. For Greece, the Pax Romanum represented three centuries of peace and prosperity during which, in many ways, the vanquished conquered the victors. The Greeks taught the Romans philosophy, poetry, sculpture, drama and sciences, and wealthy Roman families competed for the services of Greek cooks and sent their sons to study at Greek universities. In Athens, Hadrian completed the construction of the Temple of Olympian Zeus that had been started 600 years earlier, while the Herod Atticus theatre, now used for performances during the summer Athens Festival, is also Roman.

Nero competed in a rigged Olympiad (it was even more necessary to be accommodating to the superpower then than now). He also dug the first official sod in an attempt to drive a canal through the Isthmus of Corinth, but was thwarted by a combination of the terrain and the priesthood, the latter polishing skills subsequently perfected by bureaucrats with the result that ships had to wait another 2,000 years for the canal's completion.

While many works of art were shipped to Rome by anonymous predecessors of Lord Elgin and Herman Goering, the Romans were also prepared to settle, and pay, for replicas turned out by small- and medium-sized enterprises in Corinth, Patras and Athens itself.

The Roman period also saw the arrival of Christianity in the middle of the first century, with visits by St Paul to Athens, Corinth and Thessaloniki. The Greeks embraced the new faith with reformist passion, all pagan temples were closed, and in AD 393 the Olympics were abolished. Three years later the Goths arrived under Alaric.

But the Greeks did not entirely abandon their old local gods; they converted them to Christianity, and some of them were accorded sainthood. The modern visitor may easily find himself watching a procession of icons on the patronal festival of a saint whose sway extends only to that particular region or island and whose origins are lost in a pagan past.

The thousand years of Byzantium

In 395 the Roman Empire split into the Western and Eastern Empires, with the latter based at Constantinople (present-day Istanbul), the new, Roman name for the Greek city of Byzantium founded by Byzas of Megara after pondering a typically obscure pronouncement by the Oracle of Delphi. Had the Emperor Constantine not moved the capital to the shores of the Bosphorus some seventy years earlier, and had he not been baptised into the Christian faith on his deathbed, Greece would not today be largely populated by men with the name of Constantine (more familiarly, Costa or Dino) and women called Constantina (Costoula or Dina).

From the beginning, however, the Eastern Empire was Greek in spirit, language and religion. Greece itself became a province of Constantinople; Thessaloniki was the Empire's second city, and Athens declined into a minor provincial town.

After the Fourth Crusade in 1204 had disgraced itself by seizing Constantinople as an easier and more remunerative alternative to the Holy Land which it had been formed to liberate, much of Greece was parcelled out among Crusader participants. The Frankish feudal states did not survive long, but left behind them some notable castles in the Peloponnese that are well worth visiting. Rather more remains of the Venetians, who held Crete until the seventeenth century, and Corfu until they were dislodged by Napoleon.

Byzantium awaits the visitor today in the form of churches almost everywhere in Greece, but especially in Athens, Thessaloniki, Kastoria and Arta, and in the monasteries of Meteora and the ruined city of Mistras in the Peloponnese. Its supreme memorial is the self-governing Mount Athos 'Holy Community', to which access for strangers is very restricted. Less tangibly, its echoes linger in the Byzantine chant of church services and, of course, as a somewhat unflattering epithet for anything tortuous or complicated.

The latest dark age

In the early hours of Tuesday, 29 May 1453, Constantinople fell to the Ottoman Turks under Mohammed II. Greece has never been the same since. With Constantinople taken, the Turks swept quickly into Greece; they completed their conquest of the Peloponnese in 1461, and seized Rhodes from the Knights of St John of Jerusalem in 1522 and Crete from the Venetians in 1661. Only the Ionian islands escaped occupation, thanks to the Venetian presence, though in some of the more remote parts of Greece – the Mani at the southern tip of the Peloponnese and the high mountains of Crete and Epiros – Turkish power remained far from absolute.

For Greece as a whole, it was another dark age, lasting for almost 400 years, and it accounts for the enduring hatred felt in Greece for the Turks. Successive uprisings bloodily suppressed, the harvesting of girls for Turkish harems and boys for the élite Janissary corps, and village plane trees that once served as makeshift gallows are indelibly recorded in the popular memory, most of all on Crete. And yet, through religion, the Greek language and national identity were preserved, as innumerable churches dating from the seventeenth and eighteenth centuries testify. The legend of the village priest with cross in one hand and musket in the other dates from the centuries of Turkish occupation and still helps to preserve the influence of the Church. The fall of Constantinople, by forcing a flight of intellectuals to the west and in particular to Italy, paved the way for the Renaissance. Without the Renaissance it is unlikely that there could have been the same growth of philhellenism in Europe, and without the philhellene movement the Greeks would probably not have regained their freedom through the 1821 Revolution. And even in occupied Constantinople, the Greeks provided the business and administrative class, in a way that the Romans would have understood. They also supplied the Turkish name for the city, Istanbul, a corruption of *eis teen polis*, Greek for 'in the city'. Even today, when a Greek speaks of the 'polis' he is thinking of Constantinople, the 'polis' of Constantine: there is no other city in the world without the need of a proper name.

In present-day Greece, Tuesday is still considered an unpropitious day to start a journey, launch an enterprise or get married, since it was on a Tuesday that the city fell.

Freedom and afterwards

The French Revolution of 1789 provided the impetus, thirty-two years later, for the Greek Revolution of 1821. It was proclaimed in the Peloponnese on or about 25 March, the date subsequently adopted for the principal of Greece's two national days.

Success, at least to a limited degree, came six years later. Acting under the pressure of domestic philhellene agitation, Britain, France and Russia as the 'protecting powers' intervened with the Ottoman Sultan to concede national and political independence for an embryonic Greek state. An unintended naval battle in the Bay of Navarino, in which a tri-national squadron under the command of Vice-Admiral Lord Codrington sank most of the combined Turkish–Egyptian fleet, left the Sultan with no option but to agree. While Pylos is now the only name in use for the town at the head of the bay, the bay itself is written on modern Greek maps either as Navarino or Pylos. Today, Codrington has a street in Athens named after him.

The Battle of Navarino was the decisive encounter in the Greek Revolution. In the context of the 200th anniversary of the birth of Lord Byron, scholars and historians in Greece at least have been offered a new opportunity to examine whether it could have been fought if Lord Byron had not died in Missolonghi three years earlier.

In the inevitable form of street names, the Greeks remember other notable philhellenes of that era: France's Victor Hugo and Alfred de Musset, for example, and America's Samuel Grindley Howe, the Boston doctor who in 1825 became surgeon-general of the Greek Revolutionary forces, raised $60,000 for Greek relief, and as late as 1866 involved himself in one of the abortive attempts to liberate Crete.

But Byron outshone them all, and after his death Greece could no longer be left to its fate. The Greeks may not read Byron, but they have the grace to honour him.

It was not much of a country that gained its independence in 1829. It consisted of the Peloponnese, the southern part of central Greece and a few islands. When the Bavarian Prince Otto (hellenised as Othon) arrived to take up the throne which the protecting powers had created for him, his capital was the backwater Peloponnesian port of Nafplion and Athens was a cluster of hovels at the foot of the Acropolis. But Othon moved his capital to Athens, where a demonstration in 1843 forced him to grant a constitution and in the process gave a name to the open space in front of his palace in which it was staged: Constitution (Syntagma) Square.

The King's submission on the constitutional issue bought him just under twenty years; he was deposed in 1862 and replaced the following year by Prince George of Denmark, of the House of Glucksburg. As a gesture to the new monarch, Britain ceded the Ionian islands, which it had been holding as a protectorate since the defeat of Napoleon.

The rest of the nineteenth century and first two decades of the twentieth were devoted to pursuit of the *megali ithea*, the 'Great Idea', the incorporation of all territories inhabited by Greeks and restoration of Greek power on both sides of the Aegean, behind frontiers broadly matching those of the old Byzantine Empire. It was a dream that started and ended badly but nevertheless gave Greece its present borders.

After thirty years of continual revolts in Crete and parts of Thessaly and Epiros, Greece fought and lost a war with Turkey in 1897. But out of the resulting turmoil sprang the 1909 Revolution and the advent to power of Greece's most revered modern statesman, the Cretan Eleftherios Venizelos. Venizelos pushed through a general modernisation that included the reinforcement of parliamentary government and, above all, turned the army and navy into fighting forces that could look with confidence and relish to their next opportunity.

The faith was justified by the two Balkan Wars of 1912 and 1913 that secured Thessaloniki, most of central and western Macedonia, Ioannina and south Epiros. Together with Crete, which had united with Greece in 1908, and the East Aegean islands, Greece emerged from the Balkan Wars with its surface area and population almost doubled.

Most of the older parts of central Athens, the main public buildings, the National (formerly Royal) gardens and the Zappeion Park date from the first half-century of modern Greek freedom.

In 1913 the assassination of George I in Thessaloniki, after a fifty-year reign, brought his son Constantine to the throne. The outbreak of the First World War in 1914 led to a conflict between Constantine and Venizelos that the pro-German King lost. Venizelos took Greece into the war on the side of Britain and France, Constantine was deposed and the Macedonian Front was formed.

Treaties signed in 1919 and 1920 gave Greece eastern and western Thrace as well as a mandate to administer Smyrna, now Izmir, and its hinterland pending a plebiscite. The result was a foretaste on a small scale of what was to occur later in Germany because of the Treaty of Versailles: too much was demanded of the vanquished Turkey for having fought on the losing side. While the Greeks were voting Venizelos out of office and restoring Constantine through a plebiscite, Mustapha Kemal, subsequently Kemal Ataturk, was preparing Turkey for its day of revenge.

The 'Great Idea' in its last flowering led to the Greek–Turkish War of 1922; the Asia Minor disaster; the sack of Smyrna and massacre of its inhabitants; the arrival in Greece of a million and a half refugees whom it took thirty years to assimilate fully and house properly; and, through the Treaty of Lausanne, the return of eastern Thrace to Turkey. Understandably, the Greeks took their defeat badly. The army revolted, Constantine was deposed for a second and final time, and the five political leaders and the army commander-in-chief judged chiefly responsible for the disaster were tried and executed.

The executions opened a schism that led to successive military revolts; the proclamation of a republic that lasted only eleven years; the restoration of the monarchy in 1935 under Constantine's elder son, George II; the flight of Venizelos to exile in France and his death there in 1936; and, in August 1936, the establishment of a dictatorship under General Ioannis Metaxas.

World War, occupation and civil strife

The Second World War began for Greece on 28 October 1940, when Metaxas rejected an Italian ultimatum (his 'No! [*Ochi*!]', gave Greece its other national day). Greek victories over Mussolini in Epiros and Albania, the first to be gained by the Allies, forced Hitler to invade in 1941. It is possible to assert, as the Greeks frequently do, that had the Germans not had to rescue their Italian allies the invasion of Russia would have been launched well before June 1941, Moscow would have been captured before the onset of winter, and the war might have had a different outcome, or at least taken a different course.

The three-year occupation by German, Italian and Bulgarian forces left Greece in ruins. It was followed almost immediately after liberation by the first of two communist attempts to seize power, in December 1944: the so-called 'December Days', when Greece's freedom was preserved by British troops.

The communists' second attempt, the 'second round', took three years of hard fighting to defeat, despite American assistance under the Truman doctrine of the cold war. Clearly having studied the example of the Janissaries, the communist guerrillas as they melted away across the Yugoslav and Albanian frontiers took with them a round-up of children for indoctrination and training for an eventual third round. These wounds have yet to close completely.

Meanwhile, another referendum had confirmed the monarchy, George II had died and been succeeded by his brother Paul, and the Dodecanese islands, occupied by Italy since 1912, had been ceded to Greece under the terms of the Greek–Italian peace treaty. Greece had thus reached its present dimensions. There is still a hankering for northern Epiros, now part of southern Albania, but this is currently a question of the human rights of the Greek minority, and is not being pursued as a territorial claim.

The Aegean divergence

You may find it strange, as you move around the islands, that so much more has survived from the Middle Ages than from Ancient Greece. On the mainland, it is exactly the opposite.

The explanation lies in the extent to which, for centuries, Greece *was* its islands. Once the Romans had left the mainland, little else happened there; baronial fiefdoms came and went, leaving behind the occasional castle, and monasteries were built, but scarcely anything constructed during the 400 years of Turkish occupation was to prove enduring. Structurally, the Greek mainland missed out on the age of faith that built the great cathedrals of Europe and on the Renaissance. At the same time, since the Turks did not build they had no need to pillage the stones of earlier structures; neglected, gradually covered and ultimately forgotten, the famed sites and sanctuaries of Ancient Greece survived, to await rediscovery after the liberation.

The pattern was different on the islands, which were at once desirable, defensible and of strategic importance to the naval powers competing for dominance in the Mediterranean.

They were desirable as handy-sized dukedoms in an ideal climate, sizable enough to support the conqueror in the lifestyle to which he aspired, but not so large as to require unwieldy, expensive and inherently unreliable masses of men either to seize or hold them.

They were defensible most of all because the horse-borne hordes that regularly swept into mainland Greece from what are now the Balkans, destroying whatever they were unable to carry off and leaving behind them only ruins and corpses, invariably stopped when they reached the sea. The Venetian, Genoese and Crusader castles that you will find on almost every island were built not because of the threat of Goth, Vandal or Slav invasion, but to provide security against pirates. Only a naval power could attack the islands in force.

The strategic importance of the Aegean islands lay in their position along the trade routes to Constantinople and the Black Sea. That of the Ionians was a matter of primary concern to the Venetians, who held them as bulwarks against Turkish expansion westward from mainland Greece.

It was natural in the circumstances that when the time came to build a castle, or a church, use should be made of the material most conveniently to hand. As often as not that meant the stones of ancient temples, the destruction of which was not simply excusable, but could be regarded as a form of service to the Christian faith. On the Aegean islands it is not really surprising that so little has survived from the ancient past; it is more surprising that anything has remained at all.

The Crusade that ran amok

Much of what you see on the Aegean islands today is the curious legacy of an ambitious pope and an avaricious Venetian doge.

At the very end of the twelfth century, Pope Innocent III proclaimed the Fourth Crusade, with the stated and actual aim of recovering the Holy Land from the infidels.

A Crusader force, without ships, gathered at Venice in 1202 and negotiated an agreement with the blind Doge Henry Dandolo, then over ninety years old, to transport an army of just under 35,000 men 'across the sea'. The Venetian price: 85,000 silver marks plus half the land to be conquered.

In the event, for reasons that seemed obvious afterwards, the Crusaders took Constantinople and not Jerusalem.

● The Crusade had assembled at a time when the Adriatic was becoming a Venetian lake. Its naval power destroyed, the Byzantine Empire was already dwindling. The Venetians saw themselves as the natural successors.

● Constantinople was in the throes of one of its frequent dynastic disputes. The Emperor Isaac had been deposed, blinded and imprisoned by his brother, and Isaac's son, Alexis, was in Europe, seeking aid for the restoration of legitimacy.

● In Rome, the permanent ambition of popes for more than a century had been to bring the Greek Orthodox Church back under the spiritual jurisdiction of the Roman Catholic Church, from which it had broken with the 'schism' of 1054.

To encourage the Crusaders and to blunt any papal objection to the use of a Christian force to attack a Christian city, Alexis joined the Crusade and entered into an agreement by which he undertook, if placed on the Byzantine throne, to submit Constantinople to Rome, pay the Crusaders 200,000 silver marks, and provide 10,000 men for a subsequent expedition to the Holy Land.

The Crusaders, who in any case had been unable to raise the price agreed with the Venetians for their transport, swallowed the bait. In the spring of 1203 they sailed for Constantinople in the Venetians' ships, pausing on the way to seize the island of Andros for Alexis.

A year later, Constantinople was stormed and a Latin Empire was set up that was to last for fifty-eight years.

The question of whether greater destruction was caused to the treasures of Constantinople by the Crusader sack or the Turkish conquest of 1453 is incidental to the story of the Aegean; what is of greater relevance is that the Byzantine Empire never recovered its former mastery of the Aegean sea, and never regained the islands.

In the division of the spoils, most of the Aegean islands, including Crete, went to the Venetians; they were to hold them, building castles and churches, until dislodged gradually by the Turks in the fifteenth and sixteenth centuries.

The Knights of St John

Events followed a slightly different course in Rhodes and the rest of the Dodecanese islands. With the establishment of the Latin Empire in 1204, Rhodes declared its independence, and subsequently control of the island was secured by the Genoese. In 1304, after a two-year siege, the island was stormed by the Knights Hospitallers of St John of Jerusalem.

The order had been founded in Jerusalem in the middle of the eleventh century to provide shelter for pilgrims, and was recognised as a military order early in the twelfth century. Driven from the Holy Land in 1291, the Knights sailed first to Cyprus and from there to Rhodes. They held Rhodes, and by extension the rest of the Dodecanese, until the city of Rhodes fell to the Turkish Sultan Suleiman in 1522; they then withdrew to Crete, and in 1530 to Malta.

With a few exceptions, such as the magnificent acropolis of Lindos, the buildings that today make Rhodes the medieval showplace of Greece date from the 200 years of rule by the Knights (see also Rhodes, pp. 157–9).

The Greeks and the Sea

The Greeks took to the sea because of their islands – and because of the nature of the Aegean. Even if you, the modern tourist, prefer to fly to your chosen holiday destination, you will nevertheless appreciate the inevitability that such an archipelago should have produced a seafarer nation.

Though lashed by sudden squalls that are still predictable at least as reliably by fisherman's lore as by the most advanced meteorological instruments, the Aegean on most days of the year is a blue, tranquil and inviting stretch of water. The distances are scarcely daunting; the modern yachtsman, like the Ancient Greek, can travel from island to island without ever needing to be at sea after the sun has set, and in a couple of easy days, three at most, can have crossed from mainland Greece to the Anatolian coast of Turkey in daylight all the way. The ferries from Piraeus to Crete and Rhodes make their crossings by night for the convenience of the holiday-maker or businessman, not because the journeys are too long to be completed between the dawn and sunset of a summer's day.

The Aegean is a pool without fogs, in which the islands are stepping stones, and has been likened to a single great city with a multitude of suburbs. You do not need to be the world's greatest navigator to feel yourself in familiar waters when almost always there is land in sight somewhere. What is perhaps most surprising about the Greek islands, given their number and relative proximity to one another, is that each should be in some way different from all the rest, and in some specific feature unique.

The Ancient Greek, with his indisputable eye for beauty, may have gone to sea because he, too, found the Aegean enticing, but he was equally driven by necessities: the obvious one represented by the trading needs of island populations, and the less obvious one, to the modern eye, by a mainland that as little as half a century ago could still be travelled as easily by boat, from harbour to harbour, as through the mountain ranges of the interior. Long before Greece was a country, let alone a nation, the mainland and island states were home to a homogeneous people united by the sea, and speaking a common language.

On some of the smaller islands you will still find that the caique, not the bus, is the more commonly employed means of travel from one village to another.

It is certain that there were ships before there was a recorded history, and probable that the Greeks were seamen before they were farmers or shepherds. Obsidian tools and cutting edges discovered in a cave in the Peloponnese have been dated to around 8000 BC: they were used by a people without knowledge of iron or bronze, and could only have been manufactured from the glass-like volcanic stone taken to the cave from deposits on the island of Milos. An imaginative reconstruction of such a Stone Age voyage, using the ship technology of the earliest Aegean frescoes and vase paintings, was carried out in the summer of 1987 under the sponsorship of the Aegean Foundation; its successful conclusion provided evidence that the obvious was also possible. The Aegean coastal ferry that takes you to Milos today plies much the same route as the primitive merchantman that 10,000 years ago was engaged in the earliest known transportation of the raw materials of warfare.

The Greeks were building wooden ships, with prows and keels, sails and oars, and using them for exploration, conquest and trade, at a time when people of the Middle East were floating down rivers on round wicker-and-skin coracles which then had to be dismantled and carried back upstream on pack animals.

If you happen to be in the right place at the right time you will see replicas of two Ancient Greek ships constructed in the past five years – a warship of the Classical period and a merchantman of the fourth century. Eventually they are to become museum exhibits, but for the moment they are still engaged on trial and show-the-flag voyages. But wherever you go among the islands you will see, and probably travel in, gaily-painted caiques that differ little from those of 1,000 years ago except that they now have engines. The more glorious ships of the age of sail – the Byzantine dromonds, Venetian galleys and galleasses and the galliots of Psara – have gone forever, but the humble *trechandiri*, in its various forms including the caique, can be seen in every island harbour.

A maritime mythology

The origins of Greek seafaring are at some points inextricable from Greece's maritime mythology. Obviously, Delos never was a floating island until anchored to provide a refuge on which Leto could give birth to Apollo, nor did Nisyros start out as a piece of rock hurled at Poseidon by the giant Polyvotis. It is equally improbable that Orpheus turned the pirates that captured him into dolphins, so that they leapt into the sea and left him to sail their ship single-handedly. It may even be doubted by the unimaginative that there was a god, Poseidon, who could raise and quell tempests depending on his mood and the obsequiousness with which he was invoked. But Jason and the Argonauts? And the wanderings of Odysseus?

Remove from the search for the Golden Fleece the magical events and wondrous irrelevancies and you are left with a voyage that almost certainly was made, to a Black Sea country that now forms part of the Soviet Union (it was indeed duplicated in 1985 by an Irishman, Tim Severin, in a boat built on Spetses that was as close an approximation as possible to the kind that Jason would have had to use). Perform a similar defoliation on the *Odyssey* and you have in part a sailing manual and in part a compilation of seamen's tales spun around the wanderings of a single great hero.

There was certainly a Trojan War, expedition, siege and conquest, regardless of whether the fleet that gathered in Aulis at the behest of Agamemnon consisted of 1,186 ships or rather fewer, and really carried 140,000 men. Whatever the actual numbers, it is unlikely that so large a combined operation could have been mounted more than 3,000 years ago unless the independent states and islands that participated had been linked by at least an incipient sense of nationhood as well as a common tongue. It is only natural that the *Iliad* and *Odyssey* should have much to say about ship types and construction, since Homer was writing long after the Minoans had gained and lost command of the Aegean through their naval power.

The frescoes discovered in the excavations at Acrotiri on the island of Thera and now on display in the Athens Archaeological Museum include one, 'The Fleet', that shows that the Minoans made use both of sails and oars. Reconstructed from the Thera fresco, the Minoan warships of 1500 BC had a length of approximately 34 m and a beam of 4 m, and were propelled by a single square sail and twenty oars on each side. There was a combination bridge and fighting platform, a distant precursor of Nelson's quarterdeck, in the stern immediately behind and above the two long steering oars (development of the rudder principle was still more than 1,000 years in the future).

The Minoans of the second millennium had fleets of merchant and passenger ships, a system of ship and cargo insurance, and representative offices in the main trading areas. On the basis of Inca symbols of very much later date identical with Minoan ones found at Knossos, it has been maintained that the Minoans may even have reached the Americas, or at least that there was some form of trade links.

A model of the Thera ship, the earliest depicted terror of the seas and carver of colonies, is on display in the Aegean Maritime Museum on Myconos. Set up in 1985 by Myconos-born shipowner George M. Dracopoulos, the museum is the newest and finest of several in Greece dedicated to the seafaring tradition.

The trireme then and now

From the eighth to the sixth centuries BC, a colonisation movement took the Greeks into the Sea of Marmara and the Black Sea, and westward in the Mediterranean to Sicily and Southern Italy, North Africa and what is now the South of France. These expansionary pressures created the need for larger vessels, and for a clear distinction between the warship and the merchantman.

The Golden Age of Pericles was founded on sea power and above all on the trireme (it was also a golden age for Piraeus: the main port where the ferries and cruise liners anchor today was the principal commercial centre of the ancient world, handling the trades in goods and slaves, while the present yacht harbour of Zea was the naval base), and control of the sea was also basic to the expeditions of Alexander the Great.

Since the summer of 1987 the Greek Navy has included one Athenian trireme, the *Olympias*, and since 1985 an Alexander the Great merchantman has voyaged to Cyprus under its own sail-power and to the United States in the hold of a larger ship. If insufficiently fortunate to see either of these startling anachronisms as you travel about Greece, you can settle for the models of both in the Myconos museum.

The *Olympias* was reconstructed by British ship designer John Coates and Professor of Classics John Morrison, and built in yards near Piraeus with British and Greek financing. It is a long, sleek vessel that made its maiden voyage off the Athens coast in 1987 with a combined crew of British and Greek oarsmen, before its formal incorporation into the Greek Navy.

Described as the masterpiece of Ancient Greek shipbuilding, the trireme was about 37 m long and 5.5 m wide, was manned by 170 rowers seated on three different levels, and was armed with a ram as its main offensive weapon. Using its single sail, it is believed to have cruised at 5 knots in a fair breeze; with the oars, it could travel at 7 knots over long distances, and probably reach a ramming speed of more than 9 knots. Ancient writers make the point that it was crewed by free men, never by slaves.

The triremes were the original 'wooden walls', long before the British appropriated the term for the ships that guarded the Channel. When the Persians returned to Greece in 480 BC, a decade after their defeat at the Battle of Marathon, the natural Athenian response was to consult the Oracle of Delphi. 'Trust to your wooden walls,' it said. Themistocles provided the interpretation, and persuaded the Athenians to use the reserves of the Lavrion silver mines to construct the fleet of 200 triremes that was to smash the Persians at the Battle of Salamis. For the next seventy-five years, until the destruction of the Athenian fleet by the Spartans, the trireme ruled the Aegean.

The Alexander the Great merchantman

The so-called *Kyrenia II* is altogether a more modest but in some ways a more evocative ship: unlike the trireme, which was built 'the way it must have been', the *Kyrenia* is an exact replica of an original workhorse of coastal shipping in the days of Alexander the Great, discovered off the coast of Cyprus. It too is the fruit of bi-national cooperation, this time between Greece and the United States.

The Kyrenia ship was discovered in shallow waters in 1967, and was raised and assembled with the assistance of the Institute of Nautical Archaeology of Texas A and M University and UNESCO. It is now on display in Kyrenia castle, in the Turkish-occupied north of Cyprus.

The Kyrenia ship, the oldest merchantman ever discovered, had a length of just under 15 m and a cargo capacity of 30 tonnes. It was propelled by a single square sail attached to a mast that could be moved to several different positions along the keel, in accordance with the balance of cargo and wind and sea conditions, and carried a crew of four – a master and three seamen.

The ship was steered by port and starboard oars that could be linked together or lifted free of the water independently. Traces of bulkheads suggest that the fore and stern decks provided enclosed space for sensitive cargo or shelter for the crew, with a catwalk around or over the open hold to enable crew members to get from one deck to another.

The ship had been built in the middle of the fourth century BC and sailed until the end of that century, frequently patched after minor accidents. Lettering cut into some of the timbers indicates that it was Greek, and the Rhodian origin of the crew's dishes and plates points to its home port. On the basis of its cargo – which included wine and olive oil in amphoras, olives in sacks, and twenty-nine millstones to serve as ballast – it has been surmised that on its last voyage it had called at the islands of Samos and Nisyros as well as Rhodes, and was bound for Cyprus when attacked and sunk by pirates.

Piracy is deduced from the place where the ship was found – it was buried in soft sand at a depth of 30 m, in a part of the sea with no natural hazards – as well as the large hole in its bottom. Also, there were eight iron spearheads beneath the wreckage and another stuck in lead sheeting over the hull. The discovery of olive pits, fig and grape seeds and cloves of garlic suggests that the crew was surprised during lunch.

The name of the original ship has not survived: it is known simply as the Kyrenia ship from the port off which it sank, and for that reason the replica is the *Kyrenia II*. The intention of those who built the replica was to shed new light on Ancient Greek ship construction, but the trial voyages already made have been equally enlightening on Ancient Greek seamanship.

They also made maps

The Ancient Greeks were cartographers as well as seafarers, and the waters and islands of the Aegean were among the first in the world to be accurately mapped. For the most part, the islands you visit today bore the same names 2,000 and more years ago.

The earliest known map of the world was drawn by the Greek philosopher, Anaximander of Miletus, who died around 550 BC. Herodotus, the fifth century BC 'father of history', was the first to attempt detailed descriptions of the inhabited world, in a melding of geography and history, while the campaigns of Alexander the Great provided contemporary geographers with a wealth of new information.

Eratosthenes, who lived in the third century BC, laid the foundations of mathematical geography and Ptolemy, during the second century AD, took the system further and produced maps which were used by explorers and travellers up to the time of Columbus and Magellan, being updated as new countries were discovered.

Geographical knowledge and maps possessed by the Byzantine navy passed into the west either directly or through the Crusaders and Venetians, and into the east by way of the Arabs. Columbus himself studied Byzantine maps in the library of the island of Chios.

From Rome to Independence

Though the Romans incorporated Greece into their Empire they were never at home on the sea, and the Greeks carried much of their trade. Surviving crew rosters of Roman ships lost at sea almost invariably contain a proportion of Greek names. Some of these lists were found on the island of Delos, where there was a Roman community that numbered shipowners among its members.

The Byzantine Empire began to build up its navy in the fifth century AD, and by the sixth century was the dominant sea power. After 1204 and the Crusader rape of Constantinople, control of the Aegean passed first to the Venetians and Genoese, and then gradually to the Turks during the two centuries that followed the fall of Constantinople in 1453.

Like the Romans, the Turks were poor sailors: the Greeks lose no opportunity to tell the story, possibly apocryphal but universally believed, of a Turkish admiral who, sent to Malta on an official visit, eventually informed the Sultan that 'Malta yok' – 'There is no Malta!' When your Greek waiter replies that vanilla ice-cream 'yok', he is not taking you for a Turk but simply indulging in a little good humour.

Though nominally the Turks ruled the sea, actual control of the Aegean was the object of competition at one time or another among the Venetians, Russians, French, Dutch and British, all of whom made use of Greek seamen. Also, the single-sailed caique in its various adaptations was for centuries the ubiquitous ship of the Aegean.

The Napoleonic Wars gave the Greeks their opportunity to branch out first into Mediterranean trade and then, in part by virtue of their skills as privateers and blockade-runners, to venture beyond the Straits of Gibraltar to Europe and South America. As early as 1804, ships from the island of Hydra were carrying cargo to Montevideo in Uruguay. Able to outsail even Nelson's warships, the Greek blockade-runners supplied wheat to Napoleonic France and returned with silver ballast. Records show that by 1813 Greek island and mainland ports could muster 615 merchant ships, armed with 5,878 cannon; by 1816 the fleet totalled 700 ships.

The black thread of piracy

Piracy has its place in the Ancient Greek myths, and was finally eradicated only after the 1821 Independence Revolution. Without piracy, Greece might have had to wait rather longer to secure its freedom.

Pirates are mentioned by Thucydides, and in the fifth century BC Athens mounted an expedition against one of their strongholds, on the island of Skyros.

Go to almost any of the smaller Aegean islands and you will find that its capital, Hora, is situated not in the most convenient place but on a hill some distance from the sea. This is because it had to be defensible, and also sufficiently far from wherever pirates could land to allow time for its inhabitants to gather behind the walls. The Venetian and Genoese castles guarding the Hora were built primarily for defence against pirate raids, and the monasteries were fortified for the same reason.

For centuries, pirates could go anywhere with impunity, seizing ships and attacking coastal towns. In 1537, Barbarossa (Redbeard) massacred the menfolk of the island of Aegina and sold 6,000 women and children into slavery. In 1570, the Algerian Kemal Reis similarly depopulated Skiathos, Skopelos and Kythera, while in the same century Salamis was a pirate lair.

In a curious reflection on the morality of the times, piracy was at once a scourge, and an honourable profession to which fathers apprenticed their sons. It also provided what today would be described as a developmental incentive in that, as early as the Byzantine period, it led to the construction of fast warships to protect the larger and slower merchantmen. In the centuries that followed, it equally required those Greek islanders who were not pirates to learn how to build and handle swift, manoeuvrable and well-armed ships.

By 1803, Hydra had a standing fleet of pirate-chasers, the cost of which was shared with other maritime islands. These ships, and others like them, proved invaluable during the 1821 struggle for independence.

The modern Greek shipowner, in his mellower moments, will own up to a privateering instinct, and it should scarcely have caused surprise that when the British imposed an embargo on trade with Ian Smith's breakaway regime in Rhodesia some twenty years ago, the richest of the pickings from blockade-running went to Greek shipping enterprises.

Independence and afterwards

Visit Syros today and you may find it strange that the island's elegant but unimportant neo-Classical capital, Ermoupolis, was Greece's principal port and the centre of its shipowning and construction activity until less than a century ago. However, there were sound historical reasons for this.

Because of its Roman Catholic community, Syros had enjoyed an unusual degree of autonomy from the Turks even before 1821, under Venetian and French protection. Ermoupolis itself – named after Hermes, god of commerce – became a commercial city in the fifteen years from 1821 to 1835, when refugees moved there in particular from the islands of Chios, Psara, Andros and Kassos.

The majority of the shipowners came from Chios, where for generations they had been both merchants and seafarers. The Chios caiques were owned by their captain and crewed by his family and friends, who earned their living from the boat and also made it their home. They took advantage of their knowledge of the Aegean to act as merchants for the cargo they carried, and many of them built up connections with traders of Greek origin in Black Sea ports who dealt mainly in grain.

The growth of Syros was especially damaging to Galaxidi, the tiny mainland port in the Gulf of Corinth near Delphi where the best Greek ships had traditionally been built: new yards on Syros competed successfully in the construction of the latest two- and three-masted passenger-cargo vessels.

Nevertheless, the primacy of Syros was to prove short-lived. The bell tolled, first for its shipyards and then for its shipping industry, with the arrival of steam in the middle of the nineteenth century. Steam and its corollary, the iron ship, placed Greece in a doubly disadvantageous position as a country with neither coal nor iron ore.

Though the first Greek steamship was purchased in 1857 for a state-owned company established on Syros, which by 1893 was operating fifteen steamships on Greek island services, steam and the simultaneous growth of Athens made it inevitable that the shipping industry should move gradually to the mainland.

A final Syros challenge – a New Hellenic Steam Navigation Society founded in 1893 by ten of the island's wealthier merchants – petered out in bankruptcy after only twelve years, by which time the focus of Mediterranean and Black Sea trade had shifted firmly to the Greek capital and its expanding port, Piraeus.

Despite this, sail died slowly in Greek waters. As late as 1888, the Greek registry contained 5,731 sailing ships of 216,649 gross registered tons (crewed by 21,063 seamen) and 98 steamships of 32,325 GRT (using 1,380 seamen). Pure sailing ships were still in service in the Aegean during the 1920s, and caiques using sail and engine until the 1950s.

The Greek genius

It was during this reluctant transition from sail to steam that the foundations of the modern Greek shipping industry were laid in terms of families and fortunes and also of the attitudes of mind that make up what is loosely but tellingly epitomised as the 'Greek genius'.

Greek shipowners like to describe themselves as the scions not of an aristocratic but of an axiocratic profession, one based on merit demonstrated by the fact of survival. A captain-owner of a caique would first venture into trading by purchasing cargo he would otherwise have been chartered to carry and then, when the cumulative profits of successive voyages were sufficient, invest in a quarter- or half-share of a second-hand steamship. New blood still flows continuously into the industry through the channel of deck and engine-room officers who graduate into management on their way to the final plunge into ownership (ashore, the same determined pursuit of independence has given Greece its unusually high proportion of self-employed). Similarly, Greeks acknowledge no peers in sale-and-purchase; if there is a killing to be made in the second-hand market, they will sniff it out.

The stories handed down from this twilight of sail in the secondary trade routes, which essentially came to an end with the First World War, tend to focus on the little man with a hunger for success that required him to cut corners, besting the competition and beating the odds, just as the favourite character in the *karaghiozi* shadow theatre, armed only with his cunning, routinely outwits the pasha.

Revealingly, none of the classic tales that shipowners tell concerns the late-comers Onassis and Niarchos, who rose from nowhere on the strength of a single brilliant idea for exploiting an unrepeatable opportunity – the demand for unprecedented quantities of oil at a time when neither the means of transporting it nor the traditional sources of finance for ship construction was sufficient – and who never had been nor ever became a part of the mainstream of Greek shipping nurtured by its Aegean heart. Greek shipowners wince at the idea of living conspicuously, and would find it unbearable to be the butt of jokes centred on personal or business vulgarity.

On the subject of empty bellies and the knack of filling them with finesse, there is a story told of one Antony Angelicoussis, who in the early days of the present century moored his caique in what was still known as Constantinople to load cargo for Chios.

Soon afterwards, a spruce British steamer docked in front of him and, while winching in, snapped off a protuberance that Captain Angelicoussis was pleased to describe as his bowsprit.

The British captain, ever correct, reported the mishap to his agent and suggested that a half-sovereign would be more than adequate recompense.

The agent hesitated. 'Unfortunately, captain,' he said, 'Angelicoussis has already been here with his lawyer. He claims you damaged his bow as well as the bowsprit, and says the repairs will cost between thirty and forty sovereigns.'

'We'll fight,' was the British master's first reaction. But warned that the steamer was threatened with arrest, he agreed to attend a meeting with Angelicoussis and his lawyer. The discussion was brief and far from amicable.

Lawyer: 'The damage is far more serious than you maintain.'
Captain: 'Very well then, two sovereigns.'
Lawyer: 'No, we insist on forty!'
Captain: 'Four, and that's my last offer.'
Lawyer: 'Forty, or we arrest your ship!'

The British captain began to walk out, but was restrained by his agent, who warned that an arrest could cause expensive delays. Quivering with rage, the captain returned to the table and threw down a purse that, from the thump it made, could be concluded to contain around twelve or fifteen sovereigns. 'Take it,' he said, 'or leave it!'

As the lawyer resumed his 'We want forty!' refrain, Angelicoussis, who spoke no English but could assess situations and the likely value of a small bag of gold, picked up the purse and slipped it into his pocket.

'George,' he told his lawyer, 'you are absolutely right, and we are being treated most unfairly. But we know the British are a fine people, and if they owe us something we can be sure they will pay us one day, when they have the money. So for the moment we shall content ourselves with this advance . . .'

Angelicoussis made a fine profit, and the immaculate British master was left feeling just a little bit guilty.

The Greeks also have a sporting instinct, which leads them, all other things being equal, to derive greater satisfaction from outwitting a fellow-countryman than a foreigner, in the same way as a truly amateur fisherman would rather use a rod than a stick of dynamite. The fairest of game is another Greek who has got slightly ahead.

At roughly the same time as Captain Angelicoussis was mining British gold from the loss of his bowsprit, the captain-owner of a steam freighter, Michael Pnevmaticos (the family is still in shipping) was passing north of Chios on his way to the Dardanelles when he overtook a caique sailed by an acquaintance of his, Yanni Frangos.

As the two ships drew level, Frangos hailed Pnevmaticos.

'Say, old friend, would you throw me a line and tow me a bit of the way, until we get some wind?'

In an incautiously benevolent mood, Pnevmaticos stopped, threw Frangos a new line, and began the tow.

A couple of hours later the wind freshened, and Pnevmaticos sent his first mate aft to signal Frangos to cast off.

'Just a few more miles, old friend,' Frangos shouted back.

Each time the request was made, with increasing force, the reply was the same: 'Soon!' For Frangos knew well that, for Pnevmaticos, a choice between slow-steaming and loss of a new rope was no choice at all. Arriving outside the Dardanelles port that was their common destination, Frangos cast off the rope and, while Pnevmaticos was engaged in retrieving it, slipped into harbour first.

Whenever he told the story afterwards, Pnevmaticos would conclude: 'And that was the last time I ever offered anybody a tow.'

For the stories of the bowsprit and the rope I am indebted to Michael Peraticos, a pillar of the Greek shipping community in London, joint General Secretary of the Union of Greek Shipowners in Piraeus, a yachtsman with unexcelled knowledge of Aegean coves and currents, and a raconteur of note in a profession more commonly associated with taciturnity.

Peraticos also has a story, this one based on his personal knowledge of its heroes, concerning the entry of new blood and the indomitable optimism required of a first-generation shipowner.

Some thirty years ago the late Stavros Livanos, for a time the father-in-law of both Onassis and Niarchos and almost certainly the richest Greek of his generation, was walking to his office in the City of London, trademark silk handkerchief flopping from his breast pocket, when he was stopped by two of his officers, a captain and a first engineer.

'Excuse us, Captain Stavros . . .'

'What do you want?', in his brusquest manner.

'A minute of your time, and the favour of your advice.'

They recalled that they had worked hard for his company for a great number of years, assured him that they were properly grateful, and explained that they had just heard of a 6,000-tonner for sale at a good price and were wondering whether to commit their combined nest-eggs and risk the passage into ownership.

'Forget it! You're crazy! All you know is the sea, and that's only a tenth of shipping! You'll be eaten alive!'

They thanked him, and bowed themselves out of the presence.

On his way to his office a couple of weeks later, Livanos bumped into them again, by chance.

'You boys ready to sign on again?'

'Not exactly, Captain Stavros.'

'You don't mean you went ahead, after all I told you?'

'Well, Captain Stavros, it's like this. We listened to what you said, and decided you were probably right. So what could we do? We made the sign of the cross, and bought the ship.'

On the subject of faith, a few years ago Aristomenis Karageorgis, then the President of the Union of Greek Shipowners, regaled his table companions at a press lunch with the story of the caique and the storm off Chios.

As the vessel rolled and shipped water in desperate quest of a lee shore, the captain made the customary promises to the Virgin and Aghios Nikolaos, patron saint of Greek seamen, and invoked the name of Alexander the Great in the proper formula. Eventually, the wind dropped and the waves fell. Relaxed, he rang for coffee.

When it arrived, he took a sip and spat it out.

'You forgot the sugar,' he roared at his cook-steward.

'No I didn't, captain! If you remember, just before you promised all the profits of the voyage to the church if we got through the storm safely, God sent a particularly great wave. It went right through the galley and took the beans and the olives and the bread and cheese, and the sugar too. In fact, all I managed to hold on to was the coffee.'

The captain stared at him, purple-faced.

'To Hell with you and God!'

And finally, back to Peraticos for an example of the way in which Greek shipowners a century or more ago were already developing crude prototypes of systems that today would be cloaked in the respectability of 'productivity bonuses'.

The caique captain-owner would present an occasional hard-boiled egg to his crew members, separately and surreptitiously, instructing each of them to keep the gift secret and eat it in private – an egg was then a rare delicacy in a diet of bread, tomatoes, onions, olives and white *feta* cheese.

Later, when there was routine maintenance work to be done, he would call out from the bridge: 'Hey, look alive, you who got the egg!' All four would redouble their efforts.

Greek shipping goes international

During the last two decades of the nineteenth century, Greek merchants living abroad – particularly in London, Marseilles, Istanbul and Black Sea ports – had embarked on a policy of buying steamships and entrusting their operation to Greek captains, usually former owners of sailing ships, who were eventually given the opportunity to buy the new ships and set up in business for themselves. The great Greek shipowner families, many of them still active today, built up their fleets in this way in the quarter-century between 1885 and 1910. One result was that, around the turn of the century, the emerging Greek-flag fleet consisted mainly of fairly new ships, since even the second-hand vessels were as a rule no more than five or ten years old. Already, the focus of shipping activity was moving away from Greece.

The First World War saw the virtual destruction of the Greek fleet (it lost 270 of its 475 ships), and the 1920s that of its reputation: when compensation was paid out for tonnage lost in Allied service the Athens government, ill-advised and short-sighted, enlisted the weapon of punitive taxes to force Greek owners to reinvest immediately, at a time of extraordinarily high prices. As the government had been warned they would, ship values plummeted between 1920 and 1922, and the Greeks lost 80 per cent of their investment. Shipowner distrust of state intervention is based on solid foundations.

Throughout the 1920s, because of their financial losses and the disappearance of the wealthy merchants, Greek owners could afford only very old vessels, prone to accident, subject to scuttle in insurance frauds and bearing the stigma of 'hellships'. Greek shipping had reached its nadir.

Recovery was prompted, and the basis laid for future development, by the Greek shipping offices in London. Shipping businesses in Athens had at least a representative office in London, which bought ships on their account. Piraeus was little more than a port at which cargo was handled.

Though the Greeks had become active in northern European and South American trades during the nineteenth century, until the First World War the majority of Greek ships still plied the Mediterranean and Black Sea. Real worldwide trading in its present form developed during the 1930s.

In terms of family origin, Chios is still the main Greek shipowner island, along with Oinousses, Andros, Kassos and Syros in the

Aegean, and Cephalonia and Ithaki among the Ionian islands, without this meaning that the mainland, including Piraeus and the Mani region of the south Peloponnese, has not contributed sizable contingents of seamen and owners.

Shipping developed later in the Ionian islands because the Venetians had carried their own trade, and it was then built up through connections with Black Sea merchants of Ionian origin. However, the Ionians have always produced seamen rather than shipowners.

The Second World War and the 'Greek miracle'

The Second World War cost Greece three-quarters of its ships, two-thirds of its tonnage and about 6,000 seamen: recovery this time dated from the sale by the United States in 1946 and 1947 of 575 of the welded Liberty cargo ships that had helped win the Battle of the Atlantic and keep the armies supplied. Greek owners took up 98 of the Libertys, a figure that put them second only to the British among purchasers from thirty-three countries, and they would have bought more if their allocation had been larger.

At about the same time, the late Aristotle Onassis, most colourful of all the 'Golden Greeks', issued himself a licence to print money that Stavros Niarchos and others were quick to copy. Among the first to appreciate that oil was about to displace coal as the primary source of energy, he discovered that if he could obtain a long-term contract from an oil company to carry oil he could then, on the strength of that contract, get a loan from a bank to build the ship to fulfil the contract. The loan was repaid from the proceeds of the first few voyages, and the rest was pure profit.

Obviously, it was a sleight-of-hand formula that worked only for those who got in first; this explains why, even in the balmiest days of cheap oil, there were still Greek shipowners who were only moderately rich.

The Greek-owned merchant fleet, by no means all of it flying the Greek flag, peaked in the mid-1970s at almost 5,000 ships and more than 52 million GRT. Although by 1988 these figures had been almost halved, the Greek-owned fleet was still the largest in the world: in flag terms, Liberia, Panama, Japan and Russia were ahead of Greece, but the first two traditional 'flag of convenience' countries owed their position essentially to Greek-owned tonnage.

The importance to Greece of its shipping industry as measured by invisible receipts has also approximately halved in the past seven or eight years, from almost 2 billion US dollars a year to just over 1 billion. Nevertheless, shipping remains second only to tourism as a source of invisibles. Also, it is scarcely less important as a provider of work: counting the estimated 80,000 Greek seamen and the thousands of jobs provided in shipping-related industries and services, owners calculate that one Greek family in every ten derives at least part of its income from the merchant marine.

With little national cargo to carry, Greek shipowners live by tramping: the ability to have ships available where needed, at competitive rates. This makes them supreme champions of free competition, and implacably hostile to national cargo reservation or inter-state cargo sharing arrangements in any guise.

Except, of course, in Greek waters! Greek owners and successive Greek governments are firmly agreed on the desirability of preserving their country's coastal passenger and freight services for Greek-flag ships exclusively, and thus of defending cabotage to the last ditch and final gasp. The arguments employed range from the archipelago nature of the Aegean to national defence considerations. For this reason, and also because cabotage is like a pillar of salt – if water is allowed to seep in at one point, the whole structure may topple – you will find that you can take a cruise from a Greek port only on a Greek liner. British cruise ships are free to call at the islands, but their passengers must begin and end their cruises outside Greece.

Walking along the Akti Miaoulis (Miaoulis Quay) to where the Piraeus ferries and cruise liners dock, and observing how new most of the taller buildings are, you will begin to appreciate the extent to which the 'miracle' of post-war Greek merchant shipping has transformed the appearance of Greece's principal port.

Come back in ten years, and in all likelihood you will see even greater changes. It has finally been appreciated that Piraeus cannot be at the same time the largest passenger terminal in the entire Mediterranean and the sole cargo port for a region of Greece containing a third of the country's population and half its industrial base. A choice has now been made, in favour of people: if plans are implemented on schedule, within the next decade the whole of the central port will have been dedicated exclusively to passenger movement, with new reception facilities, greater expanses of greenery and hopefully even a solution to the traffic problem.

The Greek merchant fleet will continue to be run from offices in Piraeus, London and New York, but in Piraeus itself the tourist will hardly realise that it is engaged in trading at all. Also, if present trends continue, more than half the Greek-flag fleet will consist of coastal freighters and passenger-cargo ferries, fussing about in the same Aegean sea where open-sea shipping may be said to have begun.

Greece Today

Though Greece today, in 1989, appears to have weathered its self-generated economic crisis of four years ago, and wage restraints have been relaxed, it is still the EC member with the highest inflation rate and the most obvious symptoms of social discontent. The Greeks now know, after their experience of austerity, that no matter how affluent their country may be by the local standards of thirty years ago, it is not yet sufficiently rich to be able to afford a welfare state of the Anglo-Danish type and, like its people, must live more or less within its means.

It was not a lesson attended with pleasure, as will almost certainly be brought to your attention during your stay. It required that living standards must fall, not far perhaps, but for the first time in three decades. The natural reaction was and still is resistance in the form of strikes. You may well find that if the buses are running the trains are not, and if the banks are open the bakeries are closed. You may also observe indications of unemployment and under-employment. Though nothing compared to the times just after the Second World War when close on a million Greeks were driven to permanent or temporary emigration, it is a persistent problem and for that reason disturbing.

If you were in Greece three or five or seven years ago, you will remark how much more crowded the shops and tavernas were then. Only the video clubs, then a rarity, have blossomed since and are continuing to flourish. The Greeks spend more time at home now, not from choice but of necessity, weighed down by bills and taxes and deprived of the assurance that wage increases would be at least in step with inflation and usually a little ahead. However, to appreciate Greece today a rather longer perspective is needed: say thirty years.

Through the eyes of children

In the immediate aftermath of the Second World War and the Greek civil war, and to a diminishing extent until the early 1960s, only an American relief organisation, the Foster Parents Plan, stood between several thousand Greek families and a possibility that normal deprivation could turn at any moment into actual starvation.

In return for $8 a month, then 240 drachmas, and the occasional parcel of food and clothing, the children supported by the Plan had to write a monthly thank-you letter to their 'foster parent'. The letters were translated in Athens, and copies were kept on file. Through the eyes of children between the ages of five and fifteen from every corner of mainland and Peloponnesian Greece and the large and small islands, they made up a body of testimony of what it was like to be alive and poor in Greece in the days when Britain was painfully emerging from austerity, Germany was rebuilding its gutted cities, Australia was welcoming monthly boat-loads of Greek immigrants, and Greece itself was slowly recovering with the help of aid under the Marshall Plan.

Though the files may no longer exist, the tenor of the letters remains in the mind:

- Yesterday I was beaten when I went to school because I had missed lessons for three weeks. But I couldn't return until the chicken laid an egg, because they laugh at me when I haven't got a pencil.
- Thank you for the second blanket. Now that we have two, my sister and I can sleep in one bed and mother in the other.
- Last week we went to father's grave and laid some flowers. It's just three years since the bandits (communist guerrillas) came and shot him because he wouldn't join them. Mother went straight to bed when we got home, and won't stop crying.
- In reply to your question, yes, we did sell our tobacco, but the merchants paid only half as much as last year. So now we shan't be able to buy a goat, to have milk this winter.
- Last week something terrible happened. Mother got a sudden pain in her side in the morning and went to bed, and in the afternoon she died. The doctor came next day so she could be buried, and now we are going to an orphanage.

By the middle of the 1960s Greece had outgrown the need for this form of direct charity, and 240 drachmas had lost their value. The Plan moved elsewhere. But Greece was still a very poor country. A family expected to spend between a third and a half of its income on rent. Jobs were precious, and the unemployed could look only to their families for support; it was not altogether unusual for unsuccessful beggars, or those whose heart was not in it, to be found dead in shop doorways or public conveniences in the depths of winter. Regardless of what the law said, children in the villages, girls especially, were lucky to finish primary school, and to dream of a university education required a courage divorced from reality. There was no health service, or right to a pension, outside the main towns. As late as the 1967–74 military dictatorship, Brigadier Stylianos Pattakos, a country boy himself, could describe the five-day week as a 'Marxist invention'. The trade unions were docile, in the grip of 'fathers of labour' appointed by government, and a six-day week of sixty hours was far preferable to no work at all. On Saturdays, shops did not close till 10 p.m.

In Athens, the present-day apartment blocks were beginning to be built – for the most part, they date from the 1960s. But the mistake should not be made of attributing them to money: they were the result of poverty. Had the state been wealthier, it could have imposed at least elementary town planning regulations. The blocks would not have been constructed side-by-side along narrow streets, each occupying the site of the one- or two-storey house it replaced with never a thought of greenery, simply because the faster they were completed the sooner the tax was collected.

Greeks had always been ambitious to own their own homes; for the poorer, and particularly for those flooding into Athens from the provinces, the construction of a dozen or more apartments on the site of a former one-family house made this an attainable ambition. The condition was that costs should be held down by building small and cutting standards.

The availability of mortgages, through a specialised state bank and some trade union organisations, helped solve the problem of downpayments. The blocks themselves were built under a system that required little or no capital: the owner of a site would exchange it for one or two of the more desirable of the apartments to be built and then move into a rented home for a couple of years, while construction would be financed from the down-payments and ongoing instalments paid by prospective apartment purchasers as the work progressed. Final payments, due on presentation of the key, represented the builder's profits – provided he had managed to keep out of debt.

It meant that apartments were purchased while the block still existed only on paper, or as a hole in the ground; work could begin only when enough down-payments had been received to finance the cost of cement and reinforcing rods. Obviously those who bought the apartments had little control over quality; they were committed to the purchase, had scant hope of recovering their money in the event of a dispute with the builder and, in any case, were concerned above all to move in as quickly as possible to avoid the double haemorrhage of payments and temporary rent which, as likely as not, was driving them into debt.

One result of this lack of planning, and above all of the lack of greenery, was seen in July 1987, when more than 1,000 inhabitants of the 'cement city' which Athens has become died of the effects of a heatwave compounded by air pollution.

Had the purchasers been wealthier, they would not have herded themselves into the apartments out of desperation. They would also have been able to afford the time and money for commuting from satellite towns that the governments would have had the budgetary facility to create. The few architects with vision and a sense of responsibility who saw and drew attention to what was happening to Athens were simply advised to be 'practical'.

The face of change

A quarter of a century ago, the Greeks had heard of television but not yet seen it, dreamed of owning radiograms and considered themselves fortunate if they had a small radio and a separate gramophone. In much of the countryside there was still no electricity. The farmers, with the cooperative movement and collective cultivation emerging only slowly, and with no means of borrowing from banks, either sold their crops at the prices offered or lived by barter among their neighbours.

The city Greek had a 'quarter-pillar' of ice delivered to his home in the morning to help preserve food. Unless it could be done in a saucepan, the housewife took the family's midday meal to the baker for cooking; if she had an oven, she could afford to use it only on Sundays. There were so few cars that Panepistimiou Street, the main Athens thoroughfare, could accommodate two-way traffic with a double tramline down the centre and still have room for bus terminals. The villages were still effectively managed by the old triumvirate of priest, schoolteacher and gendarme; the first two taught acceptance as a spiritual and temporal duty, and the third ran sheepdog on the flock.

Politically, Greece was in the grip of the stern conservative movement, sometimes under one name and sometimes another, that had won the civil war but found difficulty in coming to terms with peace. It correctly assumed that recovery could result only from hard work and foreign investment, and that the latter required compliance with the will of the USA as the new and this time indispensable 'protecting power'. In the allocation of budget resources, successive governments gave absolute priority to electrification, road construction, irrigation and the creation of an industrial infrastructure. Hospitals, universities, public transport and pensions were luxuries that could be deferred.

If this was scarcely a populist policy, elections could usually be won with the help of priest, schoolteacher, gendarme, trade union official, the armed militia (now disbanded) and, if need be, judicious manipulation of the military vote. In any case, it hardly mattered if the occasional election was lost, since the centrist opposition differed only in degree, the Communist Party was in exile until its legalisation in 1974, and the last of the Aegean island internment camps were still a functioning threat. A most effective weapon, cheap and ubiquitous, was the 'certificate of political reliability'. This was a police document testifying, in effect, that its holder was untarnished by left-wing associations; without one, it was impossible to obtain a job in the public sector, a passport or, for a time, even a driving licence.

Eventually, of course, these pressures had to be relaxed. Almost inevitably, the moment was delayed beyond the point of safety. Constantine Karamanlis, who held it all together during eight years that changed the face of Greece and made its ultimate admission to the European Community 'club' a realisable vision, was manoeuvred out of office by the Palace in 1963. Greece descended into political chaos, and in 1967 the fallen fruits of power were picked up by the Colonels; they did not even need to shake the tree.

You should be careful in discussing the dictatorship with casual acquaintances: the scars still itch, and bleed easily. For one thing, there is the question of whether, and to what extent, the Greeks resisted. On the morning after the tanks rolled into central Athens the Greeks discovered from their radios that they had lost their freedom, theoretically their most prized possession. Helen Vlachou – who preferred to close her daily newspaper, *Kathimerini*, rather than submit to censorship – caught the mood of that morning in her book *House Arrest* (1971):

'The night's work had been perfectly timed, admirably well executed, and of a lightning rapidity; but the next day the shrugging indifference of the population of Athens helped it more than military efficiency had done. The people in the streets did not show any kind of concern, did not seem to care one way or the other. It was not a victory for anybody, man or party; it was an all-round defeat for all politicians of all denominations, a philosophically accepted overthrow of a situation that evidently did not appeal to the majority. "Let them have a go," was the feeling of the day.'

The triumvirate of middle-ranking officers – Colonels George Papadopoulos and Nicholas Makarezos, and Brigadier Stylianos Pattakos – had one supreme flaw: they knew how to seize power, and hold on to it, but not what to do with it afterwards. The plot and its execution were everything; they proved themselves simple opportunists, without policy or programme.

The trio held power from April 1967 to November 1973, when they were overthrown by a second junta led by the sinister commander of the Military Police, Brigadier Dimitrios Ioannidis. In more than six years, ruling by the formula 'decide and decree' and with neither Parliament nor public opinion to consider, they had failed to solve even one of the 'structural problems' of Greece's economy and society that still torment elected governments.

Some Greeks will insist that the task was inherently impossible for any dictatorship; others take the view that for this failure alone the three and Ioannidis are deservedly serving sentences of life imprisonment, though these were imposed for the seizure of power, not its misuse.

Certainly they were given a credit of time, by the Greeks and internationally. With some honourable exceptions – far fewer than those who afterwards laid claim to resistance activity – the Greeks preferred to fight back with humour. One of the classic dictatorship jokes may be more revealing than its authors intended. A man on a crowded bus taps a fellow passenger on the shoulder. 'Excuse me, sir, but do you happen to be in the army?' 'No!' 'Perhaps you have a brother in the army?' 'No!' 'Or a son?' 'No!' 'Then in that case, sir, would you mind not standing on my foot?'

The ordinary Greeks had their livings to earn, and their children to educate. They knew how easily they could find themselves ordered to live on an Aegean island, dependent on a family that would be both hungry and harassed because of them. It should cause little surprise if they left the heroics to those who were safely out of the country. But this is not always the way it is told today.

Be careful also when you talk to Greeks about the Polytechnic, the uprising of students at the Athens Polytechnic in November 1973 which was, beyond doubt, the supreme act of resistance, but at the same time was peculiarly inappropriate in its timing and unfortunate in its results.

Bending to pressures from outside Greece, Papadopoulos had already appointed a civilian government that, on the Turkish model and under his guidance as first President of the newly-established Greek republic, would supposedly lead the country back in careful stages towards parliamentary rule. It was this government, and Papadopoulos, which the uprising overthrew; it brought to power a man, Ioannidis, who cared nothing for world opinion and had no fear of killing. There were no more outbreaks of resistance.

Many Greeks had said from the beginning that it was pointless to resist the dictators since in the end they would fall by themselves, thus demonstrating their awareness of their own history. They were proved right in July 1974 when the Ioannidis junta suicided. After it had brought Greece to the edge of a war with Turkey that could have led only to disaster, wiser officers brushed it aside and requested the formation, without conditions, of a civilian government.

Karamanlis returned in triumph from eleven years of self-exile in Paris to restore and consolidate government by the people. Armed with the authority of successive election victories and an unequalled international prestige, he jumped the queue in Brussels and secured Greece's accession to the European Community ahead of Spain and Portugal.

This second time round he lasted for six years. In 1981, failing to appreciate that the 'great change' that had become a national longing had already been made inevitable, though not yet manifest, by Community membership, the Greeks voted for socialism. For four years they were handsomely rewarded; then the bill was presented, late in

1985, and is still being paid.

Since 1974 Greece has been a republic; in a plebiscite late that year 70 per cent of Greeks voted against the monarchy, confirming in a free vote the outcome of a rigged referendum staged by the Colonels the year before. The monarchy, really, had only itself to blame: King Paul, who had succeeded his brother George II, forced the 1963 resignation of Karamanlis shortly before his own death, and two years later his son, Constantine, did the same to the Centrist Prime Minister George Papandreou, the late father of the present Prime Minister Andreas Papandreou. Constantine himself went into exile in December 1967 after the failure of an ill-planned attempt to overthrow the dictatorship that, in any case, was undertaken too late to earn his redemption; he had to fight his 1974 campaign from London. In the circumstances, it was surprising that even three out of every ten Greeks voted for him.

Under the 1975 Constitution, presidents are elected by Parliament for five-year terms: that of the present head of state, Christos Sartzetakis, expires in 1990.

The political situation

In view of the Greeks' obsession with politics and their sense of deprivation if a year goes by without an election – general, local or European Parliament – it may seem strange at first that they are only now beginning to acquire a recognisable party system. In a country where everything is politicised, the professional politician can sometimes appear curiously apolitical to those accustomed to equate politics with parties of principle.

Except for the Communist Party of Greece (KKE), which until 1974 was illegal anyway and depended on front organisations, all the parties now represented in the 300-seat, single-chamber Greek Parliament were formed after the fall of the dictatorship.

The conservative New Democracy party, which Karamanlis set up as his vehicle for the 1974 elections, has already established a local record: it has survived three changes of leadership with only minor defections and without a change of name. Its nucleus was the pre-dictatorship National Radical Union, which Karamanlis had created in 1955.

The present ruling party, the Panhellenic Socialist Movement (PASOK), was formed in 1974 by Andreas Papandreou, the Prime Minister, from the left wing of what his father George Papandreou had named the Centre Union when he established it for the 1961 general elections. There is nothing yet to indicate that PASOK will emulate the New Democracy party in outlasting its founder.

The kind of party with which the older, non-communist, Greeks have been brought up, and feel comfortable with, consists of a gathering of Deputies, solidly based in their own constituencies, who have adapted to the parliamentary system the precepts of the racecourse. Usually, but not necessarily, within the broad confines of right, left or centre, the Deputies identify the one among their peers with the most promising actual or potential track record and place their loyalty at his disposal for as long as he goes on winning. They are students of form, which in politics is graced by the name of charisma, rather than of content. Thus Karamanlis was succeeded as New Democracy leader by George Rallis, who lost one election and went. The same fate awaited Rallis's successor, Evangelos Averof, and would have befallen the present leader, Constantine Mitsotakis, if he had not come close to victory in 1985, and if, by then, New Democracy had not been running short of heirs of the older generation.

Political fluidity is assisted by the absence of a party tradition and the method of leadership elections. The 'parliamentary group', namely the party Deputies, chooses the party leader, and there is no such thing as an annual party conference. Even the architecture of the Parliament building helps party positions to be trimmed: the semi-circular chamber provides benches to be slid along, rather than floors to be crossed.

New Democracy, recognisably conservative under Karamanlis, today follows the policies of the liberal centre in which Mitsotakis served a long apprenticeship. Thanks to the dictatorship, the old right is now associated in the popular mind with neo-fascism, draws a steady three to five per cent of the vote in general elections, is without representation in Parliament and can safely be ignored. For economic rather than political reasons, the ruling Socialists have swung sharply into social democratic channels since 1985, abandoning at least temporarily the policies that brought them two successive election victories in the hope of eventually obtaining a third. This is not found at all confusing: on the contrary, it is the way things have always been.

There is a comparable instability about the voting system. Traditionally, the one under which the next elections will be fought is decided by the government in power a few months before polling day. Since the Second World War, the Greeks have tried all the tested systems: the British winner-takes-all (hurriedly dropped after one experience); simple proportional representation; reinforced proportional representation, and the dictatorship's gun-on-the-table ('Please, sir, would you move your revolver from that pile of papers so that I can take one and vote against you?').

Reinforced PR, which gives bonus seats to the larger parties, appears to have become established, but there is no legal impediment to a switch to the simple PR system demanded by the Communists and the minor parties. The government will decide, shortly before

Parliament is prorogued, on the basis of whether it can reasonably hope for another overall majority under the present system or should reconcile itself to leadership of a coalition and therefore let the smaller parties into Parliament.

Nevertheless, changes are under way, presented as reform. In particular, Deputies have had their wings clipped. The number of seats won by each party is still determined by the votes received, but which of the candidates will actually be returned to Parliament is decided by their positions on the party tickets, which in turn is a matter for the leader. Also, in the name of transparency, parties now receive financing from the state budget, in the form of 1,000 million drachmas shared out annually among those represented in Parliament, in return for which they are theoretically required to reveal their other sources of income. Transparency, however, has not yet been extended to campaign spending. Parliaments are elected for four years, and the next general elections are expected in June 1989.

The national issues

Taking it for granted that you do not intend to adopt a vow of silence while in Greece, there are two issues on which it would certainly be useful to be able to converse intelligently. They are not only at the forefront of Greek attention but, to a remarkable extent, above and outside the daily political battle. They are *Ta Turkika* and *Ta Kypriaka*, matters connected with Turkey and Cyprus. They are closely interwoven, and it is unlikely that either can be solved except as part of a package.

Ta Turkika   Despite the legacy of smouldering animosity, the present confrontationary situation in Greek–Turkish relations arises directly from the events of a single year, 1974. On a winter's day early in the year the Prime Minister of the Ioannidis junta went to Kavala in northern Greece to announce, with the equivalent of a clash of cymbals and roll of kettledrums, that Greece had struck it rich.

An international consortium of oil companies working under a Greek state concession, he proclaimed, had located immense quantities of commercially exploitable oil offshore near the island of Thassos – the so-called 'Prinos' field. Oil had indeed been found, but not of a particularly good quality (it was heavily larded with sulphur) and not in particularly large quantities (an estimated nine million tons). It was enough to cover about 10 per cent of Greece's annual requirements until the early 1990s. And it was enough to whet the appetite of Greece's neighbour across the Aegean.

At that time, not one Greek in 100,000 would have known what you were talking about if you had tried to interest him in the 'continental shelf'. Now, it is you who will be expected to be familiar with the *ifalokripida*. Weather maps on Greek television show an Aegean Sea that has no eastern shore; beyond the Greek islands, nothing. In fact, of course, there is the whole Anatolian coast of Turkey, at some points only an easy swim from the closest Greek islands. So who owns the continental shelf?

On the basis of a 1958 Geneva Convention and the 1982 Law of the Sea, the Greeks do, since islands have their own continental shelves. Turkey, which has not ratified the Law of the Sea (but neither has the United States), responds that the Aegean is a special situation since the mainland coast of Turkey is as long as that of Greece. Refusing to concede 97 per cent of the shelf to Greece under the Law of the Sea formula, it demands half on the principle of equity, and proposes political negotiations on a division.

The Greeks are ready to go to the International Court of Justice at The Hague, but solely for demarcation of the shelf under the provisions of the 1982 law. The result is a stalemate, broken by occasional flares of crisis. In effect, each country has had to desist from further exploration outside its own territorial waters, for fear of starting a war, and whatever oil the shelf may contain remains undiscovered.

More emotively, to the Greeks the Aegean, with its 2,000 Greek islands, is a Greek archipelago through which the Turks are free to pass, but no more. To the Turks, it is intolerable that they should be confined to the eastern edges of a 'Greek lake'.

The dispute provides an obvious temptation for Turkey to occupy the islands east of the mid-Aegean, including the Dodecanese group, Chios, Samos, Mytilene, Lemnos and Samothrace. Convinced that Turkey would if it could, and asking why else it has an 'Army of the Aegean' along the Anatolian coast supplied with landing-craft, the Greeks have fortified the islands and spend a greater proportion of their gross national product on defence than any other NATO country except the United States.

Inability to resolve the main dispute has encouraged the emergence of secondary issues. Thus, *Ta Turkika* today also embraces questions of airspace and civilian air corridors over the Aegean, command control on and over the sea, the militarisation of Greek islands close to the Turkish coast (Greece insists on the supremacy of the unwritten law of self-defence), and allegations by Ankara concerning Greece's treatment of the Moslem minority in Thrace.

But the brush with disaster in the spring of 1987, when the two countries came closer to war than at any time since 1974, was over oil exploration. The Turks moved a seismic research ship into the North Aegean, the Greeks said it would be 'prevented' if exploration were carried out beyond Turkish territorial waters, and Ankara responded that force would be met with force. In the end, the vessel engaged in no tests outside Turkish waters, and the countries' Prime Ministers embarked on a form of 'dialogue' through an exchange of letters. But the letters addressed one issue only: the continental shelf.

The shelf remains at the heart of the dispute, the most likely spark of a war in cold blood, and the essential component of any eventual package agreement.

As a direct if delayed result of the 1987 confrontation, the Greek and Turkish Prime Ministers embarked early in 1988 on a continuing series of 'summit' meetings that appear to have led only to an unwritten agreement that war should be avoided! None of the specific problems has yet been resolved or, on the evidence of official announcements, even discussed in depth. Nevertheless, there does appear to have been an improvement in the atmosphere of bilateral relations.

Ta Kypriaka

In the watershed year of 1974, as the late Archbishop Makarios once told them pointedly from a balcony overlooking Constitution Square, the Greeks recovered their democratic freedoms but the cost was paid by Cyprus. In July of that year the Ioannidis junta mounted a coup in Cyprus intended to depose and murder the Archbishop and make the island part of Greece – the old dream of *enosis* (union) which had been quietly abandoned in favour of statehood once the British had left in 1960.

The Turkish response, theoretically justifiable as a police action under the treaties that established the independence of Cyprus, was to invade and occupy the northern third of the island to protect the 18 per cent Turkish-Cypriot minority of the population. Greece and Turkey stood on the edge of war, the junta collapsed, and Karamanlis returned.

The Turks did not withdraw from Cyprus once the danger of *enosis* had been averted; instead, they are still there in defiance of a series of United Nations resolutions stacked up both by the British Commonwealth and the non-Aligned movement. They have established an 'independent state' in the north of the island that only Turkey itself recognises, have introduced thousands of settlers from the mainland to take over expropriated Greek-Cypriot property, and have built up an armed presence that is a clear threat to the rest of the island. Athens has warned that any attempt to move south will lead to a Greek–Turkish war.

The Cyprus stalemate explains Greece's determination to erect barriers against any improvement of Turkish relations with the European Community and, above all, to block Turkish membership. To the Greeks, the only military threat they face comes from Turkey, from a member of the alliance that they believe to be favoured by the USA and NATO because of its geographic proximity to the USSR and its supposedly greater strategic and numerical contribution to western defence. In these circumstances, a degree of anti-Americanism is understandable. But this never extends to the individual American visitor; the Greeks personalise their politics, not their animosities.

Current economic distress

Though it is easy enough for the government to demonstrate statistically that the Greek economy is now in far better shape than seemed possible four years ago, it is another matter to persuade wage-earners and pensioners that they are much better off with 'only' 12 or 14 per cent inflation than they were when prices were rising by 24 per cent a year or more. If the economy has been 'stabilised', so too has the discontent engendered by the painful years of austerity that stabilisation entailed; this you will observe for yourself – from strikes, protest marches and conversation – as you move about the country. The Greeks might have been more forgiving had they not been duped: in October 1985, three months after winning a second four-year term under the slogan 'even better days to come', the socialist government was forced to initiate an austerity programme amounting to adoption of basic New Democracy policies that the electorate had just been persuaded by Mr Papandreou to reject.

Internationally, Greece was approaching the position where it could no longer borrow the $3,000 million a year that it then needed to cover its foreign deficits and loan servicing. Domestically, the government faced one of the highest public sector deficits in western Europe (18 per cent of gross domestic product) and a 25 per cent inflation rate matched by wage indexation (the automatic adjustment of incomes to the consumer price index) that was making Greek products unsaleable abroad and vulnerable on the home market to European Community imports.

The government faced the choice of either restoring the competitiveness of Greek products internationally, or re-erecting the old tariff barriers that had had to be dismantled with Community accession. Despite campaign promises of a referendum on continued Community membership, there was really no choice at all: far too much money was coming in from Brussels to make withdrawal a practical option, and without withdrawal there could be no return to protectionism. The stabilisation programme adopted in October 1985 had the apparently modest aims of reducing the foreign borrowing requirement to the amount needed to service existing debt, bring inflation down to 10 per cent, and cut the public sector deficit also to 10 per cent of gross domestic product, by 1988.

In pursuit of these aims, the drachma was first devalued and then allowed to depreciate by the difference between Greek and average Community inflation so as to make exports more competitive and imports more expensive (and also your holiday cheaper in terms of your own currency). Indexation was watered down by the imposition of ceilings well below inflation on permissible wage increases, taxes were increased, and the public utilities and state corporations (electricity, water, telephones, the post office and most forms of public transport) were required to come closer to balancing their budgets by charging more for their services.

Inevitably, this placed a disproportionate burden on lower- and middle-income Greeks, especially on those living on wages, salaries and pensions. The result was a predictable discontent. New Democracy, unable to attack the policies directly since it had advocated them, could only complain that they were not accompanied by cuts in state spending and did not address the larger problem of development through stimulation of domestic and foreign investment and reducing the size of the public sector by privatisation. Certainly there has been only insignificant investment for at least the past ten years, but whether this is due to a shortage of money or a lack of trust in the socialist state is a matter of dispute.

Since the middle of 1988, there have been indications that Greek and foreign investment is beginning to pick up again. The balance of payments has ceased to be an acute problem: though the trade deficit continues to widen, the gap is bridged by increased receipts from tourism, shipping and emigrants' remittances to their families in Greece, and by inflows of foreign capital for deposit in banks and purchase of shares as well as for construction of factories and hotels and establishment of offices. The foreign debt is no longer growing, and should soon begin to shrink. Conversely, with polling day approaching, the government is understandably in no hurry to launch an assault on budget deficits that are acknowledged to be the main source of inflation. Whether its policy of putting the international half of the house in order first and leaving the domestic half for later will prove sufficient to give it a third successive election victory remains to be seen.

Black and shades of grey

There are three permanent peculiarities of the Greek economy, which stem from a deep-seated contradiction in the Greek character and the readiness of successive governments to swim with the current.

- Every Greek dreams of owning his own business, or at least of being self-employed. If he has to settle for something less, he wants to work for the state.
- Though Greece owes all its very considerable industrialisation over the past quarter-century to private enterprise, every government since the collapse of the dictatorship has sought votes through expansion of the public sector.
- Greece has a black economy that is not only unusually large by any standards but those of Italy, but that is also the mainstay of state budgets to which, theoretically, it makes no contribution. Greece

would very probably be bankrupt if it were not for tax evasion.

The black economy is something which you, as a visitor, will make contact with at every turn of the road. On a beach, you will rent a chair and sunshade from someone of whom the tax authorities know nothing. Buy something from a small shop, not a supermarket, and you will probably see your money go into an ever-open till underneath a cash register that is there only in case of inspection. If you need to visit a doctor, do not expect a receipt. If you have the misfortune to break a tooth or lose a filling you may be offered two prices, one with and the other without a receipt.

Bowing to the inescapable, the government taxes members of the liberal and fix-it professions – in essence all the self-employed from physicians to plumbers and from engineers to electricians – on the basis of their declarations only if they are above an assumed minimum income that is arbitrarily determined. Effectively, therefore, all income above the minimum level may well be untaxed: to the victors go the spoils. Addressing a Foreign Press Association lunch a few years after the collapse of the dictatorship, a conservative Finance Minister lamented the fact that, 'to the ordinary Greek, tax evasion is a form of national resistance.' He should scarcely have found this surprising.

Between black and white there is a large grey area. Agricultural income in practice and bank interest by law are exempt from tax, the former because of the difficulty and cost of collection rather than any remaining poverty gap, and the latter because otherwise the Greeks would not save the money the government needs to borrow to finance budget deficits. (Supposedly farmers are taxed, but the exempt allowances are set so high that few admit to reaching the ceiling.)

Greek wage and salary earners and pensioners, meanwhile, taxed to the limits of their endurance, cannot see all that much difference between the plumber who gives them no receipt and the neighbour who lives comfortably on the tax-free 18 per cent annual interest, paid monthly, from his nest-egg of five million drachmas that he probably accumulated through tax evasion in the first place. It scarcely gives the dodger a bad name.

The Greek who cannot work for himself wants to work for the state because of security of tenure and a guaranteed pension after thirty-five years of service, regardless of age. The wider public sector now embraces all the utilities, all forms of public transport except taxis and some coastal ferries and provincial buses, 90 per cent of the banking system and, through nationalisation and the creation of state and local authority enterprises, an increasing proportion of manufacturing. Though New Democracy talks of privatisation, when it was in government it too proved unwilling to forgo the political advantage of expanding the public sector.

Even the Greek who has achieved his ambition of personal incorporation into the public sector will very possibly have a second part-time job in the evening. A bank clerk may keep the accounts of a small business; teachers give 'cramming' lessons, and also turn up as taxi drivers and hotel pianists; your wine waiter could be a lawyer in a state corporation by day. Greeks collect jobs as a security against total unemployment, and because aspirations are higher than salaries. The working hours make it feasible, and the income from the secondary occupation, normally, is not declared; if it were, Greeks would probably stay at home and watch television. The money they now earn would not circulate, and the government would have to look elsewhere for the income from indirect taxes, essentially on consumption, which today accounts for close on two-thirds of budget revenues.

Shortly after the 1981 general election the government successfully outlawed the holding of two jobs in the public sector, but recoiled from its own proposal to extend the prohibition to two jobs in the private sector, or one in each. Though hours are staggered to some extent to relieve traffic congestion, Greeks employed in the public sector can expect to go to their offices around 7.30 or 8 a.m., work through without a formal break, and be home for the day by 3 p.m. Lunch and siesta still leave time for a second job before the 11 p.m. late-show at a cinema or the 1 a.m. closure of the cafés.

This explains how a Greek with a wife and two children, earning a good average salary of around 100,000 drachmas a month of which almost half may well go on tax and mortgage payments, can afford to engage a language tutor for his children, run a car, spend weekends at his country home, dress himself and his family in imported clothes, and eat well at home and frequently in restaurants. He can also buy a colour television set, hi-fi system or video recorder that still cost twice as much as in London, even though in theory the tax difference has been whittled away under EC regulations. The government pockets the fruit of a special 'luxury consumption tax', and does not enquire where he found the money.

If he has been a little too ostentatious, he may run foul of life-style criteria when he reports his income. He will then, complainingly, pay the extra tax demanded on the basis of the way he lives, but will insist that the money he has been caught spending came from bank interest. Since banking secrecy is strict in Greece, the assertion is not open to challenge. Any pricking of conscience is quickly anaesthetised by observance of the prodigality with which governments spend tax money, *his* money, in ways that he can easily persuade himself are scandalously wasteful, and that New Democracy now tells him are indeed deplorable. The man outside the system is encouraged to seek not its destruction but his own niche inside it, so as not to be left behind by his neighbours.

The black and grey economies do not simply keep the white one going; they are also the great social safety valve.

Different on the islands

One of the main concerns of all Greek governments since the Second World War has been to persuade the million and a quarter Greek people who live on islands, and particularly the younger generations, to reject the temptation to migrate to urban centres on the mainland. The key to achieving this is to erode any sense of isolation felt by islanders, and at least to reduce, if not eradicate, distinctions between islands and mainland in terms of standard of living and quality of life.

More specifically, this breaks down into equal expectations of year-round income; as well as equal availability of educational opportunities and health care, locally in their most basic forms – clinics and primary schools – and reasonably close in the form of hospitals and access to higher education and vocational training. Also, there must not be a gross inequality in regard to entertainment: at the most basic level this means radio and television, which in turn means electricity.

The newest government department is the Ministry of the Aegean, set up on Lesbos to coordinate island development in all forms: its current programme covers shipping and air communications, water and electricity supply, radio and television and even the provision of liquid fuels. In addition, the islands feature prominently in seven Integrated Mediterranean Programmes (IMPs) approved for Greece by the European Community and involving investment in infrastructure, agriculture, industry and energy, fishing and aquaculture, and tourism. If all seven programmes are implemented on schedule – something that unfortunately cannot be taken for granted, even though the determination exists – projects will have been completed by the end of 1993 costing ECU 3.41 billion, with more than half of the money provided by the Community.

One of the IMPs is for Crete and another is for the Aegean islands: the stated goals of the latter, in broad definition, range from the development of agriculture, fishing and tourism to the creation of conditions in which the islands, individually or as members of a group, will be able to confront competition from mainland Greece and beyond the Greek borders.

The Aegean Ministry is strongly sold on communications, and looks to the establishment of new ferry lines, the improvement of connections between small islands and nearby larger ones, and the better coordination of Olympic Airways flights to large islands with local ferries to nearby small islands which are currently not provided with regular air services. Subsections of this programme foresee relatively rapid and frequent coastal services linking the northern port cities of Thessaloniki, Kavala and Alexandroupolis with the islands of Lemnos, Lesbos, Chios, Samos, Patmos, Kos, Rhodes and Crete. Also, a greater subsidisation of shipping to islands too sparsely populated to support freight and passenger services of the quality and regularity they must have if they are to cease to be the backward regions of a two-speed Community.

The ultimate vision is of a kind of 'Aegean national highway', along which modern ferries will provide services comparable to those offered by trains and buses between provincial cities on the mainland.

In conjunction with the Civil Aviation Service and the National Defence Ministry, the Aegean Ministry has also drawn up plans for the construction of heliports on twenty-eight islands: Koufonisia, Amorgos, Anafi, Aghios Efstratios, Ikaria, Fournoi, Psara, Oinousses, Donousa, Ios, Heraklia, Schinousa, Sikinos, Folegandros, Kimolos, Sifnos, Serifos, Andros, Kea, Kythnos, Kalymnos, Nisyros, Simi, Tilos, Halki, Agathonisi, Patmos and Leipsi. This will leave very few island inhabitants (or tourists, for that matter), more than a short hop away from a well-equipped general or maternity hospital. The alternative would be to convert dozens of small island clinics into full hospitals: even if the money could be found, staffing would be an insurmountable problem.

In addition to the heliport programme, those airports on the larger islands that are still too small to accept charter flights from outside Greece will be enlarged, and others will be built on such islands as Syros, Naxos, Samothrace (Samothraki) and Astipalaia. By 1989 or 1990 this should have brought the number of Greek mainland and island airports to more than forty.

Though the improvement of sea and air communications will open up the islands to greater numbers of tourists, and stimulate the construction of hotels, a realistic claim to more than an inconsequential share of the visitors obviously depends to an even greater extent on the assurance of uninterrupted and sufficient supplies of electricity and water. For power, aeolic (wind) has been preferred to solar energy – it is cheaper and simpler, and in the Aegean the wind is even more faithful than the sun – and domestic and Community programmes are already being implemented that will provide the islands with a hundred or more wind generators of 55 and 100 kw output. Similar programmes for water foresee drillings for artesian supplies, desalination when economically feasible, and improved shipments by tanker to islands where no other solution has been found. Direct-dial telephoning, important psychologically, is now available to all of the inhabited islands.

The Greeks laugh at themselves for their belief in '*tha*', the syllable that converts the present into the future tense and a harsh reality into a vision. However, there are two persuasive reasons why the promises for the islands are likely to be kept: they have to be, if social problems are to be averted, and the money from the European Community will be forthcoming only if identifiably used for the stated purposes.

Whether the changes that this will entail for island life and traditions will be wholly for the better is a question that is unlikely to be answered for ten or fifteen years. But those familiar with small Aegean islands in the winter find it hard to challenge the need for the programmes.

The Greek and the family

Though family ties have weakened in the quarter-century that has seen Greece change from a basically agricultural country to one standing on the tripod of agriculture, manufacturing and services, they remain powerful by European comparisons. Traditionally, the family that sticks together in Greece lives in a village, goes to church in a group on Sundays and saints' days, may hold a council to decide anything from the purchase of a cow to a suitor's application for the hand of a daughter, and considers itself collectively responsible for the well-being of all its members. At its worst, this can lead to 'honour killings' and vendettas, of which rare and isolated incidents occur even now in Crete. At its best, it means that the family looks to its own resources, not to the state, when one of its members becomes unemployed, ill or disabled. Twenty-five years ago it had no alternative.

That the Greek family today is in a state of transition and gradual attenuation is explained by the drift to the cities, the growth of a welfare state and the changing position of women.

● **Population drift.** In the thirty years between the census of 1951 and that of 1981, the population of Greater Athens grew by 1.64 million to 3.02 million. With the population of the whole country around 10 million, broadly one Greek in three is an Athenian. Much the same happened in Thessaloniki, and to a lesser extent in the other main cities. There was never any mystery about the reasons for the drift of population to the urban centres: job opportunities, greater financial security and the availability of state services. And at the end of the day, somewhere to go at night.

Clearly, this had to be fought. If the villages were to be abandoned, who would feed the rest of the country? If the lesser islands were depopulated, who would keep out the Turks? There was occasional talk, apparently serious, of imposing a licence requirement for a move to Athens, or some form of 'internal migration tax'. Fortunately, Karamanlis and his successors, including in this instance the Colonels, were wiser than those who offered free advice from coffeeshop tables. They chose the developmental route: new roads, electrification, irrigation, secondary schools first and then universities, rural clinics at least if not full hospitals, and subsidised transport to counter isolation. The process is continuing today in the form of administrative decentralisation. But while it has halted the drift, it has not reversed it, and families remain separated.

● **The welfare state.** Though this is definitely a misnomer in comparison, for example, with Britain or Denmark, Greece may already have overtaken such socially retarded countries as the USA and West Germany. The government's ambition, close to realisation, is that no Greek should be without some form of national insurance cover, providing at least health care and a basic old age pension; less than twenty years ago, this was still the prerogative of the urban worker.

Unemployment relief is patchy, with entitlement to benefit and duration of cover strictly circumscribed. The point has yet to be reached where even those qualifying for maximum family allowances could live better on relief than if they were working. Also, the national health service exists rather on paper than in the realities of new hospitals. However, malnutrition in its various disguises is no longer a common cause of death, and anyone requiring hospital treatment can be sure at least of a bed in a corridor. The Greek in need can now look to state as well as to family.

You may wonder, however, why you are accosted by so many beggars – in crowded buses, the underground to Piraeus and at street corners. Without doubt, some are simply exercising the only profession they have ever known, on beats they have found remunerative, and are unwilling to deprive their regular clients of the opportunity of contentment through charity. At Christmas and Easter they are reinforced by gipsies with babies, some of the latter allegedly rented. But regardless of what you may hear about blind beggars changing into their rags in the stock exchange toilets when the markets close (even the Greeks who give most regularly will often insist that they are being taken), there are undoubtedly isolated pockets of genuine hardship. Whether you give or not is your decision: you will be invited, but at least you will no longer be pestered.

● **The ascent of woman.** The old family was patriarchal in concept, and Greece was a man's world. A family that bred prolifically but with the wrong balance would say it had 'two sons and five burdens', and pitying glances would be cast on the husband of such a wife. The sons had it both good and bad. It would be unthinkable that they should assist with the household chores, clean their own shoes or fetch their slippers. In the fields, the girls picked and they carried, assisted by their donkeys; afterwards, they relaxed in the coffee-shops while their sisters cooked. But they had a price to pay. The daughters had not only to be provided with dowries but married off first; a son would be regarded as disloyal to his family, the worst of charges, if he took a wife before he had secured husbands for his sisters. It made for late marriages, and incessant subdivisions of family land into smaller and smaller holdings.

Women acquired the right to vote only in 1952, and the first woman Deputy took her seat in Parliament the following year – the honour of electing her, in a by-election, went to Thessaloniki; the Parliament elected in 1985 consists of 289 men and 11 women.

The battle for sex equality has already been won legislatively, and remains to be fought only in the psychology of the Greeks. Sex discrimination in career opportunities and at the place of work has been outlawed, and the principle of equal pay established. There are women judges and professors as well as taxi and bus drivers, and women's branches of the police and armed forces; women are theoretically subject to conscription too, but have not been heard to complain over the fact that only volunteers are taken. Women have acquired the right to separate ownership of property after marriage and, in the event of divorce, an equal share of communal property acquired during marriage. They may also, if they wish, retain their maiden names. Other legislation has removed adultery from the category of criminal offences, so making divorce easier, and has placed controls on the 'exploitation' of the female body in advertising.

Far more importantly, all legal underpinning has been removed from the dowry system, while the establishment of thousands of low-cost day-nurseries has made it possible for married women in practice to make use of the equal opportunities provided for them in theory. At the same time, there has been a widening appreciation that the most durable form of dowry, and the only one protected against inflation, is a working wife's salary and eventual pension.

● **The result.** The family today, in the tribal sense, is no longer an economic necessity. It has been dispersed, among towns and villages and from the family home into the cells, in both senses, of small apartments.

And yet it survives. On holiday weekends and in the summer it reunites in the village of origin. In ways that the state cannot, it looks after its own: family influence will be used to find young Costas a job or get him a posting closer to home during his conscription, and it is a rare parent who will be consigned to an old people's home if there is a corner in the city apartment where a bed can be unfolded at night. The difference is that it is now a matter of blood, not survival. To many a modern Greek, his family has become a useful organisation to belong to, but there is definitely life outside.

Religion and the church

Like the family, and because of the same liberation process, the Church too is in a state of flux. Statistically, of every 1,000 Greeks 974 are Christians, and of these 967 belong to the Greek Orthodox Church. Orthodoxy is the established religion and other faiths and creeds are tolerated on condition that they refrain from proselytism –

a mandatory abstention with which only Jehovah's Witnesses find difficulty in complying.

The Greek Church is autocephalous, divided into seventy-eight dioceses, headed by an Archbishop of Athens and All Greece, and governed by a synod of the hierarchy of which all serving bishops are members. Day-to-day administration is handled by a small 'permanent holy synod' of twelve senior bishops and the Primate. The separate Church of Crete, the bishoprics of the Dodecanese and the Holy Community of Mount Athos are spiritually and administratively subject to the Ecumenical Patriarchate of Constantinople.

The Greek Church derives its income from its very considerable real estate and directly from the state budget; in certain civil matters it is subject to the Ministry of National Education and Religious Affairs. Married men may be ordained as priests, but celibacy is a requirement for higher office.

That said, it becomes a question of influence and power, and of why the Church is being drained of both.

A reformist movement is believed to exist among a section of the clergy, but appears to be dormant: nothing has been heard for several years, for example, of the proposed liberalisation of priestly dress and appearance. Thus the priest continues to be seen only in black ankle-length cassock and pillbox hat, full-bearded and with hair uncut. You may occasionally observe a priest driving a car or sitting, in his canonicals, enjoying a glass of wine in a taverna. But you will not find one serving on a local authority as an elected member, or getting out among his parishioners in ways you would expect at home. This is both natural and peculiar for a Church that, while never producing missionaries, was the defender of the faith during the Turkish period.

Aloofness at a personal level, at a time of rapid changes in society, has been accompanied by misfortune in the choice of issues on which the Church has taken a stand in relations with the state. Two particularly significant and popular reforms instituted since the socialist election victory in 1981, both initially resisted by the Church hierarchy but finally accepted under threat, introduced civil marriage as a second ceremony or an alternative to religious rites, and legalised abortion.

Civil marriage, apart from relieving the irreligious of compulsory hypocrisy, had the side-effect of legitimising the position of thousands of Greeks in the communities abroad who, having been married only in civil ceremonies, were regarded under Greek civil law and in the eyes of the Church as unmarried when they came to Greece; their children were therefore illegitimate, and had only restricted inheritance rights.

Legalisation of abortion amounted simply, but emotively, to recognition of an existing situation. Though figures of 250,000–300,000 abortions a year and 'three abortions for every live birth' quoted during debate on the legislation were obviously no more than estimates, there has never been any doubt that abortion was, and is, the most common form of birth control and family planning in Greece. The Church understandably regards it as tantamount to murder, but could offer only doctrinal arguments to the basic observation that if the embryo was going to be slaughtered anyway at least the mother should be protected from the danger of botched interventions carried out secretly, and both parents should be protected from the risk of blackmail. The only real losers from legalisation were those doctors who saw their income fall, as the fees for abortions plummeted and also became reportable for tax.

It is partly in deference to the Church that even now, despite AIDS, the condom is neither mentionable on television, advertised nor displayed for sale: *profylaktika* is still a whispered purchase, whether from a chemist or a newspaper and cigarette kiosk.

In 1987 the Church again found itself on the losing side in an argument with the state over compulsory distribution of unexploited agricultural land. Technically, the dispute was over whether the land should go to individual landless farm workers or to farm cooperatives, but this was a finer point lost on most Greeks, to whom it seemed simply that the Church was resolved to keep what it held.

Not surprisingly, given its militant traditions, the Church does not support pacifism, and accepts the need for continued conscription. The lack of a 'but' to soften the 'yes' costs it sympathy.

In the last thirty years the Church has lost much of its authority within a rapidly developing society, and has seen its regular Sunday congregations become increasingly elderly. Even Easters are no longer what they used to be: the midnight resurrection services on the Saturday, held in the open air, are still heavily attended, but few now stay longer than ten minutes to hear the *Christos Anesti* ('Christ is Risen'), light their white candles, exchange kisses and set off fireworks. And a growing number of them go to church after, not before, they have eaten their Easter soup – the traditional breaking of the Lenten fast that only their grandparents will have observed. Athens municipality has ceased to drape the street lamps in black tulle on Good Friday and lovers of classical music, to whom Holy Week was an annual oasis in the desert of Greek television and radio, no longer enjoy a respite from soap operas and politics.

If you had been travelling in a crowded bus in Athens a few years ago, and a priest had got on, you would have remarked the alacrity with which the passengers competed to offer him a seat. Now, unless he is very old and of saintly appearance, his entry has the peculiar effect of turning a humdrum city street, observable through the windows, into a fascinating panorama. Eventually, someone will catch his eye, and the offer will be made; the fact that a younger priest will occasionally reject it may well be a good sign for the future.

The impact of tourism

The rapid changes in Greece over the past thirty years have been accompanied, and to some extent influenced, by the growth of tourism from a movement of a few hundred thousand to close on 8 million a year. But first, a clarification: to the Greek National Statistics Service, a tourist is anyone entering Greece on a foreign passport, including Greeks from the communities abroad and foreign businessmen operating out of Athens who, if they happen to travel monthly, become twelve tourists a year. But while this may swell the numbers, it scarcely affects the growth rates. It certainly does not alleviate the responsibilities which you, the holiday-maker pure and simple, must share for what you have wrought.

Thirty years ago you came to Greece by boat from Marseilles (there were no ferries from Italian east coast ports to Patras), by the old Simplon Orient Express (the part of it that ended in Athens and not Istanbul), or by air to Athens, the only Greek destination to which you could fly. If you were adventurous, you might then hazard the twenty-four-hour voyage from Piraeus to Rhodes or Corfu; otherwise, you would settle for a visit to one of the offshore islands – Aegina, Poros, Hydra or Spetses. There were no day cruises. In Athens you had a choice among six deluxe hotels; in Rhodes or Corfu you had to settle for much less.

In those days you did not come for the swimming, and probably did not come at all unless you were drawn by the antiquities. If you did pack a swimming costume, you took your dip from a free public beach that did not provide any facilities.

In Athens at least, you could eat well – possibly better than today in terms of quality and service. Apart from your hotel there were about a dozen really excellent restaurants (barely half of them in existence today among the scores of new ones), and in the evening Plaka awaited you. Since the restaurants relied on Greek business they had to be good.

You could not have dreamed of a cruise. Andreas and George Potamianos, whose Epirotiki Lines is today the world's largest family-owned cruise-ship company, had still to purchase the long-gone Semiramis that, waddling across to Myconos, became the first Greek cruise liner ever to sail out of Piraeus on a regular schedule.

In the villages, you were such a rare sight that you could expect to be greeted by old ladies with cries of *Evghè* ('Glory be!'), on the assumption that you had sprung from that legendary tribe of British aristocrats of Victorian and Edwardian days, known sometimes as 'Lordi' and sometimes as 'Imiluds'. Since you were presumed normally to ride a horse, you would at least be offered a donkey. In short, you made no impact on the economy or on Greek society.

But now, to accommodate you, hotels have been built in every corner of the mainland and on all but the tiniest of the islands. There is no part of Greece you cannot reach easily, safely and quickly. You have become a principal support of the Greek economy: you bring in well over $2,000 million a year, double the contribution of the Greek merchant marine and half as much as Greece's total exports.

By coming earlier and staying later (from Easter to October instead of June to late August), you are the great safety valve against unemployment. The Greeks who serve you would be delighted to see you in the winter also, but in the meantime are prepared to consider themselves employed if they have well-paid jobs for seven months of the year.

Because of you, at least a smattering of English has become almost essential for a young Greek seeking a job in any of the businesses or services with which you are likely to come into contact. European Community accession has accelerated and expanded this process, but you began it. You have also brought with you some of your modern ways, and to some extent have disfigured the landscape and disoriented society.

Possibly the worst and best thing you did was to make the ordinary young Greek feel, first, a sense of inferiority and then, when he sat down and thought about it, a determination to reach your standards. It was not your fault that you made him feel poor in his own country; you could not be expected to live austerely just because he had to, especially when you were on holiday. But he looked at your ample wardrobe (you yourself travelled in style in those days) and thought of his one Sunday suit. He contrasted your meals with what he got at home, and observed the equanimity with which you paid bills that would have bankrupted him for a month. He did not always appreciate that when you hailed a taxi for a thirty-mile drive it was because you had no idea where to find a bus.

As you grew in numbers, the socialist and communist parties pounced on the opportunities you offered. One of the central themes of their campaign against European Community accession (others included the alleged interdependence of the Community and NATO and the unpreparedness of the Greek economy) was that membership would turn Greece into 'the holiday camp of Europe' and the Greeks into 'a nation of waiters'. For considerations that were never made entirely clear, this was presented as the ultimate degradation.

With similar innocence, and equally unknowingly, you were also chipping away at what some Greeks regarded as their moral standards. What was normal for your beaches was revolutionary indeed for theirs. Before your arrival, the bikini was unknown. Now you have imposed the monokini, and it is only a matter of time before your *pankat* (the Greek for skinny dipping, from the words for above and below, *epano* and *kato*) bursts out of its Myconos beach-heads. Before you came, a nipple in a photograph could get a newspaper editor arrested. Just look at the kiosks now!

You helped to liberate young girls and widows, the former from their chaperone brothers and the latter from everlasting black. You even taught the Greeks to drink between meals, and introduced them to beer; just about the last barrier still to fall is that against public drunkenness. Before tourism, one small nineteenth-century brewery in central Athens covered Greece's total needs in beer and still relied for solvency on the manufacture of household ice. Wine was the daily drink with meals, and ouzo the only aperitif. Beer was for celebrations, whisky was exclusive to snob bars, and the customary order at a café or cinema, if not coffee, was a lemonade, ice cream or cake.

Now, it is an underprivileged family indeed that does not make its regular contribution to keeping Scotland afloat. Beer is drunk as often as wine. Even the coffee has changed, from what was then Turkish and subsequently rechristened Greek to ordinary instant. Though Greek coffee by law is available wherever any coffee is served, not one of the cavernous coffee-shops of central Athens which used to serve no other form, and which were the places where politicians gathered to consult the electorate across a table, has survived your invasion.

On the principle that nothing can be envisaged until it has been seen, hotels of concrete and glass had to be erected along beaches and in tiny bays before it was appreciated what they were doing to the landscape. Controls then followed, but the eyesores remain.

So too does the neon lighting, in which the economical Greeks invested only because word-of-mouth requires a common language. Thirty years ago Plaka in Athens was a peaceful nineteenth-century haven; fifteen years ago it was a garish nightmare, in which every nightclub and taverna competed against its neighbour with the brightness of its lights and the volume of its amplifiers; today, because even you were frightened away along with the Greeks, it has become quiet and tranquil again. There is one charge, however, of which even the most partial Athenian jury would have to acquit you: co-responsibility for the picture presented by modern Athens. To the contrary, if it had been even suspected that one day you might vote with your airline tickets, bypassing the capital at least on return visits to Greece, some of the worst offences against town planning might not have been committed. If so, your invasion came thirty years too late to save the Athenians from themselves.

In summary, you have rescued the economy, provided sufficient jobs to make emigration unnecessary, helped to narrow the divisions between Athens and the rest of Greece by going everywhere and needing to be supplied with the means of spending your money, ruined some of the most beautiful landscapes, inculcated discontent, promoted communism and, on the islands at least, built a new Greece more or less in your own image. God bless and shame on you!

National and regional characteristics

While Greece is too small and compact a country to have major regional characteristics, the Greeks themselves tend to differentiate among three main groupings: mainland Greeks, island Greeks and 'overseas' Greeks. The last-named are not so much those still living in the communities abroad, who are flattered and supplied with the means of preserving their ethnic identity as if they were indeed a potential fifth column, as those who have repatriated either from choice or by force of circumstances.

Mainland Greeks

The mainlanders are the ordinary Greeks; those who have become modern in their pursuits and ambitions at the cost of their sense of comradeship, feel themselves oppressed, insult one another with vociferous abandon, and frequently give the impression of regarding any government, even one they voted for, as an occupying power. When you get to know them better, you may find they are not altogether unjustified. It naturally follows that the mainland is particularly disorganised.

Island Greeks

The islanders are reputedly calmer, shrewd rather than crafty, and closer to nature and the sea; their young menfolk are the mainstay of the Greek merchant navy. Until fairly recently, they were only too frequently ambitious to convert themselves into mainlanders; they have now been given less reason to feel isolated, through improved communications, better services, the expansion of the tourist movement and the levelling effect of television. For the most part, they still contrive to live at a more leisurely pace.

Within the islander context, those of the Ionian islands regard themselves as the more cultured – the readiness of considerable numbers of other Greeks to concede this suggests that there might be some truth in it – while inhabitants of the more numerous Aegean islands, from Thassos and Samothrace in the north to the most southerly of the Dodecanese, retort that they at least can keep their women in better order.

Overseas Greeks

Greeks from the communities abroad, for the obvious reasons of education and fluency in languages, are already disproportionately represented in Greece's managerial class; their share is likely to increase still further if governmental hopes of attracting high-technology industries and more international business and services bear fruit. As may be imagined, Greeks from the *'diaspora'* are not particularly well-liked by those who see the plums go into their baskets in the multinationals, the travel industry, foreign and Greek banks and foreign diplomatic missions.

To some extent, they are only living up to their reputations: any

Greek will tell you that the Greeks 'do better' abroad than in their own country, work and study harder, are more law-abiding and pay their taxes with greater willingness and honesty. The conclusion drawn is that there must be something wrong with Greece, as state and society; the reaction is a widespread ambition among Greek families of even modest means to send at least their sons abroad for advanced studies and character-building.

Except that Cephalonian names tend to end in *-atos* and Cretan in *-akis* or *-yannis*, inferences of origin cannot safely be drawn from surnames.

Considering all Greeks as one people, some broad generalisations may be hazarded:

- They are such great complainers that they even find fault with the Greek weather. They complain about taxes and the way they are spent, prices and incomes, state services, the bureaucracy and politicians. When all these subjects have been exhausted they will complain about one another and, as a last resort, about themselves.

Karamanlis once made a joke of it, in the days when he was winning one election after another: 'The Greeks', he said, 'swear on the day before that they will never vote for me again, when they go to the polls they re-elect me, and on the morning after they say they will cut off the hand that did it.'

As he almost said, you should beware of taking them too literally. You do not need a particularly close relationship before someone will say to you, 'We are the worst race in the world [*heirotera ratsa tou kosmou*].' A gentle disclaimer is the proper reaction; at most they only half-believe it, in moments of despair.

- They criticise everything Greek, a tendency that leads them to prefer an import, at prices they often cannot afford, to the quite possibly superior and certainly cheaper local equivalent. This explains the profusion of 'boutiques' and the contents of supermarket shelves; it is a characteristic that has resisted years of governmental assault in the form of 'buy Greek' television campaigns based on ridiculing the snobbishness of not doing so.

As a natural corollary, they are outgoing towards foreigners and have a desire to be liked even greater than that of the Americans. They really do have only one word, *xenos*, for both foreigner and guest. Thus they are polite and helpful to the tourist even when inordinately rude to one another.

In this context, hospitality is frequently offered and should be accepted, but with caution. The shared bill is an alien practice to the Greeks. It touches on *philotimo*, literally love of honour but rather closer in meaning to 'face', since an offer to pay half impugns a host's ability to pay all. So accept only what you will be in a position to reciprocate later.

- For a country that invented philosophy, you will find an odd lack of curiosity – except about your personal affairs – and a propensity to view everything in terms of black or white. The idea of fact defined as generally accepted theory does not appeal, and argument, including parliamentary debate, is usually a recital of fixed positions. Very often, a sight not yet seen cannot be worth seeing since otherwise it would have been seen already, and a dish not part of an established household menu cannot be worth tasting for the same reason. Foreign restaurants would die without the foreign community.

● Because there has so often never been quite enough to go round, the Greeks are only now, and reluctantly, learning to wait in line, and given half a chance will still jump a queue. Boarding a bus is a free-for-all, with victory to the sharpest elbows, and you would be unwise to assume a taxi is yours until you are actually inside. A Greek would rather take his custom elsewhere than wait in a queue for service.

● Possibly because of 'the 400 years', the Greeks are curiously reluctant to commit themselves and are not altogether comfortable with a clear situation. 'Protecting one's rear' can often be an excuse for looking only backwards. A civil servant, for example, wants 'the papers' before he will act and 'the papers' generally require at least three signatures because of the safety that numbers provide, so do not expect to complete any business expeditiously. Similarly, you should not assume you can manage anything at all on the telephone; business is transacted face-to-face, across a desk and preferably over coffee.

For similar reasons, a question is likely to be answered with another, leaving to you the responsibility of drawing a conclusion. For example:

You to your hotel porter: 'Will it rain today?'
He: 'Isn't the sun shining?'
You: 'Yes, but will it last?'
He: 'Isn't it August?'

He knows very well it hardly ever does rain in August, but wants to protect himself from the faint possibility that it might.

In a restaurant, you may ask a waiter if there is any roast veal. If he replies, 'Is it on the menu?' instead of 'Certainly!' he probably means there isn't. A Greek takes no pleasure in causing disappointment to a foreigner, so it is for you to judge when his 'tomorrow' should be interpreted as 'never'.

Attitudes towards the law

Though it has no serious crime problem, Greece is notoriously not a law-abiding country, for reasons that spring from history and are reinforced by tradition. Despite a common tendency to exaggerate the degree to which the 400 years of Turkish hegemony that ended more than 150 years ago may still be blamed for modern attitudes, the period of 'the yoke' was one in which, for the ordinary Greek, the only available expression of patriotism between revolts was quiet defiance. He learned the importance of stubborn non-cooperation, and outlooks that have become part of the national subconscious are difficult to eradicate. He learned also to distinguish between laws that must be obeyed, and those that can safely be ignored.

The axiom that bad money drives out good has been demonstrated more than once in Greece (barely twenty years ago the most respected currency, welcome in restaurants and alone acceptable in sale and purchase of real estate, was the British gold sovereign); Greek experience suggests that something similar may apply to legislation. One result of European Community membership and economic difficulties has been the emergence of 'productivity' as the catchword of the moment. For Parliament, productivity is measured by the yardstick of laws enacted. Provided their number is sufficiently impressive (the October 1987 to June 1988 tally was sixty-two), the 300 Deputies can feel themselves secure against accusations of indolence; the content and enforceability of the laws are of lesser importance.

Names and language

Thousands of shops in Athens and the resort islands flout a law that was passed with a flourish of trumpets but will probably never be applied; the conflict arose out of concern for the Greek language. As the tourist movement grew in numbers and expanded in destinations, it was only natural that shopkeepers, restaurateurs, proprietors of fast-food outlets and bar and nightclub owners should be moved by their sense of politeness and business acumen to anglicise themselves. This led to expressions of concern among academics and in the correspondence columns of the quality press, which in the early 1980s found an echo in Parliament. The conviction spread that a stand must be taken, the tide must be turned – the names must be *Greek*.

It was not the kind of suggestion to be opposed frivolously, especially since a similar campaign was being fought in France at that time. When realism collided with patriotism, it was no contest. Language is at least as sensitive an issue in Greece as in France. It is commonly asserted that Greece as a nation might not have survived 'the 400 years' but for the secret schools, mostly run by village priests, which preserved the Greek language. It is less than a century since the last language riots in Athens, over the encroachment of spoken 'demotic' Greek into the preserves of the formal *katharevousa*. Even in the last fifteen years there has been sometimes bitter argument over the adoption of demotic by the state services and the simplification of written Greek through the use of a single uniform accent to indicate stress.

It was therefore only to be expected that once the new threat from foreign names had been identified, legislation should follow. Parliament decreed that, from a specified date, all foreign names above business premises or in neon advertising would become illegal unless surmounted by a larger sign giving the name in Greek. The final date for compliance, though several times extended, has long since passed. Nothing has changed, and there has not been one reported instance of prosecution.

Knowing which

When a country wallows in legislation, the trick is to identify which law is being applied at any particular moment. A driver may park his car on the pavement outside his home for years with perfect impunity, and then receive three tickets within a week and possibly find his plates removed as well. So he seeks out another pavement, until his own recovers its immunity.

At another moment, he may find it temporarily expedient to wear the seatbelts that are legally compulsory at all times. When word spreads that decibels are being measured again, boys with their first motorcycles replace the silencers that take away half the fun. Similar whispers tell householders when it would be safer to put out their rubbish in specially purchased black plastic sacks instead of supermarket carrier-bags.

Of greater relevance to the tourist, it has been quietly impressed on the individual policeman that his ambitions will not be furthered if he allows himself actually to notice certain things that in law he is required to prevent, such as toplessness on beaches anywhere, or nudity even on the most remote.

In Athens there are now more than twenty cinemas, five of them in the immediate vicinity of Omonia Square, showing totally illegal hard-core pornography from 9 a.m. to midnight, for very low admission fees. They used to be raided at regular intervals, but now a policeman is more likely to be found in the audience than clamping handcuffs on the projectionist. The pornographic magazines displayed by Athens kiosks are equally illegal, though only a shop that sold them in the privacy of a back room, away from the gaze of children, would today run any risk of being raided.

Much of the blame or credit for these changing attitudes lies with tourism, and Greece's reluctance to expose itself to adverse publicity abroad. Also, the advent to power in 1981 of the first socialist government in Greek history has brought with it an increased emphasis on personal freedom. This is seen in the view now taken of homosexuality and also in the protest marches, once a rarity, that disrupt Athens traffic two or three nights a week in fine weather. The government may appear to be more unpopular than any of its predecessors, but in fact it is simply less protected from sidewalk dissent.

Crime – and the lack of it

Crimes 'against the person' are definitely not something you need worry about while in Greece. You may have your pocket picked, especially on a crowded bus, but it is almost inconceivable that you should be mugged.

Consider the average householder. Increasingly, he is learning to secure his apartment with expensive steel-lined doors imported from

Italy, triple locks and safety chains. But he is moved by fear of burglary, which is common; not of assault, which is rare. Affluent New Yorkers on Aegean cruises have been known to ask if the gold earrings worn through pierced lobes for formal dinners can safely be retained during trips ashore. The answer is yes: if something cannot be taken stealthily it will not be stolen at all. The grab that takes the ear lobe with the earring simply could not happen in Greece, not so much because it would turn a sentence of six months into one of six years but because it would be wholly out of character. For the same reason you will never be threatened with a knife. Once I was startled to see two officer cadets, one naval and the other air force, in dress uniforms, resort to their ceremonial dirks to determine which was the better service. But that had to do with honour, not crime, and anyway it was a very hot night.

If this is so, you may ask, then why is every bank branch or post office with safety deposit boxes guarded by uniformed police armed with sub-machine guns? The answer is provided by a short but concentrated spate of Chicago-style robberies in the early 1980s. Greek opinion was genuinely shocked, for this was something that had not happened before. Neither has it happened since the guards were assigned.

Police

Until four or five years ago, law enforcement in Greece was shared between the grey-uniformed city police in Athens, Piraeus, Patras and Corfu and the green-uniformed gendarmerie everywhere else. The two forces have now been unified into the blue-uniformed Greek Police (EL-AS for *Elliniki Astonomia*). This obviously makes for greater efficiency and less duplication.

Within the police, there are subdivisions for traffic (white belts and gloves); 'protection of the national currency' (they may check your money when you leave the country); narcotics and the smuggling of antiquities, and 'markets control' (they keep tabs on shops, restaurants and such).

The aliens police, to whom you must apply for a residence permit if you are planning more than a holiday in Greece, are a branch of the plain-clothes 'General Security', the detective department. For everyday use, there is the *Ekato* ('One Hundred', named not for its exclusivity but for its telephone number); they make up the flying squad, and are equipped with prowl cars and motorcycles.

Duty officers at the *Ekato* can handle enquiries and requests for assistance in English, and should be dialled if you witness a crime, need an ambulance, accidentally start a fire or are disturbed by noisy neighbours in the 'silence hours' of the night or afternoon siesta. They are polite, patient and seemingly never ruffled, but you should not hold your breath until the car arrives.

There is also a riot squad, equipped with helmets and transparent shields and backed up by water cannon.

Greek police are equipped with pistols and truncheons (known in Greek as 'globs'), but are under strict orders to use the former only if their lives are in imminent danger and the latter with the minimum force required in the circumstances. Most of them, in the cities, also carry two-way radios. A surprising number of policemen now understand enough English to help you if you have lost your way; if they don't, they will usually find someone who does. Instructed since the collapse of the dictatorship to become polite and unfearsome, they now tend to wear their hair proportionately long and bushy.

To avoid unwanted contact with the police, it should be sufficient to observe speed limits, use your seatbelts on the motorways, never put a child in the front seat of the car, and stay sober. Should the worst happen, remember that the policeman's attitude will most probably reflect yours, so stay polite and keep smiling. If you tense up, he will – and then you are halfway towards arrest for the second worst crime a visitor to Greece is ever likely to commit: 'Insulting the Authorities'.

The worst? Just try offering him a bribe!

Drugs

The Greek authorities hope and believe they have succeeded in eliminating any lingering international belief that their country is 'soft' on drugs. But the visitor should bear in mind that, apart possibly from length of sentence, no distinction is made among types of drug, and it is no defence to claim that even a tiny quantity of cannabis was intended solely for personal use.

Although Greece's drugs problem has not attained anything like United States or European dimensions, anxiety over the use of drugs among the young has been made more acute by the AIDS connection. Also, Greece has traditionally been one of the routes along which heroin has reached Europe from the Middle East or Turkey, concealed in cars, trucks, yachts and suitcases.

Two principal weapons are deployed against drug trafficking: close surveillance, including the use of sniffer dogs at airports and land border crossings, and sentences of as much as twenty years if large quantities are involved. Even the shortest sentences are not convertible into fines. In addition, a car in which drugs have been discovered is confiscated.

Purchase of antiquities

If you should decide to purchase an expensive replica of an Ancient Greek statuette or a Byzantine icon, you will be given a certificate that it is a copy. This should be retained in case questions are asked when you leave the country. This rule does not apply to cheaper purchases from handicraft shops.

Greece is concerned to protect its archaeological heritage, a definition covering anything more than a couple of centuries old; sentences for attempted smuggling of antiquities are not much shorter than those for drugs offences. The concern is easily understood: a lucrative market is provided abroad, by private collectors and the less scrupulous museums. The demand is met through finds made by farmers and articles recovered from ancient shipwrecks or stolen from small provincial museums, isolated churches and under-occupied monasteries. While international gangs form the normal link between source and destination, use has occasionally been made of tourists and for this reason the police are watchful.

It should be borne in mind that a pebble picked up at an archaeological site and slipped into the pocket as a souvenir can be regarded as part of the protected heritage. While a guard who sees the action will normally insist only that the pebble or chip of marble be replaced, tourists have been taken to court in Athens for pebble-pocketing at the Acropolis. Though they escape with a fine, they can expect to spend a night in the cells awaiting trial.

It was a 'bad hour'

A last line of defence in a Greek court, one that will secure at least a sympathetic hearing when the situation seems hopeless, is that it was a 'bad hour' (*kaki ora*). This amounts to non-premeditation hung with bells.

In its wider uses, it once kept a British Council teacher out of court. A taverna cat had been importunate, as cats are, and became the subject of a complaint. A waiter, believing in direct action, kicked it out of the door. The teacher walked slowly across to where it had been, and kicked the waiter.

By the time order had been restored, the taverna was abuzz with whispers of *kaki ora*. The teacher apologised, and the waiter agreed not to press charges. Had it gone to court, the outcome would probably have been acquittal or a token fine. For every Greek judge is aware of the narrow line between a threat and its realisation, between a fist brandished and a punch thrown; though few Greeks actually cross that line, those who do have only to say it was a 'bad hour' to be certain they will be listened to with understanding.

Intent is also relevant: 'You surely don't imagine I did it on purpose?' You may expect to hear this from the driver of a car that emerges from a side-street, in defiance of the halt sign, and crashes broadside into your car. You may as well say no more – the 'bad hour' is yours, too.

It does serve to humanise the system.

Women travelling alone

Greece is a country where an unaccompanied woman can stroll along a dark street late at night without fear of anything worse than a sprained ankle. The authorities, including those responsible for tourism, take justified pride in the safety of the individual everywhere in Greece.

A woman need not be particularly attractive to anticipate the disguised compliment of a pinch, pat or surreptitious caress in a crowded bus or while waiting to cross a busy street, and she will hear whispered invitations that really amount to no more than the reflex action of young Greeks who consider themselves attractive to all women. A response is not expected, and she will not be pestered.

However, it would be unusual for an entire tourist season to pass without one or two cries of rape. It usually turns out that the rapist had the mistaken impression, in the absence of any other common language, that he was acting on invitation. So beware of any dress or behaviour that could be taken as a come-on. Young Greeks have been known to believe themselves irresistible, and the naïve woman visitor to Rhodes who enquired of a passing Adonis the nearest way to the Colossus should not have been as surprised as she seemed to be when she received the reply, 'But you're looking at me!'

There are occasional outbreaks of bag-snatching in Athens, by youths working in pairs from motorcycles, but increased penalties have made these less frequent in recent years. No woman will be refused service in a restaurant, bar or nightclub because she is unaccompanied.

Homosexuality and unmarried couples

The Greeks like to believe themselves without hypocrisy, which they describe as the 'English vice'; therefore, whatever they may feel about homosexuality in private, in public they behave as if it did not exist.

There are a few 'gay' bars in Athens and the resort islands, and rather more on Myconos. An Athenian woman of sufficient means will enjoy the 'frisson' of being dressed by a homosexual couturier or combed by a homosexual hairdresser, and happily married couples throughout Greece share jokes about homosexual priests and actors. But overt hostility is rare; so too are cross-sector invitations.

These unmalicious attitudes are to some extent threatened by the AIDS virus; there is concern, amounting almost to panic on Myconos, that homosexuality may be about to become bad for tourism and therefore bad for Greece. You should not suggest to a Myconian, even in jest, that his island may be the future AIDS capital of Europe.

As for unmarried couples, most Greeks really neither know nor care, and would consider it impolite to enquire. They display the normal curiosity over who, in the higher echelons of government and the world of the theatre and cinema, is this week living with whose wife, and are enthusiastic gossips, but ostracism over lack of formal marriage is a rare phenomenon. For a man, the companion of the moment is treated as a wife would be; for a woman, rather greater discretion is required – modern Greece, no matter what the law may say, is still a man's world in spirit. The children of single parents, if not always the parents themselves, now have equal rights in law with those of married couples, and illegitimacy is no longer a social stigma.

Almost every office block offers a 'garconiere' or two – a bed-sitter with kitchenette and bathroom for which the Greeks use the French word, having none of their own; it may be a place of tryst, the establishment of a mistress, the working quarters of a prostitute or the home of a student from the provinces. For those who can afford it, or whose position in society is more sensitive, there are hotel rooms available for indefinite lease. It is almost impossible for a Greek career, even one in politics, to be wrecked by sexual indiscretions.

Arson and terrorism

If you do not wish to contribute towards giving tourism a bad name, you should try to avoid starting fires. Greece is a hot, dry country, with little rain between May and October. It is also intent on preserving the little that remains of its woodland. In July and August in particular, when the *meltemi* wind blows hot from the north, a spark can cause a conflagration; as television spots point out, one tree can make a hundred thousand matches and one match can destroy a hundred thousand trees.

Since the penalties are proportionately high even for accidental arson, care is obviously needed with campfires and cigarette ends; it should also be borne in mind that sunlight focused through a broken bottle can burn down a forest. There are tourists in jail today for forgetting that!

Similarly with terrorism, the Greeks are understandably displeased when visitors who, since they are not resident, are technically tourists, make use of their streets for murdering one another. So you should not take it personally if your bags are searched when you enter Greece.

Gestures

You neither need nor could hope to pick up the deaf-and-dumb language of Greece in the course of a short visit, but there are two gestures which it is advisable to know if you want to avoid misunderstanding. Most Greeks are by now aware that the foreigner's raised right hand to signify 'no, thank you', 'please don't' or 'that's enough' is not to be confused with the almost identical Greek 'sign of the five' that means, in its most polite interpretation, 'damn your eyes!' But in the villages it could still occasion a moment of frigid misapprehension.

If you really do intend to 'give him five', named for the four fingers and thumb that stab in the direction of the face, all you need do is reverse the direction of the gesture for refusal from defensively backward to aggressively forward. You have then administered the worst possible insult that can be offered without use of words; obviously this should be done sparingly, and after due consideration.

The gesture you should not misinterpret is the blown kiss. The head jerks back, the lips open with a sometimes audible pop, and you have been informed that the answer is no, there isn't any, or he's not interested. You have neither been insulted nor made the recipient of an improper proposal.

A few words of Greek

Since the Greek with whom you come into contact has had to struggle hard to learn your language – it would be a mistake to think he picks up a foreign language more easily than the Englishman does, and the only slight advantage he may have is exposure to English through films subtitled in Greek in the cinema and on television – it is only polite to offer him a few words of Greek in exchange. For example, 'thank you' (*efharisto* or, if you prefer, F. Harry Stow), 'good morning' (*kali mera*), 'good evening' (*kali spera*) and 'good night' (*kali nichta*).

Also, you might remember that there is a feminine form for surnames. As a rule of thumb, you convert a man's name ending in -*as* or -*is* into that of his wife or daughter by dropping the final letter (Dimas to Dima, Kapsis to Kapsi); if it ends in -*os*, you convert with an -*ou* and shift the stress one syllable on (Papadopoulos to Papadopoulou). If a man's name ends in -*ou* (for example, Fotiou), obviously his wife's does too. If your guide introduces herself as Miss Papadopoulos, she is simply catering to your assumed ignorance.

A knowledge of Ancient Greek is of little use, except possibly for reading street names and bus destinations.

English is the principal second language, commonly spoken in hotels, restaurants, main post offices and the larger department stores as well as in the upper echelons of the public services. French is the second language mainly of the elderly. Italian is widely understood in the Ionian islands, particularly Corfu, German is spoken by thousands of repatriated migrants, and surprisingly large numbers of Greeks are fluent in Arabic.

An effort should be made to master the alphabet, so you can find your way around and have a better chance of getting on the right bus.

BACKGROUND INFORMATION

The alphabet

Alpha	A α	Short as in 'pat'
Beta	B β	Pronounced as V
Gamma	Γ γ	Gutteral G
Delta	Δ δ	Pronounced as soft TH as in 'father'
Epsilon	E ε	Short E
Zita	Z ζ	The English zed
Eta	H η	Long E as in 'heat'
Theta	Θ θ	Pronounced as hard TH as in 'thanks'
Iota	I ι	I as in 'pit'
Kappa	K κ	Simple K
Lambda	Λ λ	Simple L
Mu	M μ	Simple M
Ni	N ν	Simple N
Xi	Ξ ξ	KS as at the end of 'thanks'
Omicron	O o	Short O as in 'hot'
Pi	Π π	Simple P
Rho	P ρ	Simple R
Sigma	Σ σ	Simple S
Taf	T τ	Simple T
Ipsilon	Y υ	Another I as in 'pit', or Y as in 'pity'
Phi	Φ φ	Simple F
Hi	X χ	Simple H
Psi	Ψ ψ	Psee
Omega	Ω ω	Long O as in 'hope'

Note A hard D is written NT, as in Ken Ntontnt (Dodd)
A hard B is written MP, as in Mpomp Hope
OI is pronounced as a long E
AI is pronounced as a short E

The following words and phrases – a vocabulary cut to the bone – should see you through (the second column gives a phonetic transcription, with the stressed syllable underlined):

The courtesies

Good morning	kallym<u>e</u>ra
Good evening	kallysp<u>e</u>ra
Goodnight	kallyn<u>i</u>chta
Goodbye	ad<u>io</u>
Hello, goodbye, cheers!	yi<u>a</u>sas (yi<u>a</u>sou singular or familiar)
Please, don't mention it!	parakal<u>o</u>
Thank you	F. Harry Stow
All right	end<u>a</u>xi
Yes	n<u>ai</u>
No	<u>o</u>chi
Maybe	<u>ee</u>sos

Basic encounters

Where is …?	p<u>ou ee</u>nai …?
How much is …?	p<u>o</u>so (or p<u>o</u>so <u>ee</u>nai) …?
Too much!	pol<u>ee</u>
Have you …?	<u>e</u>hees?
I want (would like) …	th<u>e</u>lo …

One's bearings

Street	thr<u>o</u>mos (soft TH)
Avenue	leof<u>o</u>ros
Square	plat<u>ee</u>a

Sustenance (see also 'Eating and Drinking', pp. 103–115)

Food	fagit<u>o</u>
Bread	psom<u>ee</u>
Water	ner<u>o</u> (closer to the late Pandit than the Roman emperor)
Wine	kras<u>i</u>
Beer	b<u>ee</u>ra
Coffee	kafè
Coca Cola	Coca Cola
Waiter	gars<u>o</u>nn

Moving about

Restaurant	estiat<u>o</u>rio
Hotel	xenothoh<u>io</u> (soft TH)
Room	thom<u>a</u>ti (soft TH)
Post Office	tahithrom<u>ee</u>o (soft TH)
Letter	gr<u>a</u>mma
Stamp	grammat<u>o</u>sima
Police	astinom<u>ee</u>a
Customs	telon<u>ee</u>o
Passport	diavat<u>ee</u>rio
Grocery	bak<u>a</u>li
Pharmacy	farmak<u>ee</u>on
Doctor	yatr<u>o</u>s
Dentist	odondoyatr<u>o</u>s (tooth-doctor)
Entrance	<u>ee</u>sothos (soft TH)
Exit	<u>e</u>xothos (soft TH)
Car	aftok<u>i</u>nito
Bus	leefor<u>ee</u>on
Train	tr<u>e</u>no
Boat/ship	pl<u>ee</u>o
Aeroplane	airopl<u>a</u>no (first syllable as in ire for anger)
Garage	gar<u>a</u>ge
Train station	stathm<u>o</u>s
Bus station	afet<u>i</u>rio

Port	lim<u>ee</u>n
Airport	airolim<u>ee</u>n (first syllable as in ire)
Taxi	tax<u>ee</u>
Ticket	eesit<u>i</u>rio
What's the time?	t<u>ee</u> <u>o</u>ra <u>ee</u>nai?
Do you speak English?	mil<u>a</u>tè anglik<u>ee</u>?
I don't speak Greek	th<u>e</u>n meel<u>o</u> ellenik<u>a</u>
Help!	vo<u>ee</u>thia!

Counting

One	<u>e</u>na (m<u>ee</u>a with feminine noun)
Two	thi<u>o</u> (soft TH)
Three	tr<u>ee</u>a
Four	t<u>e</u>ssera
Five	p<u>e</u>ndè
Six	<u>e</u>ksi
Seven	eft<u>a</u>
Eight	okt<u>o</u>
Nine	enn<u>e</u>a
Ten	th<u>e</u>ka (soft TH)
Eleven	<u>e</u>ntheka
Twelve	th<u>o</u>theka (initial TH also soft)
Thirteen	th<u>e</u>katria (continue in the same way up to twenty)
Twenty	<u>ee</u>kosi
Twenty-one	eekosi-<u>e</u>na (or m<u>ee</u>a) (continue in the same way up to thirty)
Thirty	tri<u>a</u>nda
Forty	sar<u>a</u>nda
Fifty	pen<u>ee</u>nda
Sixty	ex<u>ee</u>nda
Seventy	evthom<u>ee</u>nda (soft TH)
Eighty	ogth<u>o</u>nda (soft TH)
Ninety	enen<u>ee</u>nda
Hundred	ekat<u>o</u>
Hundred and twenty-one	ekatoeekosi<u>e</u>na
Two hundred	thiak<u>o</u>sia (soft TH)
Thousand	heeliès
Two thousand	thioheeli<u>a</u>thas (both soft TH)
Million	ekatom<u>i</u>ria
Billion	thi<u>s</u>ekatomiria (soft TH)

The Weather and When to Go

Except that the Aegean is definitely a windier sea than the Ionian, Greece is not a large enough country to have noteworthy climatic differences between regions. It enjoys a typical Mediterranean climate: a short spring, a long, hot summer and a generally mild winter. The best time of the year to go is between mid-May and the end of September. Rains and cold snaps can be expected from October, but even then they will be interspersed, until around Christmas, with warm, sunny days on which foreigners continue to swim.

January, February and March are likely to be cold and damp everywhere in Greece. The Greeks like winter so little that if they could hibernate they would; when the black arrows on television weather charts denote invasions of 'cold masses' from Russia via the Balkans, the wind strikes far closer to the bone than the actual temperatures would suggest. Any remaining tourists, like the Athenian cats, then find themselves preoccupied with the unhellenic necessities of warmth and shelter.

At the opposite end of the climatic spectrum, July and August lend themselves more to a form of gradual suttee on the beaches than to exploration. If you have to travel in peak season, your objective should be enjoyment of the sea in all its forms – on, in and under the water – with a sunshade to cower beneath during the mad-dog hours.

Increasingly, like everyone else, the Greeks are having to take their own holidays in the heart of summer. In recent years, since a month's holiday became a legal entitlement regardless of length of service, industries have tended to substitute a one-month closure for the previous system of staggered leave. With their regular clients away, many shops and tavernas in the urban centres now follow suit – anyone familiar with a Parisian August will feel at home in a Greek mainland city. Naturally, this does not apply to those islands where holiday-making by tourists and city Greeks is the main industry.

Greek holiday snobs – senior executives and self-employed professionals – still contrive to make their disappearance in September, not just because the crowds are thinner on the resort islands but out of a desire to saunter comfortably in the sunshine. If your aim is mobility the ideal months are May, June and September; April can be showery and in October the rains, if they arrive, are likely to be more purposeful.

Average temperatures in Athens and southern Greece range between 12°C/52°F in January–February and 33°C/92°F in July–August. Extremes can be just below freezing point in winter and 40°C/102°F and more in an August heatwave. Hours of sunshine are not officially recorded, but the tourism authorities speak loosely but probably correctly of around 3,000 a year. In northern Greece, summer temperatures are about the same as in Athens but winter averages are a couple of degrees centigrade lower.

The edges of mainland Greece and the islands tend to be slightly cooler in summer but also more humid, especially at night.

Rainfall

Over a ten-year period, as reported by the National Statistics Service, Athens averaged 406 mm of rain annually, with 374 mm falling between the beginning of October and the end of May, and only 32 mm in the summer months, largely in the form of thunderstorms. In Thessaloniki, the average was 452 mm: 357 mm from October to May and 95 mm from June to September.

Corfu holds the record for the wettest part of Greece: 1,179 mm in winter and 139 mm in summer for an average annual total of 1,318 mm. It follows that Corfu is also the greenest of the Greek islands.

Still on the ten-year basis, rain fell in Athens on an average of 105 days a year, only 14 of them between May and September. The corresponding figures for Thessaloniki were 112 and 15, and for Corfu 139 and 17, suggesting that in Corfu the summer rain was heavier or of longer duration rather than more frequent.

The meltemi

The summer visitor should be aware in advance of the *meltemi*, which the Greeks both love and hate. For those to whom nothing is worse than savage heat, the *meltemi* is Greece's saving grace. It is a stiff north-westerly wind that sweeps the east coast of mainland Greece (including Athens) and the Aegean islands almost every day from the middle of July until the end of August. The result of pressure differences between North Africa and the Balkans, it springs up at around 8 or 9 a.m. and drops abruptly after sunset.

Undeniably, it does reduce the humidity. On the other hand, not even those who profess to love it could describe it as cooling; at its worst it is suggestive of a blast from an oven with an open door. It can make a beach umbrella unusable anywhere, and whip grit into the best-protected sandwich; for the eyes, the recommended defence is a pair of wrap-around sunglasses. Though it forces cruise passengers to the sheltered sides of the deck, the *meltemi* is the unqualified friend of yachtsmen.

Western Greece, including the Ionian islands, knows nothing of this particular wind. As a result, mid-summer there is a stickier season; also, though you escape the sand-papering you may acquire a closer acquaintance with the local wasp and fly populations.

The conclusion is self-evident: if you have the freedom of choice, go to the Greek islands between Easter and the end of June or in September and the first half of October. You will then reduce the likelihood of suffering from seasickness, either your own or others'. You will also find better service in hotels and restaurants, since they will be less crowded and their staffs more patient, and you will travel in greater comfort whether by land, sea or air.

Swimming

Average sea temperatures are measured, but are virtually meaningless for the swimmer. Whether your dip will be in bracing or tepid water is a matter of the depth of the sea, the strength and direction of wind and current and, to some extent, whether the sea bed is sandy or covered with weeds. Probably the warmest water in all Greece laps the east coast of Corfu; even there, however, there are chill patches above the clumps of seaweed.

If a warm sea is your weakness and you have a choice of beaches, check with your hotel porter; he will generally be able to tell you which will be warm and which cool, which sheltered and which not, on any particular day.

Final advice

● When visiting an island, do not book your return in advance on a ferry that will theoretically get you to Piraeus a couple of hours before you have to be at Athens Airport for your flight home. Apart from the normal unpunctuality, Greece is subject to sudden gales with winds of force 8 or 9 that can keep ferries in harbour for a day or two at a stretch.

It would be a mistake to believe you could then simply tear up your boat ticket and jump on an Olympic Airways flight to Athens. Hundreds of others will have the same idea, including the well connected, and you may find yourself at the end of a very long queue in which promotion depends on influence. Since there is no gale-free season, you need to be a little flexible.

● Even in July and August, you should pack a sweater. The nights can be chilly and, once the *meltemi* has retired to bed, damp also.

Travelling Around

Only a generation ago, you would have thought twice before going to an island. It was difficult enough to reach Athens, without the conveniences of packaged travel. From there, or more precisely from Piraeus, you would have taken a slow, hot, uncomfortable, overcrowded and in many respects unreliable boat, with no real certainty either of when you would arrive or whether the cabin for which you had paid would be without rival claimants.

You can now fly, either direct in a charter aircraft or on an Olympic Airways domestic service from Athens, to eighteen of the islands. If incorrigibly reluctant to entrust yourself to the water, Olympic Aviation will take you to most of the rest by light aircraft, air taxi or helicopter.

Though there is still room for improvement, and fleet renewal is a perennial intention, the ferries from Piraeus are for the most part larger and more comfortable, with a wider range of cabins for overnight journeys and higher standards of catering. Unpunctuality has ceased to be characteristic, and double-booking is no longer a problem.

On the larger islands you will find good bus services, a wide selection of coach and caique excursions, and taxis, cars, mopeds and sometimes bicycles for hire. On the smallest, if there are few roads and no buses, there will be motorboats, lifts to be hitched on farm vehicles, and probably a donkey if you ask around.

Also, it is usually not appreciated just how small a small island can be. An easy walk from where you stay to where you swim is exactly that, and bears no relation to a hike – except, perhaps, in the midday heat after a morning in the sea, when one side of the road can seem a long way from the other.

But be very careful indeed if equipping yourselves with two wheels rather than four. Motorcycles and mopeds tend to be poorly maintained, as do road surfaces, and narrow, winding lanes lose something of their romance when behind every blind corner there could be a tourist coach in the act of overtaking a sauntering car. Greek driving standards are not among the world's highest; the accident rate is unusually high, and young tourists on scooters make up an unfair if explicable proportion of those carted off to hospitals. If you must take the plunge, drive like a worrier, not a warrior; over-confidence is just another form of hubris.

Island-hopping

Inter-island communications, once skeletal and chancy, are steadily being improved, not so much for the convenience of holiday-makers as for that of the island inhabitants, and it is rarely necessary to return to Piraeus first in order to reach another island in the same group.

The Piraeus, inter-Cycladic and inter-Dodecanese ferries are in effect bus services, ideal for island-hopping. The Ionian islands are less well served.

In addition, the larger islands have their own boat and caique services to their closest neighbours and 'satellites', some of which can be reached from nowhere else.

The essential requirement for island-hopping is flexibility. On the one hand, you have no need to book in advance; on the other, you can never be certain that a sudden storm will not delay your departure for one or several days.

Unfortunately, there are still only very limited opportunities for island-hopping by air.

On the subject of reservations generally, they are always advisable for Olympic Airways domestic services. By sea, unless you will need a cabin, they are really required only for weekend travel in July and August. Hotel accommodation on the larger islands should always be booked in advance, if only to avoid a choice between a frustrating search and emergency shelter in the kind of room that can spoil a holiday. An unscheduled arrival on a smaller island entails less risk, as well as a greater possibility of a delightful surprise.

By sea

Travel by water in the Aegean is for the most part slow. In addition, since very few islands are big enough to be linked individually with the mainland, and the ferries must instead serve chains or groups of islands, reaching them can also be tedious.

The islands need communications in the winter too, not just in the holiday season, and these as a rule cannot be profitable and so must be subsidised. Greek taxpayers do not subsidise foreign companies. Therefore, you can travel only on Greek ships.

New roads built throughout mainland Greece since the Second World War have made it cheaper, simpler and more reliable to supply the Ionian islands by short-sea crossings from west-coast ports than by larger ferries from Piraeus, so you now get to the Ionian islands that way, or by air, and can no longer board a ship in Piraeus that will deposit you in Corfu twenty-four hours later.

FERRY ROUTES

Times given are approximate maximum sailing durations, depending upon the number of scheduled stops made. To save space, times for connections with Piraeus are shown only under Piraeus.

FROM	*TO*	*hrs/mins*
Aedipsos	Arkitsa	50 mins
Ag. Marina	Almyropotamos	1 hr
	Euboia	1 hr
Aghiokambos	Glyfa	30 mins
Ag. Constantinos	Alonysos	8 hrs
	Kavala	16½ hrs
	Lemnos	11 hrs
	Skiathos	3¼ hrs
	Skopelos	4½ hrs
Ag. Efstratios	Kavala	7½ hrs
	Kimi	6 hrs
	Lemnos	1½ hrs
Alexandroupolis	Samothrace	3 hrs
Almyropotamos	Ag. Marina	1 hr
Alonysos	Ag. Constantinos	8 hrs
	Kimi	3½ hrs
	Volos	5 hrs
Andros	Rafina	2½ hrs
Arkitsa	Aedipsos	50 mins
Astakos	Cephalonia:	
	Ag. Evfymia	2¼ hrs
	Ithaki	1¾ hrs
Cephalonia		
Ag. Evfymia	Astakos	2¼ hrs
Argostoli	Kylini	2¾ hrs
Fiskardo	Lefkas	1¼ hrs
Poros	Kylini	1½ hrs
Sami	Ithaki	1 hr
	Lefkas	1½ hrs
Chios	Psara	3¾ hrs
	Samos	4¾ hrs
Crete: Kasteli	Gythion	6 hrs
Corfu	Igoumenitsa	2 hrs
	Patras	10¼ hrs
	Paxi	3 hrs
Eretria	Oropos	25 mins
Euboia	Ag. Marina	50 mins
	Rafina	1 hr
Gythion	Crete: Kasteli	6 hrs
Igoumenitsa	Corfu	2 hrs
Ithaki	Astakos	1¾ hrs
	Cephalonia	1 hr
	Patras	2 hrs
Kastellorizon	Rhodes	6 hrs
Kavala	Ag. Constantinos	16½ hrs
	Ag. Efstratios	7½ hrs
	Kimi	12½ hrs
	Lemnos	6 hrs
	Lesbos	12 hrs
	Samothrace	3¾ hrs
	Thassos: Limena	1½ hrs
	Prinos	1 hr
Kea	Lavrion	2½ hrs
Keramoti	Thassos	45 mins
Kimi	Ag. Efstratios	6 hrs
	Alonysos	3½ hrs
	Glossa	5 hrs
	Kavala	12½ hrs
	Lemnos	7 hrs
	Skiathos	5½ hrs
	Skopelos	3½ hrs
	Skyros	2 hrs
	Volos	8 hrs
Kylini	Cephalonia: Argostoli	2¾ hrs
	Poros	2 hrs
	Zakynthos	1½ hrs
Kythera	Astakos	2 hrs
	Patras	4½ hrs
Kythnos	Lavrion	4 hrs
Lavrion	Kea	2½ hrs
	Kythnos	4 hrs
Lefkas	Cephalonia: Fiskardo	50 mins
	Sami	1½ hrs
Lemnos	Ag. Constantinos	11 hrs
	Ag. Efstratios	1½ hrs
	Kavala	6 hrs
	Kimi	7 hrs
	Lesbos	6 hrs
Lesbos	Kavala	12 hrs
	Lemnos	6 hrs
Lixouri	Argostoli	30 mins
Myconos	Rafina	5 hrs
Naxos	Rafina	7 hrs
Oropos	Eretria	25 mins
Paros	Rafina	5 hrs

FROM	*TO*	*hrs/mins*
Patras	Corfu	10¼ hrs
	Ithaki	5½ hrs
	Paxi	9 hrs
	Sami	3½ hrs
Paxi	Corfu	3 hrs
	Patras	9 hrs
Perama	Salamis	15 mins
Piraeus	Aegina	1½ hrs
	Amorgos	18 hrs
	Anafi	19 hrs
	Astipalaia	17 hrs
	Chios	11 hrs
	Crete: Chania	12 hrs
	Iraklion	12 hrs
	Ermioni	4 hrs
	Folegandros	11 hrs
	Hydra	4 hrs
	Ikaria	10 hrs
	Ios	11 hrs
	Kalymnos	13 hrs
	Kastellorizon	40 hrs
	Kimolos	8 hrs
	Kos	15 hrs
	Kythnos	4 hrs
	Leros	10 hrs
	Lesbos	15 hrs
	Methana	3½ hrs
	Milos	8 hrs
	Myconos	6½ hrs
	Naxos	8 hrs
	Paros	7 hrs
	Patmos	10 hrs
	Poros	2½ hrs
	Porto Heli	4 hrs
	Rhodes	19 hrs
	Samos	12 hrs
	Serifos	6 hrs
	Sifnos	8 hrs
	Sikinos	12 hrs
	Spetses	5½ hrs
	Syros	5 hrs
	Thera	12 hrs
	Tinos	4¾ hrs
Poros	Kylini	2 hrs
Psara	Chios	3¾ hrs
Rafina	Andros	2½ hrs
	Euboia	2 hrs
	Marmari	1 hr
	Myconos	5 hrs
	Naxos	6½ hrs
	Paros	5 hrs
	Syros	4 hrs
	Tinos	4 hrs
Rhodes	Kastellorizon	6 hrs
	Simi	1½ hrs
	Tilos	5 hrs
Salamis	Perama	15 mins
Sami	Patras	3½ hrs
Samos	Chios	4¾ hrs
Samothrace	Alexandroupolis	3 hrs
	Kavala	3¾ hrs
Simi	Rhodes	1½ hrs
Skiathos	Ag. Constantinos	3¼ hrs
	Kimi	5½ hrs
	Volos	5½ hrs
Skopelos	Ag. Constantinos	4½ hrs
	Kimi	5 hrs
	Volos	5 hrs
Skyros	Kimi	2 hrs
	Volos	11 hrs
Syros	Rafina	4 hrs
Thassos: Limena	Kavala	1½ hrs
Prinos	Kavala	1 hr
	Keramoti	45 mins
Tilos	Rhodes	5 hrs
Tinos	Rafina	4 hrs
Trikeri	Volos	1½ hrs
Volos	Alonysos	5 hrs
	Glossa	4 hrs
	Kimi	8 hrs
	Skiathos	5½ hrs
	Skopelos	5 hrs
	Skyros	11 hrs
	Trikeri	1½ hrs
Zakynthos	Kylini	1½ hrs

Deterring migration to the mainland is an overriding priority and explains why the interests of tourism take second place in the planning and execution of Aegean sea communications, why hydrofoil availability is still surprisingly limited, and why Olympic Airways has to make up from its international services the losses it incurs from below-cost fares on domestic routes.

At the same time, however, there is an indirect benefit to the tourist travelling outside the package system, deriving from governmental determination to meet urgent medical and social needs of island inhabitants: within the next few years, almost every inhabited island will have been provided with an airport or landing strip, or at least a heliport. This twenty-year-old programme was not launched primarily with tourists in mind – the possible divergence of a small part of the tourist movement to previously unvisited islands was simply regarded as a bonus in the overall context of keeping the islands economically viable and socially attractive to their inhabitants. Nevertheless, it does give the independent traveller a wider selection of destinations in the framework of a one- or two-week holiday than those generally available through group tours (see also pp. 57–8).

When the faster hydrofoils, with their considerably higher fares, were introduced in 1976 they created their own, new clientele, consisting of tourists in a hurry and Athenians for whom short breaks on the nearby islands, even weekend commuting, had been made feasible by the Ceres Hellenic fleet of 'Flying Dolphins'.

Ceres Hellenic now operates eighteen Soviet-built Kometa and Kolhida hydrofoils, giving it the world's largest privately-owned hydrofoil fleet, covering the Saronic islands and ports along the west coast of the Peloponnese (including Nafplion, Ermioni, Porto Heli, Neapolis and Monemvasia) down to the island of Kythera. There is a second service from the eastern mainland ports of Volos and Aghios Constantinos to the North Sporades islands of Skiathos, Skopelos, Alonysos and Skyros, and a limited non-Ceres hydrofoil availability in the Cyclades, Dodecanese and Ionian groups. But overall, the impact of the hydrofoil on Aegean sea transport has been far less than might have been anticipated.

It has to be admitted that the Greeks, and many tourists, still prefer to travel on a ship that looks and feels less like an aeroplane, and that may roll but is incapable of vibrating; one on which they can stroll about, and lean on a rail in hope of seeing dolphins play.

Though eminently suitable for Greek waters, the hovercraft has yet to make an appearance, in part because of the Turks. The Defence Ministry can well appreciate the value of a fleet of 150-capacity, 32-knot hydrofoils as troop-carriers in a national emergency, but has no comparable regard for hovercraft.

Although coastal shipping is not nationalised, the Merchant Marine Ministry exercises close control over it, establishing routes,

Ferry Routes

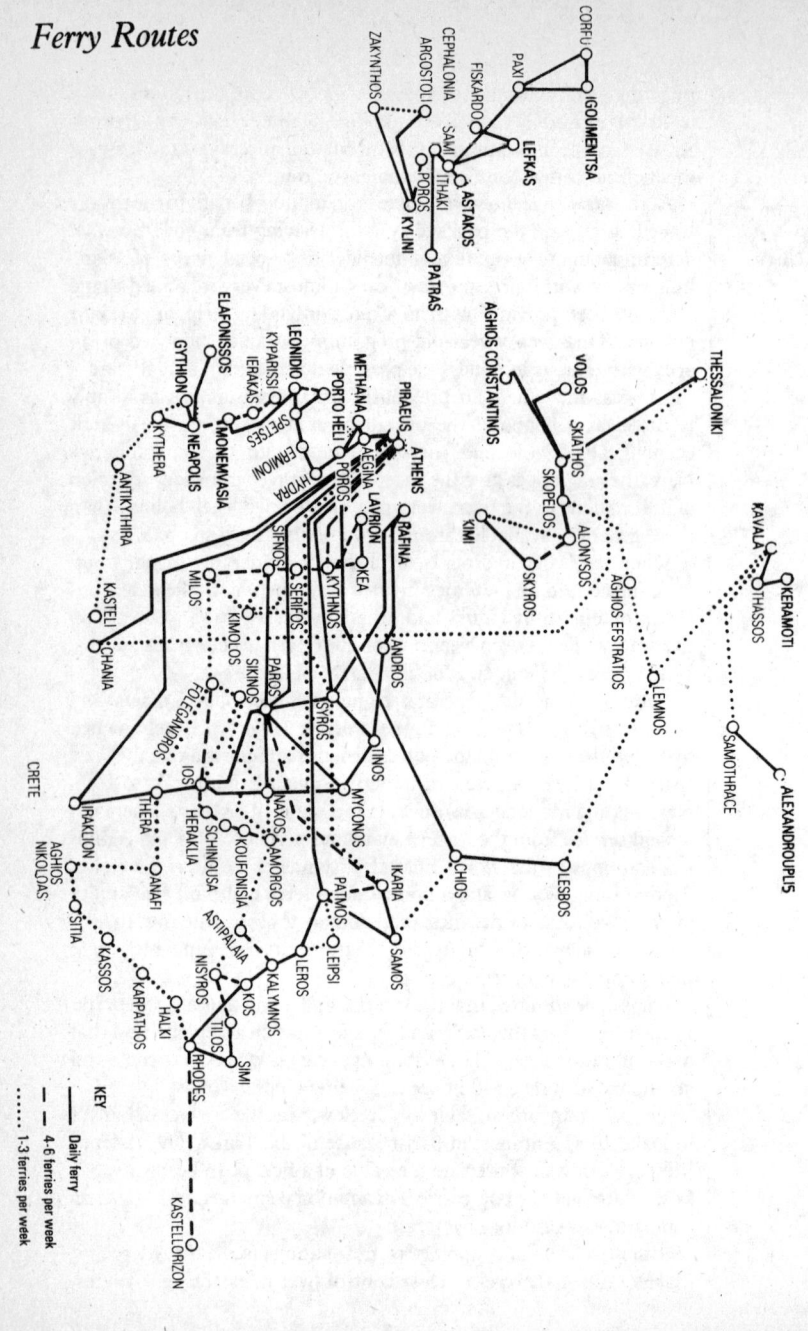

licensing ships and setting fares and frequency requirements.

You may therefore have to travel on older and less comfortable ships than would be available if their owners were free to charge the fares that the summer market could support and to reduce winter services to economic frequencies, building up the kind of reserves needed for fleet renewal without regard to social considerations.

However, in the absence of a sudden gale, you can be fairly sure that the ship you are planning to take will sail on time, no matter how few passengers it may be carrying (this was not always a safe assumption), and, conversely, that it will not sail in dangerous conditions. This decision is no longer left to the ship's master, who may be torn between his own hesitations and the demands of his owners, but is taken for him by Coastguard officers with every reason to play for safety.

Greek coastal ferries other than those to Rhodes and Crete have to be small, since otherwise they would be unable to enter many of the island harbours – cruise liners can disembark passengers by tender, but it would scarcely be feasible to provision a petrol station with jerrycans or a supermarket with toilet rolls handed package-by-package into a motorboat. So if the sea is at all choppy, you will have no doubt that you are on a ship.

Again with the exception of the Crete and Rhodes ferries, you should expect neither the comfort in the lounges nor the standard of catering to be found, for example, on a cross-Channel ferry; even when the ship has a dining room most passengers content themselves with snacks at the bar, and in all but the harshest weather the deck is generally more pleasant than the saloon.

While it is always safer to buy a ticket a day or two in advance from a travel agency, reservations are really essential only if you are making an overnight journey, and therefore will need a cabin, or are proposing to travel on July or August weekends or around the 15 August Feast of the Assumption holiday. Otherwise, you can turn up half an hour before the ferry is due to sail and buy your ticket at the foot of the gangplank. Most ferries have two or three classes, depending on their size and whether there is a 'deck' category: on the shorter crossings of two or three hours, there is usually only one class.

A word on fares

Rounded up to the nearest hundred drachmas, typical fares on Aegean ferry services at the time of going to press (one-way, second-class) included:

From Piraeus to: Crete Dr 3,500 (cars Dr 6,000 to 15,000 depending on size); Rhodes Dr 4,500 (cars Dr 6,000 to 11,000); Myconos Dr 2,000 (cars Dr 5,000 to 9,000); Patmos Dr 3,300 (cars Dr 6,400 to 11,000); Chios Dr 2,900 (cars Dr 5,200 to 8,900).

From Kavalla to Thassos: Dr 250 (cars Dr 1,200).

From Igoumenitsa to Corfu: Dr 330 (cars Dr 2,300).

From Kylini to Zakynthos: Dr 420 (cars Dr 2,300).

From Volos to Skiathos: Dr 1,300 (cars Dr 3,700 to 5,200).

Car rates and fares from second-class downwards are subject to Merchant Marine Ministry endorsement: first-class fares are not controlled, and vary widely from ship to ship. It can safely be anticipated that fares will rise by about between 10 and 15 per cent a year, to keep pace with domestic inflation.

From Piraeus to the Saronic islands: Aegina Dr 500 (hydrofoil Dr 600); Poros Dr 800 (Dr 1,200); Hydra Dr 900 (Dr 1,500); Spetses Dr 1,100 (1,700).

Cruises

It is not often that so precise a date can be put on the birth of an industry as it can with Greek cruising. However, in the early summer of 1954, Epirotiki Lines of Piraeus in a joint operation with the National Tourist Organisation of Greece took the 3,000-ton *Semiramis*, with a 150-passenger capacity, off the Greece–Italy ferry run and launched it on a trial Aegean itinerary to Hydra, Myconos and Delos.

Previously, of course, even before the Second World War, ships had been chartered for special cruises, but the *Semiramis* was the first to be dedicated to an entire season of cruising for which anyone could buy a ticket.

The idea had been made feasible by the development of air travel to Greece, which was opening the country to upper-income tourists not attracted primarily by the antiquities; it caught on, and other companies followed the Epirotiki lead.

Today, though operating the world's largest privately-owned fleet of cruise liners, Epirotiki is just one of half a dozen Piraeus-based companies offering holidays afloat in the Aegean, and beyond, into the Mediterranean and Black Sea. In an average summer, you have between fifteen and twenty ships to choose from – the exact number depends on how many are on charter or laid up for renovation or other reasons – and a choice of three-day, four-day, one-week and two-week voyages.

The Aegean islands are still the mainstay of the cruises: Crete, Rhodes, Thera (Santorini), Myconos/Delos, Patmos and sometimes Kos. Most of the cruises include a call at the Turkish port of Kusadasi for an excursion to Ephesus, and those lasting a week generally allow one day for Istanbul.

Further afield, there are cuises to Egypt and Israel; the South of France, Italy, Sicily and the Dalmatian coast of Yugoslavia; and the Soviet ports of Yalta and Odessa. At the other end of the scale, one-day cruises can be taken to the Saronic islands of Aegina, Poros and Hydra.

Whether cruising is expensive is a subjective question, but certainly it is not the cheapest way to see Greece. The cruise companies quote fares only in US dollars and payments in other currencies are adjusted according to the current exchange rates. For 1988, Epirotiki was quoting prices in a range from 945 to 1,855 US dollars per person for a seven-day cruise depending on the type of cabin (from four-bunk inner to two-bed outer) in its one-class ships; while quoted rates include meals, it would probably be wise to budget another 50 dollars a day for bar bills, shore excursions and tips.

On the other hand, the companies observe with justification that accommodation in the better cabins is equivalent to a deluxe hotel, the meals are lavish, the evening entertainment is nightclub standard, and passengers are coddled as they rarely are ashore, where the opportunity to merit a handsome tip is more restricted.

It may also be pointed out that you pay for your cruise when you book it; therefore, if you never touch alcohol, never gamble, never tip, buy nothing from the duty-free shop and go ashore on islands only by yourself, you need be no poorer on your return than when you started out!

Though all the companies still rely heavily on Americans, the fall in American travel over the past few years has forced them to devote greater attention to European markets. A common claim is that they carry up to a hundred nationalities during a full season, and as many as twenty on a single cruise; nowadays, the British are well represented.

If the idea that only Americans take cruises is one lingering misconception, another is that an average passenger list is overwhelmingly made up of elderly couples on a retirement fling and newly-weds on their honeymoon. You will find as wide a cross-section in terms of age as of nationality.

(Greek captains, incidentally, are not authorised to perform marriages. However, a few years ago an Epirotiki ship's master decided to entertain his passengers with a mock wedding, for which he recruited the services of a jovial American travel writer in a press group and a startling blonde from public relations. A couple of years later, the travel writer was back on the ship, this time with his wife. As he tells the story, they were stopped by a passenger with a question that froze the air: 'Married again already?')

Whether a cruise is worth the cost is another subjective question. It is certainly the easiest way to see the pick of the islands in only three or four days, provided you are satisfied with three or four hours ashore on each, and the only convenient way to see Ephesus and Istanbul as part of a Greek holiday. It is also a way of making fleeting or even lasting friendships. A cruise of three or four days can give an extra dimension to a longer holiday in Greece; one of seven or fourteen days should probably be regarded as a holiday in itself.

BACKGROUND INFORMATION

By air

Olympic Airways, the Greek-flag carrier, is far more useful for travel to the islands than for getting around mainland Greece: from Athens, it flies regular services to eighteen islands, as against ten mainland destinations, and from Thessaloniki to six islands compared with only one mainland town. Additional islands are being slotted into the network as their airports or landing strips are completed, and inter-island flights are also being expanded.

In addition, Olympic Aviation, a light aircraft subsidiary set up by the late Aristotle Onassis in 1971 to provide his son Alexander with business experience, and kept in being after Alexander was killed in an air crash at Athens Airport, offers air-taxi services by small aircraft and helicopters.

From Athens, Olympic Airways has regular flights to Cephalonia, Chios, Corfu, Crete, Kos, Kythera, Lemnos, Leros, Lesbos, Milos, Myconos, Paros, Rhodes, Samos, Skiathos, Skyros, Thera (Santorini) and Zakynthos. You can fly from Thessaloniki to Crete, Corfu, Lesbos, Lemnos, Rhodes and Skiathos, and from Rhodes to Crete, Karpathos, Kassos, Kastellorizon, Kos, Leros, Myconos, Paros and Thera. In addition, there are services from Chios to Lesbos, Myconos and Samos; from Crete to Myconos, Paros, Rhodes and Thera; from Myconos to Thera; from Karpathos to Kassos, Rhodes and Crete; from Lesbos to Chios, Lemnos, Rhodes and Samos; and from Kos to Leros, Samos to Myconos, and Cephalonia to Zakynthos.

Olympic Aviation, which uses thirty-seat Shorts, nineteen-seat Dorniers and fifteen-seat Skyvans on some of the scheduled services to small islands, makes Ecureuil helicopters and five-seat Piper Aztec aircraft available as air taxis.

Reservations can be made through the Olympic head office at 96 Syngrou Avenue, Athens, tel. 9616 161, or the booking office in Othonos Street, beside Constitution Square, tel. 9292 489, and at the Olympic offices on all the islands served.

Fares

At the time of going to press, typical Olympic Airways fares from Athens to the islands included: Crete Dr 7,500; Corfu Dr 8,200; Myconos Dr 5,020; Lesbos Dr 6,000; Rhodes Dr 9,200; Skiathos Dr 5,300; Thera Dr 6,400.

Inter-island rates included: Crete to Myconos Dr 6,710; Crete to Thera Dr 4,610; Corfu to Cephalonia Dr 5,100; Myconos to Lesbos Dr 8,000; Lesbos to Rhodes Dr 10,460; Rhodes to Myconos Dr 7,270. As on the Aegean ferries, and for the same reasons, fares will probably rise by between 10 and 15 per cent a year.

Olympic Aviation does not publish air-taxi fares.

A word on yachting

At this point, a confession should be made – one of necessity couched in the first person singular. Over a period of close on thirty-five years I have travelled by choice or editorial instruction to all corners of Greece by all forms of public or semi-public transport, the latter including lifts in ministerial helicopters and on the wooden saddles of friendly farmers' donkeys, but I have never made use of a yacht. The closest approaches have been a trip by motor cruiser to Syros for the opening of a hotel and a morning spent on a shipowner's catamaran tacking between Piraeus and Salamis! On both occasions, the availability of a well-stocked bar was more than usually appreciated; neither experience left any inclination to camouflage ignorance with a net of enthusiasm.

Therefore, what follows is an attempt to winnow a few grains of accepted wisdom from the chaff of hyperbole contained in brokers' brochures and an elegant NTOG publication, *Sailing the Greek Seas*. Appended as a footnote are the addresses from which you can obtain the brochures, booklet, and lists of the fifty or so registered Greek yacht brokers.

● Although yachting is generally associated with island-hopping, and no one would charter a yacht without the intention of visiting at least a few islands, it should also be borne in mind that Greece is a country of small mainland ports and that none of its famed archaeological sites is more than a fairly short taxi-drive from where a yacht can drop anchor. Of fifty-one designated entry and departure points, twenty-five are on the mainland and twenty-six on Aegean or Ionian islands.

Yachts of any nationality entering Greek waters and intending to cruise in them have to put in at one of the designated ports first and last, to receive and surrender their transit log. All harbours except the large commercial ports provide anchorage space for yachts. The expanding network of NTOG marinas now numbers twelve (six in the Athens/Piraeus area and the others at Thessaloniki, Halkidiki, Patras and Methana in the Peloponnese and on the islands of Corfu and Rhodes), with others due to be added (fairly soon) on Crete, Kos, Cephalonia, Paxi, Zakynthos, Chios, Ikaria, Skyros, Thassos and Lemnos. The NTOG enthusiasm for yachting is easily explained: there are no longer any goldmines on the mainland.

● For those not sailing to Greece, there appears to be general agreement on a number totalling more than 2,000 yachts available for charter locally. These consist mainly of crewed vessels of more than 15 m, and auxiliary sailing yachts of up to 15 m which can be chartered without crews (provided that at least two members of the charter party hold skipper's papers or equivalent certificates from a recognised yacht club). Also, especially in the Dodecanese, the flotilla system is creeping in – groups of eight to ten craft with between four and six berths each, guided and mothered by a lead boat.

- Though it is assertedly possible to negotiate a charter for as little as three days, you will obviously be of greater interest to a broker if he can anticipate a charter of two or three weeks.
- The yachting season runs from April to October, but July and August are preferred by those who like their breezes stiff (these are also the months of yacht races and regattas in Greece).
- There seems no reason to challenge the description of the Aegean as an 'easy' sea for skilled yachtsmen. The reasons cited include some that applied also in Ancient Greece – good shelter within thirty miles of even the most exposed patch of water, negligible tides, few currents, deep water except close to the coasts and scarcely ever any fog – plus such modern aids as navigation lights, radio beacons and the regular broadcasting of weather forecasts.
- While entry and exit formalities and log-book requirements appear complex in comparison with renting a car, it may well be that they are no more so than in other countries: the obvious difference in the 'rules of the game' is the stringent prohibition of swimming with breathing apparatus, which is defined as anything that enables the diver to stay underwater beyond his natural capabilities. The reason is the number of ancient shipwrecks found but not yet explored, and presumably the many more not yet located, at fairly shallow depths.
- Prices differ according to type of craft and month required, but appear to be within a general band between 100 and 5,000 US dollars a day; it is tempting to suspect that for the former price you would be negotiating the rent of a motorboat with a canvas awning. . . .

Addresses for further inquiries

The Hellenic Professional Yacht Owners' Association, 43 Freattydos Street, Marina Zea, 185 36 Piraeus; The Greek Yacht Brokers' & Consultants' Association, 36 Alkyonis Street, Old Phaleron, 175 61 Athens; The Greek Bareboat Yacht Owners' Association, 56 Vass Pavlou Street, Kastella, Piraeus; NTOG, 2 Amerikis Street, Athens.

Where to Stay

Introduction

As an independent traveller moving about the Greek islands as the whim takes you, without firm plans and therefore without hotel reservations, you need have no fear of spending a night under the stars provided only that you are prepared, if necessary, to do without the normal luxury of a private shower and toilet.

At the end of 1987, Greece as a whole, mainland and islands, had 5,771 hotels, furnished apartments, inns and hostels offering 375,367 beds in 199,583 rooms. A little less than half of these units – 2,475 – were on Crete and the Cyclades, Dodecanese and Ionian islands. With the construction boom continuing, at least in the middle and lower categories, the overall total is now comfortably above 5,800 units and probably around 400,000 beds.

The National Tourist Organisation of Greece (NTOG) estimated at the beginning of the 1988 tourist season that Greece was in a position to accommodate 8.5 million visitors in 380,000 hotel beds, 140,000 beds in licensed supplementary accommodation, 65,000 in campsites, 12,000 on cruise liners and another 12,000 on yachts.

With a few exceptions attributable to local initiative or the desire of a wealthy businessman to contribute to the progress of his island of origin, you will find deluxe and first-class hotels – the equivalent of five- and four-star units elsewhere – only on the resort and semi-resort islands. But almost any island you are likely to visit, unless your priority was isolation, will have some fairly new third-class hotels built within the past twenty years. Everywhere, rooms will be offered in private houses. You will sleep on a beach only by choice.

Rooms in private houses
To the official bed total should be added beds available in private houses, estimated at anywhere between 100,000 and 400,000. These unreported beds, which for obvious reasons cannot be booked in advance, are to be found in almost all parts of the country except the two major cities of Athens and Thessaloniki. On arrival anywhere else, through a port, train station or bus terminal, you will be approached by old women and young children enquiring in broken English whether you have a place to stay. If not, you will be led to perfectly adequate, basic accommodation in a room with at least an old-fashioned washbasin and jug, access to the family toilet, and showers by arrangement. Depending on the season, a two-bed room

will probably cost you between Dr 1,000 and 1,500 a night, without breakfast but almost certainly with the offer of coffee as a friendly gesture and an invitation to converse. The bill you pay, if in foreign currency, will be exchanged on the unofficial market; in no matter what form, it will remain unknown to the tax authorities.

This so-called 'para hotel' cottage industry is a cause of acute distress to professional hoteliers and to NTOG; the latter, despite evidence to the contrary, likes to maintain that it is gradually being eradicated. It dates from the 1967-74 dictatorship when, to confront a sudden growth in tourism that far outpaced hotel capacity, the Colonels offered low-interest loans to householders to refurbish a room and hold it in readiness for visitors when all the hotels in the area were full – something that then applied through most of the holiday season.

With the hotels now built in generally sufficient numbers, the original justification no longer applies. But it would be a strange businessman, and in particular a strange Greek businessman, who would quietly liquidate a profitable enterprise within the black economy just because the state told him to, at a time when the product – the room – remains in demand for reasons of cost and availability. Price-conscious Greek families and budget tourists use the rooms because they are cheap, not because the hotels are full. Others, planning a stay of only a night or two, prefer to save themselves the trouble of searching for a hotel.

So you may go with confidence anywhere, at any time; even in the most crowded resort on the busiest holiday weekend you will find somewhere to spend the night. In my personal experience, acquired on Spetses one Feast of the Assumption, there will at least be straw in a stable, vacated by a donkey 'bounced' to the shade of a fig tree, and a welcome warmer than you will receive from some hotel employees.

If no one accosts you with a whispered offer of accommodation, the tourist police department, if one exists, or otherwise the ordinary police station will have a list of hotels and registered private rooms and, as a rule, a good idea of where vacancies are likely to exist.

Otherwise, try the coffee-shop or grocery, or enquire at the kiosk selling cigarettes; the boy who fetches the woman who has a room to offer will be well satisfied with a Dr 100 tip.

A word of advice Do not try to save money on hotels. If you wish to economise, avoid expensive-looking restaurants; you will then eat better anyway.

The 'real' hotels

The following table from NTOG, correct to the end of 1987, tells you something.

Number of hotels in Greece (mainland and islands)

Category	Number of units	Number of beds	Average number of beds per unit
Deluxe	41	19,078	465
1st class	233	74,378	319
2nd class	607	81,547	134
3rd class	1,767	105,793	59
4th class	966	30,565	31
5th class	726	16,622	22
Sub-totals	4,340	327,983	
Bungalow complexes and motels	70	8,523	
Apartments	598	18,367	
Inns, pensions, etc.	763	20,494	
Grand total	5,771	375,367	

Miscellaneous information

NTOG offers an estimate that seven out of every ten hotels in Greece are less than twenty years old, built in response to a steady growth in package tour holidays dating from the early 1960s. On the one hand, this accounts for the unusually high proportion of rooms with private toilets and bath or shower facilities. On the other, it explains why you so often find your accommodation in obvious need of renovation, with scratched and possibly broken furniture, plumbing systems that sometimes dribble and sometimes flood, shutters that refuse to close properly, peeling paint and radios that have long since ceased to convey piped music at the touch of a button.

Hoteliers blame low profit margins, high state and municipal taxes, and an inflation rate – matched by the cost of borrowing money and public utility bills – that for more than a dozen years has ranged between 15 and 25 per cent. They say they simply cannot afford to refurbish as often as they should.

NTOG, responsible for supervision of hotels, acknowledges that this is an unsatisfactory situation, but observes that allowance must be made for the fact that an average 55 per cent of a hotel's turnover goes to meet payroll costs. For this reason, its supervision has to be directed mainly towards honesty of operations, cleanliness and standards of meals, and it is unable to push hard on quality of furnishings and plumbing. You may find your sheet is patched, your pillowcase is discoloured and your towel is frayed, but none of the three is likely to be dirty.

Also, outside the main cities, the vast majority of hotels operate only seasonally, from just before the western Easter to around the end of September or early October. This is reflected in the standard of personnel. A hotelier with jobs to offer for only five months of the year is fortunate, and unusual, if he can secure the services of trained, multilingual waiters and barmen; more commonly, he has to recruit where he can among the local population, taking on whoever happens to be unemployed in that particular season. Obviously, it is easier to find chambermaids than adequate head waiters. Similarly, on the islands, you should not expect too much from your hall porter; if he is entitled to wear the crossed keys he will not be working in a hotel open for only five or six months every year.

The concentration of new hotel construction on mainly small units of middle and lower categories reflects two tendencies that the Greeks regret but are powerless to combat. The first is the average hotelier's reliance on package business negotiated with a limited number of European and United States tour operators, whose primary interest is in the final cost of the package, not the quality of services, and who are in a position to impose their demands. The hotelier simply dare not rely on independent travellers. The second is the increasing preference for self-catering holidays (in 1988 peak season, deluxe and first-class hotels throughout the country had empty rooms, second and third class were just about full, and it was almost impossible to obtain a room or bungalow with self-catering facilities).

The independent traveller taking a room in a first- or second-class hotel pays a full rate far higher than the portion of a package that goes to the hotelier from group travel. So he may legitimately be disappointed when he has to queue for a self-service meal that offers a choice between two or three warmed-up dishes to which chips have apparently been assigned by numbers, and canned peas and carrots by the teaspoonful. The hotelier would like to offer him full restaurant service and an à la carte menu, but numerically he is simply not a sufficiently important part of the business to justify the expense.

A new trend, not yet widespread but beginning to be observable, is for hotels to retain their restaurants but close their kitchens. They find it cheaper to buy ready-made dishes from a local caterer and warm them up in a microwave oven. If airline passengers do not mind, why should hotel guests? This explains the basic advice offered in 'Eating and Drinking' (p. 106): if you are not on a half-board arrangement, eat in your hotel only if you are too tired to look for a nearby restaurant or taverna.

A word on categories

In theory, and usually in fact, the classification awarded to a hotel is determined by the size of its rooms and public areas, including the lobby, the décor and furnishing of the rooms, and the services provided. Hotels of deluxe, first and second class (also called L, A and B) have dining facilities on the premises.

With a few notable exceptions in the main cities and islands, most surviving pre-war hotels are now of fourth or fifth class (D or E), do without lift, lobby or lounge, and may have added private showers but still have one toilet per floor. In the cities, they are unlikely to be in the newer and pleasanter suburbs (in Athens they are particularly thick around Omonia Square and the railway stations). They can so easily spoil a holiday and, except for a possible overnight stop in a village, should be regarded as last-resort accommodation. There are some whose most permanent guests are cockroaches.

For more than ten years NTOG has had the intention of switching to the star system, and officials say the changeover may finally be made during 1989. The difficulty, and source of hoteliers' opposition, is that this will require the adoption of international criteria, and will lead to the relegation to a lower category of a considerable number of units. Nevertheless, officials are confident that all of Greece's deluxe hotels and at least some in first class will be in a position to claim five stars.

NTOG, concerned to prevent excessive competition at the expense of services, which could bring the entire industry into disrepute, decrees only minimum room rates by hotel category. It leaves the hotelier free to charge whatever higher figure the market will stand, subject to registration of rates with NTOG in advance of each season and their posting in every hotel room.

For this reason, it frequently happens that, say, a third-class hotel may be considerably more expensive than another, even in the same area, of second class. The difference is explained by the age of the hotel, its furnishings, and sometimes its position, and should be eradicated through the star system.

In these circumstances, and bearing in mind also the sharp difference between off- and peak-season rates even in hotels open for only five months each year, and the surcharges imposed at times of local festivals or fairs, it is possible to give only the very roughest guidelines to prices by category. For example, in 1988 peak season a double room in a deluxe hotel could have cost anywhere between Dr 6,000 and 30,000 a night. While the spread was less in first class, a double room still ran at between Dr 5,000 and 8,000 a night. At the other end of the scale, there were any number of fourth-class hotels offering rooms for Dr 1,500 a night, as against Dr 2,000 or more asked by some obviously superior fifth-class units.

In general, outside Athens, you should be able to find a comfortable room in an upper-bracket hotel at between Dr 5,000 and 7,000 a night. A likely third-class price is around Dr 3,500 a night, and a hotel of last resort should leave you change from Dr 2,000.

Purely as an indication of the best you could hope for, these are the minimum rates set for 1989 for a double room with private bath, in drachma: deluxe 5,520, first class 4,090, second class 2,630, third class 2,120, fourth class 1,590, fifth class 1,570, inns, etc 1,140.

Similarly, minimum 1989 rates for a continental breakfast run from Dr 480 in a deluxe hotel to Dr 250 in a fourth-class unit; corresponding minima for dinner/lunch (soup or pasta, a meat dish with salad, and ice-cream or fruit) range between Dr 1,790 deluxe and Dr 910 fourth class, with beverages charged extra.

Most hotels will offer the independent traveller a rate for the room, with breakfast and lunch or dinner as optional extras. If you are quoted only a half-board rate, you could consider looking elsewhere! You may legally be subjected to a surcharge for a stay of less than three nights.

Avoiding groups

In the main cities and resort islands, it is almost impossible to avoid groups, unless you use the kind of hotel that will make you miserable for more substantial reasons, since even one too small to have business with a European or United States tour operator will probably be linked with a Greek agent for domestic groups. However, Greek groups do not normally arrive or leave in the middle of the night.

Also, some comfort may be derived from the fact that only a handful of deluxe hotels in Athens, Thessaloniki and on the islands of Rhodes and Crete are equipped to go after convention business.

Air conditioning

Although Greece is a hot country, air conditioning in the home and in any but the most modern offices is still regarded as the ultimate luxury. It should not be taken for granted in hotels below second class, or in bungalows of any category.

If you are travelling in the provinces, you can expect to sleep with open windows. You might therefore consider bringing with you your own personal mosquito-killer, or buying one on arrival from a grocer or chemist – preferably electric. The Greeks use them all the time. An appliance plus a two-week supply of poison should not set you back more than Dr 1,000, and should save a lot of scratching.

Traditional settlements

Greece has a large number of villages and buildings that have retained their traditional characteristics. To protect this national heritage, NTOG has pioneered a programme based on conservation of selected settlements or individual houses through their conversion into tourist guest-houses and complexes. Eight settlements have been chosen for the first phase, on the islands of Thera (Santorini), Chios, Cephalonia and Psara and, in mainland Greece, at Makrynitsa and Vizitsa on Mount Pelion, Zagorohoria in Epiros, and Areopoli in the Mani region of the Peloponnese.

The largest of the island settlements is at Oia on Thera (Santorini), where fifty-seven beds are on offer in the twenty-eight rooms of ten houses. Fiskardo on Cephalonia provides fifty-one beds in twenty rooms of four houses. The settlement at Mesta on Chios also consists of four houses, with twenty-three beds in nine rooms. The Psara settlement so far is a matter of a five-room house with fifteen beds, but there are plans for expansion. Room prices range between Dr 2,000 and 8,000 a night, depending mainly on the number of beds. Reservations may be made by writing to NTOG at 2 Amerikis Street, Athens.

Accommodation is somewhat basic, usually without a private bath. While there are no restaurant facilities, a degree of self-catering is possible. In strict value terms the rooms may be somewhat overpriced, but they are intended for those prepared to pay a little extra to experience Greece as it used to be.

Youth hostels

To obtain accommodation in any youth hostel in Greece requires a membership card from a national association of youth hostels or an international guest card; the latter may be obtained by application to the youth hostel itself or the Greek Association of Youth Hostels at 4 Dragatsaniou Street, Athens; tel. 3234 107.

There are four youth hostels in Athens and, on the mainland, one each in Thessaloniki, Delphi, Litochoron (Mount Olympos), Mycenae, Nafplion, Olympia and Patras.

Both Athens and Thessaloniki have YMCA and YWCA hostels.

Tents and caravans

There are organised camp-sites in most parts of Greece, some set up and run by NTOG or the Hellenic Automobile and Touring Club (ELPA) but the majority privately owned. All are enclosed and guarded. Legally, camping is allowed only in these organised grounds. Pitch your tent or park your caravan elsewhere and you will be moved along if the police choose to notice you or if their attention is drawn to your presence by a householder or hotelier.

Ex-officio police action is more certain if you are found in places with a high risk of woodland fires than, for example, at the edge of the sea in a remote cove.

While camping equipment can be purchased in the main towns, there are as yet no shops specialising in camping equipment rentals. However, two-person tents with beds can be hired by the night at some of the sites.

Before going to Greece for a camping or caravan holiday, it is advisable to write to NTOG, or ELPA (Athens Tower B, Athens) for lists of sites and detailed regulations.

Time-sharing

Time-sharing was legalised in Greece only in 1986 and has so far made little impact on the hotel picture. But several hotels – on Corfu and Myconos and in the Peloponnese – now offer time-shares, and the situation could develop quickly. NTOG is much in favour; one of its permanent goals is to increase the number of regular visitors travelling independently to Greece.

Eating and Drinking

Greece offers some delightful surprises to those who still retain a secret affection for the simple things of life. In relation to Greek cuisine, that means charcoal.

The Ancient Greeks taught the barbarian world how to cook – wealthy Romans employed Greeks to tutor their children and prepare their meals – and the barbarian world took it on from there, but at home the Greeks just went on grilling.

They set up their grills in the monasteries of the Byzantine era, including those on Mount Athos, which bequeathed to the modern world not a host of new dishes or rare brandies, but the one thing that no self-respecting chef can do without: his white hat.

'The 400 years' are held responsible for a number of 'Turkish' dishes, most notably sweets, though it is more than likely that many of these had simply been appropriated by the conquerors along with much else that was appreciated in old Constantinople. Throughout the four centuries, the Greeks grilled.

Neither European Community nor medical questioning of the long-term effects of charred food on the health will stop them now. There may be a place for Wiener Schnitzel, Bœuf Bourgignon and fish and chips, but the taverna the Greeks will choose for a family outing will be pungent with blue smoke and the perfume of oregano.

If an Ancient Greek could be resurrected today, with his language intact, he would understand little or nothing of what he heard and at best would be able to communicate only with the occasional professor or more learned bishop. But he would feel completely at home in the corner taverna, and would find much that he recognised. His staple foods in particular would all be there: olive oil and olives, fish, lamb and goat, goats' milk cheese, wine and bread, beans, peas, cabbage, lettuce, lentils and garlic, honey, nuts and, come August, figs.

Unless your luck is running on an ebb tide, you will eat better on an island than in Athens. Theoretically this ought not to be so, since Athens restaurants have a regular clientele to consider while the island *tavernaris* must cover his year's costs in five or six months, from customers whom he can have little expectation of seeing a second time. The explanation lies in the freshness of the fish, the simplicity of traditional dishes prepared with ingredients produced locally and purchased recently, and a sense of pride in well-deserved praise that is more marked in the smaller communities. While the family that runs an island taverna may hope to get rich, wealth has a different definition, just as giving satisfaction has a different priority.

The taverna

As in any country, what you eat and how much you pay will depend on where you go and whether you are in search of a meal or an evening's entertainment. Tavernas (and, for that matter, restaurants and bars) can be broken down into arbitrary but workable divisions between the traditional, the transitional and the new.

The traditional taverna

This will have its large charcoal grill near the entrance, or in summer just outside, tended by the owner. Close by will be a glass-fronted refrigerator displaying plates of veal and pork chops, lamb and goat in joint or cutlet form, 'village' sausages, and hamburgers the size of squashed tennis balls made up of ground meat mixed with bread.

Another display, not refrigerated, will be of cold appetisers (*mezedes*) and whatever meat dishes the owner's family may have prepared during the day; one member will be seated at a table collating the orders, keeping the tax records and manning the till, and others will be serving. Though in the main cities the taverna may have become large enough to require the employment of staff, it will still be a family operation catering to families that are also friends; children old enough to sit up will be at the tables, and there could well be a couple of babies sleeping in prams.

The tables themselves will probably be covered by white cloths, which will not be changed for the next client; instead, a fresh sheet of paper or plastic will be spread over the cloth. Scraps of food left on the plates at the end of the meal will be emptied on to the table and gathered up inside the 'cover'.

The *tavernaris* would be surprised if you sought to make a reservation; he would obligingly lean reversed chairs against one of the tables, but would be unlikely to hold it if a regular customer turned up before you did and no other table was free.

There is no such thing as a non-smoking corner in a taverna, though a number of restaurants, especially in hotels, are now beginning to introduce them.

The traditional taverna is not, above all, the place for a quick meal. If it is eight o'clock and you have a ticket for folk dancing at nine, either go to a restaurant or eat after the show. Leisurely service is a matter of life-style and economics. The Greek goes to his taverna to spend the evening and the owner, knowing he must count on a limited turnover, has no reason not to economise on waiters, while the waiters themselves rely on the percentages from a relatively small number of bills.

The average Greek family will prefer to 'give a table' at a taverna than to entertain at home. Their apartment is probably small, air conditioning is still a luxury, and at the end of the night the bill for six at a taverna is probably not much higher than the cost of the raw materials of a similarly varied menu prepared in a cramped kitchen.

The taverna offers, therefore, exactly what the customer requires: not an aperitif, since he will have had that at home, but a wide range of starters, and a choice among a small number of familiar main dishes. It follows that a taverna is a place in which to talk. It is unlikely to have music, except possibly from a tape-recorder, though it might be on the beat of a strolling player or singer who will wander among the tables, collect his tips and leave. If it has a piano, it is definitely a restaurant.

A menu, probably handwritten, may be displayed somewhere near the entrance, but there is unlikely to be one on the table and no need to become anxious if you can neither read the menu brought to you nor make yourself understood by the waiter. You are not simply welcome but expected to point to what you want from the dishes on display or stroll into the kitchen. The Greeks do that themselves: they know very well what a moussaka is, but they want to see what this taverna's moussaka looks like before venturing an order.

Suppose you order half a dozen starters to be followed by grilled steak. The waiter will bring you the *mezedes* and then, unless he acquires the impression that you are in a hurry, he will wait for a reminder before telling the *afentiko*, his boss, to put the steaks over the charcoal. The meat will probably reach you extremely well done; the Greeks prefer it that way. Medium rare is better hazarded in an expensive restaurant or steak house, where the meat will probably be imported and almost certainly will have been hung; the *tavernaris* will only have beaten it with a metal weight.

There is no compulsion in a taverna to order what you do not want. You can sit all night with a glass of wine and a plate of beans if you wish, though you will be regarded as eccentric if you open a book.

The taverna is identifiable by its decor: bright lighting, quite possibly from naked bulbs if the owner is of the older generation and regards it as a sign of extravagance not to obtain the full value of what he has paid for. Walls will be covered with whitewash or plastic paint, the monotony broken by an occasional picture in an unglassed frame or secured with tacks. Somewhere, there will be a line of barrels: wine is part of the meal, but in the taverna it is also definitely part of the decor.

You call the waiter by clapping your hands or tapping a knife against a glass. When you want your bill, you can either use the word *logariasmó* or, having caught the waiter's eye, move the hand rapidly from side to side on a horizontal plane with thumb and forefinger holding an imaginary pencil. The bill will be handwritten, probably indecipherable, and honest; the Greek customer at his regular taverna will at most only check the addition.

In the grey area of the taverna in transition, you can expect a fresh tablecloth without a plastic topping, subdued lighting or even a personal candle, a printed menu in several languages, and no sign of wine other than in bottles. The plates may be warm though the helpings will probably be smaller; the bill will probably be higher but at least will be the legible production of a cash register. Whether this is more romantic depends on your personal views.

Some tavernas are uppity

The elegant taverna will be found mainly in Athens and the resort islands, occasionally in the larger provincial towns, and rarely in the countryside. Unlike its more humble relatives which tend to be named after their owners, their principal feature, speciality or location, its name will lean towards elegance also. It may boast a small combo with a lady vocalist, but if it has a dance floor and a live orchestra it should be regarded as a nightclub.

At the elegant taverna you will be under greater pressure to sample the whole range of starters. If a waiter brings them to your table without being asked, you can at that point reject anything you may find unattractive in appearance and it will be removed without objection. Main dishes can still be selected during a visit to the kitchen.

At some point during the evening, the musicians will circulate among the tables singing requested numbers. They do not need to be tipped unless you ask for something special – if you put them to the test, you will find their repertoire may well include *Waltzing Matilda*. The tip, a couple of hundred drachmas a song, is slipped into the leader's pocket as your signal that he is released.

But are there no restaurants?

Certainly there are restaurants, and of as many categories as there are types of taverna. If you are staying in a deluxe hotel, you will have direct access to some of the most elegant restaurants in Greece, offering the kind of dishes you are accustomed to when in funds in your own country. You will almost certainly be impressed by your surroundings, and may even eat well. Also if you are in Corfu with deep pockets, you could dine at the Achilleion, once the summer palace of the Empress Elizabeth of Austria and Kaiser Wilhelm of Germany, and now one of Greece's three casinos.

It is rather more probable that you will be staying in a hotel of lower category, on a half-board basis. In that case by all means take the meal you have paid for, but give earnest consideration to doing so at lunch, when you will probably not want to fill up anyway.

Crusades have been fought in Greece, not least by NTOG, to impress on hoteliers that not every visitor is a weight-watcher, and some improvements have resulted. The Commerce Ministry has now decreed minimum rations, by ingredient and weight, plus unlimited bread. But you will certainly not eat as well as you would in an equivalent hotel in Italy, Germany, France, England or Turkey.

To do them justice, hoteliers who live from package tours, which most of them do, have a genuine grievance: their contracts are stipulated a year in advance in drachmas, leaving them to confront inflation without the cover that would otherwise be provided by currency depreciation (when the drachma slides, the profit goes to the tour operator). However, they appear to have been persuaded that economies can better be made on waiters' salaries, through introduction of canteen-style self-service restaurants, than by counting the chips.

Outside hotels, the possibilities are wide and varied. Athens all year round and the resort islands in season are well provided with French, Italian and Chinese restaurants; on the islands there will also be restaurants catering to Scandinavians or offering fish and chips (though not quite in the English manner) to cautious Britons. And everywhere there are steak houses.

The Old Contemptibles

More Greek, in style and menu, are the longstanding restaurants whose clientele is divided equally among Greeks, resident foreigners and tourists. They open early for the foreigners, midday for lunch and 7 p.m. for dinner, and stay open late for the Greeks, to 4 p.m. and 1 a.m. They employ mainly elderly waiters by whom it is a pleasure to be served, and offer a wide range of Greek and European dishes at middle-range prices – say Dr 1,500–2,000 a head for a three-course meal with wine.

You will also find restaurants where only grilled meats are served as main dishes. At the entrance or in the display window, serried ranks of chickens will be turning on spits; other grills will be processing sucking-pig or dealing with steaks, and somewhere there should be a doner kebab – veal assembled on spits and grilled vertically, so that every slice as it is carved off is succulently crisp. *Souvlaki*, the same veal on individual skewers, will be cooked to order. Except for *souvlaki*, the meat is usually sold by weight, with side helpings if desired of chips, salad or cold boiled vegetables. Chopped raw onion will be sprinkled on the kebab, and mustard is available. The meat is of reasonably good quality, and the prices are moderate.

Lamb also may be used occasionally for *souvlaki*, but will not turn up in doner form. The reason is availability, price and preference. Greece has no mutton – the pasture is insufficient and the demand is always for lean meat. Even around Easter, when it floods the market, lamb is the most expensive of all meat except fillet steak; from June to

November it can be hard to find. There is a fairly recent tendency for *psistaries* to make their doner out of pork, to save a few drachmas; since there is no legal requirement to specify the meat used, the incurious among their customers will generally assume they are eating veal.

Sizing up the opportunities

The time has come for a first foray into real food. You have familiarised yourself with what is available at your hotel, identified some likely-looking alternative in the vicinity, and are ready to lay purse and stomach on a strange table.

The purpose of this section is not to list all the familiar international dishes that can be found in Greece, while regional and seasonal specialities will be touched on only if, like the Corfu *sofrito* or the Easter *mayeritsa* soup, they are on offer also in other parts of the country or at other times of the year. And finally, since this is not a cookery book, it would be purposeless to include dishes, no matter how delicious, that are eaten routinely in the Greek home but are rarely if ever found in restaurants or tavernas – either because of their over-familiarity, the time or labour required to prepare them, or the patent impossibility of charging a high enough price to make them profitable. There is an adequate supply of Greek cookery books in English for those who would like to experiment in making bean soup (*fassolatha*), lentil soup (*fakès*) or chickpea soup (*rovithia*): these are not so much soups as full one-course meatless meals – another good reason for tavernas to avoid them. (And a fortune remains to be made by the enterprising small businessman who parks a barrow between the Cumberland and Mount Royal Hotels in London to serve cups of hot *fassolatha* and *fakès* to Greek tourists.)

Over the next few pages you will find brief descriptions of the dishes you can expect to come across throughout Greece in the middle of the summer. The intention is to provide a rough guide to their composition, with a view to preventing unpleasant surprises, disappointment or waste.

'Killing the appetite'

Mezedes

The Greeks are dedicated nibblers, to whom *mezedes* are the essential prelude to every meal, and may indeed become the whole meal in the middle of the day. At its simplest, the *mezè* (one *mezè*, two *mezedes*) can be no more than a plate containing a slice of cucumber, a few pickles, olives, a piece of cheese and a quarter of a hard-boiled egg. But usually something a little more elaborate is preferred.

This could take the form of a dip: *Rossiki* (Russian) salad, *taramousalata* (a pink paste of fish roe and potato), *hatziki* (thick yoghurt blended with cucumber and garlic), *melitzano salata* (a similar preparation based on aubergines) or, mainly but not necessarily as an accompaniment to fish, *skordalia* (from *skorda*, the Greek for garlic), a purée of potato or bread with garlic, oil and lemon.

Self-caterers will find all these dips ready-made in grocery refrigerators. The Greeks eat them spread on slices of bread, but they can also be used to improve strips of raw or salad vegetables.

Obviously, *skordalia* has to be a group activity, unless you propose to go into a twenty-four hour retreat. Two highly prized properties are ascribed to garlic: it is said to combat blood pressure and induce sleep. The strings of garlic hanging from rafters or festooning taverna walls have nothing to do with vampires, which in Greece drink only from wallets, but are intended to convey a promise of healthy eating. However, a virgin stomach may appreciate an alka seltzer after the first encounter, and, though raw parsley helps, there is really not much you can do about your breath.

The cold dip negotiated, you are ready for the hot *mezè*: *tyropita* or *spanakopita* (cheese or spinach in hot flaky pastry), or a combination of the two in the form of *spanakotiropita*, or a plate of *kolokithia* or *melitzana tiganitès* (fried eggplant or aubergine). *Patatès tiganitès* (French fries; ask for 'tsips' in Greece and you get a packet of crisps) are the most common *mezè* in the vegetable category. Cheese will be feta.

As an accompaniment to the hot *mezè*, which in many tavernas may also include *keftèdes* (meatballs), you have a choice of whatever *horta* (boiled vegetable, served cold with olive oil) the taverna has prepared that day. In the traditional taverna you may also expect *kokoretsi* in the evening, though not for lunch. This is a highly spiced preparation consisting of the offal of lamb threaded on a spit and wrapped round and round with intestine. A cut from the spit makes a helping, and it really does taste better than a description of its components might suggest.

In a fish taverna or restaurant, the *mezedes* will probably include *marides* (whitebait) and *kalamarakia* (squid). The *marides* – up to two dozen a helping – will be larger than the whitebait commonly encountered in other countries, but are still eaten head and all. For the squeamish, the taverna cat can come in useful. The *marides* will always be fresh, since they are never frozen and do not keep. The same does not apply to *kalamarakia* and even less to *garithes* (shrimps), though legally if they are not fresh they should be identified on the menu as *katapsigmeno* (deep-frozen), usually signified by a capital 'K'.

At their tastiest, *kalamarakia* are small enough to be fried whole after a simple washing; you pull out the semi-transparent bone and eat them guts, ink and all. In the more expensive restaurants they will have been filleted and sliced into rings and strips, losing much of their flavour but posing less danger to clothing from flying ink and also, it must be admitted, less danger of mild poisoning or allergic reaction. That is the real problem with *kalamarakia*: you have to try it once to be sure you can take it.

Soup

Soup, if served at all, is more likely to follow than precede the *mezedes*. Outside the deluxe hotel, the choice is limited: *kotosoupa* (chicken soup, usually thickened with egg and flavoured with lemon), *hortosoupa* (vegetable soup) and *psarosoupa* (fish soup, but definitely not a bouillabaisse). At Easter everywhere, but at some restaurants throughout the year, *mayeritsa* is also on offer. This so-called 'Easter' soup represents an alternative use of the lamb offal and intestines that more commonly go to make a *kokoretsi*; enjoyment is aided by not dwelling too much upon the contents.

Picking and choosing

In the traditional taverna, the main dish will be a choice among *brizoles* (steaks) of *moushari* (veal) or *hirino* (pork), *païdaki* (lamb cutlets) or *biftekaki* (hamburgers). Sometimes the taverna, and certainly the restaurant, will also offer what in Greece are known as 'cooked' dishes, prepared in the *tapsi* (pan) earlier in the day and kept warm.

These include veal, pork and chicken *sto fourno* ('in the oven', i.e. roast), garnished with a couple of chips or potatoes also *sto fourno*. The same meat slices or chickens quartered will turn up with spaghetti or a small heap of rice. In general, partly because of the previous *mezedes* and also to keep prices low, vegetables have to be ordered separately as side dishes.

There are three other delicious pre-prepared dishes found everywhere in Greece: *moussaka* (which has and needs no translation), *pastitsio* (much the same as moussaka but with the aubergine or potato replaced by pasta) and *stiffado* (meat stewed with onions and garlic). *Sofrito*, the national dish of Corfu, also turns up in Corfiote restaurants around the country; it is a fillet steak stewed in a garlic sauce and should be served with mashed potato, though increasingly the tourist will get it with chips.

Common though less ubiquitous are *youvetsaki* (meat stewed with tomato and served with pasta), veal *stamnas* (much the same, with vegetables instead of pasta) and lamb, kid or rabbit *lathorigani* (stewed in olive oil and flavoured with oregano). Variations are played on all these themes, so it is a good idea to visit the kitchen before you decide.

And finally a word on *dolmadakia*, meat and rice wrapped in vine leaves and served with a thick egg-and-lemon sauce. These can be eaten either as an appetiser or a main course. They bear no resemblance to those you can buy in cans in Greek supermarkets, which contain no meat, have no sauce, are swimming in olive oil, and are eaten only cold.

The finny drove

Fish is much more expensive than meat, whether ordered in a restaurant or bought from a fishmonger. Around Athens, fish restaurants are mainly to be found, as might be expected, in Piraeus, the nearby yacht marina of Mikrolimano and along the coast to and beyond Athens Airport. In the provinces, they will be sitting on beaches, and on the lesser islands you will find them close to the harbour. In the resort islands you may have to search. You can expect to pay at least Dr 2,000 a head if you have substantial appetites to satisfy.

Here again, except for slices of *synagrida* or similar white fish (any translation is open to dispute and could be misleading), you will select the fish you want from the restaurant icebox and it will be grilled or fried to order and served head and all. If grilled, it will be accompanied by an oil and lemon sauce. A scrap of paper on the dish will give weight and price: keep this so that you can check the bill.

Barbounia and *glossa* (these are indisputably red mullet and sole respectively) will usually be dusted in flour and fried. *Bakalarakia* (cod, either fresh, frozen or imported dried from Iceland or the Soviet Union) will also be fried, though in batter, and probably accompanied by *skordalia*; not a highly-regarded fish in Greece, this is relatively cheap.

You should consider yourself fortunate if you find *lithrini*, *fangri*, *sargos*, *spathari* or *melanouria*: order them grilled and do not torment yourself about what they may be called in English since no two experts agree.

Apart from *marides* and *kalamarakia* as a *mezè*, you may also be offered *ktopodi* (octopus, grilled or stewed) or *garithes* (shrimps, grilled, fried or boiled, and sometimes with tomato sauce). If in funds you could also go for a lobster, boiled or grilled, though unless it twitches when you shake hands you should assume it is frozen. Greeks eat them only after winning a lottery.

Winding up on the way home

With the possible exception of an ice or a cream caramel, you will not find dessert or coffee on the menu of the traditional taverna and middle-ranking restaurant. The Greeks end their meal with fruit, then go to a patisserie if they want more.

Cakes are either recognisably international or *sto tapsi* ('in the pan'); the latter may once have been Turkish, but should certainly not now be described as such. Essentially, they comprise the *baklava*, *kataifi* and *galaktobouriko*. The first is the nut-filled and honey-flavoured pastry now familiar around the world, the second is much the same but in the form of a 'shredded wheat', and the third is a custard pie. The Greeks will prefer them for safety if they are in any doubt about the reliability or freshness of the cream-and-chocolate confections, and you might well do the same for these and two additional reasons: they are more 'Greek' and less likely to cause an upset stomach.

On the subject of coffee

You may still, if you wish, order a *turkiko* but it would be more polite to your hosts if you requested an *elliniko*. A few years ago, what is now 'Greek' coffee began to disappear from patisseries, though not from the working-class coffee-shops. This was because its prices were, and indeed still are, set by the Commerce Ministry under regulations covering 'products of wider popular consumption' while those of 'French', 'American' – espresso, cappuccino and the rest – were not. But responding to protests, the Ministry eventually made it illegal for any kind of coffee to be served unless 'Greek' coffee was also available.

You are over the first hurdle when you request Greek and not Turkish coffee, but to earn the respect of the waiter and therefore a better result you should be familiar with at least the three basic subdivisions: *variglyko* (heavy and sweet), *glykivrasto* (sweet and boiled) and *metreo* (medium sweet). Order one of these and the coffee should reach you hot, accompanied by a glass of iced water; use only the generic term and you may get instant tepid in a small cup.

All too often, your hotel will expect you to brew your own, at least at breakfast and after meals, from the cup of lukewarm water and the packet of Nescafé in the saucer. If a patisserie does the same, go somewhere else next time.

Water

A carafe of iced water will normally be put on your table along with the bread; if not, you ask for *neró*. Is it safe to drink? You will observe that the Greeks consume it by the gallon, and normally regard bottled water as the ultimate extravagance. But since there are sharp regional differences in water content and quality, even the Greeks will sometimes order a bottle when away from their home town. You might wisely do the same, since it would be a pity to lose a day's wellbeing for so little reason.

You can buy water in one-and-a-half litre disposable plastic bottles from a *kava* (wine and spirit merchant), grocery or supermarket: you will find Ivi, which comes from springs at Loutraki near Corinth, in most parts of the country, but there is no agreement among the Greeks themselves on which is better and which not so good. All bottled water is 'natural', never aerated.

Drinks before, during and after

If you are to stay with the local product, Greece offers ouzo as an aperitif, wine or beer with the meal, and brandy afterwards. Ouzo is the aniseed-flavoured national drink that has now been joined in the Greek home, though rarely superseded, by imported Campari and even the occasional gin and tonic. Distilled from grape, it is colourless in the bottle but turns cloudy when water is added. The Greeks prefer it on ice with water, at most half-and-half. With an alcohol content of 42 per cent vol it is not particularly potent but nevertheless it is always accompanied by something to nibble, even if only a biscuit and a piece of cheese. In quantity and without food, it has the un-Greek habit of attacking the stranger on two fronts, but at least the condition of your stomach then helps to distract your attention from the state of your head. Try it, but with caution!

More than 90 per cent of all wine consumed in Greece is white, and the Greeks prefer it *heema* ('loose') from the barrel, not just because it is cheaper but because they believe it is less likely to have chemical additives. With comparatively rare exceptions, if it's from a barrel it's resinated. Most Greeks will tell you retsina got that way because the barrels had to be caulked with pine resin, but even earlier, resin was applied to the inside of earthenware wine jars to guard against seepage. Now, it is simply the preferred flavouring. The first sip may suggest turpentine but a taste for retsina is not hard to acquire. However, for the faint-hearted, tavernas keep a few bottles of drinkable non-resinated white wine in the ice-box. Restaurants will offer a choice between resinated and non-resinated carafe wine, or will not offer *heema* wine of any kind. Restaurant retsina is likely to be of reliable quality, neither so excellent nor so atrocious as that supplied in some tavernas. As a rule of thumb, be wary of retsina that is cloudy, and of any kind of 'loose' red wine.

Bottled wines

Though no accurate count exists, there are said to be close on 500 wines now available in bottles; the number is increasing annually as an effect of European Community membership, which has created new markets abroad, and the growth of cooperative production and bottling. Also, standardisation procedures are being improved, though there is still no real conception of vintage. Similarly, there are no little vineyards to which the passing stranger will be invited for the trampling. The closest approximation is the summer wine festival at Daphni, on the outskirts of Athens, where the price of admission gives the right of unlimited tippling. But if one goes there at all it is for quantity, not quality.

Among the bottled whites, those you will find on sale everywhere in Greece include Kambas (retsina or unresinated Hymettus), Santa Helena, Cellar, the Kourtakis 'Apelia' and Boutari's Lac de Roches and, at the more expensive end of the spectrum, Porto Carras. Boutari also markets the most popular of the reds, under the name Naoussa, closely pursued again by Porto Carras. There are also a few dessert wines, heavy and sweet. The best of these are probably Samos, which Byron implored the Greeks to 'dash down', and the darker Mavrodafni that inspired Henry Miller in *The Colossus of Maroussi* to prose even purpler than the wine itself, bemusing some Greeks and amusing others. Sweet wines are simply not drunk except by tourists.

Three wine industries, Cair of Rhodes, Achaia Klaus of Patras and Zitsa of central Greece, now market sparkling dry and medium-sweet wines that are acceptable approximations to champagne at far more reasonable prices, but these too have not really caught on and are more likely to be found in supermarkets than in restaurants. However, if you are treating yourself to a lobster . . . .

Probably the best wine you will ever drink in Greece, if you are lucky enough to be offered a small glass, will accompany a couple of olives and a piece of cheese in the refectory of a monastery. But for that you not only have to go to the monastery but to arrive on a day and at a time when the monks are receiving. You will then get an idea of what wine used to be like when its production was still a cottage industry and it didn't matter whether it travelled or not since it wasn't going anywhere.

You will find the better-known international beers on sale in Greece, but only in pale or lager form, in cans or bottles. You might come across a supermarket with cans of Guinness.

There is no reason to fear Greek brandies, provided you go for the five-star, seven-star or VSOP: Metaxas and Votrys are the most ubiquitous.

A word on bars and pubs

Except in hotels or nightclubs, Greek bars bear no relation to bars in other countries, and even less to pubs. You go to one if you want to sit down with beer, wine or ouzo and eat a fairly substantial meal but without a main course. Typical orders might be chips, baked beans, meat balls, cheese in slices or fried in flour, fried eggs, omelette, Russian salad, olives, or a cold plate of ham and salami. Many bars are open only during shopping hours, which gives an idea of the reason for their existence, while there is usually a small one, also serving coffee, on the mezzanine floor of an office block. This explains why eating at his desk need not be a particular hardship for a businessman, and there is no such thing as a packed lunch.

The pub in Greece is really a myth. Certainly there are places that call themselves pubs, sometimes whole clusters of them in areas of concentrated British tourism, such as the Glyfada suburb of Athens and Benitses or Cavo in Corfu. They will have a polished bar and bar stools, and possibly even a rail for the feet, along with a barman in some kind of uniform, a selection of whiskies, gins and brandies, and beer in bottles or possibly even drawn from small metal barrels and presented as 'draught'. The music will be piped or provided by a pianist, and the lighting will be equally subdued.

These pubs have been opened, sometimes by British or Irish immigrants, to offer a home-from-home to the British tourist and to persuade him to leave some of his money in the hands of his compatriots; occasionally they will employ a couple of barmaid–waitresses recruited from among the British girls who arrive with the swallows with the intention of financing a protracted summer holiday through part-time work. What should not be anticipated is a recognisable pub atmosphere. Like the acoustics in some concert halls, this is a problem that has so far eluded solution. There are too many barriers to its creation.

One is the climate. Between May and October, which is when the pubs must cover their costs for the year and is the only time many of them are even open, the idea of a pub as a place of shelter and warmth is untenable. It has to remove its windows, and may well spill on to the pavement. So there is no cosiness.

Another is the Greek lack of interest at best, and antipathy at worst. The Greeks do not drink standing up, do not drink at all without eating, and do not like to be served by women except in quality cafés. Not being drunks themselves, they have a natural nervousness at the prospect of confronting a possibly drunken foreigner. Greek men, though kings in their castles, rarely go out at night without their wives, and would be hard put to persuade a woman to enter a place so inherently unsympathetic as a pub with all the connotations of immorality inherited from its predecessor, the 'girly bar' that survives mainly in the docklands and the vicinity of American military bases.

Greeks can occasionally be found in pubs and may genuinely have been attracted there by a liking for foreign ways acquired during studies, work or holidays in England; but it is equally likely that their objectives will be business or a pick-up. You need not boycott them; simply do not expect too much.

There are no licensing hours in Greece for the sale of alcoholic beverages. All places of entertainment are required to close at 1 a.m. except on holidays, but under legislation governing staff working hours and for the sake of economising on electricity, not because the Greeks cannot be trusted to decide for themselves when they have had enough.

Entertainment

Entertainment in Greece falls into two broad categories: eating while talking, and watching while eating. Culture, on the other hand, at its most pure, is when you cannot even get a bag of crisps. On that definition, the cultural highlights of the Greek tourist season are certainly the Athens and Epidavros Festivals. Theatre runs them pretty close, since cakes and sandwiches are available only at the intervals. At the cinema, by contrast, you can slip into the bar for a hot or cold snack at any time, and some of the open-air summer cinemas provide waiter service while the film is running.

Unless you attend a performance of folk dancing by the Dora Stratou company in Athens, you will be exposed to this most picturesque form of callisthenics at the luxury tavernas where, of course, you have to eat. At nightclubs and bouzouki tavernas you will be offered food, but would probably be wiser only to drink. You will probably enjoy the Sound and Light spectacles in Athens, Rhodes, Crete and Corfu: to these, since Greeks rarely go unless accompanying foreigners, you have to take your own sandwiches.

Greek folk dancing

Folk dance in Greece in its purest form, which is not what you see in tavernas and nightclubs, owes much to the late Dora Stratou, who died in 1988 at the age of eighty-four. Some years ago, in an interview with me spread over two days, she told of how she came to form her Society of Greek Folk Dancing and Songs, which throughout the summer performs nightly at a theatre on Philopapus Hill across the road from the Herod Atticus, and of what the spectator should look for:

- 'I was always very fond of the folk gatherings, the folk festivals that used to take place – and are still taking place – around the country on saints' days. The people there have a religious festival; sometimes they spend the night around the cloister or the church and they follow the ritual of the church, but then they have a great festivity and dance and sing all night probably. It lasts one or two days . . . . You can understand much more about what is called a nation if you get together with the people while they are having a festivity. And, of course, the first expression of the human person is the music, the dance, something that is practically inarticulate.'

The historic continuity of the Greek race, Miss Stratou explained, can be found not only in the works of art and writings of the Ancient Greeks and Byzantines, but comes alive in the dances, songs, customs, superstitions and festivals of the people. As an example she offered the simple circle, a characteristic of most Greek folk dances. 'The circle means most probably the closing up of the people so as to throw out evil, a kind of defence against evil. It has most certainly to do with the seasons – for instance, to have a good season or to avoid the rain.'

One of the principal difficulties facing the Society in its early days was to find the dances and the performers. 'When I started, everything was dying out with that excitement of the Greeks to go forward and to progress. After we became a nation, after centuries of occupation, it was quite natural that the Greeks should want to throw away everything that reminded them of slavery. It was the same with Greek folk dancing. But the Greeks were forgetting that what they had been doing all these years was keeping their characteristics and the historical traces of the Greek ways.'

Miss Stratou sought out the dances, located the instrumentalists, recruited the dancers and rescued the costumes. The Society considers that its 'moment of recognition, when the people accepted their heritage', came in 1961 at the first of its annual panhellenic folk dance and song competitions.

'The Cretans danced their proud, eagle-like dances, the men of Naoussa came with chests ablaze with coins, the people of Pontus showed their Homeric war dances, the tender girls of Cephalonia sang their lively melodies, timidly the women of Macedonia punctuated with their rhythmical steps a tragic lament. The costumes, the work of love and wonderful taste, shone like jewels, and the art and talent of the dancers enthralled the audience.'

Greek folk dances are basically divided into two types, the *syrtos* or drag-dances and the *pedektos* or hop-dances. Almost always, the men have the more important role and the more intricate steps. By tradition, the women are modest, with downcast eyes; this, and the weight of their costumes, explains why most of the women's dances are of the quiet *syrtos* type.

The *syrtos* itself is believed to be the oldest of the Greek folk dances; it is the round dance depicted on many ancient vases and Byzantine frescoes, with the leading dancer twirling a handkerchief. The *kalamatianos*, a panhellenic dance, and the *tsakonikos*, are variations of the *syrtos*. In the *tsakonikos* the dancers hold tightly to one another's arms, as if striving not to lose each other on their way out of a maze. Plutarch describes a similar dance performed by Theseus and his Athenian companions when, during their return voyage to Athens from Crete after the slaying of the Minotaur, they anchored at the island of Delos to sacrifice to the gods.

The *sousta*, best known of the hop-dances, is performed mainly on Crete and the Dodecanese islands, with differentiations peculiar to each island. On Rhodes, for instance, it is 'undulating', with limited hopping; on Halki it is all hops; on Karpathos it is danced heavily, as if Doric columns were in motion; on the sponge-diving island of Kalymnos, the hops of the *mechanikos* dance are implied rather than achieved, as a symbol of the crippled diver struggling to repeat what he can no longer perform.

On Crete, the basic dances are the *pentozales*, the *sousta* and the *syrtos*. The *pentozales* is a war dance, performed in older times by fully-armed fighters; the dancers hold one another by the shoulders while the leader (a role often played by the dancers in turn) displays the virtuosity on which his right to command is established.

On the Ionian islands, the music and dances retain recognisable Venetian influences; in the cities in particular, the *kantades* (serenades) are suggestive of Italian folk music. Though the Greek traditions are more obvious in the countryside, there is still a greater lightness of colour, tone and movement than in the dances of the Aegean generally.

An interesting throwback to the days of Alexander the Great can still be found in villages of the region of ancient Pella, Alexander's birthplace: there, a heavy ceremonial dance is performed by village girls who, alone of all women in Greece, wear a headdress vaguely reminiscent of an Ancient Greek helmet. According to legend, Alexander bestowed this privilege because of their prowess on the battlefield; he was about to be defeated when the women seized arms, rushed on to the field, and turned the tide.

No programme of Greek folk music is complete without some of the dances of Pontus, brought back to Greece by the refugees from Asia Minor. One of them, the *serra*, is the nearest surviving equivalent of the Ancient Greek Pyrrhic dance, and even now ends with two warriors duelling with swords.

Folk music is usually performed by a small orchestra consisting of a clarinet (which has replaced the shepherd's pipe), violin, lute and santouri, sometimes enriched with a drum or tambourine or both. The lyre is still widely in use on Crete, and the bagpipe can be heard in parts of Macedonia.

Ari, Zorba and the bouzouki

To the regret of many Greeks, who profess to find it unbearable, bouzouki music was made respectable by Zorba 'the Greek', with a little help from Alan Bates and Aristotle Onassis. In the film, Anthony Quinn created his *syrtaki* to the music of Mikis Theodorakis and finally got his young English friend doing it too. Onassis, who for all of twenty years set many paces in Greece, helped to take the bouzouki out of the waterfront dives in which it had languished and on to the dance floors of hotel ballrooms and luxury liners. But you can still find establishments where plates are smashed to cries of '*Spasta!*', though it is rare now for the more exuberant to burn a banknote or a jacket.

Broadly speaking, bouzouki defines an instrument, a club, a dance and a form of entertainment; more strictly speaking, it is an instrument like a mandolin, but with a harder tone and an elongated stem. It has three pairs of strings each tuned in unison, the first pair to A, the second to D and the third to A flat, and is played with a tortoise-shell or feather plectrum. As a form of music, bouzouki is of disputed origin; some claim it is an offshoot of Greek folk music while others dismiss it contemptuously as 'refugee' music, assert that it was brought to Greece after the Asia Minor disaster, and blame it on the Turks.

At a bouzouki taverna, the orchestra and singers sit in a straight line along a narrow stage, with ferocious amplification, and sing of the pathos of life, disappointments in love and the faithlessness of women: misery is rampant. Never at any moment does a true bouzouki instrumentalist or singer stand up, and never is there a moment of pianissimo. The floor show is provided by the customers, usually men, moved to dance by themselves and for themselves the intricate steps of the *zeimbekiko*, *tsifteteli* or *hassapiko*. Piles of plates are kept in readiness for audience participation, which can be an expensive indulgence.

Though you may at times believe you are listening to Radio Cairo, you have no hope of seeing belly-dancing.

Shopping

If you came to Greece for the shopping, which would imply a certain eccentricity, your best buys would probably be gold jewellery and silverware, fur coats and antiques. Converted back into your own currency, you would find the prices of these reasonable. Also, with the exception of the fur, they could be regarded as minor diversifications in an otherwise humdrum investment portfolio. Since Greece in effect went off the gold standard in 1965, when restrictions were placed on the purchase and sale of gold sovereigns that made them unattractive to the hoarder, the Greeks have collected their favourite metal in the form of rings, bracelets and chains.

But if your interest lies in souvenirs, you will have a wide choice of quality work ranging from ceramics, woodcarving and metalwork to rugs, embroidery and articles of marble, alabaster and onyx.

Clothes But first, a few things to bear in mind: Greece is not and probably will never be a serious contestant in the world of *haute couture* or a major producer of high-quality ready-to-wear clothes. Certainly you can buy women's dresses off the peg in wide varieties, but as a rule the patterns are either undistinguished or so excessively 'archaeological' that the dresses are more likely to serve as a conversation piece than to create an impression of tasteful elegance. Except for the wealthy who patronise specific designers, Greek women buy from boutiques, which in turn do their shopping in Italy, or from department stores that are stocked by such as Marks & Spencer; what might seem a bargain to them would scarcely seem so to you.

Leather Similarly, Greece is no rival to Italy or France in the production of quality leather goods, or even to Turkey in that of hard-wearing leather coats and jackets. Your best buy in this area would probably be a pair of sandals or leather slippers, to be found especially in Athens and Rhodes.

Imports Finally, Greece is not the place to buy anything at all not actually made there. Though Community membership has played havoc with tariffs, Greece is still an expensive country for imported goods because of the cost of transport, the small market and high taxes and mark-ups. The sole exception is whisky on Rhodes and Kos; because of special tariff dispensations harking back to the incorporation of the Dodecanese after the Second World War, hard liquor is cheaper there than in many duty-free stores.

The casual buy

Rugs

If weight is no problem, you could do much worse than pick up a *flokati*. These luxuriously soft, shaggy rugs are one of the few indigenous cottage-industry products that the Greeks themselves prize highly; in the past they were routinely included among the contents of a dowry chest. You will hear from dealers that they are both uniquely Greek and the direct descendants of the rugs that covered the walls and floors of Agamemnon's palace at Mycenae and the bed of Helen of Troy.

The best *flokati* are still made by women in their homes. They twist the yarn on special spindles to give it a fluffy texture, then weave it on looms to produce a rug with a matted base and a surface of long wool strands. The completed rug is immersed in running water for several days, to soften the wool and shrink the pile to a length of about four inches. It is then dyed, traditionally in flaming red or soft shades of brown or blue, or left in its natural cream colour.

Cottage production is concentrated in the mountain villages of central and north-west Greece, where the *flokati* tradition was kept alive during 'the 400 years' and into the first century of the present Greek state by families whose only concern was warmth and who learned subsequently, often with astonishment, that they were also artists. Factory *flokati* are lighter and less closely packed than those made by hand, and therefore cheaper. Both can be used on beds as well as floors, or hung on walls.

The *arachovas*, wool carpets with brilliant patterns named after the village near Delphi that used to be the centre of production, are slightly cheaper, as well as far lighter. *Arachovas* are mostly tacked to walls, often above a divan, but strips of them can be sewn together to make larger rugs. Most dealers can arrange shipment of the purchases home, for those travelling by air.

Carpet shops also offer *tagari* bags, which hang from one shoulder by a thick cord. While not very practical for general shopping, they make a bright accessory for the young and slim and a highly-regarded, inexpensive present. With the shoulder cords removed, they can be used as cushion covers.

Pottery

While Athens and Rhodes are the twin centres of Greek ceramics, many of the islands have their own specialities and you could usefully set aside an hour for browsing wherever you spend the night.

On Rhodes you will be invited to the Ikaros factory, where you can watch the girls painting the intricate designs and make your purchases from the display rooms.

Other crafts

For the trinket, you can go almost everywhere: a degree of gentle haggling may, for larger purchases, result in a 5 or 10 per cent discount.

Serious shopping

This can best be done in Athens, Thessaloniki, Rhodes and Myconos. The two co-capitals have the concentrated shopping areas, to which products are brought from all parts of Greece. And Rhodes and Myconos are the indispensable ports of call for almost every liner on an Aegean or Mediterranean cruise; they have reciprocated with a determination that no passenger on a shore excursion should experience difficulty in supporting the local economy.

Gold and silver People on cruises do seem to go for gold. When, as in 1986 and to a lesser extent in 1987, the Americans failed to arrive, the cruise companies fought back with special rates for Greek passengers but still the goldsmiths languished.

As little as twenty-five years ago, a mention of Greek jewellery would bring to mind the silver filigree work of Rhodes and Ioannina, a kind of embroidery with silver wire, and gold bracelets of 18 and 22 carats worked in a similar way and known locally as Smyrneika. Since the early 1960s, Greek goldsmiths have learned to visit the museums for their inspiration. The result has been a new flowering of a 4,000-year-old art, to be seen in rings and earrings, necklaces and bracelets, and articles for use and display – bowls, chalices and plates. They are of guaranteed quality and, considering their workmanship, not particularly expensive. It is unlikely that this would have happened to such an extent without tourism, in particular cruising, and the withdrawal of the gold sovereign from circulation.

Fur Fur – essentially mink, chinchilla and stone marten – may seem a curious specialisation for a hot country, but it is indisputably one of the better buys. If you intend to pick up a coat, jacket, stole or hat, you will probably make the purchase in Athens, Thessaloniki or Rhodes.

Antiques A degree of caution is required in buying antiques and antiquities; above all, it is necessary to know the difference between the two. As a rule of thumb, anything pre-dating the 1821 War of Independence is likely to be classified as an antiquity, and to require an export licence. In practice, difficulties arise most frequently over Byzantine icons.

If a traveller is found with antiquities in his luggage without a covering export permit, the articles will be confiscated and he will become liable to prosecution. So buy only from a reputable dealer, who will provide you with the necessary documentation and tell you where to go if confirmatory signatures are needed.

General Basics

Banking and shopping hours

Banks work a five-day week, from 7.40 a.m. to 1.30 p.m. Some in central areas stay open in the evenings and at weekends for currency exchange only.

Shopping hours vary slightly according to category and season. As a general rule, in the summer shops are open by 9 a.m. and close between 1.30 and 2.30 p.m.; on Tuesdays, Thursdays and Fridays they reopen for three hours in the afternoon, from around five to around eight. From October to May inclusive, when afternoon heat is not a problem, they are open throughout the day, roughly from 9 a.m. to 7 p.m., with personnel working a forty-hour week.

Restrictions on shopping hours do not apply to folk art and souvenir shops nor, in practice, to groceries in tourist resorts. Newspaper and cigarette kiosks can also work the hours they wish, and some in central Athens never close.

Barbers and hairdressers broadly follow the same hours as shops, but may stay open later on Saturdays. Men can expect to pay Dr 700–1,000 for a haircut, and women Dr 2,000–4,000 for a trim, shampoo and set; tipping is optional but expected.

For pharmacies see 'Health', p. 127.

Clothing suggestions

Carry lightweight, easily washable clothing, with a shawl, jacket or sweater for the evenings. You will need a jacket and tie or a cocktail dress only if you are planning to go on a cruise or lose money at one of Greece's three casinos on the outskirts of Athens (in the Mount Parnes Hotel), on Corfu and on Rhodes.

Swimming costumes may not be worn at archaeological sites. To enter a monastery or church, men should wear long trousers (not shorts) and shirts, and women a dress or full-length skirt (not mini) and a top with sleeves. Shawls can often be borrowed at the entrance. Heads need not be covered.

Currency and currency regulations

Greek currency The Greek currency is the drachma (Dr). While the drachma for purposes of commercial calculation is divided into 100 lepta, inflation has overtaken the old lepta coins and they are no longer in circulation. Coins in actual circulation are of 1, 2, 5, 10, 20 and 50 drachma.

Banknotes are in denominations of Dr 50 (now being phased out and replaced by the Dr 50 coin), 100, 500, 1,000 and 5,000.

Restrictions Visitors are permitted to enter Greece with up to Dr 25,000 in Greek currency, in banknotes of up to Dr 1,000, but may not export more than Dr 10,000 in Greek currency.

There are no restrictions on the amount of foreign exchange, including gold in coin or bullion, which may be brought into Greece. However, sums in excess of US $1,000, in any form other than travellers' cheques made out in the name of the bearer should be declared on entry since otherwise re-export will not be permitted. This is logical, since the Greek authorities are delighted to see money enter the country but loathe to see it leave; for that reason, you should not neglect to make a currency declaration if you calculate that you may still be carrying more than $1,000 at the end of your trip.

Plastic money All major credit cards are accepted in hotels, top restaurants and many shops, and money can be drawn against them through cooperating banks, but they are not yet extensively recognised on the smaller islands. Most useful are American Express, Diners, Visa, Access and MasterCard. Travellers' cheques and Eurocheques can be exchanged at banks and used in most hotels; elsewhere, expect a polite refusal.

Exchange rates For currency exchange, banks usually offer a slightly better rate than hotels; their rates for the day will be posted prominently near the main door. It is not worth shopping around among banks unless large sums are involved. You will note the unusually wide spread between the buying and selling rates (as much as Dr 6 on the dollar and Dr 10 on sterling); in buying drachma, of course, you get the lower figure. In resort areas, currency can also be exchanged in shops displaying Bank of Greece authorisation; these may not always keep their rates up to date, especially when the drachma is on one of its slides.

Foreign currency You can pay in foreign exchange at most souvenir shops (though the rate may be poor), but other shops, restaurants, bars and taxi-drivers are becoming less willing to accept dollars or pounds. Greece's once flourishing currency black market is in the doldrums, mainly as a result of the general easing of restrictions on movement of capital required by Greece's EC membership and also because of fifteen years of double-digit inflation; while this may have turned the drachma into a 'sunshine' currency, it has also enhanced the attractiveness of the 'positive' interest rates – slightly above inflation – with which banks have had to defend themselves.

Documents needed to enter Greece

Nationals of European Community countries, the United States, Canada, Australia and New Zealand require only a valid passport for a stay of up to three months.

For a longer stay, you need a temporary residence permit from the aliens police (in Athens, this service is a department of the security police in Alexandras Avenue). In practice, first and second extensions are normally granted without much formality.

The holders of passports bearing a visa, stamp or other indication of a visit or intention to visit the Turkish-held part of northern Cyprus are liable to be refused entry to Greece (see 'National Issues', p. 52).

Electrical current

Greek current is standard 220 volts A/C, and therefore transformers are not required for European appliances. However, you will need a plug adaptor if your appliance has a plug with square, not round, pins.

Embassies and consulates

- **Britain:** 1 Ploutarchou Street, 106-75 Athens; tel. 7236 211-219. The beautiful white house behind it, possibly the finest remaining example of a neo-Classical home in Athens, is the British Ambassador's residence.

- **United States:** 91 Vassilissis Sophias (Queen Sophia) Avenue, 115-21 Athens; tel. 7212 951-959. Once a kind of modern Parthenon crowning a grassy knoll and symbolising the open society, it has now been surrounded by high steel fencing and concrete tank-barriers disguised as flower pots and has become part of fortress America. This is not only a matter of terrorism; it was costing too much to scrape away the paint after Greece's routine anti-American demonstrations. It is on the left past the Hilton Hotel and adjacent to the permanently uncompleted concert hall; expect to be searched if you want to get in.

- **Canada:** 4, I. Gennadiou Street, 115-21 Athens; tel. 7239 511; suitably modest premises in a residential street.

- **Australia:** 37 D. Soutsou Street, 115-21 Athens; tel. 6423 186 or 6411 712. Now occupying its fourth home in twenty years, this is easily Greece's most walk-about embassy; telephone first in case it is still wandering, then hail a taxi!

- **New Zealand:** 15–17 An. Tsoha Street, 115–21 Athens; tel. 6410 311–315. Hard to find, but not much looked for; you will need a taxi.
- **South Africa:** 124 Kifissias Avenue, 115–10 Athens; tel. 6922 125.

Flora of the Aegean

An Ancient Greek or even a Byzantine, returning to the Aegean today, would find many differences: the islands as a whole are less verdant than in the past, because of the depredations of foreign conquerors and the ravages of fire, but at the same time there is a far greater variety of tree and bush.

Typically, the vegetation up to a height of 800 m includes the holm oak, laurel, myrtle, mastic tree, oleander, pear and olive. Though usually associated with mountains, pine trees can be found at the very edge of sandy beaches; there is also a profusion of fir and cypress.

Thyme, always considered the best flavour for honey, is one of the links with Ancient Greece; curiously, it is little used in the modern Greek kitchen, where oregano is preferred, and is never to be found in a city market. The Ancient Greek would also find his familiar olives, figs, pomegranates, almonds, vines and cereals, the 'gift' of Demeter. But he would not previously have seen the oranges, tangerines, apricots and peaches introduced from east Asia, the lemons, cotton, sugar cane, rice and quinces from central and southern Asia, the bananas, water melons and papyrus from Africa, the tomatoes, peanuts and potatoes from South America, and the maize and tobacco from Central and North America.

Much of the flora was brought to Greece by natural means from Asia and Africa. Other plants now considered typical of the Aegean were introduced by man and flourished because of the climate, in a process going back at least to the Minoan period and continued by Alexander the Great.

Health

Vaccination or inoculation certificates are not required for entry to Greece from the European Community, United States, Canada, Australia and New Zealand.

The prohibition of import of narcotics and drugs does not extend to internationally recognised medications in small quantities which are clearly intended for personal use.

First aid

There are no endemic dangerous diseases in Greece, nor any dangerous insects or wildlife. However, it is advisable to ensure that anti-tetanus injections are up to date. Mosquitoes and gnats can be an irritant, and a first-aid bag might include a repellant and ointment, in addition to a laxative and a medication for diarrhoea. Because of the danger of allergic reactions (for example, to fish or seafood, or unfamiliar dust or pollen) an anti-histamine might well be considered. At some point you can expect to need an elastic bandage (if the pavements don't get you, the archaeological sites probably will).

Sun oils and creams can be bought everywhere in Greece, but are expensive. Beware of over-exposure to the sun at the beginning of a holiday.

If you are dependent on glasses, carry a spare pair or at least your prescription.

Pharmacies

Pharmacies are open normal shopping hours, but closed on Saturdays as well as Sundays. In every city, one or several will provide an all-night and weekend service, on a roster system: the lists are displayed, in Greek, in pharmacy windows. Hotels should be able to provide the information in English.

Most of the larger pharmacies have one or two English-speaking staff, who will advise on simple remedies for minor indispositions. Prescriptions are not required for the milder antibiotics and anti-histamines. You can also go to a pharmacy if you need an injection.

Aspirin can be bought at any newspaper and cigarette kiosk.

Doctors and dentists

In the event of illness, your hotel will be able to call a doctor; embassies and consulates (including vice- and honorary consulates outside Athens) can supply lists of English-speaking doctors. You can expect to pay at least Dr 5,000 for a consultation.

It is definitely advisable to stay away from the Greek National Health Service, which is still in its formative stage. The Greeks resort to it only if their first concern is over the cost of the treatment.

Consult your hotel if you suddenly need a dentist. A simple extraction or replacement filling ought not to cost more than Dr 5,000.

The best advice on hospitals is to try to avoid accidents or major illnesses! The treatment will probably be adequate, since Greece is well supplied with doctors, but you will not enjoy the overcrowding nor be impressed by the standards of cleanliness. Preliminary examination may well be carried out in a corridor. However, most large hospitals now have intensive care units for victims of heart attacks.

Risky foods

How to avoid the nuisance of an upset stomach? Play safe and drink bottled water; be careful of milk and milk products, including ice-cream and soft white cheeses (start with a sip or nibble on your first encounter); show a similar respect for cooked seafood (particularly *kalamarakia* (squid) and boiled shrimps), and decline all uncooked seafood no matter how tempting. You should be all right with salads but, in any case, you could hardly avoid eating them in Greece. You have to assume the grapes have been properly washed, but you should peel other fruit.

Flies you have to learn to live with.

Laundry and dry-cleaning

This is generally quick and efficient, though somewhat expensive, in the hotels that provide the service and on cruise liners; you will be told in advance how much it will cost, and how long it will take. Dry-cleaning shops generally need at least forty-eight hours, and do not expect to serve tourists. You are unlikely to find a launderette.

The wise tourist washes what can be washed in a hotel bathroom, and leaves the rest for later.

Nudism

Except at a few particularly remote hotels in the Peloponnese and mainland Greece, if you want to take your clothes off in public you have to go to an island.

Nudist camps became legal in Greece only in 1985, after a discreet ten-year struggle between the National Tourist Organisation of Greece and the Orthodox Church. The final hurdle was cleared by a ruling from the Council of State, watchdog of the Greek constitution, that the legalisation of nudism by Parliament did not infringe constitutional provisions on public decency.

The preamble to the NTOG bill declared bluntly, if somewhat apologetically, that the benefits of nudism obtained by rival tourist countries (a reference mainly to Yugoslavia) made it necessary for Greece to follow suit. Authorising nudist camps in Greece, it said, would ensure high-capacity occupation of large hotels over a lengthy season by 'people belonging to the better-educated, more cultured and wealthier classes of society'.

Under the law, licences for the operation of nudist centres are granted by NTOG for renewable periods of two years, subject to agreement of the local authority of the area concerned. Hotel grounds and private beaches may be used 'provided that optical isolation is guaranteed' – a requirement interpreted as meaning that nudists must be invisible not only to the casual passer-by, but equally to the most ingenious 'voyeur'.

While not many hotels have yet thrown in their lot with foreign naturist clubs, passage of the bill has had an effect on the general outlook towards nudism in Greece. Though technically illegal outside the approved centres, it no longer draws police intervention on sufficiently remote beaches; in practice, this means on small islands or at the 'back' of larger ones.

Also, toplessness is now acceptable on beaches anywhere.

Photography

Photography with a small, portable film camera, without flash or video, is unrestricted and free of charge in museums and archaeological sites. A complex scale of fees, obtainable from NTOG, applies for photography with tripod and lighting, or which involves the use of power supplies or requires the assistance of personnel.

In moving about Greece, you will sometimes encounter signs in Greek and English warning that it is not permitted to take photographs. This means there must be military installations somewhere in the vicinity, even if you cannot see them, and the prohibition should be obeyed scrupulously. A useful precaution is never to photograph anything that looks like a landing strip, even if there are no warning signs.

The Greek authorities are suspected of being philosophical about resident agents of intelligence services; they are said to find it simpler to watch those they know than to expel them and then have to identify their successors. However, this tolerance does not extend to amateur or freelance spies.

If you are arrested for photographing what is not permitted to be photographed, you can expect to be lodged in jail on a holding charge of espionage until the film has been developed and scrutinised by experts at the National Defence Ministry. This can take several days.

Post offices

Most post offices (in Greek, *tachydromion*) work a five-day week, as do postmen, closing around 2.30 or 3 p.m. Main cities usually have one that stays open in the evenings and on Saturdays.

Letters can be sent ordinary airmail, express (the same word in Greek) or registered (*systimeno*); they all need to be weighed, and letters sent by registered mail have to be presented open for inspection.

You should expect a long queue, since post offices also accept payment of public utility bills. If you are mailing numerous letters or postcards, it is advisable to check both the addition and the change. Parcels have to be mailed from special offices. If you know your letter weighs less than 20 g, you can buy postage stamps (*grammatosima*) from most cigarette and newspaper kiosks, at a small surcharge.

Letters may be mailed in any of the yellow boxes along main roads and in squares; some of the larger have two slots, one for domestic (*esoteriko*) mail and the other for foreign (*exoteriko*). Express letters should be put into the red boxes.

Siesta

The siesta is part of the Greek way of life; European Community membership is clearly not going to change it. Outside the main resort areas, Greece is a quieter country from three to five in the afternoon than in the middle of the night. Police can be called to deal with noisy neighbours during the period of 'afternoon quiet', and one of the worst examples of ill manners would be to make a telephone call to a household when it is presumed to be sleeping.

The siesta governs and is governed by Greek working hours. Though these have been staggered to some extent to reduce traffic congestion, by 8 a.m. most offices are hard at work and the banks are open; shops follow from around 8.30 a.m. Office workers and bank clerks are away for the day by 3 p.m., and shops also take a siesta in the summer.

The only real exception to the general picture is the nine-to-five day introduced by foreign businesses and branches of multinationals and, in particular, shipping and shipping-related offices in Piraeus. If you smile at the siesta, you will be reminded – all Greeks know this – that 'Churchill won the war while sleeping in the afternoon'.

Smoking

Greek governments, for sound economic and social reasons, are ambivalent in their attitude towards smoking. In deference to medical opinion, they do not permit cigarette advertising on radio and television, and smoking is officially prohibited in public buildings and public transport except taxis. At the same time they are not unconscious of the thousands of provincial families living from tobacco production and cigarette manufacturing, nor of the foreign exchange receipts from tobacco exports and revenues from cigarette tax.

In public buildings

So you may not smoke in an indoor cinema or theatre (except in the foyer or a special *kapnisterion*, smoking room), in a bus or train (except in the corridor of the latter), or in a department store. But feel quite free to light up in a bank or post office; if there isn't an ashtray beneath

In restaurants

the no-smoking sign you may use the floor. The first no-smoking sections are just beginning to appear in restaurants, but so far it is the abstainers who are assigned the out-of-the-way tables. The Greeks are fond of the story of the American woman in a restaurant who asked the party at the next table if they objected to her eating while they smoked. Their reply: not at all, provided they could still hear the conversation.

Price of cigarettes

Greek cigarettes made of local oriental leaf sell at around Dr 80–120 for a packet of twenty, between a third and half the price of imported brands. There is a popular theory that Greek cigarettes are less hazardous to the health because Greece, as a hot country, has no need to lace its tobacco with combustibles; if you place a lighted Greek cigarette to your ear you will hear no crackle, and if you lay it in an ashtray it will go out.

For tax reasons, you cannot roll your own cigarettes in Greece; the prohibition is applied indirectly through a ban on the sale of cigarette paper. Pipes and cigars are not a Greek weakness; if they are yours, you can obtain your supplies at any kiosk.

Telephoning home

International telephone calls can be made far more cheaply from any office of the Hellenic Telecommunications Organisation (*Organismos Telepikoinonion Ellados*, or OTE) than from a hotel, which will add a surcharge.

Country codes include:
- **United Kingdom and Northern Ireland:** 0044.
- **United States and Canada:** 001.
- **Australia:** 0061.
- **New Zealand:** 0064.

Cost per minute or part of a minute for calls placed through OTE:
- **United Kingdom and Northern Ireland:** Dr 157.
- **United States and Canada:** Dr 415.
- **Australia and New Zealand:** Dr 523.

You should also go to an OTE office to send a telegram or a telex.

Time differences

Standard Greek time is two hours ahead of Greenwich Mean Time; between the last Sunday of March and the last Sunday of September, it is three hours ahead. Thus, except for possible jagged edges caused by different changeover dates, when it is midday in Greece it is 10 a.m. in London.

To calculate the time in the United States, subtract seven hours (eastern standard), eight hours (central), nine hours (Mountain) or ten hours (Pacific).

Australia and New Zealand are ahead of the Greek clock. For Australia, add eight hours (Melbourne and Sydney), seven hours (Canberra, Brisbane and Hobart), six and a half hours (Adelaide and Darwin) or five and a half hours (Perth).

For New Zealand, add nine hours.

Tipping

The tipping situation is not the only disorderly mess in Greece, but simply the one to which the tourist is most regularly exposed. The main thing is to avoid doubling the tip by adding 15 per cent to a bill that already incorporates a 15 per cent service charge. Greek practice is to leave the waiter the loose change on the plate in an ordinary taverna, restaurant or patisserie, and perhaps Dr 50 for each member of the party at a more expensive establishment. Don't add 15 or 20 per cent to the total bill unless you have received exceptionally good service – you'll ruin the market. The waiter picks up what is on the plate; some additional coins or a small note may be left on the table for the boy who lays the table and serves the water, bread and wine.

Your hotel bill will include service, and anything else is a matter of choice. The barman expects something, the doorman hopes for Dr 100 when he finds you a taxi, and chambermaids like to be remembered on the last day.

On cruises, where you sign for everything, you definitely do not tip as you go along. Your final bill from the purser's office will be accompanied by an envelope and a printed suggestion of a fair tip per person per day.

Tour guides may be tipped on the basis of Dr 100 per person per day, on the assumption that you have received only routine service. Give more if it has been better.

Porters may show you a rate card, and you pay accordingly; if they do not, you should allow Dr 100 per suitcase.

At a cinema, you do not tip the usherette but buy a perfectly useless 'programme' on entering for, say, Dr 10 or 20. At a theatre or concert, where you will be shown to a numbered seat, the usherette will be happy with Dr 50 for a couple.

You may add 10 per cent to a barber's or hairdresser's bill as a fair tip.

Greeks definitely do not tip taxi drivers; at most, they may decline the change if only a few coins are involved. But if you happen on one who speaks your language, or takes you to a taverna that he can recommend, he hopes to be rewarded.

You do not tip shop assistants, nor in banks or post offices.

Toilets

The best advice, though it is not always practicable, is to use only your own; this alone would justify insistence on a hotel room with private facilities.

The customary marking in Greece is WC, though sometimes the word *apohoritirion* is used. Usually there is a single entrance for men and women; sex separation, if any, takes place inside.

In the larger cafés, you may find an old woman seated at a table at the entrance to the toilet. Her responsibility is cleanliness and replenishment of paper, and Dr 5 or 10 should be dropped into her plate. This is not, however, as in some Balkan countries, an admission fee!

Public toilets tend to be relatively clean, at least in comparison with some of those compulsorily provided even by the smallest restaurant, coffee-shop and bar. In older buildings, you will occasionally happen on a survivor of the once ubiquitous 'Turkish toilets'. These are holes in the floor, flanked by guidance in one form or another as to where the feet should be placed. To the extent that they are more easily swilled, they may inspire greater confidence than those with bowl and seat. The trick is to retain your balance.

Carry some toilet paper in your bag, and you are one strike up before the game begins.

Wildlife

Greece has none that is dangerous, unless you are allergic to bee and wasp stings or put flies in that category. Village dogs are nature's bullies; accustomed to regular beatings, they require resolute confrontation. Should you actually be bitten, you may take comfort from the thought that there is no rabies.

Occupants of bungalows may anticipate inspection by families of newts; these should be left in peace, since they are said to discourage mosquitoes.

In areas of particularly high mosquito concentration, many open-air tavernas have installed an electrical appliance that looks like an inefficient blue light but massacres what otherwise would make you itch. At peak immolation periods, the noise can be distracting – but every 'crack' means one enemy less. It may put you in mind of a gnatcracker suite for muted kettledrums.

Gazetteer

Introduction

For the reader's convenience, the islands that follow are placed in alphabetical order according to their group: the Cyclades, the Dodecanese, the East Aegean, Euboia, the Ionian, the North Aegean, the North Sporades and the Saronic.

An exception is made only for the three resort islands – Corfu, Rhodes and Crete – which are presented first, and separately, because they are the destinations of the great majority of visitors to Greece. Any newcomer to Greece is most likely to go to one of them, saving the less familiar islands for subsequent holidays.

In the presentation of the individual islands:

- The population (1981 census figures) is given as a guideline to expectable standards of accommodation and facilities, and equally to where you may hope to find 'unspoiled' surroundings away from crowds and groups.
- Area and length of coastline are noted, not just because they are available from the unabridged yearbook of the Greek National Statistics Service, but also because of a theory (which it must be admitted is not infallible) that the greater the ratio of coastline to area, the greater the number of secluded beaches is likely to be.
- 'Best beaches' and suggested hotels and restaurants should be regarded only as indicative. There are always far more beaches than could possibly be mentioned without the mind buckling under the weight of unrememberable names. Very few Greek hotels outside the main cities are positively uncomfortable. And, as any traveller knows, the never-to-be-forgotten restaurant is the one where he happened to be in the mood to enjoy an unforgettable meal on a day when the proprietor chanced to serve one; the same perfect mesh of food and mood may never exist again at the same restaurant.

- While an attempt has been made to indicate basic island-hopping opportunities, a call should still be made at a local travel agency; new boat schedules and caique excursions are constantly being introduced, and sometimes old ones are dropped or amended.
- The term Coastguard (reflecting the American meaning of the word) has been preferred as the translation of the Greek *Limeniko Soma* (literally Harbour Corps), since this conforms more closely with the function of the white-uniformed force. Established in 1919, the Coastguard does police the harbours, but it also mans the Merchant Marine Ministry and consular port offices abroad, and is responsible for the protection of Greek waters from illegal fishing, the pursuit of drugs- and antiquities-smugglers and the prevention of sea pollution. The Coastguards carry out ship inspections in Greece, authorise departures, ensure against overloading of passenger vessels, and can provide information (as a rule, only in Greek) on all ferry timetables.
- On islands with only a modest tourist movement – a definition applying to the majority of them – opening hours of small museums and minor castles tend to be not only variable but also erratic. For this reason, only the established opening hours of important sites have been included. Information on the others should be obtainable from hotel porters or, if not, from local travel agencies.

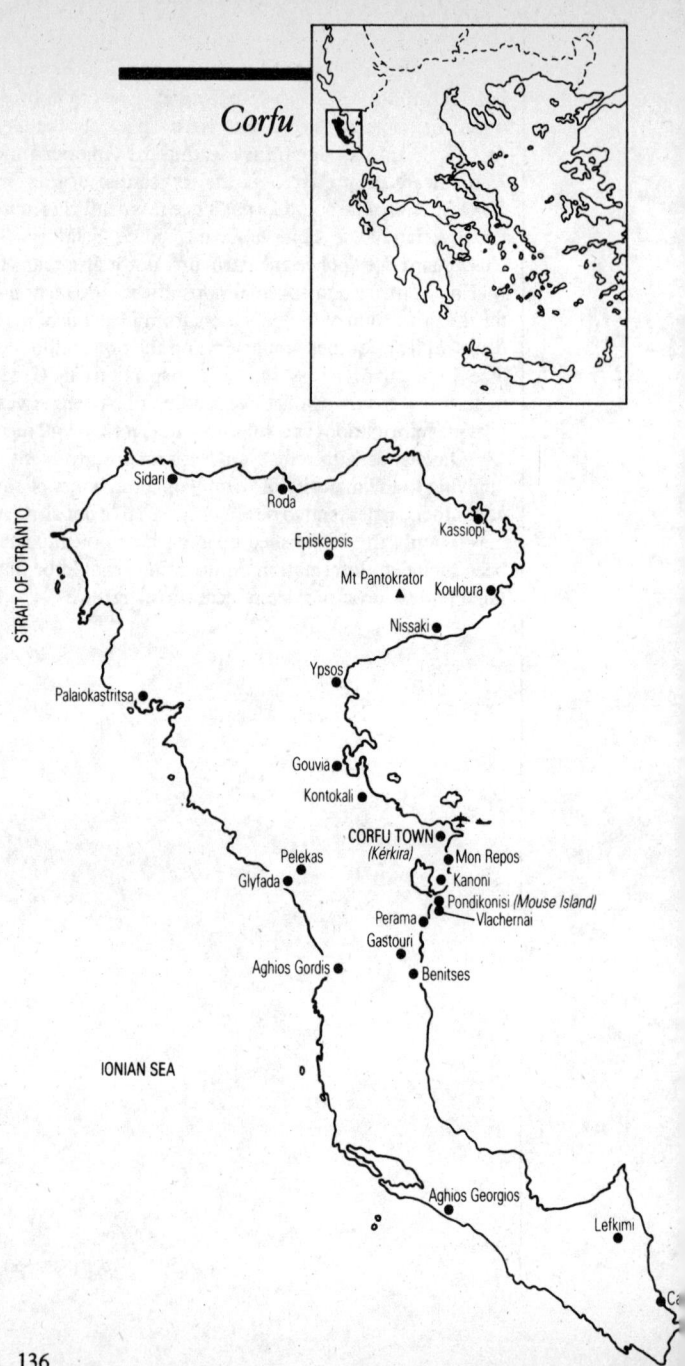

The Resort Islands: Corfu, Rhodes and Crete

Corfu

See also The Ionian Islands, pp. 296–315.

Introduction If the British Empire had been dismembered in inverse order to the beauty of its parts, Corfu would have been the last to go – not the first. However, the very grace of the gesture, the only one of its kind Lord Palmerston ever made, and one not to become standard until after the Second World War almost a century later, ensured that the legacy of British rule took the form not only of roads and public buildings, cricket, ginger-beer and statues, but also of good will towards the British.

Corfu is an island that the Greeks call Kerkyra and that once was generally known as Corcyra; the name Corfu dates from the Byzantine era and derives from the Greek for 'the city "at the peaks"' (*stis koryfes*). The two hills are the first features that strike you as you approach the city from the sea.

Area: 592 sq km. Length of coastline: 217 km.
Population: 97,102 (36,901 in Corfu town).
Area telephone code: 0061 to 0063 depending on district.

Corfu is the second largest of the Ionian islands, after Cephalonia, lying at the entrance to the Adriatic. At its closest point to the mainland, in the north-east, it is only 2½ nautical miles from the Albanian coast.

To be strictly accurate, Corfu never acquired the full glory of colonial status, but was only a British protectorate, and even that for not quite fifty years – from the end of the Napoleonic Wars in 1815 to the surrender of power in 1864. However, the distinction was a fine one for the imperialists of Victorian England and was entirely lost on the Greeks, whose cry for *enosis* (union) bore fruit a century before Britain's graceless withdrawal from Cyprus, its other outpost in 'Greater Greece'.

With apologies to the Greeks, Corfu in the summer is more of a British colony now than it ever was in the days of the Raj, as well as the greatest of all British overseas holiday resorts. As good Europeans the British will let in occasional French and Germans, but clearly they regard it as *their* island.

Since January 1988, with the expiry of the seven-year transitional period, EC freedom of movement regulations have also applied to Greece – for nationals of the other Community countries wishing to live and work in Greece and for Greeks ambitious to try their luck elsewhere in the Community. Despite pockets of nervousness in some of the trade unions, it quickly became apparent that Greece had no cause to fear an invasion of unemployed Britons seeking work in Athens. However, there have been some effects on the islands, particularly Corfu, and there are likely to be more, now that the nationality barrier to finding employment has been demolished and only the language barrier remains in place, to be surmounted by personal effort.

Within the next few years, you will probably be able to stay in a hotel on Corfu owned and staffed by Britons, eat in a British restaurant that flies in British sausages and North Sea cod, drink in a British bar and be amused at night by British entertainers. It is to be hoped that you will not want to do any of these things, but the possibilities will exist: to some extent (accommodation, cod and sausages excluded) it already does in Cavo, an outpost of the new-style Empire on the southern tip of the island.

Unfortunately but predictably, as the only place in Greece that receives plane-loads of young Britons as defenceless as babies against the temptation of cheap beer on sale at all hours, Corfu is also the only part of Greece with a nightly problem of public drunkenness, and sometimes hooliganism. The Corfiots (or you might sometimes see this written as Corfiotes) try to take this philosophically, although their feelings may sometimes be expressed in letters to newspapers and quiet complaints to their friends.

There is no doubt that Corfu is a 'fun' island for youth, even if possibly to a lesser extent than Myconos and Ios, where the skinheads more obviously outnumber the naturally bald. Listen to the cleaning women of Benitses and Cavo as they exchange experiences on the early morning buses and you might conclude that fun consists largely of fornication at night and brandy for breakfast; on the other hand, if sexual revelry were the rule it would scarcely be found worthy of remark.

The British connection

Recent history

A quarter of a century ago there was still a very old waiter at one of the Liston cafés in Corfu town who claimed to be aware, on the word of his grandfather, of the actual linden tree beneath which W. E. Gladstone, 'the people's William', the Acting Lord High Commissioner in 1858, used to sprawl at his ease across five chairs, lazing the afternoon away with his hat tipped over his eyes.

Parenthetically, the Greek five-chair trick was always a difficult one to pull off, and has now been made impossible in most places through the substitution of plastic armchairs for the older straight-backed, rush-bottomed type of seating. To try it today, you need to go to one of the more isolated villages. You sit on one chair, spread your arms over another two and hook your feet into the backs of numbers four and five. You can then tip and rock on the semi-circle of three chairs, using the two in front of you for preservation of balance. Though it seems complicated, it is considerably easier than learning to ride a bicycle. Obviously you should practise on someone else's furniture.

Whether precariously on five chairs or sedately on one, young Mr Gladstone's advice, which went unheeded, was that Corfu should not be handed over to Greece: this did not prevent the Greeks eventually naming a street after him, but it probably cost him a square.

In 1858 Corfu and the rest of the Ionian islands had been a British protectorate for forty-three years. In the meantime, the Greeks had fought and won their Independence Revolution, expelling the Turks from the Peloponnese, the southern part of mainland Greece and some of the islands. Their desire for the Ionians was growing, and becoming more vociferous.

For the British, Corfu was a useful Adriatic base for the Mediterranean fleet, covering trade routes to the Middle East. However, even those who were prepared to forgo the base drew back before the prospect of a Russian succession.

Corfu had become part of the Grand Tour for young gentlefolk, cricket had been introduced along with British weights and measures, and even Disraeli had dropped in as a young and promising politician.

In 1848, revolutionary turmoil in Europe had provided encouragement in Greece for the Ionian *enosis* movement. On the other hand, the close connections that King Othon's government in Athens maintained with tsarist Russia scarcely endeared it to Westminster, especially in the circumstances of the Crimean War. The situation changed with the 1862 uprising in Athens, which cost Othon his throne. A delighted Palmerston offered the Ionians to Greece in return for Greek acceptance of a monarch designated by Britain – Prince William of Denmark, subsequently King George I of Greece. The Greeks accepted with alacrity and the British, with Disraeli opposing in Parliament, honoured their undertaking: in 1864, the Ionians became part of Greece.

The British scarcely disgraced themselves during the protectorate. They constructed roads, bridges and lighthouses throughout the Seven Islands, built hospitals and schools, looked to the water supply and improved agriculture. On Corfu itself, they founded a university, the Ionian Academy, that for several decades was Greece's principal centre of higher education (it was destroyed in a Second World War Italian air-raid and never rebuilt), laid out the Esplanade and used it for cricket matches and band concerts, and built the two palaces – of St Michael and St George and Mon Repos. They irritated by being there, but they left no hatred behind them when they went.

Odysseus and his successors

Mythology and history

Known in antiquity as Skeria and Drepani, Corfu is identified as Homer's island of the Phaeacians, where Odysseus was shipwrecked and succoured by Nafsicaa. In 734 BC it became a colony of Corinth. Subsequently, when conflict broke out between Corinth and Athens, it allied itself with the latter. After being part of the Macedonian Empire, it passed to Roman rule in 229 BC. Octavian mustered his fleet there before the naval battle of Actium, at which Mark Antony and Cleopatra came to grief, and Nero called at Corfu on his way to compete in the Olympic Games.

Later still, Corfu was incorporated into the Byzantine Empire. As on mainland Greece and in the Aegean, the Byzantine grip was weakened during the period of the Crusades and in 1386, fearful of the Moslem encroachment, the Ionian islands requested the protection of Venice. This, and a later inflow of Byzantine scholars after the fall of Constantinople and a second wave after the Turkish capture of Crete, meant that the island group was the only part of Greece to be exposed to the full force of the Renaissance. The Turks made three unsuccessful attempts to seize Corfu, two in the sixteenth century and the last in 1716.

The Venetians held Corfu for more than four centuries, from 1386 until the Venetian Republic fell to Napoleon in 1797. The older section of Corfu town and its principal fortifications date essentially from the Venetian period. The French were dislodged before they could make much of an impression on the architecture, and the British built patchily.

Corfu was bombarded and occupied by the Italians in the Second World War and then, after the Italian surrender, was damaged more extensively by German attacks. A hillside cemetery in Corfu town contains the graves of forty-five British sailors killed when two destroyers struck Albanian mines in the Corfu Narrows in 1946.

The island as a whole has little to show from its ancient past, but rather more – in the form of churches and monasteries – from Byzantium. However, there are the remains of a sixth-century BC Temple of Asclipios in the grounds of Mon Repos, the former summer palace of the Greek royal family just outside Corfu town. The present capital is built slightly to the north of the ancient city.

Corfu is the wettest part of Greece, but fortunately for its holiday reputation, the rain falls mainly in the winter. It is also the nearest part of Greece to Italy, and therefore to the European Community. Although Italian is widely understood, English is the island's second language.

First impressions

Sooner or later, if you strike up an acquaintance with a Corfiot and he elicits from you the information that you have also been to Rhodes, you will be invited to award the apple. Which, you will be asked, is the more beautiful? The queen of the Dodecanese or the princess of the Ionians?

The safe reply is that both are equally lovely in their own ways. However, you may also be a little more adventurous, and award the prize equally between Corfu as an island and Rhodes as a city.

When you go to Rhodes, you are as likely to stay in the new town as in a beach hotel; on Corfu, you would take a room in town only in an emergency, or as a member of a visiting cricket team.

The old town of Rhodes demands exploration, preferably over a couple of days; Corfu old town can be walked through in as many hours, with everything seen that is worth seeing.

However, get out into the island of Corfu and you at once encounter green hillsides, long beaches and a succession of incomparable beauty spots. Admittedly, Corfu has no Lindos, nor anything worth seeking out from Ancient Greece. But Rhodes has no Perama or Pondikonisi, Sidari, Roda or Kassiopi, Palaiokastritsa, Aghios Georgios or even Cavo. On Corfu, you really need mobility, in the form of a rented car or moped, a willingness to take coach excursions, or sufficient resilience for the local bus services. On Rhodes, old town apart, you can book a couple of excursions and then spend the rest of your time just basking.

Corfu is composed of the Esplanade and the Liston, the old Venetian town between there and the harbour where the ferries dock and yachts tie up (and where the main bus station is located), and the new town to the south along and back from Garitsa Bay.

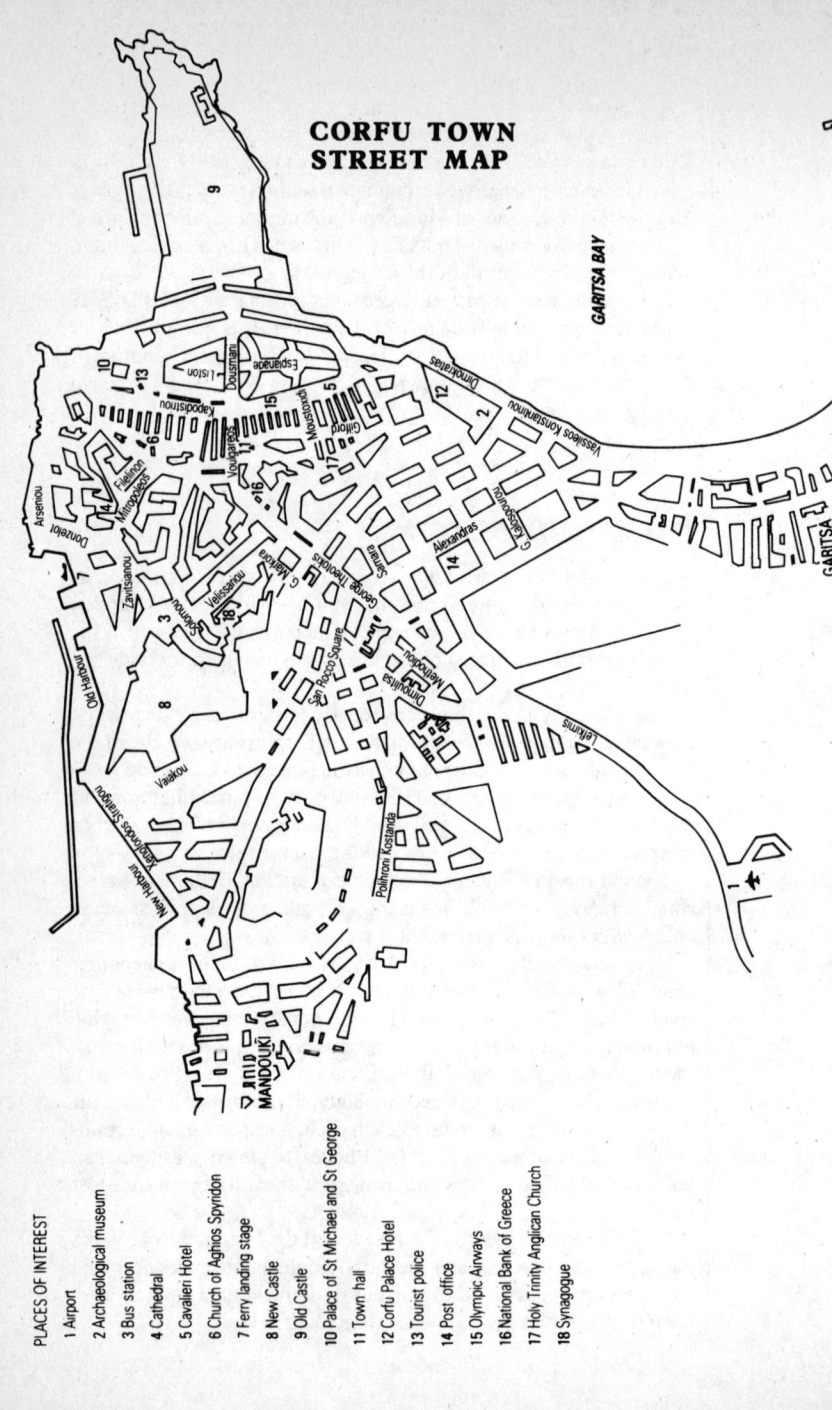

You can forget about the new town, even as a place to stay or to do some shopping: it is modern, residential, and totally without interest.

The Esplanade and Liston

Start with refreshments beneath the linden trees lining the Esplanade, known locally as the Spianada and once a Venetian parade and exercise ground, to get your bearings; Greece has no other square so French. The Liston is the row of arcaded houses forming one of its sides, laid out at the turn of the eighteenth and nineteenth centuries in imitation of the Rue de Rivoli in Paris and now housing some of the more expensive shops, the best of the cafés and a couple of adequate restaurants.

On two or three afternoons a week in summer, there will be a cricket match in progress in the centre of the square, involving local or visiting teams. According to legend, Jack Hobbs, that luminary of English cricket in the 1930s, played there once. It is all deadly serious in a befittingly casual way; there are no sight-screens, and the 'pavilion' consists of café tables beneath the trees, but there is nothing subdued about a Corfiot appeal. Reflecting the island's pace and temperament, Corfu produces deadly slow bowlers . . .

The Corfiots have never quite understood why Greek television, which devotes hours to international sports, should appear unaware of the existence of a game called cricket. Reminded that cricket is played only in Corfu, they observe that the absence anywhere in Greece of car and motorcycle racing and ice hockey does not deter television from covering those sports. However, television in Greece is a state agency dedicated to serving the government in power; responsiveness to viewer suggestions is therefore not one of its distinguishing characteristics.

When the cricket palls, you can then explore:

Old Castle

● Across the square to the Old Castle (Palaio Frurio), begun in the fourteenth century and completed in the sixteenth and used in the evenings for sound-and-light performances, and to the Regency-style

Palace

Palace of St Michael and St George, built in 1819 for the first British High Commissioner and now in part a museum, that forms the northern side of the square. Head south, past the rank of horse-drawn cabs that may be romantic but are formidably expensive, and you come to a second square with a Protectorate bandstand in the middle, where the island's brass bands take their turn in giving concerts.

'Cantounias'

● And then back from the Liston into the maze of 'cantounias': narrow, flagstoned streets lined with three- and four-storey houses that were built by the Venetians and are now divided into walk-up apartments over ground-floor shops. This part of the town may put you in mind of Venice without the water or Naples without the washing, but you will also discern French overtones and occasional suggestions of Georgian architecture. Walk far enough and you will reach either the new town along George Theotokis Street, where the buses to the closer resort areas have their terminals, or the port alongside the so-called New Castle (it dates only from the seventeenth century) and the main bus garage beneath the castle walls.

The old town is stifling on a hot day, and humid at night. The accommodation on offer in the occasional run-down hotel, or private rooms hawked by old women and children, is for those to whom proximity to 'the action' is all that matters.

Sights to see

There are several buildings in Corfu town that are worth a look, but there is only one that should definitely not be missed.

The former would include the Cathedral near the ferry landing-stage, which contains the headless body of Aghia Theodora the Augusta, the seventeenth-century town hall, the Archaeological Museum in Garitsa with finds from local excavations, the Museum of Asiatic Art in the Palace of St Michael and St George with its unusually rich collection of Chinese, Japanese and Indian exhibits, and a quaint numismatic and banknote museum near the Church of Aghios Spyridon.

Church of Aghios Spyridon

The Church of Aghios Spyridon is the building that should be sought out, in a small square two blocks back from the Liston. A sixteenth-century basilica with an Italianate interior, it contains the greatest weight of silver, in candelabra and votive offerings, possessed by any Greek church outside the island of Tinos.

It also contains the body of the island's patron saint, Aghios Spyridon, in a silver casket with glass insets that allow a view of the shrunken head and hands, and with slippered feet exposed for veneration.

As Bishop of Cyprus, Spyridon took part in the Council of Nicaea in AD 325. After his death, it is said, fragrance issued from his grave; the body was exhumed and found to be undecayed – proof positive of holiness – and was placed in a gold casket.

In the fifteenth century, to save it from Moslem desecration, the body (by this time in its silver casket) was removed first to Constantinople and later brought to Corfu. You can scarcely fail to be impressed by the devotion with which the body is venerated and the feet kissed, mainly but not only by old women dressed all in black.

Four times a year, on the saint's patronal festival and on the anniversaries of miracles attributed to Aghios Spyridon on the occasion of epidemics, famine and siege, the casket is carried through the town in a solemn litany.

Whenever you meet a Spyridon, or more commonly a Spyros, you can be fairly sure that either he or his family originated from Corfu (please do pronounce Spyros to rhyme with 'spear' and not 'spire', regardless of how one-time American Vice-President Spiro Agnew may have chosen to style himself).

Shopping

Corfu is not much of a shopping town, probably because so few of the island's visitors spend more than a couple of hours there. Best buys, though scarcely bargains, are embroidery and silverware.

Around the island

Almost certainly if you have left your accommodation to a travel agent, but very probably even if you have made the booking yourself, you will be staying along the stretch of coast extending 15 km on each side of Corfu town, as far as Ypsos to the north and Benitses to the south. The north coast, from Kassiopi to Sidari, is developing more slowly; on the west coast, your choice would really be between the Palaiokastritsa and Glyfada areas.

Some of the coach excursions claim to cover the whole island in a day, but if you have your own means of transport you will find it more relaxing, and more satisfying, to allow three days for separate tours.

Heading south: Pondikonisi and the Achilleion

Mon Repos Palace — Heading south from Corfu town you will pass, but cannot enter, the densely wooded grounds of the Mon Repos Palace, built in 1824 as the summer residence of the Lord High Commissioner and later adopted as the summer palace of the Greek royal family. The Duke of Edinburgh was born there in 1921.

Kanoni — A couple of kilometres further, where the road ends at **Kanoni**, you will come upon a view with which you may feel you have been familiar all your life, from travel articles, brochures, television and the cinema: the deep bay of Kanoni with the two monastery islands. The smaller, *Vlachernai; Pondikonisi* containing the monastery of **Vlachernai**, is linked to the mainland by a causeway; **Pondikonisi** (Mouse Island), named for its peculiar shape, is reached by a shuttle service of motorboats.

It is said that Pondikonisi inspired Arnold Boecklin's painting *Island of the Dead*, with a soul approaching the shore in a small boat, and that this in turn led Richard Strauss to the idea for his tone poem 'Death and Transfiguration'. Those who are not geniuses find the view an astonishingly cheerful one.

Pondikonisi can be reached also by the Benitses bus: press the bell as soon as you see the island, then walk across the causeway. The Corfu Hilton overlooks the bay, if you feel in need of coffee or air-conditioning; though you may then find it intriguing to watch airliners fly past slightly below you, the noise can be a distraction. Eventually a new Corfu airport is to be built at Lefkimi in the south, relieving the whole Perama resort area of what today is a definite nuisance.

Achilleion Palace — Between Perama and Benitses, among a string of excellent hotels, you will find the Achilleion Palace at Gastouri, a pseudo-Greek structure of no architectural significance whatever, but worth visiting for three other reasons: the beauty of the gardens, the view from them and the historical connections.

Built for the Empress Elizabeth of Austria (Sissy) in 1890, it was acquired by Kaiser Wilhelm II of Germany (Kaiser Bill) after her assassination in 1898, was an Allied naval hospital in the First World War, and now houses the Corfu casino.

There are several representations of Achilles. A mural over the main stairway depicts him riding round the walls of Troy trailing the body of Hector, and in the gardens there are two statues: a heroic bronze of the warrior accoutred for battle and a marble 'Achilles wounded'. On the plinth of the former the Kaiser ordered the addition of an inscription: 'To the greatest of the Greeks, from the greatest of Germans.' In one of the staterooms you can see the saddle, mounted on a stool, on which the warlord would sit to transact official business or give audiences; on the shore just outside the grounds are the crumbling ruins of an ornate pier, the Kaiser's Bridge, where the imperial yacht would tie up. The Kaiser's Bridge Restaurant beside it may look attractive, but is both overrated and overpriced; in 1987 it had one waiter whose attitude towards intending customers was apparently inspired by the Kaiser's towards the Chinese.

Benitses **Benitses** you may well find repulsive and sad; it is certainly the most grotesque example of over-development to be found anywhere in Greece in so concentrated a form. A ribbon of land between mountain and sea, with indifferent rock-and-pebble beaches, it is where thousands of youthful tourists attracted by the rock-and-pebble prices are accommodated on the sardine principle. Everything at Benitses has to be queued for, even space by the water to spread a towel, and at night the disco-shriek can be heard from many kilometres away. Pass through it quickly, but drive slowly: the other Benitses distinction is possession of Greece's single most dangerous stretch of road.

The opening to the south – and Cavo

Once Benitses is behind you – and because of the mountain there is no way around it – the road widens and the countryside becomes more open. You pass through wooded hills and valleys wispy with mist in the early morning, offering distant views of the Ionian Sea and Epirus mountains to the east and the Adriatic to the west. At this point, the Corfiot boast of 4 million olive trees on the island becomes credible.

Dirt roads branch off to a succession of long, sandy Adriatic beaches, served by tavernas and rooming-houses, although not, so far, by large hotels. **Aghios Georgios**, reached through 4 km of olive groves noisy with crickets, may be the best of them, and it is also typical; you will not find solitude, but you will find space. You will also discover how much colder the Adriatic is than the Ionian Sea. The beaches in this part of Corfu are exposed and therefore are not pleasant in westerly gales – the probable reason why hoteliers have fought shy of them.

Aghios Georgios

Pass through **Lefkimi**, a town with nothing to detain you except possibly the sight of Corfu's only semi-navigable river, and you reach **Cavo**, a most peculiar place.

Lefkimi

Cavo

Twenty-five years ago, Cavo was a long beach where Fotis Roussos built a taverna with six guest-rooms forming the upper storey. You carried your own water from the well to the washbasin in your room. Since there was no electricity, you dined by the light of acetylene lamps, went to bed early and rose at dawn. If Fotis caught fish, you ate that: if not, you had to slum it on lobster from one of his pots, grilled over charcoal and served with a sauce of olive oil and lemon. Corfu town was half a day away, seemingly on a different continent.

Today, if you want a touch of 'noble savage' isolation, you have to go to a very small island. Cavo has become a ribbon development of small hotels, self-catering apartments, restaurants and, at the latest count, more than sixty bars and discos including the 'Lady Di'. You can find 'full English breakfasts' all morning – bacon, eggs and beans in shade temperatures of 32°C/90°F – and 'fish and chips' from noon onwards.

Fotis Roussos has one of the larger hotels now, and a restaurant that can seat hundreds and still offers lobster, but he no longer bothers with the kind of fish that jumps into the pan. His explanation: the British won't eat fish with a head on it, but want slices fried in batter, so obviously it has to be frozen.

Your Greek acquaintances, who are more likely to know Cavo by reputation than first-hand, will try to warn you off. However, they overlook one consideration, which makes the place entirely different from Benitses: the beach is separated from the town by a stretch of land 200 to 300 m wide on which self-catering complexes have been built, and therefore neither the beach nor the apartments are noisy. The beach itself is so long that it is uncomfortably crowded only at weekends, when the villagers do their swimming. Also, the flow of water through the Epirus channel ensures that the sea has stayed clean, which is not an assumption you make easily at Benitses. The water is shallow and therefore spacious – 100 m out you can still touch the bottom – and the sand makes it almost tepid. The real peculiarity of Cavo, however, is the apparently inexhaustible ability of the 'town' (winter population 497) to absorb thousands of tourists and still remain, to a remarkable extent, a hideaway.

You should not arrive in Cavo without a reservation, unless you are prepared to sleep on the beach. Almost all the rooms are contracted to London tour offices, and are unbookable from Athens.

Heading north: a distant prospect of Albania

Northern Corfu

The beaches immediately north of Corfu town, along the wide bay extending to **Nissaki** 22 km away and **Kouloura** 30 km from the town, are places to stay rather than to visit. This is the area of big hotels with private access to the sea, equipped with swimming pools and offering a choice of restaurants and often a nightclub: excellent in their way, comfortable and unremarkable.

The road then winds through the foothills of Mount Pantokrator, at 906 m the tallest peak on Corfu, to the north-coast resorts of Kassiopi, Roda and Sidari.

Because Albania is only a few kilometres from Kassiopi across the narrows, the whole of northern Corfu used to be a restricted zone; to go beyond a control post at Episkepsis, on the slopes of Mount Pantokrator, required authorisation from the Corfu police. This was because of the state of war between Greece and Albania that formally existed until 1987, dating from the Italian invasion of Greece through Albania in 1940, and linked with the treatment of the Greek minority in a part of southern Albania still known to the Greeks as Northern Epirus – an appellation conveying a suggestion of pending if unpursued territorial claims. Though a war that had never been declared has now been declared over, and long before then the north of Corfu had been opened to visitors, the years of restricted entry meant that the three northern townships were late entrants to the scramble for tourists. This part of the island is still less intensively developed than the rest, for all that its beaches are among the finest.

Kassiopi; Sidari

Kassiopi, 36 km from Corfu town, also offers a sixteenth-century church and ruins of a castle, while **Sidari**, 37 km from Corfu, but reached by a different road, has the so-called **Canal d'Amour** – rocky channels through which you can swim from one tiny beach to another. The 'Canal' is one of the island's three most-photographed beauty spots (the others are Pondikonisi and Palaiokastritsa).

Palaiokastritsa

The north-western tip of Corfu appeals more to the hiker than the swimmer, at least until **Palaiokastritsa** is reached; you can get there along secondary roads as a continuation of a tour in the north, but the easiest way is by a direct road from Corfu town across the centre of the island.

Palaiokastritsa, 26 km from Corfu, will be a delight or a disappointment depending on what you have been led to expect. Come across it unprepared, and you will be struck by its loveliness; go there after a fresh reading of Henry Miller's *The Colossus of Maroussi* and you will probably experience a let-down.

Palaiokastritsa is a magnificent miniature that simply cannot absorb the hordes of day-trippers who converge on it in the summer. The best way to appreciate it is to spend a night there; then, when the coaches arrive in procession, you can slip away to look at the thirteenth-century castle and mainly eighteenth-century monastery, returning to your hotel for a lobster dinner when peace has been restored. However, despite the extent to which the controlled depreciation of the drachma protects you against Greece's perpetual double-digit inflation rate, even you may find Palaiokastritsa expensive.

Further south

Further south are the quieter and more typical west coast resorts of **Glyfada** and **Aghios Gordis**; on your way back to your base you might consider a diversion to the hill of **Pelekas**, where Corfiots take their guests to watch the sun dip into the Adriatic.

Where to stay

Corfu has almost 250 listed hotels with more than 13,000 rooms, in addition to hundreds of self-catering complexes and several thousand beds on offer in private houses. Nevertheless, it can be difficult to find a hotel room between June and August, and the self-catering facilities are booked even more solidly. If you arrive without a reservation and the tourist police cannot help you, your best bet is to go to Corfu harbour: the ferries from Igoumenitsa are met by old women and children with offers of rooms in the town that are unlikely to be particularly comfortable, but are better than nothing.

Of the listed hotels, Corfu town has only twenty-four, with 865 rooms; since the groups as a rule go to the beaches, these hotels may have peak-season vacancies. Easily the best are the deluxe **Corfu Palace** (106 rooms, tel. 39 485) and first-class **Cavalieri** (forty-eight rooms, tel. 39 336), both in Garitsa.

The nature and recent development of Corfu's holiday movement can be gauged from the number of hotels – 156 – catering to the upper segment of the market: five deluxe, thirty first class, thirty-eight second class and eighty-three third class. Their dependence on groups makes reservations even more advisable.

Purely indicatively, at Perama you could try the **Aeolos Beach** (second class, 324 rooms in the main hotel and bungalows, tel. 33 132), at Benitses the **Belvedere** (second class, 180 rooms, tel. 92 411), at Moraïtika the **Messonghi Beach** (second class, 828 rooms, tel. 38 684) and at Kontokali, if prepared to splurge, the **Kontokali Palace** (deluxe, 238 rooms, tel. 38 736). The **Corfu Hilton** at Kanoni (deluxe, 274 rooms, tel. 36 540) appeals to those who enjoy Hilton hotels, while if you must stay at Palaiokastritsa the veteran **Xenia** (second class, tel. 41 208) is still the best-sited though offering only eight rooms. (At this point, a confession of bias might be appropriate:

my wife and I honeymooned at the **Xenia** too long ago, when Palaiokastritsa was still an undiscovered village with no other hotel, and now routinely use the **Aeolos Beach**.)

Where to eat

Corfu is not a place for gourmet eating. Since the hotels as a rule insist on half-board arrangements, you can be sure that the lunch or dinner you eat there will be standard European; your other meal will probably be a lunch-time snack on the beach or by the pool (typically pizza) or dinner in the nearest restaurant or taverna.

A really memorable meal is a matter of chance. To stack the cards in your favour, seek out a shack-like taverna on a remote beach at the end of a dirt road; the fish should then be fresh, you may be lucky enough to find lobster, the wine will be local Corfiot served in the carafe, the bill will be reasonable and, if your luck is running in full flow, a strolling guitarist will provide music that will inspire the fishermen clientele to a singalong. If your luck is entirely out, you may have to settle for chicken.

In Corfu town, you can eat safely at the **Aigli** in the Liston, the nearby **Akteon**, or the **Rex** a couple of blocks back in Kapodistriou Street. While these rely on tourists, they also have a local clientele. *Sofrito*, the Corfu speciality (meat stewed in garlic sauce and served with mashed potatoes) is the usual *plat du jour*. Corfu's other contribution to Greek cuisine, *pastitsada* (a tomato stew with pasta) is less frequently encountered, and few restaurants any longer take the trouble to prepare its fancier and far tastier relative, *pastitsio*.

You can have a slap-up meal at the **Corfu Palace Hotel**, or eat more simply at the **Naftikon** near the port and the **Bekios** and **Orestes** in Mandouki. Outside the town, the **Three Stars** by the airport is well regarded, and you can combine dinner with shopping and, during the season, folk dancing at the touristy **Danilo Village** near Moraitika. The casino in the **Achilleion Palace** has a superb dining room if you wish to eat in nineteenth-century splendour and have a matching chequebook, while the **Bella Vista**, 50 metres from the palace gates, serves lunch as well as dinner on a terrace with unsurpassed views towards Corfu town, and presents a more reasonable bill at the end. The **Tripa** at Kinopiastes village is unusual in that it offers a set menu consisting of an apparently endless series of *mezedes* and also attracts Corfiots; if you propose to dine there it would be better to avoid lunch. Though you might consider that an apter name for **Chez George** at Palaiokastritsa would be Cher George, it is easily the best place to eat in that environmentally degraded former beauty spot. Throughout the island there are hundreds of eating places to choose among, and it is as much a matter of luck as judgement.

Local wine and other drinks

Corfu produces some excellent wine, especially red, but also a sea of plonk. Unless you are prepared to pay for Theotokis, treat bottled Corfiot wine with a degree of caution. Much of the really good wine is produced in insufficient quantity to justify bottling, and you might be fortunate enough to stumble on some; if not, at least a carafe is cheaper than a bottle.

You might also venture a glass of *kum kwat*, a kind of brandy made from tiny oranges that is produced nowhere else. If you find it halfway palatable, a barrel-shaped bottle of it makes a cheap souvenir.

The only thing worse than Corfu coffee is Corfu tea.

Getting there

Almost every foreign visitor to Corfu arrives by air, either on a charter flight or by Olympic Airways from Athens (up to seven flights a day in summer).

If you are driving to Corfu from Athens following the bus route from the capital, you will take the road along the north coast of the Peloponnese to Patras, cross to the mainland on the Rio-Andirrio ferry and then drive along the west coast to Igoumenitsa, from where ferries depart almost hourly for the two-hour crossing to Corfu. In total the journey will take you eleven hours by bus and rather longer by car. The occasional boats from Patras cater mainly to haversack tourists.

It is possible to reach Corfu direct from Italy, on some of the Brindisi-Patras ferries, or from Dubrovnik in Yugoslavia.

Transport

Buses run half-hourly to the resorts nearest to Corfu town, and from six to ten times a day to those in the northern and southern parts of the island. Those to the nearer resorts leave from San Rocco Square in George Theotokis Street, in the new town; for the others, go to the garage near the ferry docks. Buses to Kanoni have their terminus at the Esplanade.

Corfu has 1,800 km of roads, mostly narrow and requiring care because of poor maintenance and the amount of traffic. Cars and mopeds can be rented in Corfu town or through most of the hotels.

Radio-taxis can be ordered through your hotel, and cost about twice as much as in Athens and not much less than in London. Your best chance of a taxi in Corfu town is at the rank across from the ferry dock.

From Corfu

Take the ferry to Igoumenitsa and from there the whole of Greece is open to you. Boat excursions are organised to Paxi and Antipaxi islands, and less regularly to Parga on the Epirus coast. There are also boats to Cephalonia.

Telephone

Police 30 265
Tourist police 30 669
Coastguard 32 655
NTOG 30 360
Olympic Airways 38 694
Hospital 37 105/30 562

Rhodes

Introduction

See also The Dodecanese Islands, pp. 234–65.

Rhodes is an island of sunshine and flowers, with a magnificent medieval town and one of the finest archaeological sites on any Greek island. It is also desperately overcrowded in July and August, and pitifully dependent on staying that way: other parts of Greece would somehow survive a bad tourist season, but the Rhodian economy would almost certainly go phut.

The capital of the Dodecanese and fourth largest Greek island after Crete, Euboia and Lesbos, Rhodes lies 260 nautical miles from Piraeus and only 10 nautical miles off the Asia Minor coast. It can be reached by sea from Piraeus, air from Athens and charter flights from most European countries, and is a port of call on almost every Aegean and east Mediterranean cruise.

Though excessively dependent on groups of tourists, Rhodes remains attractive to the independent traveller because of its easy accessibility and incomparable medieval town. If you do not intend to devote your holiday there to playing Russian roulette with ultraviolet rays on hotel beaches, you will need three days for sightseeing and could spend another two island-hopping on excursion boats. Cruise passengers manage to crowd all Rhodes into less than a day, with a few hours in the old town for shopping and a trip to Lindos, but then have no time to study the fish in Greece's only aquarium . . .

Area: 1,398 sq km. Length of coastline: 220 km.
Population: 87,833 (41,425 in the city of Rhodes).
Area telephone code: 0241.

A rose by many other names

The name of the island is today generally assumed to have some connection with the Greek for rose, *rodos* (though if you want to order a dozen of them from a florist you will ask for *triandafylla*), and it is sometimes styled 'island of roses'. In the ancient past it bore other names: Anemousa, after the Greek for breeze because of the soft winds from the north that cool it in summer and then, in winter, give their place to equally soft warming breezes from the south; Ophidia or Fidoussa, after the Greek for snakes, which the ancients eradicated by importing a herd of stags with the result that the deer is still the island's symbol; Telchinis, after the mermaid-like creatures charged with raising the baby sea-god Poseidon; Asteria or Aetheraea, for the purity of its atmosphere and cloudless skies; Makaria, from the prosperity and joy that were supposedly the inhabitants' birthright; and

Rhodes

TRIANDA BAY
RHODES
Trianda
Kremastis
Ixia
Pasida
Philerimos
Kallithea
Kameiros
Petaloudes
Faliraki
Afandou
Embonas
Monolithos
Profilia
KARPATHOS STRAITS
Vlicha
LINDOS
Vatio
Genadio
Katavia

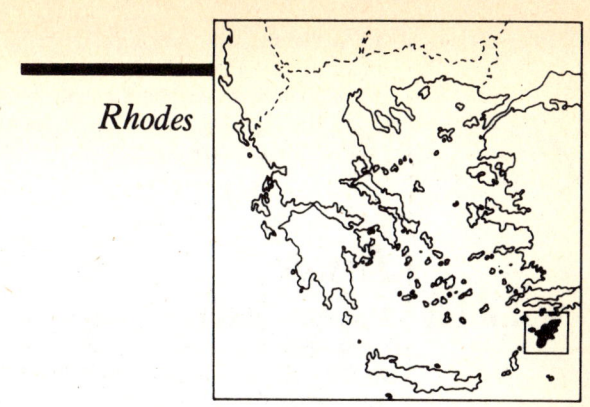

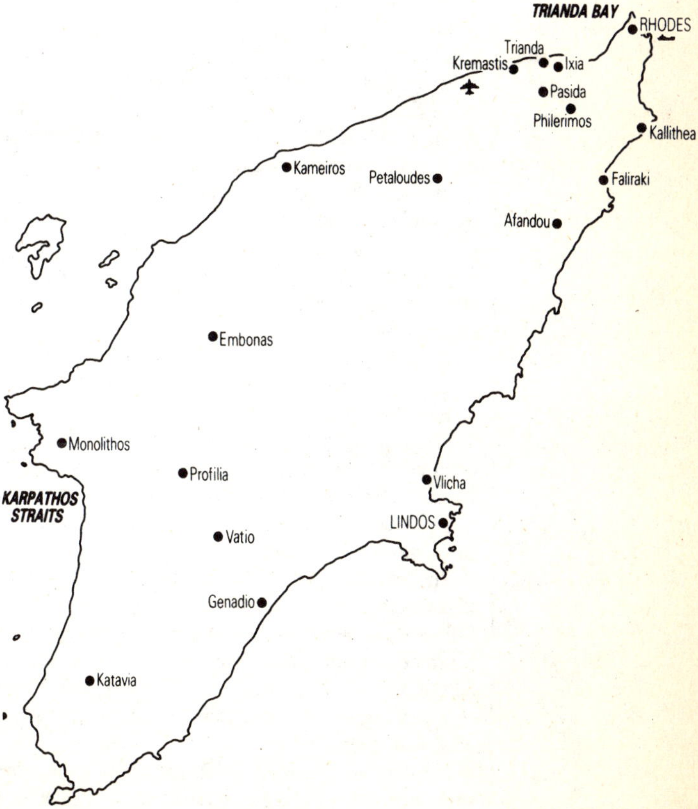

also Stadia (stadium), from its somewhat oblong shape, and Atavyris, after its tallest peak.

The Rhodian local authorities and hoteliers' association are trying to popularise the name Rodos internationally rather than Rhodes, but so far with little success.

History

Mythology

Mythology reports that the island was especially created by Zeus for the sun-god, Helios, who lived on it with his betrothed, Rodos, the daughter of Venus. He not only named it after her, but also gifted it with perpetual sunshine. Helios is not yet dead: he has become *iliaki energeia*, solar energy.

Recorded times

There is archaeological evidence that Rhodes has been inhabited since neolithic times, well before the Minoan and Mycenaean periods. When the Dorians arrived on Rhodes around 1200 BC they found three flourishing Mycenaean cities: Lindos, Ialysos and Kameiros. Along with Kos and two Greek cities on the Asia Minor coast opposite the island, these banded together to form one of the earliest known 'commonwealths', the Hexapolis (Six Cities) and, in 408 BC, decided to establish a new town as a common capital. To lay it out, they called in Hippodamos, a town-planner who had been born in Miletus in Asia Minor and worked in Piraeus. Although today everything else has changed, the streets of the old town still broadly follow the original Hippodamos plan.

The city was designed for 100,000 inhabitants, with zoning for public buildings, monuments, athletics facilities, libraries and theatres, as well as a drainage system and five harbours.

From the fifth to the third centuries BC Rhodes became a major commercial and cultural centre, founding colonies, minting its own coinage, introducing the first known system of maritime law, and setting up schools of philosophy and sculpture that were famous throughout the Ancient World.

The Colossus

Rhodes allied itself with the Macedonians during the time of Philip II and Alexander the Great. After the death of Alexander it successfully resisted a siege by one Dimitrios Poliorcetes in 305 BC and, to commemorate the victory, set up the Colossus. Described variously as between 30 and 40 m high, this is believed to have been a bronze statue representing the sun god, and to have served both as lighthouse and observation post.

Modern historians question the traditional representations of it standing with legs apart, straddling one of the harbours, since it would then have collapsed into the sea when toppled in an earthquake in 227 BC, while all accounts speak of its ruins as lying on the land. It is thought more likely to have been erected either on the northern promontory now occupied by the aquarium or on high ground at the edge of the old town.

The statue, one of the seven wonders of the Ancient World, was constructed by Chares of Lindos from the siege material left behind by Poliorcetes. It stood for a little more than fifty years, from its completion around 280 BC until the earthquake. Though the town was rebuilt, the statue was not restored – possibly because of an unfavourable prediction by the Delphic Oracle. Debris of the statue is said to have been left where it fell until AD 653, when it was sold as scrap to Syrian merchants and carried away on 900 camels.

The statue briefly became headline news in the summer of 1987, when a huge 'fist-like' stone was observed on the bed of Rhodes harbour. Supervised by the Coastguard and the Merchant Marine Minister in person, and a large contingent of journalists, the stone was raised and placed gently on the quay. Archaeologists invited to confirm its antiquity quickly identified it as a lump of twentieth-century cement left over from some forgotten harbour works. In the general hilarity a question left unanswered was whether the Merchant Marine Ministry, and for a time even the Culture Ministry, had forgotten or had never known that the Colossus was a bronze.

The Roman era

Even without its great statue, Rhodes flourished again. At the height of its maritime supremacy, it exercised sovereignty over the neighbouring islands and part of Asia Minor, and its fleet was the largest in the Mediterranean (it was said of the island, 'ten Rhodians, ten ships'). Among the colonies it established was one in Italy that was subsequently renamed Naples, and another in France that was then Rhodanoussia and is now Arles. Three thousand statues are said to have graced the temples, squares and boulevards of Rhodes, and its schools of philosophy, rhetoric and law were renowned; eminent Romans who studied there included Cicero, Julius Caesar, Tiberius, Seneca, Pompey and Cato, as well as a general named Cassius.

Sent back at the head of an army to reduce Rhodes from the status of ally to that of province, Cassius may well have exceeded his orders. Certainly, Rhodes never fully recovered from the sack and massacre that followed his invasion. Implored to leave something behind him, he is said to have retorted: 'I leave the sun!' Before burning the city, he arranged the removal of many of the statues to Rome: some still survive there, and also in Naples and Florence.

Byzantine flavour

When the Roman Empire split, Rhodes linked its fate with the Byzantines and flourished once again as a province of Constantinople. Numerous churches and monasteries, dating from the fifth to the fourteenth centuries, give the city and the island a continuing Byzantine flavour.

Rhodes was occupied in turn by Goths, Saracens, Persians, Venetians and Franks, but the predominantly medieval character of the old

The Knights of St John

town is a legacy of the two-century rule of the Knights of St John of Jerusalem, an order stemming from a Benedictine hospital for pilgrims established in Jerusalem in the eleventh century (see p. 26).

When Palestine fell, in 1291, the Order moved first to Cyprus and then to Rhodes. The massive sandstone walls, 8 km long, surrounding the old town, the Palace of the Grand Master, the inns of the eight 'tongues' (the languages spoken by the Knights), the Street of the Knights and the hospital that now serves as a museum are the more spectacular relics of their two centuries on the island.

The Turkish period

After the fall of Constantinople in 1453, the Turks advanced slowly westward. In 1522, after a six-month siege, Rhodes was taken by Sultan Suleiman the Magnificent and the Knights withdrew to Malta.

Like Cassius some 1,600 years earlier, Suleiman the so-called 'Magnificent' slaughtered the inhabitants. The gate of St John became known as 'Red Gate' from the rivers of blood that flowed down the street, while the Church of St Mary, on its conversion into a mosque, was named Kantouran Tzami (Red Mosque) for the same reason.

Oriental Rhodes lasted until 1912, when the Dodecanese came into the possession of Italy. Except for the many fountains in the old town – there was a belief that whoever built a fountain went to paradise – and a few mosques, the Turks changed little and added less. The more important of the mosques they built, as distinct from those they created out of existing Byzantine churches, were the mosques of Suleiman, Ibrahim Pasha and Reghib Pasha. A rather later mosque, dating from the second half of the Turkish period, is the mosque of Sultan Mustapha, who built both it and a *hammam* (baths, with separate facilities for men and women) after a visit to Rhodes. Also dating from the end of the eighteenth century is the Achmet Avouz public library, where a collection of rare manuscripts and books includes some donated by palace libraries in Constantinople.

The old town had begun to spread outside its walls during the Turkish period. The Italians, after 1912, continued this development, with construction of the monumental public buildings that now form the heart of the new town. The restoration work in old Rhodes, including that on the Palace of the Grand Master, also dates mainly from the Italian occupation, as do the extensive public gardens.

The return to Greece

In May 1945 Rhodes and the other Dodecanese islands were occupied by Allied troops under British command, and subsequently handed over to the Greek military authorities. On 7 March, 1948, they were formally incorporated into Greece.

Rhodes town

What to see

Except for the exhibits in the museum, the city of Rhodes has little to show for its origins. However, on Monte Smith hill just outside the city are the ruins of a temple dedicated to Athena and Zeus, near an ancient stadium, restored by the Italians, and a small ancient theatre.

The hill is named for a British Admiral, Sir Sidney Smith, who established an observation post there in 1802, at the time of Napoleon's Egyptian expedition.

Rather more survives of the Byzantine era, for all that most of the churches had their icons and frescoes destroyed after the Turkish conquest.

But it is the buildings and fortifications left by the Knights that today make the Old Town of Rhodes one of the world's best preserved medieval cities. When the Italians rebuilt the Knights' Cathedral of St John, which had been completely destroyed by an explosion, they did so not on its original site inside the walls, but next to the Governor's Palace in the new town. This Crusader replica is now the island's Evangelismos Cathedral.

Bearings

The new town, with all of the city's hotels and most of its restaurants, can be explored in a couple of hours: the yacht harbour of Mandraki guarded by its two bronze deer, the Cathedral and Italianate public buildings, a picturesque enclosed food market, an overgrown Moslem cemetery and the aquarium. To gamble at night, you would go to the casino housed in the Grand Hotel. For refreshments beneath some magnificent trees, you would go to the **Aigli café** on the quay near the Cathedral, from where the small boats leave on their one-day excursions. If you wished to be glad your holiday was over, you would swim from the public beach.

Whether you cover the old town like a cruise passenger, in a few hours, or explore it more thoroughly over several visits, will depend on time and inclination. But if you, too, believe that the only way to get to know a place is to get lost in it, you will find the old town a happy hunting-ground, once you turn your back on the three or four main streets. Whatever your method, you should be sure not to miss:

● The restored Palace of the Grand Master of the Knights. Of its 200 rooms, twenty-three are open to the public, the most impressive being the throne and ceremonial rooms. (Closed Tuesdays).

● The incomparable Street of the Knights, leading downhill from the Palace, with the inns of the eight 'tongues' that once housed the Knights according to the language they spoke: French, German, English, Spanish, Italian and the dialects of Provence, Auvergne and Castille.

● The former hospital of the Knights at the bottom of the street, now the island's main museum. Most admired of the exhibits is the kneeling Aphrodite, or 'Aphrodite drying her hair', a masterpiece of Rhodian white marble only 60 cm high. (Closed Tuesdays).

● The Byzantine Cathedral of the Virgin of the Fortress almost opposite the museum; the plane tree in front of it was used by the

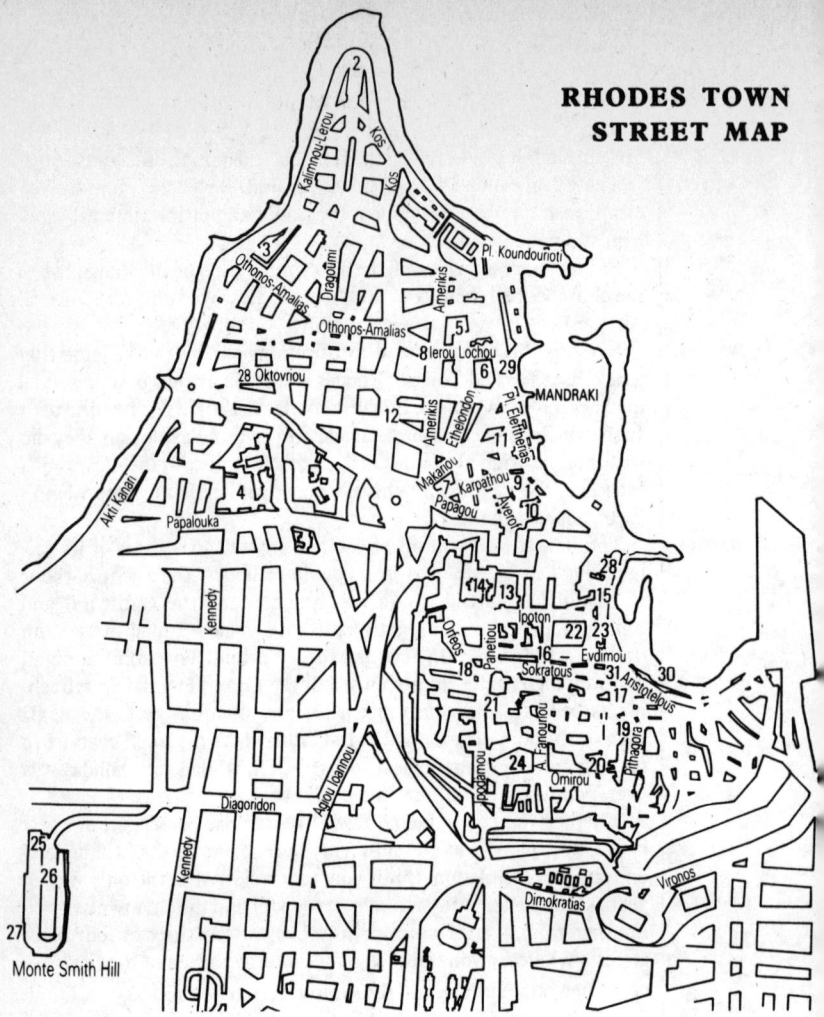

RHODES TOWN STREET MAP

PLACES OF INTEREST

NEW TOWN
1. New market
2. Aquarium
3. Grand Hotel
4. Hospital
5. Town hall
6. Post office
7. Police station (tourist office)
8. Olympic Airways
9. Bus terminal
10. Bus terminal
11. Bank of Greece
12. National Bank of Greece

OLD TOWN
13. Municipal Gardens
14. Palace of the Grand Master of the Knights
15. Inns of the Knights
16. Hospital
17. Achmet Avouz public library
18. Mosque of Suleiman
19. Ibrahim Pasha mosque
20. Reghib Pasha mosque
21. Sultan Mustapha mosque
22. Archaeological museum
23. Byzantine museum
24. Turkish baths
25. Ancient theatre
26. Ancient stadium
27. Temple of Apollo
28. Temple of Zeus
29. Evangelismos Cathedral
30. Marine Gate
31. Library

THE RESORT ISLANDS: CORFU, RHODES AND CRETE

Turks as a convenient gallows.
- Socrates Street at right-angles to the Street of the Knights, which has most of the shops and the best of the restaurants. (For shopping, see p. 161–2.)
- The Mosque of Suleiman at the top of Socrates Street, built in 1523 and reconstructed in 1808, and, close to it, the library of Achmet Avouz (open most mornings). A narrow alley from the library leads to the Turkish baths and the Mustapha Mosque.

About 7,000 people live in the old town – roughly half its population during the rule of the Knights. The town has nine gates, of which the two most frequently used are the Harbour Gate, close to where the Piraeus ferries and cruise liners dock, and the St Peter's Gate near Mandraki harbour.

For the full impact of the old town, and a downhill walk, use St Peter's Gate. Then you can admire the moat and double fortifications on the way in, pause to watch the artists at work beneath the tall plane trees (they will do a crayon portrait of you while you wait), begin with the Palace and Street of the Knights and the museum, and be suitably exhausted by the time you reach the shops of Socrates Street and ready to yield to the temptation of the cafés beside the Turkish fountains.

You may then feel you know the old town, though really you have only scratched its surface.

Around the island

Rhodes is unusually well provided with means for exploring its beauty spots: all the main car rental agencies have branches, mopeds and bicycles can be hired, and some fifty travel agencies organise coach and boat excursions.

Lindos   **Lindos** is the essential tour for a newcomer to Rhodes, and the one most likely to be taken again on a second visit. Set on a promontory on the east coast 56 km from the capital, its showpiece is an acropolis even more spectacularly situated than that of Athens itself.

Today a village of 800 inhabitants, Lindos 2,000 years ago was a city with an already glorious past. It was one of the island's three ancient cities that combined to found the fourth, Rhodes. Its acropolis stands on a flat-topped cliff that drops sheer to the sea 114 m below, and overlooks the village and tiny harbour where St Paul landed in AD 58 on his way to Rome, pausing just long enough to convert the Rhodians to Christianity.

Lindos is the kind of place that turns Christians into Rhodians. The houses, some dating from the fifteenth century, offer a mixture of Byzantine, Arabic and Aegean architecture: some of them have stone stairways leading to the upper level, from where their captain-owners could keep watch on their ships in the harbour below.

The walls of Lindos are largely Byzantine, perfected by the Knights, while the Temple of Athena dates mainly from the Hellenistic period. Alexander the Great worshipped there, and also endowed the shrine with rich offerings. (The archaeological site is closed on Tuesdays.)

The average guided tour to Lindos takes half a day. Some of the longer ones leave time for lunch, and a few include an afternoon swim from the beach where St Paul landed.

If you decide to eat in Lindos, bear in mind that the restaurants cater mainly to tourists . . .

A tour combining past and present takes in the sites of Philerimos, Kameiros and Petaloudes. Philerimos, then known as Ialyssos, and Kameiros were the other two city states of Ancient Rhodes, while Petaloudes is where the butterflies live.

Philerimos

On a hill only 15 km from the capital, **Philerimos** offers commanding views of the surrounding countryside, a part of Rhodes itself and the Asia Minor coast. There is an old Rhodian saying that anyone who has climbed the hill in the first light of dawn and lingered to enjoy the sunset has spent a day not far from paradise.

As well as a place of worship, Philerimos was always a fortified hilltop. The Dorians besieged the Phoenicians there, the Knights of St John besieged the Byzantines, the Turks besieged the Knights and, in 1943, the Germans besieged the Italians.

Principal attractions today are the remains of a temple of the Hellenistic period similar to that at Lindos but larger, the Byzantine church of Aghios Georgios, the fourteenth-century church of the Panaghia (Virgin) built by the Knights and restored by the Italians after long use as a stable, and a monastery with frescoes depicting the Knights at prayer.

Kameiros

Kameiros, the largest of the three original cities, was a lost site for centuries until its discovery just over a hundred years ago. Abandoned possibly as early as the fourth century BC, its whereabouts, only 36 km from the city of Rhodes, were unknown even to the Byzantines. What can be seen today – the ruins of houses, temples and public buildings, clearly defined streets and the remains of a sixth-century BC water supply system – is owed mostly to excavations carried out in the 1930s at a site where the first digs began in 1859.

Some of the finest statues, ceramics and jewellery on display in the Rhodes museum came from the Kameiros excavations.

Petaloudes

By contrast, **Petaloudes**, the Valley of the Butterflies, owes nothing to the ancients. A stream flows through a secluded tree-shaded valley set with rustic benches, 25 km from Rhodes. It appears to be no more than a pleasant spot for a picnic lunch. But clap your hands and at once, like waiters in training, reddish-brown butterflies that were unseen while resting on the trees rise into the air in clouds.

Naturalists believe the butterflies are attracted to the valley by the presence of a type of tree yielding an aromatic sap once used for perfuming cigar tobacco. They are said to have made their first appearance during the Italian occupation, though there is no record of their deliberate introduction. They are there from the end of May or early June until about the middle of September.

It is permitted to startle them, so as to initiate a performance, but not to torment them: a sign where the path enters the valley requests visitors to refrain from whistling!

Kallithea and Faliraki

Closer to Rhodes on the east coast are the neo-Moorish spa resort of **Kallithea** and the beachside resort of **Faliraki**, where forty-six of the island's hotels including eleven of first class have been constructed. The other main resort area is along the great sweep of **Trianda Bay**, to the west of the capital.

Trianda Bay

The half of the island south of Lindos can be toured along good roads, but is still relatively lacking in facilities. It will be many years before the southern woodlands fully recover from a disastrous fire that burned for almost a week in the summer of 1987.

Other organised tours include a 'Rhodes by Night', with dinner and folk dancing.

Beaches

Unless you are staying in the new town, your hotel will be on or near a beach and, in addition, will probably have a swimming pool. Excursions are usually timed to allow for a morning and evening dip. Like Crete and Corfu, Rhodes is not a place for secluded swimming, nor for nudists.

Shopping

Of all Greek islands, Rhodes is the place for shopping: the two centres are in the old town, based on Socrates Street, and the part of the new town between the quay and the parallel Amerikis Street. Though it would be inappropriate to speak of bargains, opportunities will come your way in the form of:

● *Fur* – the little pieces of mink, leftovers of New York workshops, that are exported to Greece for assembly into apparent whole pelts by master craftsmen and then turned into coats, jackets, stoles, gloves, hats and handbags. While the assembly is done mainly in the lakeside city of Kastoria in northern Greece, Rhodes does produce some of the garments on sale in more than sixty fur shops.

● *Jewellery* – goldsmiths and silversmiths have been working on Rhodes probably for 4,000 years and pieces crafted on the ancient models are still being produced today, along with more contemporaneous motifs.

● *Ceramics* – in which Rhodes has a tradition going back at least to the eighth century BC. Vases, ashtrays and wall-plates are the most popular buys, usually hand-painted; designs tend to be based on deer, ships or flowers, with blue the predominant colour.

● *Handicrafts* – principally embroidery, articles carved out of olive wood or onyx, and the usual run of souvenirs similar to those on sale in the Constitution Square and Monastiraki areas of Athens.

- *Carpets, shoes and sandals* – along with rugs of animal skins, mainly sheep. Along Socrates Street, you can watch the cobblers at work in their open-fronted shops. The leather slippers seem never to wear out, and freeze the feet beautifully on a cold day.
- *Whisky* – which because of the special tariff status accorded to the Dodecanese on their incorporation into Greece, and so far surviving EC accession, is cheaper on Rhodes (and Kos) than anywhere else in Greece. The same applies to all imported hard liquor.

Where to stay

Rhodes has considerably more than 20,000 rooms in around 300 hotels, and an estimated 3,000 additional beds on offer in private houses and self-catering apartments. The Hotel Chamber of Greece lists four deluxe hotels, sixty-one first class, fifty-four second class, 101 third class and only sixty-seven fourth and fifth class, which is indicative of the extent to which construction has been concentrated over the past two decades. Of the hotels, it lists 164 with 8,660 rooms in the new town of Rhodes and 123 with 11,393 rooms (among them most of the real resort units) along the east- and west-coast beaches. The resort hotels include three with more than 600 rooms each, two in the 400-to-600-room category, and twenty providing between 200 and 400 rooms.

Obviously these live on groups, so bookings are advisable.

In a game of one-upmanship with your travel agent, you could reliably insist, among first-class hotels, on the **Rodos Bay** at Ixia (611 beds, tel. 23 661; built in the style of a medieval fortress, with a salt-water pool on the roof), the **Blue Horizon** at Ialyssos (412 beds, tel. 93 484, for unforgettable sunsets), the **Apollo Beach** at Faliraki (539 beds, tel. 85 535), the **Steps of Lindos** at Vlicha on a beach just outside Lindos (310 beds, tel. 42 249) and, in Rhodes itself, the beach-side **Mediterranean** at 35 Kos Street (292 beds, tel. 24 661). Dropping down to second class, the **Plaza** (244 beds, tel. 22 501) is conveniently located in the centre of the new town in Ierou Lochou Street, ten minutes from the nearest public beach, but with a swimming pool.

Where to eat

Your first impression of the new town of Rhodes may easily be that every second block houses a fast-food eatery, and that all hope of good food should be abandoned. This is not so: you can dine well even in the new town, though better in the old town.

One Rhodes hotelier, when tired of his own catering or when entertaining special guests, says he relies on the restaurants Fotis, Alexis, Argo and Kontiki.

Fotis, which specialises in seafood, is just off Socrates Street (going uphill, you turn left at the two big trees), **Alexis** is by the fountain at the bottom of Socrates Street, **Argo** is in Hippocrates Square just off Socrates Street, and the **Kontiki** (continental cuisine) is a floating restaurant in Mandraki harbour.

Outside the town, the same hotelier heads for **Tupia** at Trianda on the west coast, **Yefira** in the village of Pasida near the old airport, or **Triton** on the beach at Lindos (definitely for fish, and certainly not cheap!).

If your weakness is ice-cream, his recommendation is the **Galeria** (in the new town, close to the Hotel Thermai), which is owned and operated by Italian specialists.

For snacks, the **Aegli** is the obvious place to go, as well as an easy place to find if your party has split up for shopping.

Local wine

Rhodian wines, marketed under the label CAIR (Compagnie Agricole et Industrielle Rhodes), are well-regarded throughout Greece, especially the red Chevalier de Rhodes, the dry white Lindos and a champagne-style 'sparkling' white.

Alternative forms of culture

- Sound-and-light performances (in Greek, English, French, German and Swedish) in the municipal gardens beside the Palace of the Grand Master from April to October.
- A wine festival at Rodini Park, 3 km outside Rhodes (buses from Mandraki harbour), from early July to the end of September.
- The casino (roulette, blackjack and slot machines) at the Grand Hotel/Astir Palace.
- Folk dance performances nightly during the tourist season in the Theatre of the Old Town.
- Numerous restaurants and tavernas with orchestras and floor shows, as well as nightclubs, discos and bars.
- Outdoor and indoor cinemas, and occasional concerts and recitals at the National and Municipal Theatres.
- An eighteen-hole golf course at Afandou, 19 km outside Rhodes (tel. 51 255).

Getting there

By air: Five or six flights a day from Athens, and five a week from Thessaloniki. The airport is at Kremastis, 15 km from Rhodes. Flights also from Iraklion, Karpathos and Kos all the year round.

By sea: Up to three ferries a day from Piraeus (nineteen hours).

Transport

There are adequate though not particularly frequent bus services, and cars, mopeds and bicycles for hire. The relatively considerable distances (for Greek islands) make the coach excursions more attractive. Taxis on Rhodes are expensive.

From Rhodes

By air (less than daily) to Crete, Karpathos, Kassos, Kastellorizon, Kos, Myconos, Lesbos, Paros and Thera (Santorini).

By sea to ports of call on the Piraeus and inter-Dodecanese ferries (in effect, most of the Dodecanese islands) and Crete, and to Kos, Simi, Halki, Tilos and Nisyros on excursion boats. There are also day-trips to Marmari in Turkey, and local hydrofoil services.

Telephone

Police (and tourist police) 27 423
Coastguard 27 690
NTOG 23 255
Olympic Airways 24 571
General emergency 100
Hospital 25 555/22 222

Crete

Introduction

Crete is a little larger than life. An island that stands in relation to the rest of Greece much as Texas does to the United States, and whose inhabitants are as clannish as the Scots but at the same time extraordinarily generous, it would be tempting to describe it as 110 per cent Greek. Zorba could only have been a Cretan.

Known as Kriti in Greek and commonly referred to as the *Megalonissos* ('big island'), Crete is the most sizable of the Greek islands and one of the half-dozen largest in the Mediterranean. Long and thin in shape (257 km from east to west and between 58 and 12 km from north to south), it is the southernmost part of the European Community and last stop before Libya and north Africa across the water.

Administratively, Crete is divided into four *nomes*, or prefectures. Iraklion (sometimes written as Irakleion or Heraklion), Chanea (Hania) and Rethymnon are the capital cities of homonymous prefectures; Lassithion (Lassithi), the fourth prefecture, has Aghios Nikolaos, Ierapetra and Sitia as its largest towns.

The main mountain range is the Lefka (White) Mountains; the tallest peak is Mount Ida (Idi), at 2,456 m. South of the mountains, the weather is slightly hotter than elsewhere in Greece, allowing the production of bananas and avocados on a commercial scale. Crete also keeps the rest of Greece and much of Europe supplied with winter cucumbers and tomatoes. Although tourism is important to Crete, which does not have much of an industrial base, a disastrous season would cause less distress than snow on the plains.

Area: 8,258 sq km. Length of coastline: 1,046 km.

Population: 502,165.

  Iraklion prefecture 243,622 (town 101,634).
  Chanea prefecture 125, 856 (town 47,338).
  Rethymnon prefecture 62,634 (town 17,736).
  Lassithion prefecture 70,053 (Aghios Nikolaos 8,130; Ierapetra 8,575; Sitia 6,659).

Area telephone codes: Iraklion 081.
  Chanea 0821.
  Rethymnon 0831.
  Aghios Nikolaos (including Elounda) 0841.
  Ierapetra 0842.
  Sitia 0843.

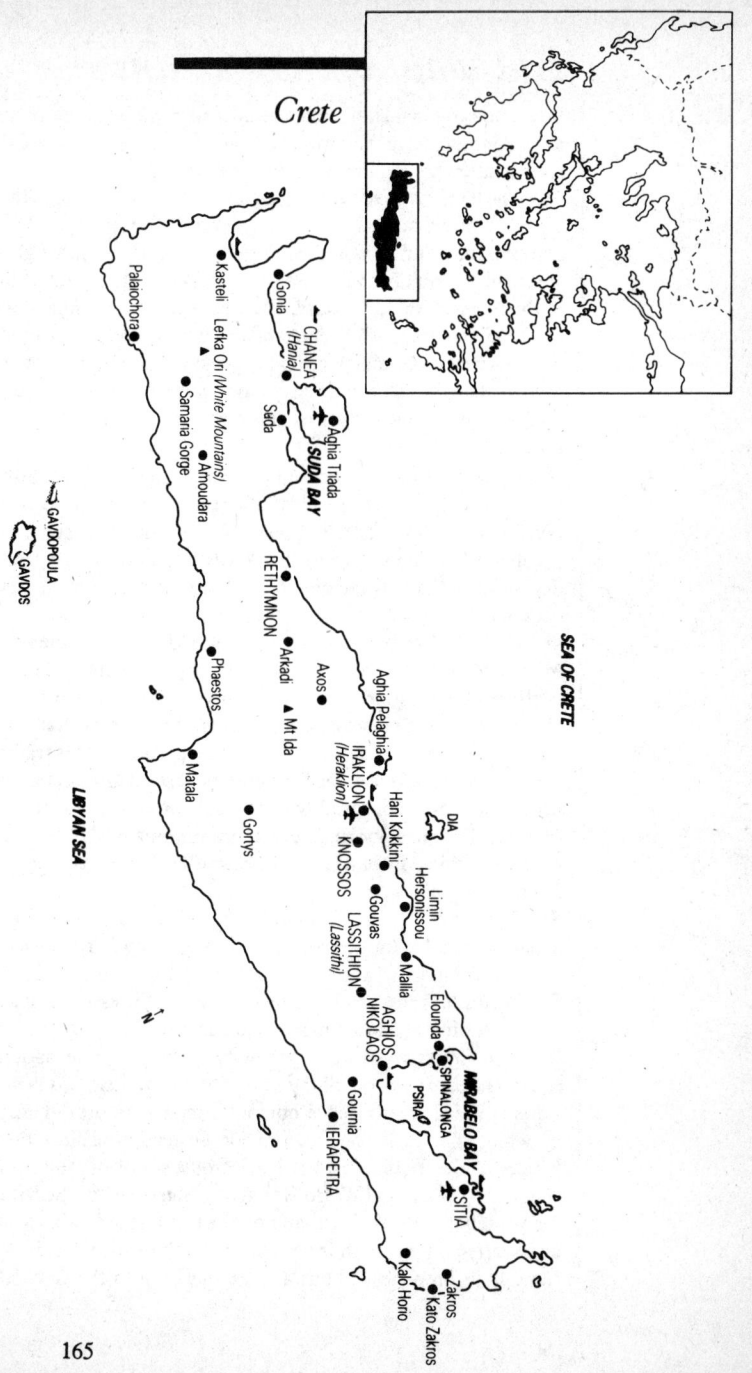

But what of the Cretans?

If you propose to talk to Cretans – and they will certainly want to talk to you – these things you might usefully bear in mind as guidelines or conversation pieces, in no particular order of importance:

● The Cretans have been compared to the Irish as well as the Scots. They are proud and quickly offended, brave and stubborn, hospitable and generous, and loyal in their friendships. They get into fights easily and tend to drink not to excess – no Greeks do that – but to the limit of their considerable capacity. They have an old-fashioned morality; the family remains the centre of the world, and its daughters are chaperoned before marriage and expected to go virgin to the altar. It follows that the Church is strong on Crete, where it enjoys a semi-autonomous status, and also that there is no welcome on the island for nudity.

● Because of the idea of family, Crete is the last stronghold of the vendetta. The present President of Greece, Christos Sartzetakis, was born on Crete but raised in Thessaloniki for safety, because of a feud involving his family. The same sense of family as clan may also explain why Crete is the only part of Greece where cattle rustling is occasionally encountered.

● Cretan surnames tend to end in 'akis' or 'yiannis'; the most common Christian names are Emmanouil (Manolis, Manola) and Eleftherios, the latter in honour of Eleftherios Venizelos.

● Because of Venizelos, Greece's greatest modern statesman and one of the island's three greatest sons (see p. 22), Crete is traditionally a liberal fortress. One of the few permanencies of Greek politics is that no cabinet could conceivably be formed without at least one Cretan member. On current form, the next prime minister should be a Cretan – Constantine Mitsotakis, who became leader of the opposition in September 1984.

● The other two famous sons of Crete were Domenico Theotokopoulos, the Renaissance painter known as El Greco, and Nikos Kazantzakis (who wrote *Zorba the Greek*, among other works), the greatest novelist produced by Greece and the essential guide to an understanding of Cretan mores and customs.

● The Cretans lose no opportunity of slipping into national costume, and some wear it all the time. For the women, this is much the same as elsewhere in Greece, but for the men it is quite different: black or white knee-high boots to provide protection against the thornbushes of the mountainsides, black trousers cut baggily in the rear (known to the Second World War generation of British Servicemen as crap-catchers), black shirts, and on the head a kind of black skullcap or sweatband hung with fringes and sometimes with beads. The costume is incomplete without a knife tucked into the belt. Black, of course, is a suitable colour because it does not show the blood. You will not see anything so effeminate as a *fustanella* (the short stiff white skirt that is male national costume elsewhere) on Crete.

● Facial adornment runs to moustaches, usually bushy, but rarely to beards. In this, the modern Cretans follow their Minoan ancestors rather than the generations immortalised by Kazantzakis who preferred death to slavery and wore beards as breastplates.

● As befits the island's history, the folk dances of Crete are stirring, robust and never flabby. You are unlikely to attend an evening of folk dance anywhere in Greece that does not include at least one Cretan troupe. Similarly, Crete has its own special type of folk song, the *matinades*, consisting of rhyming couplets that are often biting and sometimes bitter:

> Soon must this earth our bodies eat!
> Stamp it, then, with dancing feet!

Folk singers customarily compose new couplets as they go along, to express joy, sadness, love, irony or their own philosophy according to the mood of the occasion.

● If you chance to be invited to a Cretan feast, you should not be too surprised if the first dish placed before you is the whole head of a roast kid, of which you will enjoy (or pretend to) the brains, tongue, cheeks and eyes – it helps if you close your own. The intended inference is one of limitless generosity: that for every guest a separate kid has been slaughtered. While this is unlikely to be an exact analogy, Cretan hospitality on such occasions does require that the supply of food should considerably exceed the capacity of the guests; Cretan thriftiness takes over during the days that follow, with the varied means known to housewives of turning leftovers into succulent stews.

● Like their wine, the Cretans do not travel well. They are to be found in large numbers in Athens, but are not particularly well represented in the communities abroad. When those who have emigrated speak of 'home' they are thinking of Crete, not Greece. Given this common tendency to think of themselves as Cretans first and Greeks second, it follows that those who live in Athens are fiendishly well informed: if you want to learn secrets, cultivate Cretans. There would probably be a home-rule movement, if their ambitions were sufficiently modest . . .

Cretan historical eras signposted

Neolithic: 7000 to 3000 BC. Exhibits in museums.
Minoan: 3000 to 1100 BC. Knossos and other Minoan sites, and museums.

Geometric-Archaic-Classical: 900 to 69 BC. Museums.
Roman: 69 BC to AD 395. Some sites, but mainly museums.
Byzantine: 395 to 1204 (except for an Arab/Saracen period from 824 to 961). Churches, monasteries, museums.
Venetian: 1204 to 1669. Castles and forts.
Turkish: 1669 to 1898. Fortifications, mosques and fountains.
Cretan State: 1898 to 1913.
Union with Greece: 1913.
In the exchange of populations that followed the 1922 Asia Minor disaster, some 30,000 Turks left Crete and 13,000 Greeks moved in from Asia Minor.
Main Cretan revolutions: 1770, 1821, 1866 and 1897.

Mythology and history

There is not much of a chronological gap between Cretan mythology and history.

The infant Zeus, king of the gods, was supposedly concealed in a cave on Mount Ida to save him from Chronos (Time) and suckled there by the goat Amalthea. One of the sons of Zeus was Minos, whose unpleasant pet was the Minotaur (*mino-tavros*, or bull of Minos), which lived in the heart of the labyrinth and demolished its annual quota of Athenian maidens until despatched by Theseus. Just a myth, of course – but bull vaulting (seize it by the horns, swing over its back and land on your feet behind it) was fact.

Today, King Minos is a Cretan wine, and Minoan Lines is a shipping company.

Once, some 3,000 years before the birth of Christ, Minoan Crete was the first great European civilisation, with a fleet that dominated the Aegean (see The Greeks and the Sea, p. 29, and Thera (Santorini), p. 224).

Minoan remains

Minoan Crete can be seen today in the remains of the palaces of Knossos, Phaestos, Kato Zakros and Mallia, and also in Gournia, a less well known site but the most complete example of an ordinary Minoan *city* so far discovered.

Neither the Classical age nor the period of Roman occupation have left much imprint on modern Crete. Rather more remains from the Byzantine era, but the finest treasures of the past date from the 450 years of Venetian dominance, in particular in Iraklion and Chanea.

The Turkish occupation survives rather in the great deeds and legends of those who resisted it than in anything built by the conquerors although, as on Rhodes and with the same hope of paradise, they did leave fountains behind them.

As a result of the last of the string of revolutions, and also of the savagery with which it was repressed, the Protecting Powers – Britain, France and Russia had by then been joined by Italy – intervened in 1898 and Crete was granted autonomy from Turkish rule. Union with Greece was proclaimed in 1908 and confirmed in 1913, after the Balkan War of the previous year.

The island's latest contribution to world history came in May 1941 with the Battle of Crete. The Greek mainland had been seized rapidly by German forces invading from Bulgaria, but Crete held out for almost a fortnight against elite German airborne troops in some of the heaviest fighting of the Second World War up to that time.

Beyond the losses inflicted on the invaders, the incalculable effect of the Cretans' ferocious defence of their homeland also lay in the delay caused to Operation Barbarossa, the German invasion of the Soviet Union. Had the invasion been launched in the middle of May 1941 as planned, instead of on 22 June, it is at least possible that Moscow would have fallen before the onset of winter. From that point on, the hypotheses are legion: some of them are aired every May, at the Battle of Crete commemorations.

Economy in a nutshell

Two or three decades ago, Crete was definitely one of Greece's most backward regions. This began to change in the early 1960s, with the diversification of farming in the direction of market garden produce and the development of tourism, in a process that should accelerate over the next few years through special European Community assistance.

Aftermath of a shipwreck

The *Iraklion* disaster

On the night of 8 December, 1966, the ferry *Iraklion*, owned by a Piraeus company that subsequently went bankrupt, was ploughing north through an Aegean gale when a truck loaded with oranges broke loose in the hold, smashed through the side loading door and toppled into the sea.

The ship heeled over and sank within minutes, carrying more than 250 passengers and crew members to their deaths. No boats were launched, and no woman or child was among the forty-seven survivors: these were mostly crew members and a few passengers who had still been in the lounges and so were not trapped in their cabins.

The exact death toll was never established, because of the system then in force of selling tickets on the ship itself. But beyond that, a naval board of inquiry raised questions over almost everything connected with the *Iraklion*, from the manner of its conversion from a passenger-freighter into a car/truck ferry, to non-compliance with specific safety requirements and why it had sailed at all into such a gale – the inference drawn was that the ship's master, who was lost, had been under undue pressure from the owners.

Even today, Cretans speak with quivering indignation of the conditions of sea communications between the island and the mainland when they were in the hands of Piraeus companies. They decided, after pondering the report of the inquiry, that they could do a better and certainly safer job themselves.

The Metropolitan (senior bishop) of Chanea accepted the chairmanship of a committee of Chanea economists, merchants and farmers, and a fund-raising campaign was launched 'from man to man and village to village'. Inside two months, Dr 90 million had been subscribed, entirely by Cretans.

A company was founded, known as ANEK from its initials in Greek, and a Swedish tanker was bought, renamed *Kydon*, and converted into a ferry with accommodation for 1,492 passengers, fifty-five trucks and between 170 and 200 cars.

ANEK, with its shares held by 5,000 individual Cretans, was the first real joint stock company ever set up in Greece, and the first attempt ever made by an island to organise its own sea communications.

The *Kydon* went into service in 1971. Two years later, ANEK bought two more ferries, this time from Japan, and a second company, Minoan Lines, was set up on the same basis in Iraklion. Today, ANEK and Minoan Lines own all the ferries operating between Piraeus and Crete, and are branching out into Adriatic freight and passenger trades. Also, similar companies serve the communications of Rhodes and a half-dozen other Aegean islands.

It would probably never have happened if the ill-secured truckload of oranges had sunk a ferry from any island other than Crete.

Iraklion

Bearings You are most likely to arrive in Crete through Iraklion port or airport, and should try to spare a day for the city before touring the island, or as an excursion from your chosen resort.

The main towns are all within fairly easy reach of Iraklion along good roads, with frequent bus services. It is 79 km to Rethymnon, 137 km to Chanea, 65 km to Aghios Nikolaos, 105 km to Ierapetra and 143 km to Sitia. Coach tours to the island's beauty spots and historical sites can be booked from each of the towns; taxis are available; and cars and mopeds can be hired.

Iraklion is the island's administrative capital and main port, principal commercial and industrial centre, and greatest eyesore. It has only one possible rival, Mytilene on Lesbos, as the ugliest of island cities. It is cramped, hot, decaying and remarkably successful in concealing any grace or charm that it may possess. However, since seismologists and astrologers find common ground in short-listing it for a possibly devastating earthquake, it should be seen while there is still time.

It should also be visited for three other reasons: it has one of Greece's half-dozen finest museums, a splendid Venetian fortress, and it is the obvious base for a trip to Knossos.

Iraklion was founded by the Saracens in 824 under the name Handax, close to the Byzantine city of Iraklion, and at one time possessed the largest slave market in the east Mediterranean. Handax became Candia under the Venetians, but subsequently reverted to its Byzantine name.

Museums
● The Archaeological Museum displays specimens of the Minoan civilisation collected from all parts of the island, including carvings in stone, ceramics, seal-rings, jewellery and superb frescoes. Exhibits from the Byzantine, Venetian and Turkish periods, as well as of folk arts and crafts, can be seen in the city's Historical Museum.

Venetian buildings
● The city's Venetian buildings include Koules, the sixteenth-century fortress guarding the entrance to the old port, and the Chanea Gate (Hanioporta) and New Gate (Kenourgia Porta) that form the main entrances to Iraklion. The Martinengo Bastion offers an excellent view of the town and also contains the tomb of Nikos Kazantzakis, who died in 1957. If time permits, the vaulted Arsenals, the Venetian wall at the old port, the seventeenth-century Morosini fountain, the ducal palace, the Loggia and the thirteenth-century Basilica of Aghios Markos are also worth a look.

● Other churches of interest include two from the nineteenth century: the Cathedral of Aghios Minas and the Church of Aghios Titos with the head of Aghios Titos, the island's patron saint.

And then you simply have to go to Knossos.

The greatest Minoan site

Knossos
Situated only 5 km from Iraklion, and partly excavated and restored by British archaeologist Sir Arthur Evans in the 1890s, **Knossos** is an extensive site that can be visited in one of two ways. You can either troop around it in the hour or so allowed to most cruise passengers or the two hours offered by a coach tour, to say you have been, or you can arm yourself with a specialist guidebook and give it half a day. Though less of the site is now open than in the days before mass tourism and the vandalism threat, there is still a great deal to see if you care to nose around.

At its peak, when it was the capital of the greatest maritime power the world had then known, Knossos was a city with a population approaching 100,000 that needed no fortifications: in a foreshadowing of the 'wooden walls' principle, its fleet was sufficient protection.

From the excavations at Knossos and elsewhere, and the surviving frescoes and other records, much is known of daily life in Minoan Crete: of the amenities in the form of lighting, heating, drainage and bathrooms, of the role of women, fashion, jewellery and the use of cosmetics, of the sports and religious festivals. Today, Knossos is one of the most rewarding of all Greece's archaeological sites.

However brief your visit, it will certainly include the chambers of the King and Queen, the throne room, the grand staircase and the two Halls of the Double Axes, along with the Queen's bathroom and toilet. Unless you are already aware of the extent to which Evans' restorations have been criticised by less audacious archaeologists, your first impression will probably be one of astonishment that so much has survived in such perfect form and colour. The truth, of course, is different. Evans did make heavy, and probably excessive, use of his imagination, and the frescoes and furnishings are replicas. The ordinary, non-specialist visitor has cause to be grateful to him for this, however, for the result of his lavishness is a site that gives a clearer and more satisfying picture of what Knossos once was than if it had been excavated in a more conventional spirit.

A little-publicised discovery made in 1979, not at Knossos but at the minor Minoan site of Archanes, lends further weight to the belief that the Minoan Empire crashed into ruins with the tremendous earthquakes that accompanied the explosion of the Thera (Santorini) volcano (see p. 224). Archaeologists found a human skeleton, with a short sword or long dagger thrust into its chest, lying on top of an altar. At the foot of the altar were two other skeletons, in attitudes of worship. A fourth, crushed and badly burned, was found at the entrance to the temple, lying above fragments of a delicate painted bowl.

The reconstruction of what had happened is that a human sacrifice had been performed moments before the destruction of the temple by earthquake and fire. The inference is that it had been prompted by terror, as the sky darkened to the north and the earth shook.

If you go to Knossos in late summer, beware of the mulberries. They shed their berries everywhere, not sparing the shaded benches provided for weary tourists. The purple patches are more easily acquired than removed.

Rethymnon, Chanea and the Lassithion prefecture

Rethymnon

A medieval town with a long and attractive waterfront, **Rethymnon** is more picturesque and immeasurably more tranquil than Iraklion, with an interesting museum housed in a Venetian building of the early seventeenth century, a sixteenth-century Venetian castle, a couple of well-preserved mosques, and a municipal park for cooling off in.

Excursions on offer from Rethymnon include trips into the Lefka (White) Mountains or to Mount Ida for some of the hill villages, and to the Arkadi monastery. Founded in the eleventh century but dating mainly from the seventeenth, Arkadi became first a Cretan and then a national symbol during the 1866 revolution against the Turks. After a two-day siege by 15,000 Turkish troops, the defenders chose to blow themselves up rather than surrender; more than 1,000 died, in a 'holocaust' commemorated annually by services at the monastery.

In Crete in particular, the priest traditionally held his cross in his left hand, reserving his 'good' hand for his pistol: Cretan priests died on makeshift Turkish gallows almost as a matter of course.

Chanea Founded by the Venetians in 1253, **Chanea** is a mix of Venetian and Ottoman buildings along narrow streets, and of neo-Classical and modern architecture in the part of the town mostly post-dating the island's union with Greece. It has an archaeological museum housed in the Venetian church of St Francis, a historical museum with the richest collection of archives outside Athens, and a naval museum in the old port that displays exhibits connected with the island's seafaring history. Much of the film *Zorba the Greek* was shot in Chanea.

Chanea is particularly associated with Eleftherios Venizelos: his house survives in the Halepa quarter, and his tomb can be visited on a hilltop at Akrotiri, 7 km outside the town.

If you arrive in Chanea by ferry from Piraeus, you will disembark in Suda Bay. If not, you should try to find time for a look at the greatest natural anchorage in the entire Mediterranean, one of the reasons for Greece's importance to the NATO alliance in general and the US Sixth Fleet in particular.

Chanea is the town from which to reach the **Samaria Gorge**. The longest gorge in Europe, extending 18 km into the Lefka Mountains, and unforgettably majestic, it can be traversed only on foot. The full distance is a long day's walk for the practised hiker, but travel agencies arrange briefer and less tiring penetrations. Samaria may be just what you need after several days on a beach.

The Lassithion prefecture Travelling east from Iraklion, you come to the Lassithion prefecture, with the towns of Aghios Nikolaos and Sitia on the north coast and Ierapetra on the south. It is sometimes maintained – though not all Cretans agree about this, or indeed about anything – that the eastern tip of the island beyond Mirabelo Bay is the most rewarding part of Crete for those whose purpose is simply to relax on beaches. Certainly, the swimming is excellent. The danger is that once you have settled there, the rest of the island may seem dauntingly remote.

Aghios Nikolaos is both a small town and the region's main holiday resort, with a lake in the centre connected to the sea by a narrow channel, restaurants lining the sea front and lake shore, motorboats for hire to the offshore islets of Mochlos and Psira, and beaches in the immediate vicinity.

Excursions can be taken to the historic town of **Sitia**, the Minoan archaeological site of **Kato Zakros**, and **Ierapetra**, the prefecture's largest town, where Napoleon is said to have spent a night on his way to Egypt and where the beaches are on the Libyan Sea.

The long south coast of Crete is studded with small towns and fine sandy beaches, but the driving can be difficult. **Matala**, once the port of Phaestos, acquired brief fame some twenty years ago when the Flower Children were in full bloom, but now is just a dignified little holiday resort: it is no longer permitted to camp out in the cliff-side 'caves of shame' where the Flower Children sought their communion with nature.

Shopping

Crete is not really a shopping island, though it does offer attractive woven fabrics, embroidery and wood carving. Cretan sandals are a utilitarian purchase.

Where to stay

On Crete even more than on Corfu or Rhodes, because of the longer distances involved in travelling around the island, you first pick your resort then shop around for a hotel. The main resorts are in the Iraklion area, and include Aghia Pelaghia, Amoudara, Gouvas, Hani Kokkini, Limin Hersonissou, Linoperamata, Mallia and Stalis. The Lassithion prefecture offers in particular Elounda and Kalo Horio. Apart from Iraklion, the towns themselves are pleasant enough, provided your imperatives do not include a swim in the sea before breakfast.

Crete as a whole has 760 listed hotels, with around 150,000 beds: eight deluxe, fifty-five first class, 188 second class, 341 third class, seventy-eight fourth class and ninety fifth class. In addition, there are several hundred self-catering apartment complexes, and certainly not fewer than 20,000 beds on offer in private homes.

In these circumstances, mention of the following hotels is purely indicative:

● The deluxe **Elounda Beach** at Elounda (301 rooms, tel. 41 412) is where Greece's Prime Minister Andreas Papandreou escorts his entourage of bodyguards for their communal holiday.

● The **Astoria** in Eleftherias Square, Iraklion (first class, 141 rooms, tel. 286 462), almost opposite the Archaeological Museum, caters as much to business as to holiday travel and therefore is accustomed to one-night stands.

Good bets for starting a search for rooms in the other main towns might include:

● In Rethymnon, the **El Greco** (first class, 307 rooms, tel. 71 102) at Kambos Pighis, or the **Braskos** (second class, eighty-two rooms, tel. 23 721) in Daskalaki Street.

● In Chanea, the **Xenia** (second class, forty-four rooms, tel. 24 561) at the end of the old city beside the Venetian harbour and walls, or the **Santa Marina** (second class, sixty-six rooms, tel. 68 460) at Aghia Marina, 9 km outside the town.

● In Aghios Nikolaos, the **Hermes** (first class, 204 rooms, tel. 28

253) on the Akti Koundourou, or the nearby **Coral** (second class, 170 rooms, tel. 28 363).
● In Ierapetra, the **Ferma Beach** (first class, 230 rooms, tel. 61 341).

Where to eat

Most hotels on Crete require a half-board arrangement. For your other meal, the choice of restaurants and tavernas is effectively inexhaustible. To hunt one out just because it has been recommended is more often than not an unproductive use of time.

The following well-regarded veterans are therefore mentioned only in case you should chance on them:
● In Iraklion: **Maxim** beside the Park Hotel, **Delphini** in the Old Market, **Minos** and **Klimataria** in Dedalou Street, **Knossos** near the Morosini fountain, **Antigone** in Knossos Street, and **Rizes**, **Psaria**, **Gorgona** and **Mouragia** on or near the waterfront.
● In Rethymnon: **Tassos**, **Samarina** and **Zefiros** along the waterfront, and **Barbarossa** in the old fishing port.
● In Chanea: **Zepos** on Akti Koundourioti, **Dinos** (fish taverna) on Akti Enoseos, **Eftychia** at Kolymbari (traditional Cretan food), **Faros** next to the old lighthouse, **Kontosouvli** in the old harbour, **Nichterida** at Akrotiri, **Aposperida** in Kondilaki Street, **Vlahakis** in Ellis Street (Suda Bay) and the **Retro** opposite the house of Eleftherios Venizelos in Halepa.
● In Aghios Nikolaos: **Aktaion** on the lake shore, **Cretan Restaurant** in the harbour, and **Lotus Eaters** in 25th August Street.
● In Sitia: **Zorba** near the harbour and **Roussos** in 4th September Street.

Getting there

The most common entry point for Crete is Iraklion, by air or sea.
Iraklion Airport, 3.5 km outside the city, accepts international charters and is also served by up to seven Olympic Airways flights a day from Athens. There are daily flights from Rhodes and Myconos, and from two to four a week from Thessaloniki, Thera (Santorini) and Paros.

Ferries from Piraeus make the journey overnight in each direction, taking about twelve hours for the 174 nautical miles and arriving at Iraklion or Piraeus at about 6 a.m. There are also boat connections to the Cyclades and Dodecanese islands.

Chanea can be reached direct by air from Athens (five flights a day in summer to an airport 15 km outside the city) and by different overnight ferries from Piraeus (153 nautical miles, about eleven hours) to Suda, 7 km from Chanea.

Rethymnon is reached via Iraklion or Chanea, whether by air or sea. In 1988 a local shipping company announced plans for a direct service between Piraeus and Rethymnon, for which it purchased and converted a Japanese ship, and this may by now be operating.

Aghios Nikolaos is similarly reached via Iraklion, while the small airport at *Sitia* is used by Olympic only for Rhodes, Karpathos and

Kassos flights.

Transport Bus services are frequent and for the most part uncrowded between the main towns and to the resorts and larger villages. Local travel agencies offer a wide range of coach tours, and taxis, cars and mopeds can be hired. Diesel oil is available everywhere, but unleaded petrol is not.

Typical coach tours on offer include:
- From *Iraklion* to Knossos, Gortys, Phaestos, Mallia and Matala.
- From *Rethymnon* to Axos, Anoyia and the Arkadi monastery.
- From *Chanea* to Akrotiri, the monasteries of Aghia Triada, Gonia and Kasteli, and the Samaria Gorge.
- From *Aghios Nikolaos* to Ierapetra, and from either to Gournia, Zakros and Sitia.

Boat excursions include:
- From *Iraklion* to Dia, 7 nautical miles north of Crete. Now inhabited only by a few shepherds, Dia is believed, on the basis of underwater discoveries made in the 1970s, once to have been wooded and cultivated, and possibly to have served as a kind of holiday resort for the Minoan upper class.
- From *Chanea* to Aghia Theodori, Gavdopoula, Gavdos, Imeri and Agria Grambouza, Pondikonisi, Suda and Minoa. Gavdos, 24 nautical miles into the Libyan Sea with a population of around 100 in four settlements, is probably the more rewarding islet, though involving the longer trip; there are three boats a week in summer and one in winter.
- From *Elounda*, for those with macabre tastes, to Spinalonga for a ruined Venetian fortress and experience of the place where, for centuries, lepers were consigned to die in untended isolation.

From Crete Apart from the air communications noted in Getting there (see p. 175), there are sea communciations with various mainland and island destinations; for example, from Chanea to Kythera, the southern Peloponnese and some of the Cyclades islands; from Rethymnon to Thera (Santorini); from Iraklion to Paros, Naxos, Ios, Thera, Syros, Sikinos and Folegandros as well as to Italy, Cyprus and Israel; and from Aghios Nikolaos and Sitia to most of the Dodecanese and some of the Cyclades and North and East Aegean islands.

Telephone Iraklion (081):
    Police 282 031 (Emergency 100)
    Tourist police 283 190
    Coastguard 226 073
    NTOG 228 203/228 225
    Olympic Airways 229 191
    Hospital 237 502
    First Aid 222 222
Chanea (0821):
    Police 22 426

Tourist police 24 477
  Coastguard 22 600
  Olympic Airways 27 701
  NTOG 26 426
  Hospital 27 231
Rethymnon (0831):
  Police 22 333
  Tourist police 28 156
  Coastguard 22 276
  NTOG 29 148/24 143
  Hospital 27 491/27 814
Aghios Nikolaos (0841):
  Police 22 251
  Tourist police 22 321
  Coastguard 22 312
  NTOG 22 357
  Hospital 22 369/22 011
Ierapetra (0842):
  Police 22 560
  Coastguard 22 294
  Olympic Airways 22 444
  Hospital 22 252/22 488

The Cyclades Islands

Introduction

Though the name Cyclades derives from the Greek word for circle, *kyklos*, and the group is almost invariably described as a circle of islands centred on Delos, it might be geometrically more appropriate to envisage them as a square, or even a redoubt, in the middle of the Aegean.

The islands are sufficiently concentrated, one in sight of another, to give the poor sailor on a ferry in a rough sea the impression that the worst will soon be over. As soon as you head for an open horizon, you can be sure you are on your way out of the Cyclades:

- West, to the coast of mainland Greece and the Peloponnese.
- North, across wide expanses of open sea with only the occasional island (the total area of the Aegean is about 250,000 sq km, roughly double the area of mainland Greece) to the coast of Macedonia and Thrace.
- East, to Greece's 'frontline' islands strung along the Asia Minor coast of Turkey, from Samothrace (Samothraki) near the entrance to the Dardanelles to little Kastellorizon at the 'bottom' of the Dodecanese.
- South, across the stormiest part of the Aegean, to the long barrier of Crete.

The Cyclades are Greece's national colours, white on a sea of blue, and also the wellspring of much of its mythology and source of its maritime tradition.

Geophysically, they are all that remain above the sea of a land mass that once connected mainland Greece with Asia Minor. As a group (individual islands may be exceptional in one way or another), they are hilly and often mountainous, windswept most of the year, with only sparse greenery, and of little significance agriculturally or industrially. As some of them have already discovered, their future lies in tourism.

Economically deprived, the Cyclades confronted a particularly acute danger from population drift immediately after the Second World War, as the young and ambitious moved first to mainland Greece and often, from there, to the established Greek communities abroad and new opportunities in West Germany. Improvements across the whole range of social services – housing, health, education, communications and entertainment – have deterred the exodus, but it is the development of tourism that provides the real assurance of well-paid jobs for at least six months of the year. The population of the twenty-five inhabited islands, after falling steadily for three decades, actually rose by 2,000 to 88,500 between the 1971 census and that of 1981.

As even the smallest islands acquire runways for light aircraft, or at least helicopter landing pads, and hotels are constructed, the rewards of greater accessibility can only be spread more widely. Already it is easier than ever before to follow in the traces of Odysseus, the Crusaders and the pirates.

The Cyclades islands form a single department (*nome*) with its capital on Syros, divided into eight sub-departments. They produce mainly olives, figs, grapes and wine. As in Ancient Greece, some marble is still mined on Paros, Naxos and Tinos (Greek apartments have marble floors because 'that's the local stone', and is rather cheaper than quality wood that has to be imported).

The characteristic features of Cyclades architecture are the white 'cubist' houses and small blue-and-white churches, and often a proliferation of windmills: the Cyclades are the windiest part of Greece, exposed to northerly gales in winter and through much of the summer to the notorious *meltemi*, a stiff breeze that torments more than it refreshes. It follows that the best time to visit these islands is from May to the beginning of July, and from early September to the end of October.

On most of the lesser islands you will find that the capital, invariably known as *Hora* ('the place'), is situated on a hill inconveniently distant from the modern port; this is a legacy of the long scourge of piracy (see also pp. 33–4).

History Considering the group as a whole, the islands were already inhabited at least 10,000 years ago, came under the dominance of the Minoan Empire based on Crete and then of Mycenae, were colonised in the tenth and ninth centuries BC by Ionians (people from Ionia in Asia Minor, and no connection with the Ionian islands), were overrun by the Persians before their defeat at the Battles of Marathon and Salamis, subsequently experienced Athenian, Macedonian, Rhodian and Roman hegemony, became part of the Byzantine Empire without enjoying protection from raids by Goths, Saracens and Slavs, and were allocated to the Venetians after the Crusader sack of Constantinople in 1204. The Venetians set up small duchies that were conquered piecemeal by the Turks in the fifteenth and sixteenth centuries. After the 1770 Russo-Turkish war, eighteen of the Cyclades islands were briefly annexed to the Russian Empire; the Russian domination lasted at most seven years, and left few traces. The Turks

Getting there

returned, to be dislodged finally after the 1821 Independence Revolution. The Cyclades were thus the first of the Greek islands to secure their union with modern Greece.

Though many of the Cyclades islands, with the curious exception of the administrative capital, Syros, can now be reached by scheduled air services, the commonest way to visit them is by ferry from Piraeus. Myconos, Tinos and Syros are served by ferries that leave Piraeus or Rafina in the morning and return the same afternoon; those to most of the other islands sail out one day and back the next. There are summer connections also to the Dodecanese islands (see individual islands for detailed travel information). Island-hopping is feasible, though not as easy as in the Dodecanese.

Myconos, Delos and Thera (Santorini) can be visited, though scarcely explored, on the three- and four-day cruises out of Piraeus.

The larger islands of the group – Syros, Andros, Tinos, Paros, Naxos and Milos – cater to the needs of tourists (good beaches, comfortable hotels, sightseeing and a relatively lively nightlife) without giving an impression of dependence on tourism. To these you might consider taking a car, or hiring one locally.

Ios you will love or hate: while it does not offer itself to indifference, by the time you leave you will at least feel that you 'know yourself', and your limits, better than before you went.

If your quest is for isolation and the simple life you have at least fifteen islands to choose among, none more than twenty-four hours by sea from Piraeus. On the tiniest of them, where electricity, running water and flush toilets are still a novelty and the only accommodation is in islander rooms, you will be as far away from whatever your personal 'it' may be as you are ever likely to get, this side of the South Pacific.

Amorgos

Alphabetically, either in Greek or in English, Amorgos is the first of the Cyclades, but in any ordinary list of visitor preferences it would come way down. There is no reason not to go there; it is simply that, with the exception of one monastic showpiece, Amorgos has nothing that cannot be found more easily elsewhere. Its little holiday movement is almost entirely Greek.

Area: 121 sq km. Length of coastline: 112 km.
Population: 1,722 (Hora 353, Katapola 411).
Area telephone code: 0285.

Bearings

Amorgos is a long, narrow island with one road down the centre and another linking the harbour of Katapola with the capital, Hora, 5 km away.

GAZETTEER

What to see

While ferries from Piraeus may also call at Aigialis, disembarkation normally takes place at **Katapola**, a west-coast town consisting of three settlements linked by a promenade. The nearby remains of Ancient Minoas were excavated by the French towards the end of the nineteenth century and include a stadium and Temple of Apollo.

One bus makes approximately five trips a day between Katapola and **Hora**, a typical Cyclades town with remains of a Venetian fortress, a row of disused windmills and a seventeenth-century Tower of Gavra now converted into a small museum.

Aigialis, the second harbour, offers some attractive beaches and the scant remains of the ancient city of the same name. The island's third ancient city, **Arkesini**, is in the south, and difficult to reach; there, too, the remains are unimpressive.

The island's pride is the Monastery of Hozoviotissa, a few kilometres from Hora (part of the way by bus and then on foot). Dating from the early eleventh century and rebuilt after 1088 by mandate of the Byzantine Emperor Alexis Komninos, it is a remarkable white structure pressed against a sheer cliff 300 m above the sea. Its treasures include icons, church vessels, manuscripts and the charter granted by Alexis Komninos. Casual visitors are offered refreshments, and a few cells are available for any who wish to spend the night there.

At the other end of the ecclesiastical scale, the Church of Aghios Fanourios at Katapola may be Greece's smallest; at a squeeze it can hold three worshippers and a priest – the minimum number for a very private wedding.

Beaches

There is a beach within easy walking distance of Katapola, but the better ones are at Aigialis, Aghia Anna below the monastery, Paradisia, Kalotaritissa (an enclosed bay with fine sand) and Faros, where nudists congregate.

Where to stay

The only listed hotel is **Mike's** at Aigialis (third class, ten rooms, tel. 71 252). Apart from that, there are a number of small pensions there and at Katapola and Hora, and some 300 beds on offer in self-catering apartments and islander homes.

Where to eat

Recommended tavernas include **Kastanis**, **Parvas**, **Tsamboukas** and **Economidis** at Hora, and **Mourayio**, **Kamari** and **Psaropoula** (known also as **Psakis**) at Katapola. Elsewhere, quality at the mainly seasonal tavernas is patchy.

Getting there

The five ferries a week from Piraeus take between eleven and eighteen hours for the 138 nautical miles, depending on the route. In summer, there are daily boats from Naxos.

Transport

A bus service travels from Katapola to Aghia Anna via Hora. Aigialis can be reached most easily on the Piraeus ferries, and other beaches by caique or motorboat.

From Amorgos

Ferry ports of call, Naxos, some of the Dodecanese islands and the uninhabited offshore islands of Amorgos, known as the Amorgiana,

Telephone | for swimming and fishing; among them are Anydro (the name means Waterless), Kynouros, Levitha and Nikouria.
Police 71 210
Coastguard 71 259
Clinic 71 207

Anafi

Anafi is an easy place to overlook, as much by the state as the tourist movement, but in a sense it was the last and least of the Greek islands to establish a colony – more than 2,000 years after the others had abandoned the habit. Once noted for its masons (it was said that stone was the only thing that Anafi had plenty of), it supplied large numbers of them for the building of modern Athens when the Greek capital was moved there from Nafplion after Independence in 1829. They built the neo-Classical structures that still give the Athens taverna quarter of Plaka its grace and charm.

The most southerly of the inhabited Cyclades islands, Anafi lies 12 nautical miles off the east coast of Thera and 145 nautical miles from Piraeus.

Area: 38 sq km. Length of coastline: 32 km.
Population: 292 at the 1981 census (ten years earlier it was 353).
Area telephone code: 0286.

Mythology and history | In mythology, Anafi was summoned out of the sea by Apollo to provide a place of refuge for the Argonauts when they were caught in a storm on their voyage in quest of the Golden Fleece. A glance at the map suggests they must have been wildly off course at the time. Particularly subject to pirate raids during the Middle Ages, it was several times abandoned; eventually, however, its inhabitants always moved back.

Bearings | Anafi is a curious place to approach: for a small island, the cone-shaped mountain rising out of the sea (Vigla, 582 m) seems disproportionately tall. You land at the primitive harbour of Aghios Nikolaos on the south coast and from there face a 2-km uphill walk to **Hora**, the capital and, with Aghios Nikolaos, the only settlement. As the internal combustion engine has yet to reach Anafi as a form of propulsion for land transportation, the only alternative is a donkey or mule.

Hora is small and white, and as recently as the 1967–74 dictatorship was still playing its traditional role as a place of exile. Like a balcony above the sea, it is itself overlooked by its ruined castle.

What to see | Apart from the beaches, about the only place to visit is the eighteenth-century hilltop Monastery of the Panaghia (Virgin) of Kalamiotissa, named for an icon of the Virgin said to have been found hanging on a cane, *kalami*, at what became the site of the monastery.

Built at a height of 450 m, the monastery requires stamina of its visitors on a hot day; nearby are a few remains of a Temple of Apollo and an unexploited and still unnamed cave.

Beaches While you can swim close to where you landed, at Aghios Nikolaos, the better beaches are along the south coast and are reached by caiques or small boats.

Where to stay and eat Anafi has no listed hotel, but offers about seventy non-hotel beds, including six in a community guest-house at Hora.

The island's two tavernas, **Roussos** and **Maria**, are at Aghios Nikolaos; at Hora itself, you can snack in coffee-shops.

Getting there The two ferries a week from Piraeus take between thirteen and nineteen hours depending on route. The ferry's ports of call give you the opportunity to see other islands in the group on your way to and from Anafi, and there are boats to Thera (Santorini) in fine weather.

Transport Animals and small boats.

Telephone Police/coastguard 61 216   Clinic 61 215

Andros

The most northerly of the Cyclades islands and the second largest, after Naxos, Andros is only 7 nautical miles from Euboia and less than a mile from Tinos. Though for the Cyclades it is unusually green, thanks to its plentiful natural springs, it has yet to catch on as a tourist resort. One of Greece's pre-eminent seafarer islands, Andros is proud of its traditions: seeing what tourism has done to some of its neighbours, in particular Skiathos and Myconos, it has adopted a cautious approach to the travel industry and seems content to muddle along with a modest number of Greek visitors.

Area: 379 sq km. Length of coastline: 176 km.

Population: 9,020, with 1,920 in Andros town (Hora), 624 in Gavrion, 645 in Korthion and 623 in Batsi.

Area telephone code: 0282.

Mythology and history Said to have been named for Andros, a grandson of Apollo, the island became an important naval power after 1000 BC, founded colonies in Halkidiki, Thrace and Asia Minor, and minted its own coinage. Dionysos was much worshipped there, though Andros today has no particular reputation for wine. It took the 'wrong' side in the Persian Wars, and then compounded the error by allying itself with Sparta against Athens. It became a cultural centre in the Byzantine era, and developed a considerable silk industry in the eleventh and twelfth centuries. The Venetians arrived in 1207 and the Turks in 1556. It played an important role in the 1821 Revolution, and rejoined Greece with the rest of the Cyclades.

The capital **Andros** town, or Hora, is a blend of Cycladic and neo-Classical architecture half-way down the east coast. Narrow flagstoned streets, closed to traffic, lead into picturesque squares offering views over the bay. A ruined Venetian castle beside the sea was badly damaged by German bombing during the Second World War. Also worth visiting are the Goulandris archaeological museum, housing finds from all periods of the island's history, and the Goulandris art museum, which is dedicated mainly to modern art and works of the local sculptor, Michael Tombras, whose statue of the 'Unknown Sailor' stands in the grounds of the Andros naval museum. As may have been surmised, the Goulandris shipowner family hails from Andros.

Beaches

Andros town should not be missed, but for swimming you would go to Gavrion or Batsi, two small towns only a few kilometres apart on the west coast. If the main beaches there are crowded, head south and watch out for a cove to your liking. From either town you are within easy reach of Zagora.

Homer and hard times

Zagora will never be one of Greece's glamour archaeological sites – there is simply too little to be seen – but it rewards the imaginative visitor. Excavated by Australian archaeologists and students between 1968 and 1977, it is the only town yet discovered from the Geometric period that was never built on subsequently.

The last inhabitants of what is believed to have been a city-state moved out towards the end of the eighth century BC, less than two hundred years after the settlement had been founded and probably less than fifty years after its emergence as a flourishing town with a then considerable population of 4,000. As a result, archaeologists have been able to venture a fairly detailed reconstruction of how the ordinary people lived in the days of Homer, between the end of the Minoan civilisation and the emergence of Classical Greece.

It is clear that life there was hard, dangerous, and by any modern standards other than those of a shantytown, squalid.

Zagora is a flat-topped promontory, treeless and waterless, where shallow dusty soil supports only the hardiest scrub. It would be no place to build a city unless the sole criterion was defence: it has sheer cliffs down to the sea on three sides, and a narrow neck across which a wall of remarkable solidity was constructed.

The Zagora city wall ranged in thickness from 7 m to a minimum of 4 m along its 150-m cliff-to-cliff length, and probably rose to a height of about 3.5 m. Nothing else at Zagora was anything like so solid.

The armaments of the period – a weapon in the right hand and a shield in the left – determined the location of the only gate. Situated at the extreme left of the wall, it could be approached only in file, with the assault troops exposed to arrow- and javelin-fire from their right (the side not protected by the shield), and a false step leading to a plunge into the sea.

There is no evidence that the wall was ever broken. Behind it, the inhabitants lived in flat-roofed, single-storey houses of from one to four rooms, built of grey schist mortared with mud. There were no clearly defined streets. To save space, the houses were jumbled together, with access from twisting alley-ways. In what was the only apparent concession to comfort over space, not one house was found with its entrance facing towards the north wind.

The rooms were about 2 m high. Some of them were provided with a rectangular central hearth and a stone bench along one wall for storage jars. Rainwater that collected on the roofs was led into jars or troughs, to supplement water carried from springs outside the wall when the city was at peace.

Outside the wall, there was rich land watered by springs that still flow today. There, cereals could be cultivated, olives harvested and flocks pastured. Just outside the gate, a winding footpath led down to a sheltered cove where boats could moor. Fishing was carried out and so was trade, possibly in olive oil, wine and wool, with other Greek states and Aegean islands. Fragments of pottery originating from Athens, Corinth, Euboia and several Cyclades islands support the trade theory, while Phoenician imitations of early Egyptian scarabs supply evidence of contact with the east.

It is not known why the town was abandoned. However, the absence of human bones, arrowheads or any indications of pillage has led to the conclusion that its inhabitants either decided that it was no longer necessary to live in so inhospitable a site, since the world had become a safer place, or were driven away by earthquake or disease. They did not go far: evidence was found that they returned regularly, for many years afterwards, to present votive offerings at the temple of their abandoned city.

It is also not known what the town was then called: Zagora is simply the modern name of the promontory.

Considering the number of sites still incompletely excavated, and some hardly touched at all, it should not cause surprise that the Greeks are unable to do all their own digging themselves, and that the excavations there were carried out by Sydney University on behalf of the Athens Archaeological Society. There is enough work yet for many generations of archaeologists, as well as an appreciation that Ancient Greece is a legacy not for one country but for the world.

Around the island

Though Andros has a good bus service, the island is large enough, and with a sufficient road network, to repay the effort of shipping a car from the mainland or the cost of hiring one locally. You would then be able to see more of an island that is really worth only a couple of days, in the context of a holiday of normal length, and make a point of including:

● **Apikia** and **Stenies**: two adjoining villages within easy reach of excellent beaches, where some of the island's shipowners and merchant marine officers have their holiday homes. Apikia has a couple of hotels, and in summer there are seaside fish tavernas at Stenies. You

can also drink the renowned Sariza water from free-flowing springs: elsewhere in Greece you buy it in plastic bottles.
- **Messaria**: an inland village with a monastery dating from the tenth century and Byzantine churches from the twelfth and eighteenth centuries.
- **Korthion (or Korthi)**: at the head of a deep bay, with a sand-and-pebble beach, the ruins of a Venetian castle and a tenth-century monastery.
- **Palaiopoli**: a west-coast settlement at which swimming can be combined with a visit to the site of Ancient Andros, where the remains include fragments of walls, a theatre and a stadium.

Where to stay and eat

Andros has seventeen listed hotels (five second class, eight third and the rest fourth and fifth) with a total of 409 rooms. Three of the hotels are in Andros town, six at Batsi, four at Gavrion, and the others at Apikia, Aprovato and Korthion. There are an estimated 500 beds on offer in private homes, about half of them at Batsi.

The best hotels are the third-class **Chryssi Akti** at Batsi (sixty-one rooms, tel. 41 236), the second-class **Perrakis** at Gavrion (thirty rooms, tel. 71 456), and, in Andros town, the **Paradissos** and **Xenia**, both second class; the former has forty-one rooms (tel. 22 187) and the latter twenty-six rooms (tel. 22 270).

Islanders recommend the food at **Stathmos** and **Platanos** at Hora, **Stamatis** and **Karanassios** at Batsi, and **Petros** and **Karakatsanis** at Gavrion.

Getting there

Ferries from Rafina (37 nautical miles, two and a half hours, morning and afternoon sailings each way) go to Gavrion and Batsi, where they connect with buses for Andros town.

Transport

Bus services from Andros town to Gavrion, Batsi, Apikia, Stenies and Korthion. Cars and mopeds for hire.

From Andros

To Tinos and Myconos on the ferries from Rafina. There are also one or two boats a week to Syros, Paros and Naxos.

Telephone

Police 22 300 (Andros), 71 220 (Gavrion), 41 204 (Batsi).
Coastguard 22 250 (Andros), 71 213 (Gavrion).
Clinics 22 758 (Andros), 71 210 (Gavrion), 41 326 (Batsi).

Antiparos (see p. 216).

Delos

The offshore island of Myconos and once one of the world's greatest slave markets, with a reported turnover on heavy days of up to 10,000

head, Delos is today an incomparable archaeological site and a fascinating place to spend half a day even at the risk of dehydration.
Area: 3 sq km. Length of coastline: unlisted.
Population: 16 on the 1981 census-day, comprising staff of the museum, guest-house and café, and archaeologists temporarily in residence.
Area telephone code: 0289 (Myconos).

Mythology and history

Athens and Myconos bookshops offer solid tomes on Delos, with blow-by-blow accounts of who did what and when, for what reason and with what result. Chapter headings might well record that:

● Either (from mythology) it was an island raised by Zeus for Leto on which to give birth to their twins, Apollo and Artemis, or it was a floating island that agreed to shelter Leto, despite the jealousy of Zeus' wife Hera, in return for a mooring.

● By 1000 BC it was already developing into a cultural, religious and trade centre and, discounting the occasions on which its buildings were levelled and its inhabitants slaughtered or sold into slavery, remained one until well into the Roman period, when there was no place like Delos for staffing a household at bargain rates.

● There were at least two 'purifications', involving a prohibition of birth and death on Delos and the removal of bones already buried to the nearby island of Rineia; these are commonly attributed to religious fervour, but suspected by some of having followed outbreaks of plague.

Around the site

Since the objectives of this gazetteer do not include the provision of additional income for the many Myconos doctors who thrive on tourism, the kind of detail on the archaeological remains that would encourage you to hold this book open in one hand while scrambling over the ruins is left to specialist publications whose readers may be assumed to combine an insatiable appetite for ancient facts with rubber ankles and an imperviousness to heat.

In the very briefest outline:

● You land from the Myconos motorboat, weather permitting, at a small quay close to the ancient port. If the winds require a landing on the other side of the island, you reach the site by a footpath that will drain some of the juices from you before you catch a glimpse of your first pillar.

● You are unlikely to miss the Temple of Apollo near the harbour, the settlement of Limnis, the stadium, the theatre, the hill of Kythnos, the commercial port and houses there and, of course, the museum.

● You should look out for the houses near the theatre, where there are some superb mosaics, and the five surviving Naxian marble lions – one of at least four that are missing is in Venice.

Though you can visit the ruins by yourself, Delos is so extensive a site, covering so long a period, that you really need to join a party with a guide. The motorboats normally allow you three to four hours ashore; if disembarkation is from a cruise liner you may have rather less time. On your own, you will have to settle for vague impressions.

The site, and usually the museum, can be visited between 9 a.m. and 3 p.m. daily. Excavations began in the last quarter of the nineteenth century, and are still continuing.

Where to stay and eat

You don't, since the Xenia guest-house (four rooms, seven beds) is strictly for archaeologists.

You can snack badly and expensively near the quay, but would do better to carry a bun from Myconos (and a bottle of water!).

Getting there

By caique or motorboat from Myconos, a trip of 6 nautical miles taking between thirty minutes and an hour depending on speed of boat and state of sea. If the sea is rough, as it usually is, you should be deliciously tenderised by the end of the day. As for whether you should skip breakfast, the Ancient Greek advice is still the best: 'Know yourself!'

Delos is for those who are moved by the past, or enjoy an adventure.

Folegandros

Perhaps because it has so often been a place of exile, even as recently as the 1967-74 military dictatorship, Folegandros is unusually well provided with hotels and rentable rooms for an island with a population of less than 600. Its inhabitants are exceptionally hospitable, possibly for the same reason, and no one need be deterred from going by the thought that in the past others were forced to. The way the Colonels saw it, exile was not so much a punishment of an offence (if one had been committed, the jails awaited) as a precautionary removal from circulation in advance of anticipated offences; the sentence was usually 'administrative', imposed by someone's order and not after a court hearing. It amounted to a requirement to live in a certain village, or on a certain island, reporting regularly to the police, but with no state responsibility for the provision of lodging, food or means of passing the time. It followed that the place of exile had to be remote but not necessarily unpleasant, and sufficiently small to facilitate police surveillance. For this, Folegandros served very well. On the southern rim of the Cyclades facing the Cretan Sea, it is 102 nautical miles from Piraeus, 15 from Milos and 5 from Sikinos.

Area: 32 sq km. Length of coastline: 39 km.
Population: 567 (312 in Ano Meria, 248 in Hora and 7 in Karavostasis).
Area telephone code: 0286.

Around the island

You land at **Karavostasis**, a small port with a hotel, coffee-shops and fish tavernas along the beach, some rocky islets guarding the entrance, a few rented rooms and the terminal of a bus service to Hora (if this seems surprising given the population figures, it should be

What to see borne in mind that the ten-year census is taken in the heart of winter, when there is little purpose in living by the water).

The obvious thing to do is to head straight for **Hora**, the hillside capital that extends to the very edge of a cliff, is built in the same architectural style as Myconos, and is second only to Thera (Santorini) as a balcony over the Aegean; it is claimed that on exceptionally clear days Crete can be seen. The clifftop houses, now mostly abandoned, were constructed in such a way as to form a defensible wall when pirates came; back from the edge are some pleasant squares, one of them shaded by trees. A footpath leads to the Monastery/Church of the Panaghia. The ruined castle is Venetian.

Hora is 4 km from Karavostasis; the bus from port to capital continues another 5 km to **Ano Meria**, the island's third and largest settlement and centre of its livestock breeding. Though Ano Meria is inland, lifts can usually be obtained on farm vehicles to the beaches of Aghios Georgios and Vigla on the north-east corner of the island.

Folegandros boasts but has yet to exploit a cave, Chrysospilia, which can be reached by caique. Throughout the island there are seventy-three churches, many of them privately owned and most of them not in use.

Beaches Though tiny, the beaches of Folegandros are equal to any in the Aegean of comparable size. Easiest to reach are those at Karavostasis, Aghios Ioannis, Pelaghia and Livadi along the south-east corner, but the best of all is probably that at Angali, a west-coast settlement with some thirty non-hotel beds on offer in the summer. Angali, known also as Ormos Vathy from the name of the bay, can be reached by caique from Karavostasis or at the end of a quarter-hour walk from a bus-stop on the Hora–Ano Meria road.

Where to stay Folegandros has four listed hotels, three of them in Hora (of second, third and fifth classes), with a total of fifty-three rooms. Probably the friendliest is the Makkas family's fifth-class **Odysseas** (seven rooms, tel. 41 239), which is also the only one to stay open year-round. From May to September you could try the beach-side **Aeolos** in Karavostasis (third class, twelve rooms, tel. 41 205). An estimated 110 non-hotel rooms are also available, in Karavostasis, Hora and Angali.

Where to eat All the Folegandros restaurants double up as tavernas and fish tavernas. In Hora, look for the **Kritikos**, **Nikos**, **Folegandros**, **Melissa** and brand-new **Sideris**; in Karavostasis there are the **To Kati Allo** (Something Else), **Loukia** and **Kalymnios**; Angali offers **Psaromiringos** and **Papadopoulos**, and Ano Meria the **Iliovasilema** (Sunset) and **Mimis**.

Getting there The two to five ferries a week from Piraeus, depending on season and weather, take about eleven hours for the trip.

Transport There are bus services along the island's only road, from Karavostasis through Hora to Ano Meria, and caiques and motorboats are available.

From Folegandros	Ferry ports of call, irregular connections with Crete, and local boats to Sikinos and Ios.
Telephone	Police 41 249 Coastguard 41 203 Clinic 41 222

Ios

Ios, sometimes written Io (pronounced Eee-yo) and called by its inhabitants Nio, may just possibly be the most beautiful little island in the Cyclades. But those who found it first, some fifteen or twenty years ago, rarely go back any longer, deterred by its occasional resemblance in high summer to one vast, cosmopolitan youth club. Today Ios attracts those who have yet to reach the age when other people's nudity ceases to excite, rather than those to whom sleep at night is essential to enjoyment of the following morning. South of Naxos and north of Thera (Santorini), Ios is 111 nautical miles from Piraeus.
Area: 108 sq km. Length of coastline: 81 km.
Population: 1,451 (1,362 in Hora and 71 in Mylopota, the next biggest village).
Area telephone code: 0286.

Mythology and history

Ios has little history to speak of, except some brittle connections with Homer. One tradition says he died and was buried there; another, more elaborate, explains that he was driven ashore by a storm while on his way from Samos to Athens and died there of exhaustion. Either way, Ios has a so-called 'tomb of Homer', of dubious legitimacy. Those who accept that Homer had a mother may also accept that she was born on Ios.

Post-Homeric Ios was one of several way-stops on voyages between Crete and Athens; it has a ruined Venetian castle, and it endured the usual Turkish period, rejoining Greece along with the rest of the Cyclades islands.

Today, beds on offer to the tourist comfortably exceed the number of inhabitants. Unfortunately, the water supply has not kept pace with the provision of less essential facilities; in a particularly dry summer the taps may cease to run at night, with unpleasant effects on the toilets.

Hora in full boom

The beauty of Ios lies in its beaches and, for the Cyclades, the lushness of its vegetation. You disembark at the west-coast port of **Ormos** and either walk or take a bus to **Hora**, 2 km away; hotel and other beds are available at Ormos, where meals can be found in the summer, but the beach is not among the island's best.

Several years ago the Ios local authorities awoke to the threat that tourism had become, in the form of additional rooms built beside, behind or on top of existing houses as the inhabitants' personal conduit to the cornucopia. A halt was called just in time, with the result that Hora, the capital, is still architecturally attractive: it contains narrow streets overlooked by balconies and terraces, small squares where it is a pleasure to rest, and the whole set off by the castle and a row of windmills.

But Hora really booms at night, with the help of a dozen discos along the main street.

Beaches Milopota, the local abbreviation of Milopotamos, is a long beach at the end of the bus line, sheltered from the north wind, that has unofficially become an international nudist centre. Accommodation is plentiful, and so are the opportunities for unremarkable eating at memorable prices.

Caiques leave Ormos every morning for the three main beaches on the south and east coasts: Manganari, Psathi and Aghios Theodotis. The last two can also be reached on foot if you are up to a three-hour walk, and apart from the swimming offer a monastery, some Hellenistic ruins and an ancient aqueduct, along with traces of a temple.

Among the 'virgin' beaches, accessible by motorboat or on foot, are Volia, Miziri, Koumbaras, Almiros, Loretzainas, Diamoudia, Mouria, Plakoto (the 'tomb' of Homer), Kalo Avlaki, Agioupas, Kolitsani, Valma, Pepa, Kalamo, Tris Ekklesies and Yero Angeli. It is not suggested that you should memorise these names: they are mentioned as an assurance that escape is possible.

Where to stay The twenty-seven hotels, thirteen of them in Hora, provide a total of 497 rooms, and an estimated 1,200 additional beds are on offer in unlisted pensions, self-catering apartments and private homes. Nevertheless, not everyone who dosses down on the beaches in high summer does so out of choice. Conversely, not a single listed hotel stays open in winter.

Three of the hotels are second class, twelve are third class, and the rest are fourth or fifth.

In Hora itself, you could try the **Chryssi Akti** (second class, ten rooms, tel. 91 255) or the **Armadoros** (third class, twenty-seven rooms, tel. 91 201).

Outside Hora, an inquiry might be made at the **Ios** at Milopota (second class, forty-four rooms, tel. 91 224), the **Mare Monte** at Ormos (third class, twenty-seven rooms, tel. 91 564), the **Leto** at Kambou (fourth class, thirty-nine rooms, tel. 91 279) or the **Manganari Bungalows** at Manganari (second class, thirty-one rooms, tel. 91 215).

Where to eat The only real advice possible is to seek out the most promising-looking taverna close to where you are staying, or go for your swimming, and hope for the best. However, in Hora, fair words have been spoken of the **Caravanserai**, **Argyris**, **Pithari** and **Marco Polo**, as also of the **Korali** at Ormos.

Getting there From three to five ferries a day from Piraeus call at Ios, a voyage of about eleven hours.

Transport	A bus service from Ormos through Hora to Milopota; elsewhere, by taxi, small boat or on foot. Caique services to some of the main beaches.
From Ios	Ports of call on the Piraeus ferries and, in summer, local boats (for the most part daily) to Paros, Naxos, Myconos, Sikinos and Folegandros; and to other islands less frequently.
Telephone	Police 91 222 Coastguard 91 264 Clinic 91 227

Kea

Kea, pronounced Kay-a with the stress on the first syllable and known also by its Frankish name of Tzia, is the closest of the Cyclades to the Attica coast and for that reason is increasingly regarded by Athenian weekenders as an alternative to the more crowded Saronic islands. In less than three hours – an hour by bus to Lavrion and an hour-and-a-half on a ferry from there – you can be on a fairly typical Cyclades island without much fear of isolation by a sudden gale. In high summer it is obviously better to go midweek.

Area: 131 sq km. Length of coastline: 81 km.
Population: 1,652 (Hora 568 and Korissia 286).
Area telephone code: 0288.

History Excavations at Kefala indicate that Kea was inhabited at least 5,000 years ago. The Ionians built four towns: Ioulida (Ioulis) at the site of the present Hora, Korissia near the harbour of that name, Piiessa (more easily remembered and pronounced in its modern style of Pisses) on the south-west coast, and Karthaia on the south-east coast. Karthaia has more to show the modern visitor, including temples and a theatre, but is the hardest to reach – about 2 km off the road down the centre of the island.

A Titanic connection On 21 November, 1916, the British White Star liner *Britannic*, belonging to the same company that had owned the *Titanic*, was ripped open by an explosion while sailing three miles off the coast of Kea, and sank in 120 m of water. It had been converted into a First World War hospital ship, and at the time it sank was carrying British and ANZAC (Australian and New Zealand Army Corps) servicemen wounded in the Gallipoli campaign. Of the 1,061 aboard, of whom 396 were crew and medical staff, only twenty-one were lost when one of the lifeboats capsized.

In 1976 the French underwater explorer Jacques-Yves Cousteau, who had been contracted by the Greek authorities to prepare underwater films in the Aegean as part of a tourism promotion programme, decided to round out his research into Ancient Greek,

Byzantine and eighteenth- and nineteenth-century wrecks with photographs of the *Britannic*.

It took him three weeks to find it, he told a press conference in Athens at the time, because British Admiralty charts showed it eleven kilometres (seven miles) from where it actually lay. His photographs, he said, revealed a gash some 45 m long in the hull. This was sufficient to launch the Athens newspapers along two avenues of speculation, postulating that the sinking of the *Britannic* had been a propaganda weapon for the Allies. This is borne out by events of 1916 and 1917: Greece at that time was split between Venizelists and Royalists, the former seeking to take the country into the war on the side of the Allies (not altogether altruistically, since Turkey had joined Germany and Austria) and the latter anxious to preserve its neutrality, especially after the failure at Gallipoli. The impression created by the sinking of a clearly-marked hospital ship in Greek waters certainly assisted the war party, which eventually prevailed over the Royalists.

Even at the time, however, there was some surprise that so large a ship could have been sunk by a mine or torpedo of the relatively primitive kind then in use.

Cousteau's discovery of the gash in the hull led the Athens press to two basic suppositions:

● One, the more popular, that the ship had in fact been carrying munitions, and that it was the explosion of these rather than of the mine or torpedo that caused the fatal damage (a similar question was raised also after the torpedoing of the British passenger liner *Lusitania* off the south-west coast of Ireland in 1915).

● The second, that the ship had been scuttled by the British to provide a pretext for intervention against the Greek government for 'allowing hostile naval units to operate with impunity off the coasts of Greece.' Quoted in support of the second theory were the position of the ship, only five kilometres (three miles) off the coast, and the successful evacuation, to the point that no lives would have been lost at all but for the mishap to the lifeboat.

Either way, it was asserted, the British would not have wished the wreck to be located – a reluctance that would have explained the discrepancy in the Admiralty charts.

The questions were asked, but appear not to have been answered.

Bearings You land at **Korissia** on the north-west coast, where the ruins of a Temple of Apollo are partly covered by the sea, and can take a bus or taxi to the capital, Hora, 5 km away.

What to see **Hora**, despite much new construction, is still a pleasant, typical island town. It offers the remains of the Acropolis of Ioulida and an ancient wall, a Venetian castle with beautiful views of the valley, an archaeological museum and, within easy reach, both the three-storey Monastery of Aghia Marina, built around a Hellenistic tower, and the Lion of Kea, carved in or around the sixth century BC and said to be representative of a lion that dealt harshly with some nymphs because of their bad habit of killing women (one would imagine that it ought to be the other way about, but the texts do not appear to support the logical supposition; the smirk on the lion's face could equally denote satiety or self-congratulation).

Around the island

Oval in shape, Kea is unusually green, with attractive valleys and numerous offshore islets. The north-east coast is rocky, and indented with small coves; the better beaches are in the south-west.

The most impressive of the Kea monasteries, the eighteenth-century Panaghia Kastraki (Virgin of the Castle) on the north-east tip of the island, requires dedication to reach, but offers the reward of hospitality in a small guest-house.

Kean kid is snapped up whenever it appears in Athenian butcher shops.

Vourkari is a fishing village 2 km from Korissia, where American archaeologists have brought to light a Bronze Age settlement with a palace and houses. The beach there is adequate.

Beaches

Swimming is better at **Kountouros**, a fishing village on the south-west coast which has 700 inhabitants in summer but is almost deserted in winter; it is the nearest village to the ruins of ancient **Karthaia**, across the tip of the island. The best beach of all is at Pisses, just above Kountouros and 12 km south-west of Hora.

Where to stay

Kea has five listed hotels from second to fifth class with a total of 156 rooms, and approximately 250 beds on offer in islander homes. The **Kea Beach** at Kountouros (second class, eighty rooms, tel. 22 144) has a full restaurant, private beach, nightclub and swimming pool. Korissia has two beach hotels, **I Tzia Mas** (Our Kea) and **Karthea**; the former is second class (twenty-four rooms, tel. 31 305) and the latter third class (twenty-four rooms, tel. 31 222). In Hora you could try the second-class **Ioulis** (eleven rooms, tel. 22 177).

Where to eat

Islanders insist that you can eat well at any of the fish tavernas at Korissia, Kountouros, Vourkari and Pisses, but should go to the Hora tavernas for the best meat. Specifically recommended are the **Toundas** at Korissia, the **Vourkari**, **Aristos** and **Maroulis** at Vourkari, and the **Steki**, **Eleftheros** and **Morfovassilis** at Hora.

Getting there

Daily ferries from the Attica port of Lavrion, 16 nautical miles away.

Transport

Buses run frequently from Korissia to Hora and the west-coast beaches; less frequently elsewhere. Mopeds and bicycles for hire at Korissia.

From Kea

Two connections a week to Kythnos, 17 nautical miles away.

Telephone

Police 22 100
Coastguard 31 344
Clinic 22 200

Kimolos

Kimolos is a pale island of white houses and the chalk cliffs for which it is named (in village schools children still write on blackboards with *kimolia*); on the western circumference of the Cyclades islands, it is most often visited as a day trip from Milos.

Area: 35 sq km. Length of coastline: 38 km.
Population: 787 (a drop of 25 per cent in the ten years from the 1971 census).
Area telephone code: 0287.

The Franks, who left behind the inevitable castle, knew the island as Argentiera, from some small silver mines long since worked out. In the Middle Ages it exported clay for porcelain manufacture and fuller's earth for use in textile production. Some chalk is still mined.

Bearings You land at **Psathi**, a tiny village on the south-east coast that is almost deserted in winter, about 2 km from the capital.

What to see **Hora** consists of 'Old' and 'New' Hora. The most interesting feature of the former is that the group of houses in its centre make up a defensible square, with only narrow slit-windows in the walls facing outwards; it was designed as a makeshift fortress for when the pirates arrived. These houses have been abandoned since the Second World War, but there are plans to reconstruct some of them and preserve the rest. Hora has a small museum, some old churches and the better tavernas.

At **Koftou**, about an hour away on foot or by donkey but also reached by boat from Psathi, you may on a clear and windless day catch glimpses of stone blocks at the bottom of the sea; they are all that can now be seen of **Ancient Kimolos**. The island's main archaeological site, also an hour from Hora, is at **Ellinika**; there you can swim from white rocks.

For the really determined sightseer, there are caves at Vromolimni and Konsolinas, and the Monastery of Aghios Minas a full hour's hike from Hora.

Beaches Probably the best beaches are at Aliki and Prassa; smaller ones, where no one will notice what you are or are not wearing, can be reached on foot or by small boat.

Where to stay and eat There are no listed hotels, but about eighty non-hotel beds, most of them at Hora but a few at Psathi, Aliki and Prassa.

The coffee-shops double as tavernas, in that they will prepare rough meals to order, and you can also stock up on groceries and bakery products. At Hora there are the **Bohoris**, **Rampos** and **Tria Adelphia** (Three Brothers), at Psathi the **Ventouris** and **Spyros**, and at Aliki the **Passamihalis**.

Getting there Three ferries a week from Piraeus cover the 86 nautical miles in about eight hours, but it's easiest from Milos, a half-hour chug away.

Transport	There is a mini-bus, which sometimes runs from Psathi to Hora, but basically you use motorboats or donkeys.
From Kimolos	Ferry ports of call, and the Milos boats when weather conditions coincide with passenger demands. Of the three offshore islets, two – Aghios Andreas and Daskalio – can be reached by caique from Psathi, though there would seem little reason to go. The third, Polyaigos, is without a safe harbour and is difficult to approach in any but the calmest weather.
Telephone	Police 51 205 Coastguard 51 332 Clinic 51 222

Kythnos

The first island for ferries serving the western Cyclades, only four hours from Piraeus and two and a half for ships out of Lavrion, Kythnos cannot point to inaccessibility as explanation for the absence of tourism. Simply, it has not yet become a fashionable island. It offers a taste of old-style village life on a gentle island, greener than some, less windswept than others, but the swimming is only ordinary, there is little to attract the historian, and it can easily become crowded with Athenians on July and August weekends.

Area: 99 sq km. Length of coastline: 98 km.

Population: 1,502 (Driopis 701, Hora 631); the population has been declining steadily since the local iron ore mines failed to reopen after the Second World War, leaving the islanders dependent on farming, fishing and fruit.

Area telephone code: 0281.

Bearings	Ferries normally disembark their passengers at **Merihas**, the west-coast harbour below Hora and Driopis; if wind and sea are wrong, they use the east-coast harbour of **Loutra**, about the same distance from Hora but considerably further from Driopis. With a winter population of 93 (Loutra has only 44), Merihas is little more than a waterfront with adequate swimming from a sandy beach, a third-class hotel, a couple of tavernas and a few café-bars.
Sights to see	**Hora**, 8 km away, is a mix of traditional and new buildings clustered around the seventeenth-century Churches of the Metamorphosis (Transfiguration) and Aghios Savvas. Nearby is a monastery where a 'secret school' helped to keep the Greek language and culture alive during the Turkish occupation. You can also take a look at the island's new Aeolian Park, a modernistic wind-power complex created in 1981 with West German technical and financial assistance to help meet part of the local electricity requirements. **Cape Kefalas**, on the north-east tip of the island, offers the ruins

of a medieval castle, and **Kanala**, in the south-east, has a monastery and, below it, a beach with rooms for rent, summer tavernas and the island's only pine wood.

Beaches
Hora is inland: for swimming, you can take the bus back to Merihas or on to Loutra, or walk to Aghios Stefanos or Livadaki. **Driopis**, also inland and once the capital, is 5 km from Merihas and within easy walking distance of beaches at Kalo Livadi and Lefkas, or Aghios Stefanos. The usual motive for a visit to Driopis is to see the few ruins of Ancient Kythnos and the unremarkable cave of Katafiki.

At **Loutra** you can swim or take the waters. For the latter activity you would go to the Xenia Hotel, where the water from one spring is used for drinking and the other for soaking in. A local tradition says the water comes straight from Vesuvius, by an undersea conduit; whatever its actual source, it was highly regarded by the Romans.

Where to stay
The only two listed hotels, both of third class, are the **Xenia** at Loutra (forty-six rooms, tel. 31 217) and the **Possidonian** at Merihas (eighty-three rooms, tel. 31 244). Apart from that, there are an estimated 400 beds available, half at Loutra and half at Merihas, in small pensions, self-catering apartments and islander homes.

Where to eat
At Loutra you could look out for **Ta Adelphia** (The Brothers) and **Katerina**; at Hora **Ta Dendra** (The Trees), **Tzoyiou** and **Alafouzou**; at Driopis the **Gonidi**; and at Merihas the **Kalliopi** and **Yialos**.

Getting there
Daily boats from Piraeus (52 nautical miles) and five boats a week from Lavrion (30 nautical miles).

Transport
There are regular bus services on the Merihas–Hora–Loutra and Merihas–Driopis–Kanala routes. Other beaches, and the offshore islet of Aghios Loukas, can be reached by small boat. It is scarcely worth bothering with a car, especially since taxis are available.

From Kythnos
By 'ferry of the line' to Serifos, Sifnos and Milos, and by less frequent connections to Kea, Kimolos and Syros.

Telephone
Police 31 201
Coastguard 31 290
Clinic 31 202

The 'Little' Cyclades (Mikres Kyklades) – Donousa, Heraklia, Koufonisia, Schinousa, and other islands

A string of sparsely inhabited islands south and east of Naxos where you would look for footprints in the sand for reassurance that you are not entirely alone, these islands have no paved roads, no cars and no hotels, but provide you with a beach to yourself unless you are desperate for company. They lie between 114 and 125 nautical miles from Piraeus.

Area: Donousa 13 sq km, Heraklia 17 sq km, Koufonisia 5 sq km, Schinousa unlisted.

Population: Donousa 116, Heraklia 95, Koufonisia 237, Schinousa 140.

Area telephone code: 0285.

Bearings Reached from Naxos, you would go to one of these islands to find out if you should include yourself as being among those people who need people. If a storm blows up, you may have longer than you intended for the experiment. Evidence of past habitation is provided by traces of temples and houses, and Keros, now uninhabited, was once a kingdom. In the Turkish period the islands were pirate strongholds.

Donousa Donousa is the most easterly of the four islands and the most exposed, where families of shepherds and fishermen live in four tiny settlements. The fifty beds on offer in rented rooms are mainly around the harbour, as are the summer café-bars.

Heraklia Heraklia is somehow the most primitive of the Little Cyclades. You land at the harbour of Aghios Georgios, a quarter of an hour on foot from the ruins of a castle and an hour from Hora: of the ninety-five inhabitants reported in the 1981 census, Hora had sixty-two and Aghios Georgios thirty-three. The harbour has a community guesthouse with three rooms, and the island as a whole has about thirty beds on offer in private homes. The best beaches are at Aghios Georgios and Livadi, fifteen minutes away. The island's showpiece is a Cave of the Cyclops on the south-west coast.

Koufonisia Koufonisia actually consists of two islands, Epano (Upper) Koufonisia with a population of 232 and Kato (Lower) Koufonisia with five inhabitants. Epano Koufonisia, where the Naxos boats drop their passengers, has a small pension, a number of fish tavernas in the summer, a claimed 200 beds ultimately available and a dance hall! Walk along the coast in a south-easterly direction from the harbour and you come to one beach after another, at approximately five-minute intervals.

Schinousa Schinousa is an island of low hills with Hora, population 128, in the middle; landing is at Mersini, population 12, about a quarter of an hour's walk away. Though there are the inevitable ruins of a castle, the island's particular charm lies in its exquisite bays, especially the more sheltered ones along the south coast. Hora has a community guest-house, and there are about sixty non-hotel beds available.

Where to stay and eat You will probably have to settle for a room in an islander's home.

Look out for some little café-bar, and content yourself with fish straight from the sea, a plate of chips and a salad.

GAZETTEER

Getting there The three or four ferries a week from Piraeus follow inter-island schedules of such intricacy that the trip can take between thirteen and seventeen hours, and sometimes twenty-six hours to Donousa. It is more practical to use the daily Naxos–Amorgos ferries, which call at all four islands.

Transport Fishing boats, lifts on farm vehicles and feet.

From the four islands Naxos, Amorgos and ferry ports of call. If your taste runs to even smaller islets all to yourself, you can take a fishing boat to Keros, Antikeros, Drima, Aghios Ioannis, Daskalio or the three Makaries islets.

Each of the four islands has a clinic, where whoever picks up the receiver should have time to give general information, in Greek.

Telephone Donousa 61 306
Heraklia 71 388
Koufonisia 71 370
Schinousa 71 385

Milos

Associations with a kidnapped Venus, a famous atrocity, a macabre cemetery, a First World War naval base and the earliest known example of a monopoly situation are scarcely reasons to visit Milos, but they do add spice to what would otherwise be just another exceptionally beautiful island. Though almost a household name, and fairly easy to reach, Milos has not yet geared itself for tourism and still has no listed hotel above second class. Tucked away at the south-west corner of the Cyclades between Sifnos and Folegandros, it is 87 nautical miles from Piraeus and just under an hour by air from Athens.

Area: 150 sq km. Length of coastline: 125 km.
Population: 4,556.
Area telephone code: 0287.

History During the neolithic period, possibly as much as 10,000 years ago, Milos had an apparent monopoly on Aegean production of obsidian, an especially hard stone used for knives and cutting edges in general before metals were known. The practicability of the trade was demonstrated by an experiment in 1987 (see The Greeks and the Sea, p. 28).

Despite a well-argued and moving plea for forgiveness (the 'Melian Dialogue' of Thucydides), Milos was punished savagely by the Athenians for its support of Sparta during the Peloponnesian War: the men were massacred and the women and children were sold into slavery.

Milos apparently embraced Christianity early and fervently: catacombs near Tripiti, unique in Greece, contain more than 6,000 skeletons and can be visited except when 'temporarily closed'.

During the seventeenth and eighteenth centuries, Milos secured an enviable immunity from piracy by turning itself into a nest of pirates.

Venus de Milo

The Venus de Milo, now in the Louvre museum in Paris, was discovered in 1820. There is an abiding belief on the island that one day the missing arms will be found too, though no one is seriously looking for them. As with the Winged Victory of Samothrace, the Greeks are content that Venus should remain a Parisian for the simple reason that she is not integral to any particular site, in the way the Elgin Marbles are to the Parthenon. Tacitly, it is appreciated that she makes a more effective ambassadress in the Louvre than she would in an out-of-the-way provincial Greek museum attracting a few hundred casual visitors a year, or lost in the marble crowd at the Athens Archaeological Museum. Nevertheless, Milos is hopeful that perhaps, one day, 'the lady' will be back.

Though no one any longer pares his nails with a sliver of obsidian, bensonite, barium, perlite and kaolin are still mined on Milos and, with the island's agricultural production, help avert any sense that the future lies only with tourism.

Bearings

Disembarking at the port of **Adamas**, population 1,103, you appreciate at once why the bay of Milos – one that almost bisects the island – should have been a First World War naval base. Looking at the beaches on both sides of the bay, it is equally easy to understand why most of the island's villages and its holiday movement should be concentrated there.

What to see

Built in the 1830s, Adamas is 4 km from the capital, **Plaka** (known also as Milos town and sometimes as Hora) at the entrance to the bay. There are two French military cemeteries at Adamas, from the Crimean and First and Second World Wars.

Plaka, population 919, is a picturesque Cyclades village with a Venetian castle, remains of city walls, a partially restored Roman theatre, archaeological and folk museums (the former displaying a plaster replica of the Venus), and the nearby ruins of Ancient Milos where the Venus was discovered.

Within easy reach of Plaka are the third-century catacombs, once used also as a place of worship, and the north-coast settlement of **Filakopi**, winter population six, where British archaeologists in the last decade of the nineteenth century found three prehistoric towns one on top of another, dating from the third millennium to the Mycenaean era. The Papafranga cave near Filakopi, with a stretch of beach inside, is the more easily accessible of three Milos caves; those at **Sikia** and **Kleftiko** on the south-west tip make a greater impression but are hard to reach. Kleftiko takes its name, meaning 'Hideout', from the days when pirate caiques could find moorings there invisible from the sea; set among white cliffs and tiny islets, it is a ninety-minute hike from the road's end at the Monastery of Aghios Ioannis, but can be reached by caique from Adamas.

Beaches

Apollonia, population 233, on the north-east coast opposite

Kimolos, is a place to stay (though only in islander homes), eat, swim and take a caique to Kimolos or the once-volcanic offshore islets of Glaronisia (Seagull Islands). Apart from Apollonia and nearby Mandrakia, the main Milos beaches are along the sweep of the deep bay; for those along the south coast, you really need your own transportation.

Where to stay The twelve listed hotels (three second class, five third and four fourth) provide 249 rooms, and there are also approximately 600 non-hotel beds on offer. Recommended among hotels are the **Venus Village** at Adamas (second class, ninety-one rooms, tel. 22 020), beside a beach and with its own restaurant, and the third-class **Aphrodite** (Venus) **of Milos** (twenty-five rooms, tel. 22 132), also at Adamas, where you cater for yourself.

Where to eat At Adamas, apart from the **Venus Village** restaurant, you could look for the **Vamvakari**, **Ponorios**, **Themelis** and **Trapatseli**. The **Karamitsos** at Plaka has its following, as has the **Petrakis** at Apollonia, but all the beaches are served by fish tavernas in the summer.

Getting there Olympic Airways has up to three flights a day from Athens and there are from four to seven ferries a week from Piraeus, covering the distance in about eight hours.

Transport Buses between Adamas and Plaka and from both to the main villages and beaches, and caique services from Adamas. Mopeds for hire.

From Milos Ferry ports of call (including Serifos, Sifnos and Kimolos), and less regular connections with other Cyclades islands, the Dodecanese and Crete. Caique excursions to the offshore islets of Glaronisia, Antimilos and Arkouda.

Telephone Police 21 378
Coastguard 22 100
Olympic Airways 22 380
Clinic 21 222/21 218

Myconos

Written also as Mykonos, this is cosmopolitan Greece at its best and worst. Undeniably beautiful, Myconos can also be claustrophobic: you may easily feel yourself overcrowded, overcharged and, unless you are part of it, over-exposed to the younger generation. You can combine a visit to Myconos with trips to Syros, to which it belongs administratively, and Tinos; you have to go first to Myconos if you propose to make the pilgrimage to Delos.

Area: 85 sq km. Length of coastline: 81 km.
Population: 4,850 in 1981 (Myconos town 4,469), 3,234 in 1971 and

now estimated at 5,500. The steady increase is entirely due to tourism.
Area telephone code: 0289.

Mythology and history

The island is said to have acquired its name from a mythological hero named Mykonos, a direct descendant of Apollo. Also in mythology, Hercules slew and buried some giants there, whose tombs became the island's granite hills.

Inhabited since at least the ninth century BC, in ancient times Myconos basked in the reflected glory of Delos. Although an Ionian colony on the sea route between Piraeus and Samos, it played only a minor role in its own right and, on the basis of historical records, had only two cities, Myconos and Panormos on the north coast. A few remains of Panormos have been found, but it is only surmised that the present capital is built on the site of Ancient Myconos.

Curiously for an island of almost 400 churches, Christianity came later to Myconos than to most of its neighbours and worship of Dionysos survived longer; measured by the summer consumption of beer today, it would be tempting to conclude that the god of wine has simply adopted new technology.

A faithful ally of Athens in Classical times, Myconos saw its economy briefly improve during the period of Alexander the Great, became part of a Roman province, suffered constant pirate raids during the time of the Byzantine Empire, was taken by the Venetians in 1207 and the Turks in 1537, played a notable role in the 1821 Revolution, and was united with Greece along with the rest of the Cyclades islands in 1832.

The nucleus of Myconos town began to take shape in the fourteenth century, though in its present form it dates mainly from the eighteenth and nineteenth centuries.

In Classical times the Myconians (written also as Myconiotes) had a dubious reputation: 'Myconian' was a derisive appellation for avarice and miserliness, and for people who habitually went where they had not been invited or outstayed their welcome where they had been. Also, they were reputedly prone to baldness.

Myconos town

Ferries from Piraeus and Rafina tie up at a quay on the edge of the curving harbour. Since the town is closed to vehicular traffic, if your luggage is heavy you hire a man with a wheelbarrow; he will expect at least Dr 500 for a ten-minute push. Cruise liners are unable to enter the harbour, and disembark their passengers by cutter.

Myconos town is the long promenade – from a tiny beach where only the most undiscriminating will venture into the water to the Church of Paraportiani and Folk Museum at the other end of the waterfront – and the maze of narrow streets running back from the sea. The town's two squares both open on to the waterfront, and are ringed with shops, restaurants, bars and travel agencies.

Getting lost in Myconos is inevitable and part of the game: the streets are said to have been built that way to confuse the pirates, but

Shopping in Myconos

long before you become nervous you will have caught a glimpse of the sea and retrieved the waterfront.

The waterfront is given over to cafés and clothing and souvenir shops: two of the few streets that do run more or less straight, and parallel to it, house the shops selling gold jewellery, silverware, antiques and furs. The asking price of anything, but especially of the jewellery, is at least 20 per cent more than the shopkeeper hopes to get and probably 30 per cent above what he is prepared to settle for. The most desirable customers are cruise passengers, since they are likely to be wealthy and in too much of a hurry for serious haggling.

If you are staying in Myconos for, say, a week, identify what you really want to buy as early as possible and find out the asking price, chip away at it during successive visits over the next few days, and on your last morning resolutely declare what you are prepared to pay. If a bargain is then struck, it will be the best obtainable. The outcome will probably depend on the general business climate, and whether it is closer to the end than to the beginning of the tourist season.

Less expensive purchases include dresses, pullovers, lace, rugs and hats.

What to see

You might usefully spare an hour for the town's three museums: the Archaeological Museum (exhibits mainly from the necropolis of Rineia – see Delos, p. 188), the Museum of Popular Art (Folk Museum) near the Church of Paraportiani, and the new Aegean Maritime Museum set up by a Piraeus shipowner of Myconos origin, George Dracopoulos, and exhibiting ship models including the Thera ship (see p. 29) from the pre-Minoan period to the age of steam.

The two 'lady admirals'

The statue in the main waterfront square (where you go for some of the buses and all of the taxis) is of Mando Mavrogenous, a heroine of the 1821 Revolution; her house can be visited, though it rarely is except by Greeks. A daughter of the distinguished Byzantine family, she was born, raised and educated abroad, and was twenty-four when the Revolution broke out. She sold her estate in Austria and with the proceeds bought and equipped two ships and sailed them to Myconos. After helping to repel a Turkish attack on the island, she took the ships to Euboia and continued the struggle from there.

Mando Mavrogenous was one of two 'lady admirals' of 1821. The other was Bouboulina Laskari, who commanded the Spetses fleet in a series of naval engagements with the Turks. The Greeks honour them both, but waited until less than a decade ago to admit women into the modern Navy.

The Myconos churches

The Church of Paraportiani (literally, the church 'by the gates') is actually five churches in one – four on the ground floor and the fifth upstairs – each dedicated to different saints, and from that aspect is unique in Greece.

It should not be confused with the tiny Church of Aghios Nikolaos at the end of the waterfront, where Greek holiday-makers go to light candles for a calm voyage home.

An unusual church on a rooftop at the edge of the town is that of the Panaghia tou Gata (Virgin of the Cat). The story told is of a poor fisherman caught in a storm who promised to build a church for the Virgin if he returned safely to Myconos. He did – and then faced a poverty gap between the promise and its fulfilment. The answer came to him suddenly: he had said nothing in his prayer about the size of the church. So he built a miniature, 60 cm high, on the roof of his house. When a cat promptly moved in and had its kittens, the defilement forced him to remove the cross from the dome, but gave the church its lasting name.

The cubist architecture

The glory of Myconos town is the perfection of its scale and unity. Its designation as a protected traditional settlement means that new construction must accord with the basic characteristics of Cycladic architecture. As a result, all the new resort hotels are sited on south-coast bays, which is where their clients would have wished them anyway.

A locally-printed guidebook catches the essence of Myconos well: 'The streets of Myconos are narrow and cobbled with schistose flagstones, the nicks outlined in white. The white external staircases of the houses with their colourful banisters are uniformly aligned parallel with the house walls because of the narrowness of the lanes which wend their way around the houses, arranged in concentric zones. This veritable labyrinth is also a vestige of the town's protective measures against pirates, for there was no provision for fortification.'

The houses are whitewashed several times a year, and the streets are washed daily. Relief from the monotony of white is provided by flowers on balconies and stairways, and by blue and red doors and shutters.

The houses are made to seem taller by the narrowness of the streets; frequently, the ground floor is now used as a shop, or bar.

The same geometric style of architecture can be seen, possibly even better, on Sifnos and Folegandros.

An interesting suburb of Myconos which it is difficult to find except when thoroughly lost is Enetia (Venice), named for a line of eighteenth-century houses whose wooden balconies overhang the sea. They are said to have been particularly appreciated in the days before Myconos acquired an adequate sewerage system.

Peter the pelican

Somewhere along the waterfront, in between where the fishing boats tie up in the morning and the Paraportiani Church, you are likely to come across Peter and his elderly consort, Irene.

Myconos has had a pelican-in-residence for the best part of thirty years, represented by a succession of Peters. The present incumbent was a 1986 gift of a Munich travel agency, flown to the island after his predecessor had achieved an unusual feat for a town where cars are permitted only along the direct route to the ferry quay; he had been fatally injured in a traffic accident.

Since pelicans are apparently smart enough to recognise a cushy billet when they fall into one, Peter and Irene can safely be left to roam at will. They will pose with you for a photograph, but dislike having their beaks shaken.

Yehudi doesn't live here any more

The waterfront is definitely the place to sit and watch the Myconos world go by. Some ten or fifteen years ago, when the island's reputation was still unsullied, you could have expected to see Yehudi Menuhin and the ex-Empress Soraya of Iran, who had homes there, and Audrey Hepburn and Jackie Kennedy-Onassis, who were frequent visitors, while as A. E. Housman said of the doomed young lads of Ludlow, 'brushing your shoulder, unguessed-at and not to be told' would have been some of the world's more reclusive millionaires. Today, amid the procession of backpackers, you may still spot the occasional familiar face, though the figures that Greek eyes follow are most likely to be cabinet members and party leaders.

Yehudi doesn't live on Myconos any more, for reasons that he explained in a blistering letter to the then mayor of the island soon after his return in 1976 after a nine-year absence, caused by his refusal to visit Greece during the military dictatorship. He said he found the island filthy with uncollected garbage, his hideaway cottage in a remote bay at the back of the island half-destroyed, and his little piece of beach taken over by 'naked Beatniks of all sexes'. In his letter, published at the time in the Athens daily *Kathimerini*, he demanded urgent action before Myconos acquired, worldwide and irrevocably, the reputation of 'an island of ill fame'.

'In our travels around the world', he wrote to the mayor (the translation is from the Greek text published by *Kathimerini*), 'we have seen more charming places than I can possibly describe to you destroyed by the egoism and heedlessness of foreigners. In short, all the Mediterranean has been devastated, and it is exactly for this reason that the same locusts – for that is what they really are – have now invaded Greece, which they will devastate with the same heedlessness.'

When he was in Paris or London, he said, people asked him with astonishment how he could propose to live 'on this ill-famed island'.

'In less than a decade, your noble Myconos, where the visitors came for its own uniqueness and its proximity to the sacred island of Delos, has acquired the reputation of a place for all and every kind of decadence.'

He proposed a number of measures which, he wrote, could be taken quickly, without affecting the economic advantages deriving from tourism. Certain beaches should be set aside for the 'fashion' of nude bathing and heavy fines imposed for nudity elsewhere, as in France. There should be tighter controls on real estate purchase, construction and use. And shopkeepers and householders should be responsible for the cleanliness of the section of street fronting their properties.

These 'few simple things', he said, could help to dispel 'all the gossip about Myconos that is costing you the best type of foreigner.'

This was in 1976. Today, no one could deny that the streets of Myconos are spotlessly clean; this is the first thing that impresses the visitor, especially one who has stopped off in Athens on his way to the island. Zoning is strictly enforced. Nudism has been relegated to at least the comparatively isolated beaches, and elsewhere only toplessness is permitted. But Myconos has not reacquired the quality tourists it once had. Possibly fashions have changed, and possibly there are simply too many youths.

Also, the island is suffering the costs of its world-renowned tolerance of homosexuality and its suspected tolerance, which is rather a matter of outnumbered police, of narcotics carried in small quantities for personal use. Of the two main nudist beaches, Paradise is heterosexual and Super Paradise has effectively been taken over by male homosexuals. In addition, there are gay bars in the town itself and, despite greater police vigilance, there is little doubt that drugs are carried in many a rucksack.

Inevitably, the result is a connection made in Greece, and to some extent internationally, between Myconos and AIDS. Some of the wealthy Athenians with summer homes on the island have either stopped going there or, unwilling to deprive themselves of their holiday but disbelieving the medical assurances, go in spite of their hesitations but cook their meals at home. Restaurateurs have become accustomed to the sight of guests unwrapping their own knives and forks and pouring their wine into their own glasses.

Many Greeks, even now, are unconvinced that AIDS cannot be contracted from sheets, pillowcases, towels, cutlery, crockery, glassware and even contact with the sand of a beach on which an AIDS carrier has done his sunbathing. All this is damaging to Myconos.

The scepticism is a natural result of a diet of lies, half-truths and evasions on the state-controlled television channels. The Greeks feel sure they were lied to over the Chernobyl nuclear disaster, being told there was no cause for concern at a time when less-affected countries were taking urgent precautions, and recognise that they are lied to routinely on less vital matters. It would be strange if they did not assume that they are also being lied to on AIDS.

A word on the *meltemi*

No island is more savagely lashed than Myconos by this summer wind, which can be anticipated as a daily occurrence between the second half of July and the beginning of September.

Myconians accord the *meltemi* three self-explanatory classifications: Kareklaris, the chair-thrower; Kavalaris, the unseater of horsemen; and Kampanaris, the church bell-ringer.

Though the *meltemi* does help to avert airlessness in the narrow streets, it is in no way a cooling wind. Its saving grace is that it dies away at sunset: if you are kept awake all night by wailing it is not the *meltemi* but a normal gale. It can sweep your drink and cigarettes off a café table, sandpaper you on an exposed beach, and guarantee an uncomfortable voyage to Piraeus. Because of the *meltemi*, only one of the island's 'organised' beaches (beaches served by tavernas and provided with chairs and umbrellas) is on the north coast, in the deep bay of Panormos; that is preferred by wind-surfers.

Around the island

The best roads are the one across the middle of the island from Myconos town to the north-east corner, and the branches off it to the sheltered south-coast beaches.

Ano Mera (Upper Place), 8 km from Myconos, is the only village in the interior of an island that, if it were not for the absence of a distant horizon, could easily suggest moorland country: dark brown, infertile earth with sparse vegetation, and narrow dirt roads lined with walls of uncemented stone. You will see an occasional vineyard and a few flocks of sheep and goats, but you will look in vain for a tree. If you stop at Ano Mera it will be for refreshments and a visit to the eighteenth-century Monastery of the Panaghia of Tourlianos and its museum of ecclesiastical artifacts.

Beaches

The closest beaches, only about 3 km from the town by bus from the ferry quay, are at Aghios Stefanos and Tourlos, where the cruise liners anchor on windy days. They are not particularly attractive, but may be considered if you have only a few hours to spare.

Platy Yialos on the south coast is not much further, though less well served by buses: if you find it unpleasantly crowded, you can take a caique from there to Paradise or Super Paradise to join the nudists.

Ornos, at the head of a deep bay, is probably the island's most picturesque beach, and certainly the one with the largest hotels. Psarrou and Elias, further along the south coast, are quieter, and Kalafati, close to the south-east corner but still only 12 km from the town, combines a long, sandy beach with good eating at waterside tavernas. Unless you prefer surf, you would head north for Panormos only on a windless day.

Where to stay

The Hotel Chamber of Greece directory lists ninety-nine hotels on Myconos with a total of 2,053 rooms, for an average of only 20.75 rooms per hotel. By category, there are two first class hotels, twenty-five second class, twenty-eight third class, twenty-four fourth class and twenty fifth class. Only five of the hotels, all outside the town, have more than fifty rooms. Most of them are less than twenty years old, and all of them fill easily.

If you arrive in peak season without a booking, you should be able to find accommodation by walking to the ferry quay, just before the boats arrive from Piraeus, and waiting to be accosted. Myconos has a seemingly inexhaustible supply of rooms in private homes, most of them unregistered because of the general Greek reluctance to pay taxes.

In Myconos town you could try the first-class **Leto** (twenty-five rooms, tel. 22 207) or second-class **Calypso** (thirty-one rooms, tel. 23 415). Best bets outside the town would include the second-class **Alkistis** at Aghios Stefanos (102 rooms, tel. 22 332), the first-class **Ano Mera** at Ano Mera (sixty-seven rooms, tel. 71 215), the second-class **Aphrodite** at Kalafati (135 rooms, tel. 71 367), or the second-class **Petassos Beach** at Platy Yialos (forty-four rooms, tel. 23 437).

The short distances and good bus services make the beach hotels infinitely preferable, unless you propose to spend your nights in the discos of Myconos town.

Where to eat

Myconos town has any number of eating factories and a few good restaurants and tavernas. You can rely on the **Edem** (in a garden in the centre of the town) and the **Philippi**, **Eva's Garden**, **Katrine**, **El Greco**, **Alexandra**, **Ta Kymata**, **Makis**, **Sardam** and **La Scala**.

All the little beach-side tavernas are magnificently sited, and the fish is usually fresh.

Among snacks on offer all day in Myconos town you will find hamburgers, cheeseburgers, toasted sandwiches, pizzas, croissants plain and stuffed and baked potatoes.

If you wish to sleep at night in Myconos town, you may find earplugs useful. Nowhere else in Greece are there so many discos in such concentration; while they are required to close at 3 a.m., the party then continues until dawn at the Yacht Club and the Pigeon House.

Getting there

Olympic Airways has up to twelve flights a day from Athens, to an airport 4 km outside the town (flying time fifty minutes).

There are at least two passenger/car ferries a day from Piraeus in summer (six or seven hours, depending on whether the intermediate call is at Tinos or Syros), and daily ferries from Rafina on the Attica coast.

Almost every cruise itinerary out of Piraeus includes an afternoon at Myconos, for basic sightseeing, shopping, sunset and dinner. Alternatively, one of the world's finest sunset views has to be that of Myconos from the deck of a liner anchored a mile offshore: as the colours fade from white through pink to various shades of blue, and the lights flicker on along the waterfront and in the houses, the dilemma is which of the magic moments to try to capture on film. The stillness you have to remember. It is almost worth not going ashore, or getting back on board early.

Transport

Myconos has 120 km of roads, mostly dirt, and in summer conscripts all its school coaches in order to lay on a full bus service. There are then nineteen buses a day from Myconos to Aghios Stefanos, nineteen to Platy Yialos, eighteen to Ornos (ten of them continuing to Aghios Yiannis), eleven to Kalafati and eight to Elias.

Taxis are available (unless going to the airport, you should expect to share), and cars, jeep-type vehicles and mopeds can be hired. Though the roads to the main beaches have now been asphalted, they are nar-

From Myconos

row and winding and require the utmost care.

By air to Crete, Rhodes, Samos, Thera (Santorini) and Chios.

By Piraeus ferry to Tinos and Syros, and by Rafina ferry to Andros.

By local boat to Paros, Naxos, Ios, Thera and Crete, and some of the smaller islands en route.

And, of course, to Delos by caique.

Telephone

Police 22 482
Coastguard 22 218
Olympic Airways 22 490
Taxi rank 22 400
Clinic 22 274

Naxos

Lord Byron was greatly taken with Naxos, and so today are those who visit it for its beautiful countryside; the inhabitants claim, with probable justification, that no other island in the Cyclades has so lovely an interior. However, tourists drawn to Greece by sea and beaches have less to get enthusiastic about.

The largest of the Cyclades islands, and to some extent the market-garden and dairy of the others, Naxos is very much a working island and one used to managing without much of a holiday movement: Naxos cheese, of the Gruyère family (*graviera Naxou*), and the island's thick-skinned potatoes are prized throughout Greece. Since farm vehicles can operate very well on dirt roads, communications among the forty or more villages still leave much to be desired. South of Myconos, east of Paros and north of the 'Little' Cyclades islands, Naxos is 103 nautical miles from Piraeus.

Area: 428 sq km. Length of coastline: 148 km.

Population: 14,037, with 3,844 living in Hora and only two other communities – Apirathos and Filoti – claiming more than 1,000 inhabitants.

Area telephone code: 0285.

Mythology and history

In mythology, Naxos was the island of Dionysos and Ariadne. Theseus, on his way back from Crete after slaying the Minotaur with the help of Ariadne, daughter of King Minos, abandoned the lady on Naxos. Caught on a kind of rebound, she found solace in the arms of Dionysos (by interpretation, she took to the bottle?), who made an honest woman of her. Richard Strauss set the story to music in *Ariadne auf Naxos*.

In Classical times, Naxos was one of the first islands to exploit its marble, regarded as second in quality only to that of Paros, and became a home of sculptors. During the first millennium of the Christian era it was ravaged with peculiar frequency and savagery by pirates, to the point that all the coastal settlements had to be abandoned.

After the Crusader sack of Constantinople in 1204, Naxos was allotted to the Venetian Marco Sanudi along with the titles of Duke of the Archipelago and Sovereign of the Dodecanese, and became the seat of the Duchy of Naxos. The Sanudi and Crispi families held out for well over three centuries, until the island fell to the Turks in 1566.

Town and island

Ferry passengers disembark at **Hora**, known also as Naxos town, a hillside settlement of steep and narrow streets dominated by a Venetian castle. On the left of the harbour entrance is the islet of Palatia, accessible by causeway, with the ruins of a never-completed Temple of Apollo of the sixth century BC; only the gateway, the Portaria, is still standing.

The castle complex includes a Roman Catholic Cathedral (though its inhabitants are now mainly Orthodox, Naxos still has a Catholic bishop) and a small archaeological museum housed in a former French convent. Greek visitors make a point of seeing the house, once a school, where Nikos Kazantzakis was a pupil for two years. Mycenaean remains can be seen at Grotto, just outside the port, from where there is also a good view of a tiny islet just large enough to hold the picturesque Church of the Panaghia Myrtidiotissa ('smelling of myrrh').

Pretty villages

If you choose to head inland – something you can hardly avoid if you travel by road – you will find a wealth of pretty villages in the farm country to the north of Mount Zia, at 1,001 m the tallest in the Cyclades, and one white monastery after another. **Agersani**, known also as Aghios Arsenios, is a Venetian settlement with a thirteenth-century monastery and Byzantine church; **Apirathos** is a jewel of a village with notable Venetian remains, but is 12 km from the nearest beach; **Engares** spreads along the banks of a small river and was for a time the home of Kazantzakis; and **Filoti**, on the slopes of Mount Zia, is the most admired of the higher villages.

Beaches

While the best beaches, in the sense of the more sheltered ones, are strung out along the west and south coasts, the road network is such that the most accessible ones are in the north. The beaches southwards of Hora lie at distances of between 6 and 25 km, but are generally reached by boat. Apollona, a fishing village on the north coast 48 km away, is attractive but can be windy; the same applies to slightly nearer ones on the east coast.

Where to stay

Of the island's sixty listed hotels (909 rooms in total), thirty-three are in Hora and another eighteen at nearby Aghios Georgios. More than 1,500 of the island's estimated 2,300 non-hotel beds are also in Hora. The only hotel with more than forty rooms is the **Mathiassos bungalow complex** at Hora (second-class, 102 rooms, tel. 22 200). You might try for a vacancy at the **Ariadne** (second class, twenty-four rooms, tel. 22 452) or **Coronis** (third class, thirty-two rooms, tel. 22 626) at Hora, or the **Iliovasilema** (third class, twenty-one rooms, tel. 22 107) or **Naxos Beach** (third class, thirty-seven rooms, tel. 22 928) at Aghios Georgios.

Where to eat Favoured tavernas in Hora include **Voutzias**, **Koutouki**, **Tsitas**, **Kastro**, **Antonis**, **Apolafsis**, **Kali Kardia**, **Meltemi**, **Oneiro** and **Nissaki**. At Aghios Georgios look out for **Kavouri**, **Trata**, **Diogenis**, **Asteria**, **Kalyva**, **Flisvos**, **Paradissa** and **Medusa**.

Getting there At the moment, by ferry from Piraeus (up to seventeen a week, involving a journey of from six to eight hours) and Rafina (two or three a week, seven hours). But an airport should be ready in 1989.

Transport Buses run frequently from Hora to the main villages and west- and north-coast beaches, and less frequently along the east coast. Cars, Jeep-type vehicles and mopeds can be rented, taxis and small boats are available, and local travel agencies organise excursions.

From Naxos Ferry ports of call, summer connections with Myconos, Ios, Thera (Santorini), the Dodecanese and Crete, and a daily service in summer from Hora to Amorgos via the 'Little' Cyclades islands (Donousa, Heraklia, Koufonisia and Schinousa).

Telephone Police 22 100
Coastguard 22 300
Clinic 22 346

Paros

Egg-shaped Paros, of the Parian marble, the Church of the Hundred Doors, Greece's second valley of the butterflies, some of the finest beaches in the Cyclades and a nightlife that is lively enough but less concentrated and therefore less obtrusive than on certain of its noisier neighbours, is an island that promises to become a tourist resort but at the same time seems intent on preserving a balance between the traditional and the modern, between the needs of its inhabitants to pursue livelihoods that for the most part have no connection with tourism and those of its visitors for comfort and variety. On Paros, nothing is in excess. Even in July and August, when Greek and foreign holiday-makers can temporarily outnumber the resident population, Paros escapes a sense of overcrowding.

Situated in the heart of the Cyclades, Paros is surrounded clockwise from the north by Delos, Myconos, Naxos, Ios, Sikinos, Folegandros, Kimolos, Sifnos, Serifos and Syros. It is a hub of communications for the island-hopper, 95 nautical miles from Piraeus, and can also be reached by air from Athens.

Area: 194 sq km. Length of coastline: 118 km.

Population: 8,516 (including Antiparos), with 3,312 in the capital, Parikia, and 1,725 in Naoussa. The Paros–Antiparos total rose by 1,202 in the ten years to 1981, largely because of the boost to the local

economy provided by tourism.
Area telephone code: 0284.

Unlucky for Miltiades

The Minoans used Paros as a naval base; subsequently it became a sea power in its own right and a founder of colonies, among them Thassos. Miltiades, the hero of the Battle of Marathon fought against the Persians, was fatally wounded there while leading a punitive expedition after Paros had sided with the enemy. Decline followed a lost war with Naxos. Occupied by Macedonians and later by Romans, Paros then experienced a dark age until the arrival of the Venetians in 1207 and its incorporation into the Duchy of Naxos. The Turks took it in 1537 and the Russians in 1770, staying for only seven years and using it as an anchorage for their Black Sea fleet. The Turkish reoccupation was short: Paros played an active role in the Independence Revolution and rejoined Greece with the rest of the Cyclades.

Parian marble was prized in antiquity for its translucence. That from the Pendeli quarries was good enough for the Athens Parthenon, and is good enough today for household sinks and kitchen floors, but Parian marble was employed for the Venus de Milo, the Hermes of Praxiteles and, in the nineteenth century, for the tomb of Napoleon in Les Invalides in Paris. The quarries, with their winding galleries, can still be visited on the eastern slopes of Mount Profitis Elias.

Parikia and the church

The port-capital of **Parikia** lies at the head of a west-coast bay, on the site of the ancient capital. From the deck of a ferry, you see first an old windmill beside the quay and, a little back from the water in a clump of trees, a large stone-built Byzantine church with red-tiled roofs: the Church of the Panaghia Ekatondapiliani (Virgin of the Hundred Doors).

Regarded as perhaps the greatest church in the Aegean after Nea Moni on Chios, and believed to date from the reign of the Byzantine Emperor Justinian in the sixth century, it is worth going out of your way to see. According to one legend, the construction was supervised by Isidore of Miletus but carried out by his pupil Ignatios. On completion, the church so impressed Isidore that he went for Ignatios in a fit of jealous rage and tried to throw him off the roof; in the struggle, both fell to their deaths. Another legend holds that the original church on the site of the present building was commissioned by St Helena, the British-born mother of Constantine the Great, in fulfilment of a vow made to the Virgin when she was caught in a storm on her way to the Holy Land and succeeded in reaching shelter on Paros.

Though continuously restored, and substantially altered after earthquakes in the eighth and tenth centuries, the Ekatondapiliani retains its essentially Byzantine aspect. It is in fact three interlocking churches: the main church of the Panaghia, a smaller one dedicated to Aghios Nikolaos, and a baptistery. You will find a hundred doors only if you count the windows also. Icons on display include one attributed to St Luke.

The church houses the island's Byzantine museum, and a nearby archaeological museum exhibits treasures of earlier periods, including a fifth-century BC Wingless Victory.

On the hill above Parikia are the ruins of an acropolis, the Venetian castle and several old churches; an unexcelled view can be obtained from the Monastery of the Aghii Anargyri (the saints Anargyros) at the top.

The quayside windmill, which in summer becomes a tourist information centre, is where the four main business and shopping streets of Parikia converge. Hotels and restaurants are mostly along the waterfront.

Around the island

Buses from Parikia cross the island to Lefkes and Marpisa, and run north to Naoussa and south to Pounda and Aliki.

Five km from Parikia along the road to **Pounda**, a track leads left to the Valley of the Butterflies. Less well known and smaller than its Rhodian counterpart, it makes a pleasant walk: mules are available for the indolent.

Life at **Naoussa**, 12 km from Parikia, centres on the fishing port and the main square: from the square a narrow street leads through a medieval arch into the older part of the town, and eventually to the harbour. Beaches in both directions, within easy walking distance, include Kolimbithres, Platy Ammos, Santa Maria and Ambelas: at Kolimbithres curious rock formations are sometimes described as lunar, but the beach fronting them and the water are thoroughly Mediterranean.

Beaches

Local travel agents will give you lists of between eighteen and twenty-four recommended beaches. All easy to reach, they provide the explanation for the facility with which Paros copes with its holiday traffic.

Where to stay

Paros has eighty-three listed hotels with a total of 1,469 rooms: thirty-four of the hotels are in Parikia and twenty-three in Naoussa. By category, they comprise one first class, sixteen second class, forty-five third class, ten fourth class and eleven fifth class. There are also at least 3,500 beds available in rented rooms.

The island's helpful Mayor, Stylianos Frangoulis, says hotels in which he would confidently reserve rooms for his friends include:

- The first-class **Holiday Sun** at Pounda (fifty-three rooms, tel. 22 371), which combines a good beach, a view to Antiparos and the island's only tennis court.
- The second-class **Xenia** (twenty-three rooms, tel. 21 394) built in traditional style on a hill 600 m from Parikia harbour.
- The second-class **Apollon** (twenty-three rooms, tel. 22 364) on Livadia beach near Parikia, in Louis XIV style.
- The second-class **Aigaio** (twenty-four rooms, tel. 22 153) on the coastal road outside Parikia, and the third-class **Asteria** (thirty-six rooms, tel. 21 797) and **Nikolas** (forty-three rooms, tel. 22 259).

At Naoussa, the third-class **Swiss Home** (nine rooms, tel. 51 633) and third-class **Kouros** (fifty-five rooms, tel. 51 000), the former in island style and the latter neo-Classical, both only a few metres from the sea.

● And the other **Xenia**, also second class (fourteen rooms, tel. 71 248) at Lefkes and the second-class **Afrodite** at Aliki (twenty rooms, tel. 21 986).

Where to eat

Again, the Mayor has his little list:

● In Parikia, the **Parostia** 150 m from the harbour for seafood, the **Kyriakos** (in a garden), the **Tamarisko**, the **Thanasis**, the **Rodies** and the **Mouragio**.

● On the coastal road near Parikia, the **Corfoleon** and **International**.

● At Naoussa, the **Minoa** in the hotel of the same name and the **Secret Garden**.

● Especially for fish, the **Aliki** at Aliki and the **Damianos** at Ambella, near Naoussa.

For afterwards, apart from discos and bars, there are two nightclubs: the **Elitas** 2 km outside Parikia and the **Parianos** on the Naoussa road.

Getting there

According to season, there are up to five ferries a day from Piraeus (five to seven hours) and five a week from Rafina. There are also from five to eight flights daily by light aircraft from Athens.

Transport

Between 8 a.m. and 9 p.m., nine buses carry out twenty-five services linking Parikia with the main villages and beaches. All but 8 km of the 65-km road network is asphalted. Cars, mopeds and bicycles can be rented.

From Paros

Daily ferry connections with Naxos, Ios, Thera (Santorini), Myconos, Tinos and Sifnos, and four or five a week with Syros, Amorgos, Donousa, Koufonisia, Ikaria and Samos. Less frequent services to Sikinos, Folegandros, Serifos and Anafi. Crete can be reached twice a week by ferry and three times a week by hydrofoil, and there is a weekly connection with the Dodecanese.

Local boats provide eight sailings a day to Antiparos and daily excursions to Naxos, Delos and Myconos.

Telephone

Police 21 221/21 673
Coastguard 21 240
Tourist office 21 670
Olympic Airways 21 900
Clinic 21 339/21 235
The Mayor 22 078

Antiparos

The Paros offshore island, once joined to its larger neighbour but now separated by a narrow channel, Antiparos would scarcely be worth visiting if it were not for its famous cave. Despite a sudden tourist development over the past decade, its movement still consists largely of day-trippers from Paros.

Area: 35 sq km. Length of coastline: 25 km.
Population: 635.
Area telephone code: 0284.

Bearings The landing is made at **Hora**, known also as Kastro from its Venetian castle. The harbour is attractive enough; small hotels, tavernas and cafés along the waterfront and a central street leading to the main square, from where it is an easy walk to the ruins of the fifteenth-century fortress. On Saliangos, one of a chain of islets protecting the harbour, archaeologists have discovered traces of a neolithic settlement.

Antiparos' cave Caiques or the island's only bus service will take you to **Soros**: it is a half-hour walk from there to the cave, unless you prefer to rent a mule. With a maximum width of 70 m and covering an area of 5,600 sq m, the cave consists of a sloping vault, 350 m at its highest altitude, with a series of caverns at different depths. Among its stalagmite and stalactite formations is one known as the Holy Table (altar), where Holy Communion is said to have been celebrated during the seventeenth century. Some of the stalactites were removed and taken to St Petersburg for display during the brief Russian occupation in the latter part of the eighteenth century. The Church of Aghios Ioannis at the entrance to the cave dates from 1774.

Beaches The swimming at Antiparos is adequate, though hardly better than at Paros. Preferred beaches include Psaraliki and Sifnaikos Yialos only five and ten minutes respectively on foot from Hora, and, on the south coast, Aghios Georgios opposite the islet of Despotiko.

Where to stay Antiparos has four listed hotels in Hora, with a total of seventy-six rooms, as well as approximately 700 non-hotel beds. The top-category hotel is the **Chryssi Akti** (third class, nine rooms, tel. 61 206), the biggest is the **Madalena** (fourth class, thirty-five rooms, tel. 61 220), and the newest is the **Korali** (fifth class, fourteen rooms and at latest report still awaiting a telephone). This leaves the **Anargyros** (fourth class, eighteen rooms, tel. 61 204).

Where to eat Hungry day-trippers have a choice among no fewer than nine restaurant/tavernas at Hora: **Anargyros**, **Ta Asteria** (The Stars), **Klimataria**, **Bonos**, **Signioris**, **Garden**, **Marios** and the two known as **Morakis**, one run by Spyros and the other by Manolis. At Aghios Georgios in the summer there are the **Zombas** and the **Anna**.

Getting there By caique from Paros. In high summer, departures are hourly from

	Parikia (a forty-five-minute trip) and half-hourly from Pounda (a five-minute crossing). From Antiparos you can explore the islets of Saliangos and Despotiko.
Transport	There are no cars on the island, and only the one road from Hora to Soros, but mopeds can be hired.
Telephone	Police 61 202 Clinic 61 219

Santorini (see Thera, p. 224).

Serifos

Serifos is a lazy person's island; there are so many good beaches within an easy walk of the port that hotels have been built nowhere else. Though these easily get crowded in July and August, you should have little competition on the more remote beaches, where nudity is observable but not officially observed. In the western Cyclades between Kythnos and Sifnos, Serifos is a peaceful, brown island 73 nautical miles from Piraeus.

Area: 73 sq km. Length of coastline: 81 km.
Population: 1,133 (Hora 409, Livadi 247).
Area telephone code: 0281.

According to which version of the myth you prefer, Serifos is either where Perseus killed the Gorgon Medusa or where he used her severed head to petrify Polydeuces.

From a distance, it does look like a huge rock; on closer approach, Hora can be seen perched on a hill above the port, and the impression of aridity turns out to have been erroneous.

Bearings Landing is at **Livadi**, the harbour and main tourist resort, from where you can walk or take small boats to such beaches as Livadaki, Karavi, Lia, Aghios Sostis, Psili Ammos, Aghios Ioannis and Koutala. You can also take a bus to the capital, **Hora**, 5 km away; though not geared for tourism, Hora has the remains of a Venetian castle, a small museum and some interesting churches. The beaches on the north and west coasts are quieter, but likely to be windy during the *meltemi* season.

Serifos also has some picturesque monasteries which, though scarcely a sufficient reason to visit the island, are worth a look at if you happen to be staying there.

Where to stay The five listed hotels, all in Livadi, are of second to fifth class and offer eighty-five rooms. The two third-class hotels, accounting for fifty-five of the rooms and therefore most likely to have a bed available, are the **Maistrali** (tel. 51 381) and **Serifos Beach** (51 209),

Where to eat	both less than 50 m from the sea. Non-hotel beds are estimated at around 500. There are only three 'permanent' restaurants on Serifos, all in Livadi – the **Stamatis**, **Cavo d'Oro** and the restaurant of the **Serifos Beach** hotel, which specialise in fish and can usually offer lobster. Elsewhere, including Hora, small café-bars tend to change ownership every year.
Getting there	The ferries from Piraeus – at least one a day and sometimes two – cover the distance in about five hours.
Transport	Buses and caiques from Livadi, taxis, mopeds and bicycles for hire, and lifts on farm vehicles.
From Serifos	Ferry ports of call, more or less daily boats to Kythnos, Sifnos and Milos, and one or two boats a week to Kimolos, Thera (Santorini) and Syros.
Telephone	Police 51 300 Coastguard 51 470 Clinic 51 202/51 294

Sifnos

Sifnos, an island of the western Cyclades guarding the approaches to Paros and Naxos, is associated in the Greek mind with good food and Nikos Tselemendes. It displays the cubist architecture of the Cyclades in its greatest perfection, combining it with well-watered greenery, and a long time ago its inhabitants committed a historic blunder. It lies 76 nautical miles from Piraeus, and has a growing tourist movement.

Area: 73 sq km. Length of coastline: 70 km.

Population: 2,087 (841 in Apollonia and 732 in Artemonas, towns named for the god Apollo and goddess Artemis).

Area telephone code: 0284.

Mythology and history	Herodotus mentions Sifnos for its gold and silver, and supporting evidence of wealth is offered by the sixth-century Treasury of the Sifnians at Delphi. While it is not known whether the mines were worked out, flooded or sank beneath the sea in an earthquake, production ceased and Sifnos suddenly became poor. The mythological explanation is that the Sifnians were required to present a gold egg every year to their protector, Apollo. Once, in the earliest semi-recorded example of a confidence trick that came unscrewed, they tried to fob him off with a gilt imitation; in retaliation, he sank their mines. The Romans used Sifnos as a place of exile, the Slavs, Arabs and pirates raided it, and the Venetians and Turks held it longest. Meanwhile the Sifnians were expanding a reputation for quality olive oil

into one for quality cooking. Sifnian chefs were in demand in Constantinople, just as they were later in the Athens of Kings Othon and George I. Nikos Tselemendes, who was to Free Greece what Mrs Beeton was to Victorian England, was born on Sifnos: a Tselemendes cookery book, though continuously revised and expanded to a point where it bears little resemblance to the original, will still hold pride of place on any kitchen bookshelf regardless of whether the modern housewife has time, money or patience to lavish on recipes pre-dating the can-opener.

You can still eat unusually well on Sifnos. You might sample, among dishes that make up the island's 'flavour', a local *rovithia* (chickpea) soup that is stewed longer and with a greater variety of herbs than is usual in Greece, the *boureki* sweet of honey, almonds and sesame, and the local variations on *bougatsa* and *amygdalopita*, respectively custard and almond pie. You will be delving back into history, to the blissful times when a calorie was simply the amount of heat needed to raise the temperature of one gram of water one degree centigrade, and had nothing to do with obesity.

Around the island

You land at **Kamares** (population 110) on the west coast, where the long beach is by no means the island's best. Before leaving, or on your way back, you could visit one of the potteries that keep alive a centuries-old Sifnos tradition, and also take a look at the eighteenth-century Monastery of the Panaghia Toso Nero (Virgin of the So-Much Water). If you think about the name, you will be somewhat prepared for what you will see later: an island of tiny white villages in a sea of greenery, watered by an abundance of springs that relieve the inhabitants of any need to plan or plead for desalination plants.

Apollonia, the capital, is roughly in the centre of the island, 6 km from Kamares. Built on three hills, it is an unspoiled Cyclades town with a folk museum in the central Square of the Heroes, five hotels, a good supply of tavernas and two old monasteries within easy walking distance.

From ancient times until the eighteenth century, the Sifnos capital was at **Kastro** on the east coast, 3 km from Apollonia, with a population touching 2,000. Today Kastro is a medieval hillside village with only fifty inhabitants. Built for defence, the houses on the outside form a kind of wall, with tiny windows and doors only a metre high – the intruder had to poke his head through first, offering it for clubbing. Venetian emblems survive on many of the houses, and some of the churches still have both Orthodox and Roman Catholic altars. You can visit the Venetian castle and site of a Classical acropolis, as well as a small archaeological museum, and walk to quiet but pebbly beaches at Seralia and Palati.

There are particularly rich pickings on Sifnos for monastery collectors.

Beaches

For swimming, the places to go are Platy Yialos (population 52) on the south-east coast, Faros (population 21) a couple of kilometres further along the same road, or Vathy (population 72), a west-coast fishing village in a lagoon-like bay accessible only by boat or along footpaths – those who love it hope a road will never be built.

Where to stay

Sifnos has eleven listed hotels, all of second or third class, with a total of 147 rooms: five are in Apollonia, three in Kamares, two in Platy Yialos and one in Artemonas, a flourishing inland town a tidy stroll from the nearest beach. You could try the **Artemon** at Artemonas (third class, twenty-three rooms, tel. 31 303), or the **Platy Yialos** (formerly **Xenia**) at Platy Yialos (second class, twenty-two rooms, tel. 31 224). The approximately 1,200 non-hotel beds on offer include a few in some of the monasteries.

Where to eat

At Kamares, the **Boulis**, **Kapetan Andreas**, **Avra** or **Nikos**; at Apollonia, the **Krevatina**, **Sofia**, **Kypros** or **Mangana**; at Kastro, the **Tzifakis** or **Maria Menengaki**; at Platy Yialos the **Smaragdis** or **Ta Kymata** (Waves); at Faros the **Provos** or **Chrysopighi**; and at Vathy the **Korakis** or **Neroutsos**.

Getting there

The daily ferries from Piraeus cover the distance in six hours.

Transport

Buses from Kamares to Apollonia and Artemonas and the main east-coast beaches; elsewhere, on foot or by small boat. Taxis, cars and mopeds for hire.

From Sifnos

Piraeus ferry ports of calls; local boats to Paros and Naxos (daily) and Serifos and Milos (less than daily).

Telephone

Police 31 210 (Apollonia), 31 977 (Kamares)
Coastguard 31 617
Clinic 31 315

Sikinos

Sikinos is a long way from tourism: if your investments are doing only reasonably well, and you stay a week there, you should be worth more on leaving than when you arrived. Lying 113 nautical miles from Piraeus, it is 10 nautical miles from Ios and 14 from Folegandros. It would probably be appreciated best after a few days on Ios, when an opportunity to hear nature's breathing may have become a priority need. The olives are tiny, like the island, but nourishing in numbers.
Area: 41 sq km. Length of coastline: 40 km.
Population: 291 (all but sixteen of the inhabitants apparently winter in Hora, or gather there on census day, but in summer enough move down to the harbour of Alopronia to provide eighty beds for tourists).
Area telephone code: 0286.

Bearings

Landing is at **Alopronia**, known to the islanders as Limani (Port), from where a bus runs to the capital, Hora, 3.5 km away on the west coast. Alopronia has a small beach, a few ouzerie-tavernas in summer and some fishing boats for hire.

Hora is primitive and pretty, at the edge of a cliff on the rugged side of the island, where everything happens in the main square. It is a twenty-minute walk to the Castle-Monastery of Chryssopigis which, deserted since 1834, was once the local refuge from pirate raids. An hour and a half from Hora, whether on foot or donkey, are the remains of a Temple of Apollo at Episkopi.

Beaches

Swimming is found in successive bays along the sheltered east coast, reached on foot or by fishing boat: the north and west are rugged and inhospitable.

Where to stay and eat

No listed hotels, but about 100 beds on offer in summer in Alopronia and Hora.

Alopronia has three restaurant/fish tavernas, run by Loukas Mamalis, Panayotis Koundouris and Maria Mamali; in Hora there is one, belonging to Georgios Halkeas. For a change of pace, shop at the grocery and bakery and eat in the closest shade to either.

Getting there

Between two and four ferries call weekly from Piraeus, twelve hours away.

Transport

The sole bus, small boats and donkeys.

From Sikinos

Ports of call on the Piraeus ferries, and Ios and Folegandros by local caiques.

Telephone

Police 51 222
Clinic 51 211

Syros

The administrative capital and most thickly populated of the Cyclades islands, Syros is well worth a visit even though you may hesitate before spending a holiday there. For much of the nineteenth century the capital, Ermoupolis, was Greece's principal port (see The Greeks and the Sea, p. 34–5), and it still has one of the country's five main shipyards. Since Syros is the seat of the Cyclades prefecture, inhabitants of the other islands have to go there to transact any but routine business with the state, or for more complex medical treatment; as a result, Syros is particularly well served by inter-island communications, though strangely it still has no airport. It is 80 nautical miles from Piraeus, but only 62 from Rafina.

Area: 84 sq km. Length of coastline: 87 km.
Population: 19,669 (Ermoupolis 15,100).
Area telephone code: 0281.

History

After the Ancient Greek, Macedonian, Roman and Byzantine periods, Syros was incorporated by the Venetians into the Duchy of

Naxos. Because of Venetian trade and settlement, by the eighteenth century the island had more Catholic than Greek Orthodox inhabitants: this led to European, and especially French, protection and a lighter Turkish yoke than was felt on most of the islands, and enabled Syros to offer refugees a place of safety during the 1821 Revolution. The present capital was built mainly in the first half of the nineteenth century by refugees from Chios, Psara and Kassos; a second wave of refugees arrived after the 1922 Asia Minor disaster.

The islanders say they live on Syra, and claim their Turkish delight to be Greece's finest. For those who prefer a harder chew, Syros nougat, rich in nuts and sometimes enclosed in a kind of wafer, is also highly regarded.

Port and capital

Built on the site of an ancient city named for Ermes, god of commerce among other things, **Ermoupolis** is a neo-Classical town extending from the sea to the older settlement of Ano Syros (Upper Syros). From the ferry deck you see two hills, both dotted with elegant public buildings, large squares and imposing churches: one hill is largely Catholic and the other Orthodox.

The long waterfront is lined with cafés, restaurants and souvenir shops. Back from the water, the central Miaoulis Square, with the town hall, was laid out by one of the Bavarian architects brought to Greece by King Othon to design the basis of modern Athens after it became the Greek capital. A municipal band performs in the square on summer weekends.

Not to be missed

Not to be missed in Ermoupolis is the Apollon State Theatre, a miniature of La Scala in Milan, with a kind of Belle Epoque café beside it, and the Cathedral of the Metamorphosis (Transfiguration) built in the 1840s with shipowner contributions. The archaeological museum near the town hall displays mainly Hellenistic and Roman exhibits.

Ano Syros is the medieval part of the capital, dating from the Venetian occupation, with the Catholic Cathedral of Aghios Georgios, a sixteenth-century Capucin monastery, a seventeenth-century Church of Aghios Ioannis, and an eighteenth-century Jesuit monastery and Church of the Panaghia. The narrow, twisting streets, many of them linked by flights of steps, have changed little in 500 years. A British military cemetery at Ano Syros contains mainly the graves of sailors who were killed or who died in First World War operations connected with the Gallipoli and Macedonian campaigns.

The suburb on the hill to the right is Vaporia (Boats), where the nineteenth-century shipowners built their three-storey villas before steam propelled them to Athens.

Around the island

Ermoupolis apart, Syros has some pleasant beaches, interesting archaeological remains, a fairly developed tourism infrastructure and a road network that makes a car worthwhile. The island can be toured most conveniently in two excursions, one covering the north for the archaeological remains (among them traces of a Bronze Age settlement at Halandriani and an Ancient Greek city at Grammata) and the other the centre and south.

Cave-church Yialyssas, population 283, 6 km from Ermoupolis, is a market garden centre from where the cave-church of Aghios Stefanos can be reached on foot or by caique.

Beaches For swimming, you could go to Vari (population 845) at the head of a sheltered bay 8 km south of Ermoupolis, where five hotels abut sandy beaches, or to Kini (population 260), a picturesque west-coast fishing village 9 km from Ermoupolis where some fifty beds are on offer in rented rooms. On the way to Kini, hand-made embroideries can be purchased from the nunnery of Aghia Varvara.

Megas Yialos (population 94) has a long, sheltered beach on the east coast, while Finikas (population 479) and Posidonia (known also as Dellagrazzia, population 555) are west-coast settlements where many Syrans have their holiday and weekend homes. Finikas offers a succession of small beaches, some of them protected by tiny offshore islets.

Where to stay There are twenty-seven listed hotels with a total of 540 rooms: two of first class, six second, twelve third, two fourth and five fifth. At Ermoupolis you could try the **Nissaki** in E. Papadam Street (third class, forty-two rooms, tel. 28 200) or the **Hermes** in Kanari Square (second class, twenty-eight rooms, tel. 28 011). At Finikas there is the forty-room **Olympia** (third class, tel. 42 212), at Yialyssas the twenty-four-room **Françoise** (third class, tel. 42 000), at Posidonia the sixty-room **Posidonian** (second class, tel. 42 100), and at Vari the thirty-room **Alexandra** (third class, tel. 42 540) and thirty-room **Romantica** (third class, tel. 61 211). There are also at least 300 non-hotel beds available.

Where to eat Ermoupolis inhabitants speak well of the **Eleana**, **Cavo d'Oro** (for fish), **Christos**, **Gad** and **Silivanis**, while good reports have been made also of **Chez Michel**, **Tembeli** and **Folia**. All the beaches have fish tavernas in summer.

Getting there Many of the Piraeus and Rafina ferries to Myconos and Tinos call first at Syros; the trip takes five hours from Piraeus and three and a half from Rafina.

Transport There is a fairly adequate bus service from a terminus near the Customs House to the main holiday villages: Kini, Yialyssas, Posidonia and Finikas. Cars, mopeds and bicycles can be rented, and local travel agencies organise coach excursions.

From Syros Most easily to Myconos and Tinos, though almost all the Cyclades islands can be reached by less frequent services. There are six connections a week with Andros, two a week with Samos, Ikaria and Patmos, and one a week to Milos, Serifos and Sifnos.

Telephone Police 22 610
Coastguard 22 690
Hospital 22 555

Thera (Santorini)

Better known internationally as Santorini, formerly Kalistis, at one stage Denmemezlik and just possibly Atlantis, Thera (also written as Thira and Thyra but pronounced to rhyme with *beera*, Greek for beer) is one of the three most southerly Cyclades islands with nothing between it and the north coast of Crete but some of the roughest water in the Aegean. Its closest neighbours are Folegandros and Sikinos to the north-west, Anafi to the east, and Ios a little to the north. It is 127 nautical miles from Piraeus.

You would go to Thera to see one of the most spectacular islands in the world, and to visit an ancient Minoan city. You would scarcely go for the swimming. Also, the island's capital, Fira, can easily be mistaken for an oriental bazaar when several cruise liners arrive together.

Area: 76 sq km. Length of coastline: 69 km.
Population: 7,000, including the offshore islets (1,718 in Fira and 1,255 in Emborio, the main inland settlement).
Area telephone code: 0286.

History

First inhabited at least 5,000 years ago, even before the Minoans arrived, Thera was known in historical times as Kalistis (Most Beautiful) and Strongyli (Round). In approximately 1450 BC an explosion on the island changed the history of the Ancient World. The Dorians arrived in the eleventh century BC and gave it the name Thera. The Venetians, who took it in 1207 and incorporated it into the Duchy of Naxos, called it Santa Irene (after Aghia Irene of Thera who died in exile there in 304), which devolved into Santorini. During almost three centuries of Turkish occupation, until 1832, it was known as Denmemezlik.

The Atlantis question

Thera was and still is a volcanic island – the last eruption occurred as late as 1928. But the explosion that shattered the island in or around 1450 BC, giving it broadly its present shape, was comparable in power only to that which, from similar causes, destroyed the Pacific island of Krakatoa in 1883. With the collapse of the crater, the entire centre of 'Round Island' disappeared beneath the sea.

In a scenario with which most archaeologists and seismologists concur, the resulting tidal wave, possibly as high as 100 m, must have swept the northern coast of Crete and, with the accompaniment of earthquakes that levelled Knossos, dealt the Minoan Empire a fatal blow. A more ornate theory links the tidal wave and subsequent recession of the waters with the Biblical account of the parting of the Red Sea and safe passage of Moses with the people of Israel.

But was Thera Atlantis, the mythical island first mentioned by Plato and said to have finally sunk into the sea? Acceptance of this theory requires an assumption that Plato, in recording the legend, made an error of 8,000 years in his dates and, because of a blunder in the translation of Egyptian scripts, multiplied all the dimensions of the Lost Continent by ten. If that really happened, then his description fits.

The late Professor Spyridon Marinatos, Greece's most brilliantly successful archaeologist, who was painstakingly excavating a Minoan city on Thera at the time of his death in 1974, preferred not to commit himself.

'I have no opinion on that subject,' he said once. 'I have published an essay in which I explain that the idea of Atlantis comes from the legend of an island sinking after a volcanic explosion. The legend has varied through the centuries, in the same way as the legend of Alexander the Great, but it is nevertheless very possible that it started with the sinking of Thera.'

In an attempt to reconcile the discrepancies in dates and dimensions, a Greek author, Basil Paschos, argued in a book published some fifteen years ago that there were in fact two Lost Continents: the original 'Atlantic' Atlantis that sank roughly where Plato said it did and broadly corresponded to the measurements he quoted, and New Atlantis, a colony covering the islands of Crete, Thera and Delos, that survived its namesake for several thousand years until its own destruction in semi-recorded times. While this appears to be a lone view, the issue itself is far from settled

The town at Acrotiri

When Professor Marinatos went to Thera in 1967, he had already proved himself the most inspired pinpointer of ancient sites since Heinrich Schliemann dug at Troy and Mycenae almost exactly a century earlier. He had identified the location of the Battle of Thermopylae, at which Leonidas and the 300 Spartans fought to the last man against the invading Persians in 480 BC, and also uncovered the tomb of the Plataeans killed at the Battle of Marathon in 490 BC.

It took him less than a week to bring to light the first indications of an ancient settlement at Acrotiri, in the south-west corner of Thera, 16 km from Fira and 2 km from the village, the name of which was adopted for the discovery simply because no one knew, or yet knows, what the Minoans had called the town there.

During the eight excavation seasons that preceded the professor's death, he unearthed a city that has been described by others as Greece's Pompeii, along with a unique series of Minoan frescoes that have shed new light on the art and quality of life of the Minoan period.

The essential difference between Acrotiri and Pompeii is that the inhabitants of the former had had warning of the impending disaster and had been able to flee the town, if not the island, taking their portable belongings with them. They left behind their furniture, from beds to storage urns, but no gold or jewellery. Also, not one human skeleton has so far been found in the Thera excavations.

Unceremoniously ousted by the military dictatorship from his post of Inspector General of Antiquities – 'I learned of my "resignation" when I heard the announcement on television' – Professor Marinatos went to live in a small house on the edge of the excavation site so as to give his full attention to the digs. On 1 October, 1974, he returned to the site after lunch to supervise a group of workmen, climbed a 1½ m-high ancient wall to get a better view, lost his balance and fell. His head struck a stone, and he died before help could arrive. He was buried in the town he had discovered, leaving unfinished work that he once said would be sufficient for 'generations of archaeologists'.

The site and the frescoes

Apart from roofing the entire site – you enter what appears to be a gigantic aircraft hangar and then, in the diffused light, wander the ancient streets and squares – little new work has been done since the professor's death.

The excavations so far cover an area of about 10,000 sq m, and the finds include two-, three- and a few four-storey houses of unworked stone reinforced with wooden trestles. Since the Minoans did not employ street nameplates, the central street has been given the name Telchines Road and the two squares are marked on the map of the site as Mill Square and Triangle Square.

The rooms of the houses are by present standards small and low, and it is surmised from the height of the lintels that the people who lived in them were short. Apart from providing evidence of an advanced drainage system, the finds also indicate that the inhabitants engaged in agriculture, stockbreeding (sheep and goats), fishing and such home crafts as weaving and pottery. They were members of a community sufficiently wealthy to import pottery, obsidian, metals and timber from Crete, mainland Greece, other Aegean islands, Syria and Egypt.

But the greatest finds of all were the frescoes, now on display in the Thera Gallery of the National Archaeological Museum in Athens. With Minoan red the predominating colour, they show a group of antelopes, a monkey (presumed to have been a pet and therefore suggestive of a comparatively high standard of living – until the 1960s the modern Greeks regarded even dogs as non-unionised agricultural workers and therefore an absurd extravagance for a city family), a river landscape, depictions of a Minoan fleet on some festive occasion and of a shipwreck, a spring landscape and, in some ways most evocative of all, a young priestess in profile and children boxing.

The priestess, clad in a floor-length dress and carrying a censer, wears brilliant red lipstick and has her ear painted in the same red above an elaborate earring. The boxing children wear a single glove on the right hand, and a black belt; their heads are shaven except for long tresses, and one wears jewellery.

No one, viewing the Acrotiri frescoes, could make the mistake of believing them the work of a poor and primitive community.

In 1976, an attempt was made by French underwater explorer Jacques-Yves Cousteau, under contract to the National Tourist

Organisation of Greece, to find confirmatory evidence beneath the sea for the Atlantis theory. All he was able to report was that there appeared to be traces of ancient remains, but they were buried beneath a deep layer of mud.

Helice – a parenthesis

At the time of his death, Professor Marinatos was still dreaming of what would have been his crowning discovery: that of the site of the ancient city of Helice (known also as Iliki). He was convinced that he knew almost exactly where it was, on or possibly just off the coast of the northern Peloponnese, and had been back time and again to look for it on land and from small boats.

The difference between Helice and the town now known as Acrotiri is that the former had no warning of its approaching doom. According to ancient historians, when it sank beneath the sea in an earthquake in 373 BC not a single inhabitant survived; even a Spartan fleet on a ceremonial visit was lost with all hands.

It was the middle of the Classical period: Plato was still alive, Aristotle was a beardless boy, and Praxiteles was sculpting his masterpieces.

Waiting to be found, Marinatos said, were 'architectural monuments, masterpieces of sculpture in stone and bronze, including some by the greatest of artists – perhaps even Phidias – precious inscriptions and all kinds of products of the minor arts'.

Discovery of the city would also provide 'an invaluable and unique harvest of knowledge of ancient private and public life in the best days of Classical Greece'.

Quoting Strabo and Pafsanias, he said that 150 years after the disaster fishermen knew they must avoid a bronze statue of Poseidon standing erect on the sea bottom, since otherwise its trident would snarl their nets, while as late as the second century AD traces of the town were still visible under the sea.

Today, he said, Helice must lie either beneath the coastal plain, because of silting of two nearby rivers, or in relatively shallow waters not far off the coast.

Looking even beyond its discovery, he remarked: 'If modern technology could succeed in isolating the ruins from the surrounding waters, the whole town could be regained and restored, with its walls, sanctuaries, public buildings and at least some of its private houses. We should then have a second Pompeii, but this one a town from the Golden Age of Classical Greece.'

No one appears any longer to be looking for Helice, which is awaiting a new Schliemann – or a new Marinatos.

The approaches to Thera

To obtain the full impact of an incomparable study in black and white, it is definitely better to arrive by sea than by air.

The ship creeps between the black volcanic outcroppings of Palea (Old) and Nea (New) Kameni, the aptly-named 'Burned Islands', towards a crescent-shaped cliff rising 260 m almost sheer from the water. Behind the cluster of buildings around Skala, the landing stage, 587 steps lead up to the brilliant white town of **Fira**, formed of parallel streets along the ridge.

Although the town can now be reached by a funicular, all but the most timid still use one of the mules or donkeys that, until a few years ago, were the only means of transportation: the ticket for the animal, accompanied by owner or minder, includes the return by the funicular, and the price is the same whichever way you go to the top. Only those whose childhood was spent cleaning out stables would find it comfortable to walk to the top, and they would look in vain for a means of hosing down their feet on arrival.

You need a little faith, and some fatalism, for the mule or donkey ride. You will gain the impression that your mount is bent on scraping you off against the wall where there is a wall, and on murder and suicide where there is none. Also, on a hot day, you will discover how pervasive mule sweat can be, in oiliness and odour, once it has penetrated trousers or dress. But you will have had an experience to recount to your grandchildren, and who knows for how much longer it will be available? There are lobbies in Greece ambitious to see the animals retired permanently to pasture, even if the upshot should be their rapid extinction once the financial incentive for providing them with food and stabling had been removed.

The town at the top

Fira is a settlement of narrow, flagstoned streets, churches, shops, restaurants, tavernas, cafés, pizzerias, *souvlatzidikes* and fast-food outlets, unforgettably beautiful until the crowds arrive and then wholly dedicated to extracting the tourist dollar.

In the intervals between bargaining for gold and silver, semi-precious stones, onyx chessmen or vases, garments of cotton, wool, artificial fabrics and sheepskin, national-costume dolls and postcards, and between queuing for a restaurant table (in high season) and sipping ouzo or coffee on rooftops with stupendous views of the bay, you have two Cathedrals to visit, one Orthodox and the other Roman Catholic, as well as an old Dominican monastery and an archaeological museum (closed Tuesdays) that displays exhibits from Ancient Thera and Acrotiri.

Like Capri, Fira is a wonderful place to visit but not much of a place to stay. If you should wish to take a car to the island you will use one of the ferries that dock at Athinios, 10 km from the capital. No vehicles are allowed in Fira itself.

Around the island

To set foot on an active volcano, you take a caique to Palea and Nea Kameni, two islands, on the volcano, on which nothing lives. From the landing stage on Nea Kameni you will face a half-hour walk to the crater, and will need thick-soled shoes to protect your feet from the heat. Some of the caique tours (departure from Skala) also include Therasia and Aspro Nisi (White Island).

Therasia was formed by an eruption of the volcano in 236 BC,

Palea Kameni rose to the surface in the middle of the bay in 196 BC, and **Nea Kameni** appeared beside it during a protracted eruption in 1711 and 1712. Subsequent eruptions in 1866, 1925 to 1926 and 1928 had less effect on the topography, but the whole of Thera was badly damaged by an earthquake in July 1956.

Therasia, population 245, is an islet of sheer cliffs and no beaches, forming part of the western rim of the cavity on the volcano's summit; if you are not on an organised tour you may have time, and energy, for the hour's walk to the Monastery of the Dormition of the Virgin.

Oia (pronounced EE-Ah) is a fishing harbour 11 km from Fira at the northern corner of the crescent and the end of the bus-line, with a population of 300, a Venetian castle, old houses, hotels and rented rooms, tavernas and adequate swimming. It also offers an escape from the crowds. Since the 1956 earthquake it has been extensively rebuilt, but in traditional style. North-east of Oia, 7 km off the coast, is a second crater that last erupted in 1650.

Ancient Thera, with ruins of temples, an agora, theatre, baths and tombs, as well as three Byzantine churches, can be reached on foot either from Kamari or Perissa. There is one monastery dating from the Venetian period and dedicated to Aghios Nikolaos at **Imerovigli**, 3 km from Fira, and another, dating from 1711 and dedicated to the prophet Elias, at **Pyrgos**, 7 km from Fira. The latter has a rich collection of icons and books and also houses a small museum of monastic life and crafts (closed Sundays), and is not far from another Venetian castle.

The island's three main inland villages – **Mesaria**, **Vothonas** and **Emborio** – are rather to be passed through than stayed at, though Emborio is impressive in its way, with views of both coasts, and streets sometimes so narrow that two people can scarcely pass on foot without bowing to each other.

Beaches

In contrast to the sheer cliffs of the crescent-shaped west coast, the eastern side of Thera slopes gently down to the sea. The best of the beaches, all provided with restaurants and tavernas and with accommodation available in hotels or rented rooms, are at Monolithos, Kamari, Perissa and close to Acrotiri. However, you may find it disconcerting to swim from naturally black sand, even in water of crystal clarity; also, the sand gets extraordinarily hot in summer, requiring at least a thick towel to sit on, and shoes.

The Thera products

Thera is best known for its wine, *fava* (a paste of boiled chickpeas served with chopped onions and olive oil as an appetiser) and small nut-shaped tomatoes used mainly for pulping.

It is also, at least for the moment, still a producer and exporter of Santorin earth and pumice stone. Because the quarries are undoubted eyesores, the government in 1983 bowed to conservationist pressure and gave the mining company exploiting them one year to wind up its operations. As of the summer of 1988 the quarries were being worked seven days a week to build up stocks, suggesting a nervousness that the deadline might eventually expire. The figures involved are considerable: in response to a question in Parliament, the Commerce Ministry put production in 1986 at 600,000 tons of Santorin earth and 30,000 tons of pumice.

Where to stay

The island of Thera has ninety listed hotels with 1,318 rooms, making an average of 14.64 rooms per hotel, as well as approximately 3,500 non-hotel beds available for rent. Of the hotels, four are first class, seven second class, twenty-nine third class, twenty-two fourth-class and twenty-eight fifth class.

Recommended in Fira itself are the **Atlantis** (first class, twenty-seven rooms, tel. 22 232) and **Kallisti** (third class, thirty-three rooms, tel. 22 317).

At Kamari, you could try the second-class **Sunshine** (thirty-five rooms, tel. 31 394) or third-class **Kamari** (fifty-five rooms, tel. 31 243).

NTOG has a 'traditional settlement' at Oia, which it plans to expand but which at present comprises fifty-seven beds in ten restored houses; for reservations, write to NTOG, Amerikis Street, Athens.

Where to eat

Perhaps the best advice, in high season, is to eat where you find a table, and expect the service to be fast rather than personal.

However, you should be able to rely on the **Gamile Stefani**, **Kastro** and **Zorbas** (for fish) in Fira, the **Panorama** in Oia, and the **Retsina** in Perissa. Good reports have also been made of the **Nikos**, **Niki** and **China Terrace** in Fira.

There are four nightclubs and twelve discos for those who prefer not to sleep at night, or are kept awake by the noise.

Getting there

In summer, there are two or three flights a day from Athens (one hour) and from two to four ferries a day from Piraeus (approximately twelve hours). Most ferry passengers disembark by tender at Skala; the more nervous, and those with cars, get off in Athinios, where the ferries dock, and then take a bus or taxi to Fira. Many of the ferries also call at Oia.

Almost all cruise itineraries include a morning or afternoon visit to Thera (a call of three or four hours). In the mornings you have to choose between Acrotiri and Fira, but in the afternoons you can go only to Fira anyway.

Transport

The island's limited road network, a total of 30 km, scarcely justifies taking a car, especially since cars and mopeds can be rented in Fira. Also, the sixteen buses provide summer departures at approximately half-hour intervals for the main villages and beaches, from a park at the edge of Fira. Local travel agencies organise coach and caique tours.

From Thera

By air to Myconos (daily), Crete (four flights a week) and Rhodes (three flights a week).

By sea, in summer, to Tinos, Myconos, Naxos, Paros, Ios and

Telephone

Iraklion (Crete) daily, Sikinos, Folegandros, Syros and Milos three times a week, and Anafi, Aghios Nikolaos (Crete), Sitia (Crete), Kassos, Karpathos and Rhodes twice a week.
Police 22 649
Coastguard 22 239
Olympic Airways 22 493
Clinic 22 237

Tinos

Since the Greeks have only one word, *peristeri*, for pigeon and dove, and since dictionaries define doves as birds of the pigeon family, it scarcely matters whether you call those remarkable structures on Tinos dovecotes or pigeon coops. By either name, they are the closest approach in Greece to crenellated fairy-tale castles, and far more elaborately decorated than any homes the islanders ever build for themselves; they are a curious aberration for a people not generally known for kindness to animals.

They are not the only oddity about the island. The holiest of Greek Orthodox shrines and a place of pilgrimage, Tinos is at the same time the most Catholic of the Cyclades islands. Had the Greeks not been momentarily unready to take umbrage, an incident on Tinos would have brought them into the Second World War in August 1940, two months before Mussolini gave them no choice by invading Epirus.

Tinos, of the blue-tinged marble, is close to the heart of the Cyclades, roughly equidistant from Myconos and Syros, less than a mile from Andros and 86 nautical miles from Piraeus.

Area: 194 sq km. Length of coastline: 105 km.
Population: 7,731 (3,879 in Tinos town and the rest in 40 villages).
Area telephone code: 0283.

The Venetians held Tinos from 1207 to 1714, with the result that the Turkish occupation lasted for little more than a century. The 500 years of Venetian rule explains why it is one of Greece's two largest Catholic parishes; the other is Syros, where the Venetians lasted even longer.

Tinos and the Virgin

You land at **Tinos** town (Tinos is one of the few Cyclades islands – others include Myconos and Syros – where the capital is not generally referred to as Hora) and will almost certainly be unfavourably impressed by the small, square apartment blocks that have sprung up everywhere. A wide, paved street leads up from the harbour to the Church of the Evangelistria (Annunciation), a neo-Classical structure faced in white marble that is the closest modern Greece has to one of the 'treasuries' of Ancient Delphi. The icon of the Virgin is festooned with diamonds and pearls, and the church itself is hung with votive offerings in gold and silver; if all of them were counted by the Bank of Greece in the country's official reserves the economy would look a shade healthier.

The church was built in the 1820s at the place where an icon was found as a result of a nun's dream; the nun was subsequently beatified as Aghia Pelagia after the icon, sometimes attributed to St Luke, had begun to work its miracles, mainly in the form of cures.

Tinos comes into its own every 15 August, the Feast of the Assumption, when the icon is carried in procession through the town. For days before and afterwards, every room is booked and every place taken on the ferries, for all that reports of miracles have become rarities.

It was different even ten or fifteen years ago: as the icon was lifted over the prostrate bodies of candidates for miracles, there would almost always be one or two of the lame who began to walk and the blind to see. Now it is all rather formal, with the President of the Republic usually in the congregation; there is little of the old fervour, or sense of anticipation.

Whether the miracles are fewer because medical care is better now, or because of the effects of education, television and money on religious sentiment, is an area of speculation better left for others. But at least the Feast of the Assumption is still good for business.

Traditionally, the icon must never leave the island. The last time an exception was made was in 1964 when King Paul was in the terminal stage of stomach cancer; the then Crown Prince, now ex-King Constantine, fetched the icon and placed it beside the dying man's bed at the Tatoi summer palace outside Athens. There was no miracle.

On visiting the church, you will observe at once that the astonishing wealth in votive offerings dates from a time when the Greeks were poorer, and therefore more devout.

The auxiliary buildings of the church house a museum and art gallery, the latter exhibiting works of Tinos artists and copies of Renaissance masterpieces. The most famous modern son of Tinos is Nikos Skalkotas, Greece's best-known modern composer.

The Elli incident

As part of the Feast of the Assumption celebrations, wreaths are dropped into the water of Tinos harbour where, on 15 August, 1940, the destroyer *Elli* was torpedoed and sunk by an Italian submarine. The Greeks chose not to regard the incident as a minor Pearl Harbor.

The dovecotes

As soon as you get out of Tinos town you will begin to see them. They are generally two-storey fortress-like towers decorated with geometric designs, with battlements, towers on the four corners, and openings for the birds arranged symmetrically. The ground floor of the towers was, and sometimes still is, used for storage.

You are free to believe that their feathered residents are the direct descendants of the homing pigeons carried by Greek ships on Aegean trade in the days before there was wireless.

Doves have been associated with Tinos for a very long time. As usual, mythology offers an explanation. The daughters of King Aniou, a son of Apollo, had the Midas touch in reverse; whatever they held, they could turn into grain, olive oil and wine. Appreciating the value of such a gift to a Quartermaster Corps, Agamemnon conscripted the women for the Trojan expedition. However, they soon deserted, and fled to Andros. Facing drumhead court martial and a probable death sentence, they appealed to Dionysos, who turned them into doves.

The dovecotes of Tinos date mainly from the Venetian period. Numbering some 800, they are an unusual example of folk art and one of the island's real attractions.

Around the island

Most Greeks get no further than Tinos town, put off by the island's greater reputation for wind than beaches, with the result that the villages are little known. But **Kionia** is a developing holiday centre, 3 km outside the town, with a sandy beach and the ruins of a Temple of Poseidon and Amfitriti. **Pyrgos** is beautiful, among trees and vineyards, and has a museum dedicated to works of a renowned modern Greek sculptor, Yannoulis Halepas. **Isternia** is another attractive village, about 5 km from a good beach, and swimming can also be enjoyed at Kambos, Aghios Sostis, Aghios Ioannis, Porto, Kardianis and Kolymbithras, as well as along the shores of Panormou Bay.

Beaches

Where to stay

Of twenty-three listed hotels, with a total of 779 rooms, all but one are in or close to Tinos town, demonstrating the importance of the icon to the holiday movement. The exception is the first-class **Tinos Beach** at Kionia (180 rooms, tel. 22 626).

Good bets in or near the town are the **Aeolos Bay** at Agali (second class, sixty-nine rooms, tel. 23 339), the **Asteria** at Kalithea (third class, fifty-two rooms, tel. 22 132) and the **Meltemi** on Megaloharis Avenue (third class, forty-three rooms, tel. 22 881).

Tinos officially has another 1,300 beds on offer in about 500 rented rooms, but in mid-August somehow manages to shelter more than 6,000 visitors. That is not really the best time to go!

Where to eat

You could try the **Aigli**, **Zefiros**, **Typos**, **Lito**, **Kymata**, **Makedonia**, **Fanaria**, **Peristerionas**, **Dionysos** or **Xinari**, all in Tinos town. But around the Feast of the Assumption you may still need to pack sandwiches.

Getting there

On the Myconos ferries from Piraeus and Rafina (Tinos is the intermediate call); a trip of about four hours.

Transport

There are buses almost hourly to Kionia, and from four to six a day to most of the other villages. Nevertheless, the excellent road network can make a car or moped attractive.

From Tinos

Most easily to Myconos, Syros and Andros. In the summer there are connections, less than daily, to Paros, Naxos, Ios and Thera (Santorini).

Telephone

Police 22 255
Coastguard 22 348
Clinic 22 210/22 270

The Dodecanese Islands

See also Rhodes, pp. 152-63.

Introduction

All the Aegean islands outside the 'circle' of the Cyclades used to be known as the 'Sporades' (the here-and-there, or scattered, islands, from which the English word 'sporadic' derived). Today, the North Sporades are the chain of islands off the east coast of Greece reached usually from Volos; since 1908 the South Sporades have become the Dodecanese.

The literal translation of Dodecanese is 'Twelve Islands'; they have their counterpart on the other side of Greece in the Eptanisa, or 'Seven Islands', of which Corfu is the chief. The Dodecanese are named not for the number of islands in the group now – fourteen if only the larger are considered and between thirty and forty if account is taken of sparsely-inhabited dependencies and seasonally-inhabited outcrops of pastureland – but for the twelve islands that rose in revolt in 1908 after the Turkish government abrogated privileges granted to them almost four centuries earlier by Sultan Suleiman the Magnificent.

The revolt was successful in that the Turks were ousted, but unsuccessful in that it brought the islands neither independence nor union with Greece: instead, they were seized by the Italians during the 1911-12 Italo-Turkish war, at a time when Greece was occupied in one of its own Balkan Wars. They were awarded to Italy 'provisionally' by the 1920 Treaty of Sèvres as part of its reward for fighting on the Allied side in the First World War, and more permanently by the 1923 Treaty of Lausanne, in which Greece paid a second time for the Asia Minor disaster of the previous year – a defeat that had already cost it the Asia Minor port of Smyrna, now Izmir, and brought revolution to Athens (see p. 23).

The Mussolini regime sought to turn Rhodes and Kos in particular into showplaces, and many of the excavations, much of the restoration and the finest of the public buildings date from that period. So, too, does the widespread knowledge of Italian in the main islands of the group.

After the Italian surrender in 1943 during the Second World War, the Dodecanese were briefly occupied by the Germans, who had time to make only what was then their typical mark: they decimated the Jewish communities on Rhodes and Kos. The formal incorporation of the Dodecanese into Greece came in 1948, giving the country its present boundaries.

Reading from north to south, the main islands of the Dodecanese are Patmos, Leipsi, Leros, Kalymnos, Kos, Nisyros, Astipalaia, Simi, Tilos, Rhodes, Halki, Karpathos and Kassos, with tiny but ambitious Kastellorizon tucked away to the south-east. With the exception of Karpathos and Kassos, all of them lie close to the Asia Minor coast. They have a total population of 145,000, of which Rhodes accounts for 87,000 and Kos for 21,000. In a sense, all of them may be described as satellites of Rhodes, the almond-shaped island with almost half the total land area of the group: except for Kos, which has its own momentum, and Patmos, with its Biblical connections, they have been carried into the tourism picture very much on the skirts of 'mother Rhodes'.

While many of the Dodecanese can now be reached at least by light aircraft from Athens, only Rhodes and Kos are served by European charter flights. The large and comfortable passenger/car ferries operated by a joint stock company of Rhodian inhabitants link Piraeus with Kos, Kalymnos, Patmos and Leros as well as Rhodes. Other islands of the group are served by inter-Dodecanese and excursion boats, and there are summer connections also to Crete and the Cyclades islands. As a group, they offer everything from resort holidays to distant solitude, in the sunniest, driest and least windy corner of the Aegean.

Astipalaia

Astipalaia is a stepping-stone island, closer to Amorgos and Anafi in the Cyclades than to its nearest Dodecanese companions – Kalymnos and Kos – and belonging architecturally to neither group. Sometimes described as butterfly-shaped, it is really two mountain tops linked by a strip of land a couple of hundred metres wide. Not commonly regarded as a holiday island, it is attempting to overcome the handicaps of distance (175 nautical miles from Piraeus) and absence of an airport with the construction of pubs and discos rather than hotels.
Area: 96 sq km. Length of coastline: 110 km.
Population: 1,304 (800 in Hora and 108 in Analypsi).
Area telephone code: 0242.

The island's name is believed to derive from a Greek variant for 'old city'. In Ancient Greece it was known as Ichthioessa from its abundance of fish (though the modern Greek for fish is *psari*, the ancient word still makes its appearance in *ichthiopolion*, fishmonger) and *Trapeza ton Theon*, table of the gods, from its fertility and flowers.

Bearings The capital, **Hora**, and most of the population are on the butterfly's 'left wing', looking at the island from the deck of a ferry as it approaches the east coast. Hora spreads up a hill from the harbour, Pera Yialos, to a Venetian castle and line of windmills on the top. It is not a particularly attractive town; the houses are mostly small and square, off-white, with outside stairs and wooden balconies. Apart from the castle, there are three churches that are worth a glance: Aghios Georgios (the oldest on the island), the Evangelismos and the Panaghia Portaïtissa (Virgin of the Keep), which has an unusual eighteenth-century iconostasis dressed in gold leaf.

Of rather greater interest are three 'left-wing' monasteries: the Panaghia, Aghios Ioannis and Aghios Livyis.

Around the island **Analypsi**, known also as Maltezana, is the second largest village, set among vineyards 9 km north-east of Hora on the road to the island's 'right wing'. It offers good swimming an easy walk away, and the remains of some well-preserved Roman baths with mosaics depicting the seasons and the signs of the zodiac.

The only other villages of note are **Vathy** in the north, in a bay with an opening so narrow that it appears to be a lagoon, and **Livadi** in the south, 3 km from Hora, where a winter population of 78 is said to make 450 beds available to summer visitors. Ferries put in at Vathy when the wind is in the wrong direction for a landing at Hora.

Beaches Solitude can be enjoyed in small coves, many containing sand or pebble beaches, but the better swimming is at Livadi, Tzanaki and Aghios Konstantinos in the south and south-west, Kaminakia in the west and, off the road heading north, Marmari, Analypsi, Steno and Schinonda. It is possible to swim at Hora, but pointless in view of the alternatives. Nudism should not be a problem at the smaller beaches.

Where to stay There are four listed hotels (three fourth class and one fifth class) at Hora, with a total of sixty-five rooms: those that the islanders recommend are two of the fourth-class units, the **Paradissos** near the harbour (seventeen rooms, tel. 61 224) and the **Aigaion** (twenty rooms, tel. 61 236). In addition, there are some 750 beds in self-catering apartments and private homes in Hora and the other villages; some of the rooms near the castle are in renovated medieval houses.

Where to eat The locals will probably direct you to the **Vakroyiali**, **Kali Kardia** (Good Heart) and **Babis** among the seven restaurants and tavernas along the Hora waterfront, and the **Stefanida**, **Yiesenia** and **Kalamia** at Livadi. Analypsi has two restaurants, and Vathy one of the island's best fish tavernas. Among the various discos and pubs for a pre- or after-dinner drink, one at Hora, the **Faros** (Lighthouse), engages a small dance orchestra in the tourist season.

Getting there Four ferries a week from Piraeus cover the distance in sixteen or

Transport	seventeen hours. Astipalaia has 70 km of roads (15 km asphalted) and a single bus to provide communications between Hora and other villages. Small boats operate regular services to the main beaches and mopeds can be rented, though not cars.
From Astipalaia	There are weekly boats to numerous Cyclades and Dodecanese islands as well as Crete, and weekly hydrofoils to Kos and Kalymnos.
Telephone	Police 61 207 Clinic 61 222 Coastguard 61 208 Tourist information office 61 206

Halki

A Greek government ambition is to make Halki known around the world as a 'youth island', through the organisation of summer conferences, seminars and festivals by the quaintly-named General Secretariat for the New Generation. The effort is unlikely to amount to much unless it can be separated from leftist politics and the kind of peace movements that serve as a cloak for anti-Americanism. Youths who visit Greece to enjoy themselves, at their own expense, are more likely to be encountered on Myconos and Ios. The smallest island of the Dodecanese, and one of the most isolated, Halki nevertheless has an even smaller offshore islet for those attracted by the minuscule. It is most easily reached from Rhodes.

Area: 28 sq km. Length of coastline: 34 km.
Population: 334 (387 in 1971).
Area telephone code: 0246.

The island takes its name from the copper, *halkos*, mined there in antiquity, and should not be confused with the town of Halkis on the island of Euboia. It appears to have fallen during the Classical period of Ancient Greece into an obscurity from which it has not yet emerged.

Bearings — Landing is made at the capital and sole town, **Nimborio**, from where the island's only road runs uphill for 3 km to the abandoned former capital, Horio.

Rising like an amphitheatre from the harbour, Nimborio appears to be a considerable settlement, until closer examination reveals that most of the houses are abandoned. Few islands have suffered more from depopulation – Horio alone once had 4,000 inhabitants.

What to see — The sights of Halki comprise the remains of a Doric Temple of Apollo, an acropolis, a Crusader castle and a couple of monasteries, one of which, Aghios Ioannis, offers hospitality in houses forming part of its estate.

Beaches — For those wanting more than the opportunity to chew political fat, Halki is a place to eat fish and to swim; the more energetic of these

THE DODECANESE ISLANDS

activities can be performed at Pontamos (a ten-minute walk from Nimborio), at Trahia on the south coast, at a string of north-coast beaches reached by caique (trips of from ten to twenty minutes) and on the islet of Alimia.

Where to stay and eat

Halki has no listed hotels, but offers some 280 beds in rented rooms and a number of small pensions.

Though the pick of the catches goes to Rhodes, for obvious economic reasons, you cannot go far wrong at the Halki fish tavernas. The **Omonia** and **Houvardas** in particular have their advocates. A local speciality is lamb stuffed with rice and liver; surprisingly, for so small and rocky an island, the local bees produce some of Greece's most prized honey, which goes especially well with the local yoghurt.

Getting there

The one or two weekly ferries from Piraeus take up to thirty hours to meander over a tortuous course of more than 300 nautical miles. Understandably, most visitors arrive from Rhodes, 35 nautical miles away, on the daily boat service or occasional hydrofoil, or on excursion craft. There are also weekly connections with Karpathos and Kassos.

Transport

With neither cars nor mopeds on offer, you use the caique services or negotiate with fishermen.

From Halki

Alimia islet has a good natural harbour and a few houses, some scant remains of a Crusader castle and a number of excellent beaches; one of the beaches is close to the monastery of Aghios Georgios, which offers guest-house and cooking facilities.

Telephone

Police/Coastguard 71 213
Clinic 71 206

Kalymnos

Despite the advances made by the plastics industry, there is still a loyal market for real sponges: so long as it survives, Kalymnos divers will have a livelihood. Eventually the island will switch its reliance to some less hazardous occupation, but for the moment the obvious one, tourism, is still more a promise than a practical alternative. Less richly endowed than its neighbours with natural beauty, sandy beaches and remains from past centuries, Kalymnos attracts mainly the passing visitor who is stopping over on the way to Rhodes or day-tripping from Kos.

Area: 111 sq km. Length of coastline: 96 km.
Population: 14,279 (10,118 in Kalymnos town and 2,611 in Horio).
Area telephone code: 0243.

The sponges

The fishermen of other Greek islands are specialists in local coves and currents, squalls and matters of the surface; those of Kalymnos have an unparalleled knowledge of the bottom of the sea. They are especially familiar with the waters off the North African coast, where many spend the summer diving season. They also know all about the bends. The danger has certainly been lessened now, by knowledge and improved equipment, but you will still see the occasional old man, or apparently old man, almost unable to move, whose health was destroyed twenty or thirty years ago by a miscalculation, a moment of youthful exuberance, an elusive glimpse of rich pickings a little too far away, or simply one dive too many.

There is even a local folk dance, dating from the times when the causes of the paralysis were incompletely understood and it was therefore regarded as a normal and inescapable hazard: the movements, accompanying a melancholy song, depict the crippled diver attempting to dance, falling, struggling to his feet again, determined to continue the dance he had once loved so much.

Sponges have been in use for a long time, and so far as is known Kalymnos has been supplying them since the days of Ancient Greece. They are mentioned by Homer as being employed during the Trojan War to wipe away blood and sweat, and by Aristophanes as a prophylactic – a use to which they were also put in Roman brothels and, many centuries later, in respectable British homes, too.

Since emigrants go wherever any particular skills they may possess are in greatest demand, it is only natural that many of the pearl fishermen of Australia and a good proportion of the Greeks who dominate the fishing industry of Tarpon Springs, Florida, originate from Kalymnos.

You do not need to go all the way to Kalymnos to buy a sponge. In summer, a couple of elderly, white-smocked men ply beats in the Constitution Square area of Athens, so festooned with sponges as to invite comparison with the Michelin Man. No one reaches shelter faster than they if a sudden rain begins. They are no doubt familiar with the fable of the crafty donkey. Employed to carry salt from pans by the sea to a hilltop village, along a path beside a rushing stream, it discovered that it could lighten its load considerably by accidentally falling into the water. Its sense of balance was restored after its handler loaded the panniers not with salt but with sponges.

In 1988 sponges featured in European Community business when Greece asked special assistance for the divers, because of depleted catches attributed to a disease affecting sponges in beds off the coast of Libya.

Town and island

Kalymnos town, known also as Pothea, is the island's present capital and only port, at the head of the sheltered bay of Pothea on the south-east coast. A little smaller than Ermoupolis on the island of Syros, it is another of those commercial centres where the new and old coexist with relative harmony. It merits half a day, for the Castle of the Knights, the museum and, depending on time and energy, one or two of the island's six monasteries or a caique trip to the unexploited

What to see

cave of Kefalos on the south coast and that of the Seven Nymphs (or Virgins) a little to the north of the town.

There are also some medicinal springs near the capital, recommended for rheumatism, arthritis and ailments of the kidneys and digestive system.

Horio, the former capital, is on a hill only 2 km from Kalymnos town; most of its inhabitants simply moved down to sea level when the elimination of piracy made it safe to do so.

Vathi, population 570, is an oasis of citrus orchards on the coast 12 km north-east of Kalymnos town; it would scarcely be worth a visit unless in combination with one to the cave of the Nymphs/Virgins.

It makes rather more sense to head straight for the west coast:

Panormos, the first of the beaches, about 3 km beyond Horio, has a population of 550 and offers accommodation in private houses.

Myrties, a couple of kilometres further along the coast, population 100, is the resort area of better-off Kalymnos residents, who have built summer homes there. It has six hotels offering between eight and twenty-eight rooms.

Massouri, just beyond Myrties, is the island's closest approximation to a tourist resort, with a string of hotels close to the best beach on Kalymnos, the ruins of another castle, and a Monastery of the Panaghia for a change of pace.

The coastal road northward is for those to whom spectacular views are a sufficient reward.

Where to stay

The twenty-four listed hotels, of which only seven are open year-round, provide a total of 440 rooms, and there are an estimated 350 additional beds on offer in small pensions and private homes. Of the hotels, the only one with more than fifty rooms is the **Drossos** at Kantouni beach, Panormos (third class, fifty-one rooms, tel. 47 518). You might also try the **Olympic** in Kalymnos town (third class, forty-two rooms, tel. 28 801), the **Armeos Beach** and **Massouri Beach** at Massouri (the former second class, thirty-four rooms, tel. 47 488 and the latter third class, thirty-two rooms, tel. 47 555) and, at Myrties, the **Zephyros** (third class, twenty-eight rooms, tel. 47 500).

Where to eat

Kalymnos town has most of its restaurants and tavernas on the waterfront. Elsewhere, if there is a hotel there will be a fish taverna somewhere nearby, at least in the summer. In the town, you could try the **Yacht Club** (open to all) and **Svynos Restaurant** or, for fish, the **Marthas Brothers** and **Vouvalis**. Elsewhere, there are the **Stalas** at Myrties, **Antonopoulos** at Massouri and **Iliadis** at Kantouni.

Getting there

The nine ferries a week from Piraeus (in summer) cover the 183 nautical miles in about thirteen hours.

Transport

There are two bus services, one along the west coast and the other to Vathi. Taxis turn themselves into mini-buses when otherwise without customers, and mopeds can be hired.

From Kalymnos	Ports of call on the Piraeus and inter-Dodecanese ferries and local boats to Kos, a trip of about one and a half hours.
There are also caique connections with the offshore islets of Pserimos (population 72) and Telendos (population 90). The former, between Kalymnos and Kos, is reached from Kalymnos town, and the latter, off the west coast, from Myrties; the trips take forty and fifteen minutes respectively. Both have excellent beaches and a few beds on offer in private homes, while the Pserimos monastery can accommodate ten visitors in a guest-house. Telendos was part of Kalymnos until a sixth century BC earthquake.
Telephone	Police 29 301
Coastguard 29 304
Hospital 28 851/28 510

Karpathos

The largest of the Dodecanese after Rhodes, Karpathos is a green and well-watered island of pine-clad hills and peaceful valleys, an adequate road network, excellent beaches and hospitable people. Fortunately or not, depending on how you look at it, it is a hard place to reach by boat, and the air connections are via Rhodes; for that reason, it has so far missed out on tourism. Karpathos lies between Rhodes and Crete, 227 nautical miles from Piraeus.

Area: 301 sq km. Length of coastline: 160 km.

Population: 4,649 (1,266 in the capital, Pigadia, and the remainder in nine communities).

Area telephone code: 0245.

Mythology and history	Once part of the Minoan Empire, Karpathos was known as Krapatho by Homer and Skarpandos in the Middle Ages. Its history broadly followed that of the Dodecanese in general, except that it passed directly from Venetian to Turkish rule in the sixteenth century without an intervening occupation by the Knights of St John.
Around the island	Karpathos is a long, narrow island, made to seem even longer by the offshore islet of Saria, less than 100 m off the northern tip. Most of the inhabitants and the best of the roads are in the broader, southern sector, known locally as European Karpathos; the northern part is sparsely populated.
Landing is made at Possi (possibly Ancient Potidaeon), a natural harbour forming part of the capital, **Pigadia** (also written Pigadi). Most of the houses are new, built with the remittances of Greek-Americans originating from Karpathos; for the holiday-maker, Pigadia is the obvious base even though it has little to offer except the ruins of an acropolis and some barely adequate swimming.
Aperi, the former capital built 320 m up the slopes of Mount

Hamali, with a population of 457, is the richest village of the island because of its citrus and vine production and its links with emigrants; some of the homes there may put you in mind of desiccated ranches, clearly influenced by a style their Americanised owners envied but were unable or unwilling to reproduce full-scale.

Beaches On the west coast, the more accessible of the beaches are at Arkassa (population 379), Finiki (population 11) and Lefkos (population 65). In the northern part of the island, there is a pleasant beach miles from anywhere at Aghia Irene and another, most easily reached by caique from Pigadia, at Diafani, a small east-coast fishing village. From Diafani you could take a local bus or taxi to the inland village of Olympos, where the women still regard national costume as the daily wear, and are said to be learning only now that, in the wide world outside, men work too.

Islanders will tell you of at least a dozen other excellent beaches, but something to bear in mind is that the east and south-east coasts are the more sheltered when the wind is from the customary northerly direction, while those on the west coast can involve relatively expensive caique trips. Pigadia travel agencies arrange caique excursions to numerous beaches and – one well worth taking – to the northern headland of Karpathos and the Saria islet (population 4) where the remains of an ancient city can be seen. Saria, which has some fine beaches of its own, can also be reached by caique from Diafani.

Where to stay Karpathos has twelve listed hotels, three each of second, third, fourth and fifth classes, with a total of 210 rooms, and an estimated 500 additional beds on offer in rented rooms, mostly in Pigadia and Diafani. Two hotels in Pigadia where you could hope to find rooms are the **Seven Stars** (second class, thirty-four rooms, tel. 22 101) and **Atlantis** (third class, thirty-eight rooms, tel. 22 777).

Where to eat Pigadia inhabitants, when dining out, say they prefer the **Kali Kardia**, **Kazileris-Zafiris**, **Lamiranda** (especially for fish) and **Tassos**. Most of the beaches acquire shack-tavernas in summer.

Getting there The Piraeus ferries, of which there are two a week, take up to thirty-three hours to reach Karpathos depending on how many calls are made on the way.

Olympic has at least one flight a day from Rhodes, four a week from Sitia in Crete and two a week from Kassos.

Transport By bus or taxi along or across the island, and by caique from Pigadia to the coastal villages. Cars, mopeds and bicycles can be rented in Pigadia.

From Karpathos Ports of call on the Piraeus ferries, and by inter-Dodecanese services to Rhodes, Kassos and Halki.

Telephone Police 22 218
Coastguard 22 227
Olympic Airways 22 150
Clinic 22 228/22 296

Kassos

Kassos, or Kasos, has almost too much history for a small island, as if to make up for the absence of tangible remains from the past (at last, an island without a castle!). It celebrates its own holocaust every May, in commemoration of a massacre that helped to make Greece free and Syros rich. The most southerly of the Dodecanese, close to Karpathos and only 27 nautical miles from the north-east coast of Crete, Kassos is a long way on a ferry but can be reached by air from Rhodes.
Area: 65 sq km. Length of coastline: 50 km.
Population: 1,184 (504 in Aghia Marina and 375 in Fri).
Area telephone code: 0245.

History
An island that has the same name now as during the Trojan War, Kassos generally belonged to whoever held Karpathos. Because of its small size and isolation, it did rather nicely for most of the Turkish occupation: by 1779, when a French traveller spoke of it as 'a wonderful little republic where all are free and equal', it had already amassed a degree of wealth from shipping, with a fleet of around 100 medium-sized and small ships.

In May 1824, a combined Turko-Egyptian force sank the Kassos fleet, devastated the island and massacred the inhabitants, with two results unforeseen by the Ottoman court at Constantinople: philhellenes in Europe and the United States were handed another argument for intervention in support of the Greek Revolution, and those Kassos families that escaped fled mainly to Syros as the one island where refugees could feel safe (see The Greeks and the Sea, p. 34, and Syros, p. 222).

When Syros became Greece's principal commercial port and the headquarters of its first real ocean-going merchant fleet, Kassos families were in the forefront, and even today there are families still active in shipping that identify themselves as from Kassos via Syros.

Bearings
Fri, pronounced 'free' and sometimes written as Fris, is the island's capital, on the north-west coast. It has some interesting old 'captains' houses', but little to show the holiday-maker. Its 'port' is the suburb of Emborio, 800 m to the east, which is almost deserted in winter.

What to see
Possible excursions would be to the Monastery of Aghios Georgios 12 km from Fri, which offers beds in a guest-house and use of its kitchen, and two caves of minor interest at Selai and Ellinokamera; the latter, supplied with a fortified entrance, was once used as a refuge from pirates.

Kassos has always been a place to leave rather than to visit; its inhabitants began moving out in the first half of the nineteenth century, and a Kassos contingent is recorded as having worked on the construction of the Suez Canal. You would hardly be likely to go to Kassos unless you happened to be in the locality, which implies either

Beaches	a yacht or an excursion from Karpathos. There are municipal beaches close to Emborio, but the coastline as a whole is difficult to reach from the interior of the island and can be dangerous to approach from the sea. The better swimming, requiring arrangements with a local boatman, is at Armathia or one of the other offshore islets.
Where to stay and eat	There are two listed hotels in Fri, both third class, the ten-room **Anagenissis** (tel. 41 323) and seven-room **Anesis** (tel. 41 201), plus some fifty beds in islanders' homes. At one of five restaurant/tavernas in Fri/Emborio: the **Panorama**, **Milos**, **Emborios**, **Iouliou** and **Zagora**.
Getting there	The two ferries a week from Piraeus cover the 220 nautical miles in thirty-eight hours. Olympic has daily flights by light aircraft from Rhodes (some direct and some via Karpathos), and two a week from Sitea in Crete. Most visitors arrive on excursion boats from Karpathos.
Transport	A bus service links Fri with the two main interior villages, Aghia Marina and Arvanitohoro. For other destinations, you could take a taxi or hire a boat.
From Kassos	Ferry ports of call, Rhodes and Crete by air, excursion boats to Karpathos, and fishing craft to any of the twelve uninhabited satellite islets.
Telephone	Police 41 222 Coastguard 41 288 Olympic Airways 41 555 Clinic 41 333

Kastellorizon

Kastellorizon is an island that refuses to regard its condition as terminal. With a population that has sunk since the beginning of the present century from above 16,000 to fewer than 200, and, in the words of a local song, lying 'on the edge of the edges' of Greece, within hailing distance of the Turkish coast, it is fighting its fate with plans for a free port and a shipping registry. The European Community and the Greek government make favourable noises, though the odds appear to be against the materialisation of either project. Nevertheless, the mouse roars strongly: the late Despina Achladiotou (see pp. 247–8) personified its spirit. Some 330 nautical miles from Piraeus, effectively it can be reached only from Rhodes, 73 nautical miles away.

Area: 9 sq km. Length of coastline: 19 km.

Population: 222 on the day of the 1981 census, including about fifty public servants on assignment – police, Coastguards, and customs, clinic and public utility staffs; there seems no reason to doubt local

assertions that 'real Kastellorizons' number well under 200 and, because so many of them are elderly, are still a diminishing breed.
Area telephone code: 0241.

History

Known in antiquity and officially today as Megisti, the 'big island', not for reasons of irony but because it is the queen of its own little archipelago, Kastellorizon was settled by the Dorians, occupied at one time or another by Rhodians, Romans, pirates, the Knights of St John, Egyptians, Neapolitans, Turks and Italians, bombarded from the Asia Minor coast in the First World War when Turkey was allied with Germany, and reunited with Greece along with the rest of the Dodecanese. It is the smallest of the Dodecanese and the furthest you can travel south-east from Brussels while remaining inside the European Community.

Heading for the brink

Kastellorizon derives from Castel Rosso (Red Castle), the name given to the island by the Knights of St John when they built their fourteenth-century castle on a bluff of red rock overlooking the harbour and only town. Traditionally, the inhabitants have been seamen, and above all sponge-fishers – an occupation that helped to spur emigration to the United States and Australia (because of the sponges found there) in particular, before and especially after the Second World War.

It is easy to understand why the island should be characterised by a frontier spirit: it is just over 3 km off the Turkish coast, and the number of Kastellorizons is considerably less than the 300 Spartans whom Leonidas had with him at Thermopylae. There is a sentiment, on the island and in Athens, that the decline of population has to be arrested for national security as well as social reasons. While it is only common sense that Turkey would never go to war over so small a rock, the Greeks, who are not a particularly logical people themselves (if they were, Greece would be a wealthier country), place little faith in the concept of a logical world.

So how to bring the island back from the brink? It has been given medical and educational services to the degree feasible (the local primary school had nineteen pupils in 1987), construction of an airport has helped psychologically, and both electricity and its handmaiden, television, have been laid on. But still the young leave.

Neither can the answer be sought in tourism. Theoretically, Kastellorizon has more than 150 tourist beds, but in an average peak-season week only from ten to twenty of them are occupied by holidaymakers. Distance is too great a deterrent.

Stronger medicine sought

In 1983, in the search for stronger medicine, the idea occurred of a recourse to the tax bottle, in the form of a free port. The idea was floated by the World Kastellorizon Fraternity, an organisation based on Rhodes that helps Kastellorizons of the diaspora to keep in touch with the affairs of their home island, and was taken by a Greek Conservative Eurodeputy, Constantine Kaloyiannis to the European Parliament in Strasbourg, where it won Europarliament endorsement.

It was maintained that a free port would attract Greek holiday-makers and tourists for the shopping; that the assurance of tourism would stimulate the construction of hotels and restaurants, the expansion of communications and the inclusion of the island on cruise schedules; that the boom for the construction industry (hotels, homes, factories, workshops, port installations and shops) would spill over into small industry and handicrafts; and that the return of Kastellorizons would automatically lead to the elevation of social services to more satisfactory levels.

More succinctly, the Kastellorizon Fraternity declared that only a free port could guarantee the survival of 'an island that has no industry, no cultivation and no livestock, and whose inhabitants live as refugees inside the Community'.

The dream is still pursued, and still unfulfilled; the blame for EC inertia was placed until recently on the absence of Greek government pressure, but is now shared with the conflicting directions implied by the intended completion of a unified internal market for the entire Community by 1992.

Meanwhile, the Fraternity has added to the free port proposal the idea of an 'offshore registry' – a registry of shipping such as that of the Isle of Man, somewhere between a national flag and a flag of convenience. With the Union of Greek Shipowners unenthusiastic, action seems unlikely.

Wherever the answer to the 'demographic problem of Kastellorizon' may lie, eventually it will have to be found.

The woman of Ro

While technically Ro is an offshore islet of Kastellorizon, to most Greeks it is almost the other way round – because of Despina Achladiotou.

In 1975 *Kyra* ('Mother') Despina received a Greek National Defence Ministry medal for her part in a Second World War underground network that smuggled Greek and Allied Servicemen to the Middle East after the German invasion and occupation of Greece. At least, that was what the citation said, for reasons of higher politics and international relations. But there was no doubt in the minds of the Greeks, nor was there intended to be, that the award would probably not have been made, and Despina would have been neither remembered nor honoured, but for a couple of Turkish flags.

For close on half a century she had lived on Ro, the only inhabitant after her husband's death, raising the Greek flag on a staff outside her home every morning. Then, nearly eighty years old, she was forced by declining health to move back to Kastellorizon.

Soon afterwards, a shepherd arriving on Ro to pasture his sheep found a Turkish flag flying there. A second Turkish flag was found on Strongili, another Kastellorizon islet. Athens immediately raised the issue with the Turkish government, and the Greek fleet was reportedly placed on the alert. The incident was defused by a Turkish explanation that the flags had been planted by 'an unauthorised individual, in a silly exhibition resembling a farce'.

The abiding result was that Despina suddenly became a national heroine: the citation could say what was politic and necessary, but the real intention of the award was to honour her devotion to the flag.

When she died of a stroke in 1982, at the age of ninety-two, she received a state funeral, with wreaths laid on behalf of the prime minister and party leaders. After a funeral service on Kastellorizon she was buried on Ro, in a coffin draped with her flag.

What to see

The port-capital of **Megisti**, where all the island's inhabitants live, is a curiously majestic neo-Classical settlement where many of the houses are uninhabited and much of the ruin created by Second World War bombardment is still unrepaired. For the visitor, there are the remains of an ancient acropolis 2 km away, the Castle of the Knights overlooking the town and a Turkish hammam, the Gothic-style Cathedral of Sts Constantine and Helen built in the 1830s partially with stone taken from a Temple of Apollo on the Asia Minor coast, a Lycian tomb, a mosque, an archaeological museum with a small bronze Dionysos and a marble dedication to the goddess Hygeia, and a folk museum.

Accessible by caique only is a **Blue Grotto** (Galazio Spilaio) which the islanders believe will one day become a tourist attraction equal to its *smaller* namesake on Capri.

Beaches

You can swim from rocks close to the port, but nearby Mandraki has a better beach: the best swimming of all, however, is on Ro and Strongili.

Where to stay and eat

Kastellorizon has no listed hotels, but a municipal guest-house (**Xenon Dimou Megistis**) 5 m from the sea provides thirty-two beds (tel. 29 072). There are another fifty beds in five small pensions, and around 100 on offer in private homes.

Since there are only two restaurants and one taverna, you can try them all.

Getting there

The one ferry a week from Piraeus takes between thirty-four and forty hours to reach Kastellorizon. There are two ships a week from Rhodes, and also two flights a week from there by light aircraft.

Transport

The island has no roads outside the town, and therefore the internal combustion engine is used only to power caiques and fishing boats; these will take you to the Blue Grotto, the islets of Strongili and Ro and, if you wish, to small, isolated coves for really private swimming. Taxis are available only in the form of mules and donkeys.

From Kastellorizon

To Rhodes and the two offshore islets. Despite the island's proximity to Asia Minor, it is not possible to visit Turkey from there.

Telephone

Police 29 068
Coastguard 29 070

Olympic Airways 29 880
Clinic 29 067

Kos

Kos, or Ko (or Cos or Co, even though the Greek alphabet has no 'C'), is an elongated, dolphin-shaped island some 45 km long between Rhodes and Kalymnos. It is the third largest of the Dodecanese islands after Rhodes and Karpathos, second only to Rhodes as a tourist resort, and a place of pilgrimage for those doctors to whom the medical profession is as much a mission as a livelihood. Hippocrates was born on Kos, the Knights of St John built one of their finest castles there, and just over ten years ago the island was peripheral to one of the greatest psychosomatic mysteries of modern Greece – the so-called 'water of Kos' affair. It is also Greece's unofficial bicycle capital, with more than 4,000 available for hire. It lies 201 nautical miles from Piraeus, is well-connected by sea and air, but, despite the Asclepion, is rarely included on cruise-liner schedules.

Area: 290 sq km. Length of coastline: 112 km.
Population: 21,066 (11,851 in Kos town).
Area telephone code: 0242.

History

Kos first achieved fame and prosperity in the fourth century BC, when the capital was transferred to its present site and the island became a trading and maritime power renowned for its wines and silks.

Conquered by Alexander the Great in 336 BC, the island passed to the Ptolemies after his death and subsequently into Roman occupation. It retained its importance in the early part of the Byzantine era, though increasingly subjected to the ravages of piracy. In 1306 the Genoese handed it to the Knights of St John, who took possession in 1315. They then lost it to the Turks in 1522, along with Rhodes. After nearly four centuries of Turkish domination, the island was held by the Italians from 1912 until its incorporation into Greece after the Second World War.

Between the Italian surrender in 1943 and the island's liberation by the British two years later, Kos was held by the Germans: barely 10 per cent of the Jewish community survived their visitation.

Philadelphians may not be aware that Berenice, wife of Ptolemy I, gave birth to Ptolemy II on Kos; he, after marrying his sister Arsinoe, acquired the sobriquet *Filadelphios*, in this case denoting sibling rather than brotherly love.

Kos city was destroyed by earthquakes in AD 142 and rebuilt on a magnificent scale; destroyed again – and again rebuilt – in 469. But after it happened a third time, in 554, the inhabitants gave up and moved out, and the city entered into an eight-century eclipse. Since the latest earthquake, in 1933, the town has largely been rebuilt to anti-seismic standards, at the cost of some of its charm.

Hippocrates

Doctors still take the Hippocratic oath, which commits them not to practise euthanasia, not to aid in the procurement of an abortion, not to seduce their patients, and to preserve the secrecy of the consulting room even, or so it is currently argued in Greece, from the tax authorities.

Hippocrates is believed to have been born on Kos in or around 460 BC, to have spent half his life there, then to have toured the Greek world acquiring and disseminating knowledge. He is said to have died in Larisa, central Greece, at the age of 104 or 109.

Visitors in search of Hippocrates can go to the **Asclepion**, 4 km outside the town, to see the general setting in which he must have lived and worked, even though the sanctuary was built after his death. They will be taken, inside the town, to the 'plane tree of Hippocrates', a tree of undeniable majesty but certainly not more than a few centuries old.

However, acceptance that tradition can be evocative without historical exactitude does not necessarily imply gullibility; under such a tree, somewhere not too far away, Hippocrates probably did hold classes on just such a summer's day.

The Asclepion, or Sanctuary of Asclipios, built in the fourth century BC over the remains of a Temple of Apollo, occupies one of the finest sites for such 'hospitals' anywhere in the Aegean.

On the lower levels were the hot baths, the medical centre, the medicinal springs, small temples and hostels. The site extends along four levels up the slope of a hill, each level linked by wide marble staircases. On top is the second-century Temple of Asclipios, of which only the foundations and a few columns survive; compensation is offered in the form of a magnificent view of the Asia Minor coast and the peninsula of Helicarnassos, where Herodotus was born.

Although extensive, the Asclepion can easily become crowded when up to twenty excursion coaches arrive at the same time. On the other hand, if you go early to avoid the groups you will need to do some reading first, since the Asclepion is one place where guides are really useful. In discussing the importance attached by Hippocrates, as an early psychiatrist, to preservation and reinforcement of the will to live in the event of serious illness, the guides can rarely resist the temptation to observe that in antiquity the women of Kos were famous because their dresses were so thin and diaphanous that it was 'as if they were wearing the wind'.

Excavated in the late nineteenth century, the Asclepion was extensively restored by order of Mussolini.

The water of Kos

One of the dicta of Hippocrates was that 'any spring on which the sun shines' has therapeutic qualities. In 1976 this became a source of acute embarrassment to the Greek authorities, in a protracted incident that was never settled to anyone's entire satisfaction.

It began when Athens was gripped by reports of a 'Kos water' that was achieving miraculous cancer cures. An Athens lawyer who had been born on Kos, had studied the teachings of Hippocrates and had been impressed by his emphasis on natural springs, claimed to have discovered a 'radioactive' water that was effective against all forms of tumours.

At first the water was distributed, always for nothing, from a shipowner's apartment in central Athens, until the crowds outside stalled the traffic; it was then carted around in water trucks and distributed by the bucketful in squares, churchyards and soccer stadiums. When patients began to flee the hospitals, the Health Ministry pleaded with them not to abandon classical treatment but to take the water as an 'extra' if they wished.

Hysteria mounted, and politics intruded. Left-wing newspapers said the monarchists were behind the water, the right-wing press identified a Communist plot, and the journalists' union issued an anguished cry for an end to sensationalism. The government was criticised in Parliament for not ordering police intervention; its inertia, it was told, was making Greece look ridiculous around the world.

Finally, the lawyer and the shipowner were charged with illegal exercise of the medical profession and, after a two-day trial, were sentenced and ordered to pay token fines. They were acquitted of unlawfully circulating a pharmaceutical product after it was established that the water was indeed only water, as they had always said it was.

The court called no testimony from the hundreds who claimed to have been cured, nor concerned itself with the source of the water. Simply, distribution of the water was banned. However, boatloads of Athenians who went to Kos to fill bottles from the Asclepion found *that* water, at least, to be ineffectual.

It was not, of course, the first case in Greece of 'miraculous' cures; in 1955 similar claims had been made for a yellow liquid which, on analysis, turned out to consist of sugar, alcohol, cucumber juice and strawberry essence, while another a few years later proved only to be water in which spinach had been boiled.

There were two main differences between the Kos water and all its predecessors: no one made a drachma profit, nor would have from eventual patent rights, and rarely had the Greeks been so passionately divided on a non-political issue. Even now, nobody understands exactly what happened; the present assumption that it was only tapwater raises more questions than it answers. Even at the time, there was a suspicion that the medical establishment may have preferred not to inquire too closely into results obtained by unorthodox treatment, on the respected principle that no cure at all is preferable to one incapable of scientific explanation.

What to see

Kos town, on the north-east tip of the island, is a soporific modern city of wide, tree-shaded streets, dominated by the well-preserved Castle of the Knights. The ruins of the ancient town, scattered throughout the modern city, include Hellenistic and Roman housing, parts of an agora of the fourth and third centuries BC, Temples of Dionysos, Aphrodite and Irakles (Hercules), a third-century theatre with twelve rows of seats, a restored Roman villa (the 'casa Romana'), Hellenistic and Roman baths and parts of a Roman road.

Some of the Turkish mosques are still in use to serve the island's Moslem minority.

Exhibits in the Kos Museum include a statue of Hippocrates which is believed to date from the fourth century BC, while those in the castle itself are from the Classical to Byzantine periods. Kos town can be seen in a day; if you stay longer, it would probably be for the swimming.

Beaches

The most developed beaches, with resort hotels, are on either side of the town, at Lambi and Aghios Fokas. Less crowded beaches (though you would not go to Kos for private swimming) can be reached at the end of turnings from the main road running the length of the island: they include Marmari, Tingaki (popular with nudists), Mastihari, Kardamena, Neropida and, at the southern tip, Kamari.

Where to stay

Kos has 136 listed hotels with a total 6,665 rooms; ninety-four of the hotels with 3,947 rooms are in Kos town and the rest along various beaches. Nine of the hotels are first class, thirty-nine second class, seventy third class and only eighteen fourth and fifth class, demonstrating the extent to which the development of tourism on Kos is recent. Equally indicative of the dependence on tourism, only sixteen of the hotels stay open in winter. The average of 48.9 rooms per hotel is among the highest in Greece: two of the hotels have more than 300 rooms, four have from 200 to 300, and eight provide between 100 and 200 rooms.

There are major hotel-bungalow complexes in Kos town, Aghios Fokas and Marmari, and large first-class hotels in the town, Kefala and Psalidi.

In addition, there are numerous self-catering apartments, and more than 2,000 licensed beds in private houses.

While even the most inept travel agent would have difficulty in going far wrong when recommending accommodation on Kos, nevertheless you might bear in mind the following hotels:

- In Kos town, the **Continental Palace** (first class, 297 rooms, tel. 41 291), and **Aghios Constantinos** (second class, 125 rooms, tel. 23 301).
- In Aghios Fokas, the **Dimitra Beach** (first class, 134 rooms, tel. 28 581).
- In Kardamena, the **Norida Beach** (first class, 386 rooms, tel. 91 231).
- In Lambi, the **Atlantis** (first class, 297 rooms, tel. 28 731), and **Cosmopolitan** (second class, seventy-eight rooms, tel. 23 411).
- In Tingaki, the **Sunset** (third class, fifty-two rooms, tel. 29 428).

Where to eat

Though Kos tourism was to some extent pioneered by Scandinavians, the movement is now cosmopolitan.

There are well over 150 restaurants, tavernas, fish tavernas, cafés, pizzerias and fast-food establishments, and for afterwards a choice among bars, discos, nightclubs, cinemas and occasional summer performances of ancient Greek drama.

In Kos town your hotel porter is likely to direct you, with satisfactory results, to the restaurants **Sifis**, **No. 9**, **Intermezzo**, **Oscar** and **George's House**, and the tavernas **Eleni** and **Nikos**. For pizza you could try the **Kamelia**.

Getting there

Most tourists arrive on Kos by direct charter flights. For those already in Greece, there are at least three flights a day in summer from Athens and two ferries a day from Piraeus (fifteen hours).

Transport

On average, there are about five buses a day from Kos town to the main villages and beach resorts, from a terminus in Kleopatras (Cleopatra) Street. The island can also be toured in excursion coaches, and cars, taxis, mopeds and bicycles can be hired.

From Kos

By air to Rhodes (daily) and Leros (three flights a week). By sea to ports of call on the Piraeus ferries; there are also boats daily to Rhodes and less frequently to Crete and other islands of the Dodecanese and Cyclades groups, hydrofoils to Rhodes and Patmos, and excursion boats to Rhodes and other nearby islands.

Telephone

Police 22 100/22 222
Coastguard 28 507
NTOG 28 724
Olympic Airways 28 331
Hospital 22 300

Leipsi

Leipsi, which you will see written also as Lipsi (the way it is pronounced) or Leipso/Lipso, is at the north-east corner of the Dodecanese, east of Patmos, south of Samos and north of Leros. If it seems to have too many alternative names for an island of 16 sq km, bear with it: the island takes the plural form (a strict translation would be The Lipsis) as queen of its own archipelago of more than twenty-five islets, most of them uninhabited. It would not take a particularly large hotel to accommodate the whole population. However, if the sound of a distant tractor is too much for the nerves, you can take a caique to Arki, where sixty-eight people live, and, if even that is not quiet enough, slip across the channel to Marathos; there, if the whole population were musical, it could form a quintet. Throughout this miniature archipelago, the swimming is magnificent.

Area: 16 sq km. Length of coastline: 35 km.

Population: The Leipsi islands 574, the Agathonisi islands 133, the Arki islands 68, Marathos 5.
Area telephone code: 0247.

Port and capital

Leipsi town, on the south-west coast, is the port, capital and only village, which would relieve pressure on the road network if there were one and explains why the only wheels needed are those on farm vehicles. At night the male inhabitants gather in the square to drink ouzo; on summer Saturdays they have an open-air party there, a *glendi*, to which the women go too.

Beaches

The beaches begin within five minutes of the waterfront, at Lentou and then Kambos; within a 3-km radius there are also Kyra Vassilainas, Hochlakouras, Katsadia and, best of all, Platys Yialos, where there is a fish taverna in summer. On the north coast, Monodendri is a nudist beach.

Where to stay

The **Calypso Hotel**, fourth class, tel. 41 242, has twenty-eight beds, there are another sixty in four small pensions, and officially there are fifteen beds on offer in rented rooms – a figure that may be regarded as expandable, since the islanders are known for their hospitality.

Where to eat

The **Calypso Hotel** has a taverna, and you could also look for the **Barbarossa**, **Delphini**, **Kali Kardia** and, particularly for fish, the **Mangou**.

Getting there

The only logical way is from Patmos or Leros; the weekly Piraeus ferry, which carries the mail, takes fifty hours for the trip, and there is also a weekly boat from Rhodes.

Transport

You take small boats, hitch rides on farm vehicles (it is polite to offer payment even if one is not requested), or walk.

From Leipsi

There are three boats a week to the Arki islands and two to the Agathonisi islands; otherwise, you arrange your private transportation.

Telephone

Police 41 222
Coastguard 41 240
Clinic 41 204

Leros

Objectively, which means your travel agent will not know about it, Leros has less to recommend it to the holiday-maker than most of its Dodecanese associates. For the independent traveller, this can be a reason to go there. Leros is small, compact, a little out-of-the-way, and in general a good place for the undemanding to be alone in; any group you run up against is likely to consist of Athenians. Lying between Kalymnos and Patmos, it is 178 nautical miles from Piraeus.
Area: 53 sq km. Length of coastline: 71 km.

Population: 8,136 (2,462 in Aghia Marina/Platanos, 2,469 in Lakki and 1,646 in Xyrokambos).
Area telephone code: 0247.

Port and capital

The Piraeus ferries disembark their passengers at **Lakki**, the uninteresting, Italianate main port of Leros at the head of a deep bay with an entrance only 500 m wide – a geographical configuration that makes it one of the finest anchorages in the Mediterranean after Crete's Suda Bay. In the Second World War the Italians used it as a naval base, which resulted in considerable damage by German bombardment after their capitulation; a memorial on the waterfront commemorates the sinking of a Greek warship there by German dive-bombers.

What to see

There is little to detain you in Lakki unless you are irresistibly drawn by minor Mussolinian architecture, though you could take a look at four churches: Aghios Spyridon, Aghios Zaharias, Aghios Georgios at the entrance to the bay, and the partly eleventh-century Aghios Ioannis. Accommodation is available in rented rooms and swimming can be performed in small coves, but both are better elsewhere on Leros.

A 4-km drive brings you to the capital, **Platanos**, which in effect is three villages – Platanos where the big houses are, Aghia Marina which is the second port of Leros, and the fishing village of Panteli – that band together to form an attractive town.

Platanos has a well-preserved castle, begun by the Byzantines and completed by the Crusaders and Knights of St John, which shelters a fourteenth-century Monastery of the Virgin; a small museum outside the walls houses finds from local excavations. The ruins of an ancient town of the Classical period can be seen near the entrance to Aghia Marina harbour.

Around the island

The best beach and at the same time most touristically-developed settlement is at **Alinta**, a kilometre or so north of Platanos, where there are four hotels and a number of furnished apartments and rooms for rent, and three monasteries for when the skin peels or the sea palls: Aghia Sofronia, Aghios Isidoros and Aghion Saranda (Forty Saints).

Panteli is the main alternative to Alinta; there, the accommodation is simpler and cheaper and the fish tavernas are a little more basic. Also, since Panteli is preferred by youths and discos go where their clients are likely to be, the nights are noisier.

Beaches

For peaceful, uncrowded swimming from long, sandy beaches, Xyrokambos is in a bay at the southern tip of the island where the wind scarcely ever penetrates. Caiques leave from there for Kalymnos.

Finally, up in the north of the island, 8 km from Platanos, the village of Partheni occupies a less sheltered bay, with adequate beaches and the remains of a Temple of Artemis. Small boats will take you to the uninhabited islet of Archangelos, for some really private swimming.

There are organised beaches also at Blefouti, Koulouki and Gournas, but the whole coastline is studded with stretches of sand where you carry your own shade and refreshments.

Where to stay

Leros has fifteen listed hotels (two second class, seven third class, one fourth class and five fifth class) with a total of 229 rooms, as well as self-catering apartments, usually booked early from Athens, and some 160 licensed beds in private homes.

Islanders speak well of two third-class hotels at Alinta, the **Maleas Beach** (forty-seven rooms, tel. 23 306) and the **Alinta** (twenty-four rooms, tel. 23 266) for their proximity to the sea and good restaurants.

Where to eat

The islanders insist that it is not a matter of restaurant but of fish, and that the fish, even in restricted varieties, will usually be fresh wherever it is on offer; nevertheless, you should inspect it first.

For whiling away the hours between dinner and midnight, there are two nightclubs with orchestras – the **Cosmopolitan** at Alinta and **Deilina** at Vromolitho – as well as the Panteli discos.

Getting there

There are seven ferries a week from Piraeus and nine flights a week in summer by nineteen-seater light aircraft from Athens.

Transport

Though less than 20 km long, Leros would be three islands if it were not for two linking peninsulas. The 50-km road network is partly asphalted, and communications are provided by a single bus and twenty-nine taxis. It is possible to hire a car, but easier to find a moped or bicycle. Caiques and fishing boats will take you around the island, alone or more economically on organised excursions.

From Leros

By 'ferries of the line' to Rhodes, Kalymnos, Kos and Patmos, daily in the summer. By caique to Kalymnos daily and Patmos and Leipsi three times a week. By air, three flights a week, to Rhodes and Kos.

You can also visit the offshore islets of Agathonisi and Farmakonisi, the former with a population of 133 and the latter with a population of 1. Agathonisi (13 sq km, 30 km of coastline) has two settlements, but does not pretend to cater to tourists. Farmakonisi once had a most distinguished visitor: Julius Caesar was held there for a month by pirates, awaiting ransom. He later caught and crucified his captors, as he had told them he would.

Telephone

Police 22 222
Coastguard 22 224
Olympic Airways 23 502
Clinic 22 213

Nisyros

Nisyros is an optical illusion, born of a myth. Seen from the deck of an approaching ship, it appears large because of its towering volcano, then turns out to be little more than the mountain itself. Dormant but not extinct, the volcano's last eruption was in 1522, though some threatening rumbles were heard in 1888. Just over 200 nautical miles from Piraeus, Nisyros is usually reached by boat from Kos, which is only 10 nautical miles to the north.

Area: 41 sq km. Length of coastline: 28 km.

Population: 984 (650 in Mandraki, 128 in Pali and 66 on the offshore islet of Yiali). In the 1971 census the population numbered 1,289, which suggests that there has been a continuing move to reinforce Nisyran contingents in the Greek communities of New York and Melbourne.

Area telephone code: 0242.

An epic contest

Once upon a time there was the Battle of the Giants, or Titans – the gods of Mount Olympos against the forces of darkness. Poseidon, taking his stand on Kos, seized a rock hurled at him by the giant Polyvotis and threw it back; as it fell into the sea he ordered it to become a volcano, and in instant obedience it buried Polyvotis beneath a mass of lava. Thus was formed Nisyros the island and Polyvotis the volcano. The name Nisyros is believed to have derived from the Phoenician for 'observation post'. On the whole, whatever happened to Kos happened to Nisyros too.

Port and capital

Visitors land at **Mandraki**, the port and capital on the north-west corner of the island. From there, the only road – not particularly well maintained – runs along the north coast to Pali and then, skirting the volcano, south to the fishing village of Avlaki.

What to see

The Mandraki castle, founded by the Byzantines and restored and strengthened by the Knights, is still in fairly good condition, and offers sweeping views of the offshore islets of Yiali and Kandelousa. A Church-Cave of the Panaghia Spiliani (Virgin of the Cave), dating from the early seventeenth century and once a monastery, has a library and small museum, while the ruins of an acropolis and traces of a city of the fourth century BC lie just outside Mandraki.

Loutra, a kilometre from Mandraki, has some highly sulphurous medicinal springs, reputed since antiquity to be effective against rheumatism and certain dermatological conditions; there is a municipal guest-house (tel. 31 284) for those taking the waters.

However, the most obvious reason for visiting Nisyros – except, as always, for the swimming – would be to take a look at the volcano. Buses run to Emborio (population 46) and Nikia (population 84), two villages from where footpaths lead to the edge of the crater. The closer you get, the stronger the smell of sulphur becomes. While the rim of the crater is near enough for most people, there are steps leading down into it for vulcanologists and bolder spirits.

Emborio has a crumbling Byzantine fort, and there are monasteries there and at **Nikia**; from Nikia, it is a ten-minute drive or forty-five-minute walk to the road's end at Avlaki, where there is good swimming from a rather forbidding beach of black pebbles. Pleasanter

Beaches

beaches are at and near Pali on the north coast, and there are patches of sand around Mandraki itself, but the best beach of all – 2 km of fine sand – is on Yiali islet. Yiali is gradually shrinking, as a result of its pumice exports.

Where to stay and eat

Nisyros has no listed hotels (tourism is largely a matter of day-trippers from Kos) but three adequate pensions at Mandraki: the fifteen-bed **municipal guest-house** (tel. 31 204), the twenty-five-bed **Romantzo** (tel. 31 340, also a taverna) and the nine-bed **Tria Adelphia** (tel. 31 344). If the need arose, the islanders would probably make another 400 beds available in their homes, mostly in Mandraki.

Apart from the **Romantzo**, you could eat at the **Nisyros Taverna**, the **Nikos** and the **Tsardaka**, all in Mandraki.

Getting there

Two or three ferries a week from Piraeus (nineteen hours), two calls a week by the inter-Dodecanese ferries, a weekly ship from Samos, daily excursion boats from Kos, and hydrofoils once a week from Rhodes and Kos.

Transport

Bus services to the main villages: Loutra, Pali, Emborio, Nikia and Avlaki, caiques to Yiali, and caique excursions along the coasts; also motorboat, moped and taxi availability.

From Nisyros

Kos, Rhodes and ports of call on the Piraeus and inter-Dodecanese ferries.

Telephone

Police 31 201
Coastguard 31 222
Clinic 31 217

Patmos

The Blessed Christodoulos, who lived on Patmos during the eleventh and twelfth centuries, was right: it is one of the loveliest islands in the world. As the ferry or cruise liner creeps into the sheltered east-coast bay of Skala, crowned by the great fortress monastery, the silence is broken only by tinkling sheep-bells and the bark of the occasional village dog – until the anchor, unheard in an ordinary port, thunders into the water.

Patmos, half-way between Ikaria and Leros, is indelibly associated with St John and the Bible's Book of Revelation; it is also an island of wonderful beaches, with a growing tourist movement that poses a discernible threat of its becoming a resort. See it soon, while there is still time: 163 nautical miles from Piraeus, at the north-east corner of the Dodecanese, it is well connected by ferries and is a call on most Aegean cruises, but at least it does not yet have an airport or any resort hotels.

Area: 34 sq km. Length of coastline: 63 km.
Population: 2,607 including the offshore islets; 1,352 in Skala, 748 in Hora and 405 in Kambos.
Area telephone code: 0247.

Before and after Christ

In mythology, Orestes went to Patmos during his flight from the Furies after the murder of his mother, Clytemnestra. To the Romans, the island seemed a suitable place of exile for political and religious opponents and so, in AD 95, the Emperor Domitian sent the aged Apostle John there for preaching the new religion in Ephesus.

St John, known as the Evangelist, the Divine and the Theologian, took refuge in a cave half-way up the hill now crowned by the monastery, and there dictated the Book of Revelation to his disciple, Prohoros, as it was whispered to him through a crack in the roof. A slope in the rock is said to be the desk where Prohoros wrote, and silver haloes are set in the stone that was the Apostle's pillow and the grip by which he raised himself from his knees.

Though St John is referred to as the author of one of the Gospels as well as the Book of Revelation and three Epistles, there is some dispute among scholars, based on grammatical and stylistic incompatibilities, on whether Gospel and Apocalypse could have been written by the same person.

In 1088 the Byzantine Emperor Alexis I Komninos gave the island to the monk Christodoulos (subsequently Ossios, the Blessed), to found the monastery dedicated to St John, on the site of an earlier church to the same saint that had been abandoned when pirate raids forced the inhabitants to flee further from the sea. If history had gone another way, Patmos might today be a semi-autonomous monastic republic similar to Mount Athos.

The monastery was built as a fortress because of the continuing threat of piracy. Though left in peace by the Venetians and the Turks, its hold over the island gradually weakened in the sixteenth century as Patmos developed into a centre of shipping and trade. Like so many Aegean islands, Patmos fell back into obscurity with the coming of steamships.

The monastery

With its formidable array of battlements, towers, cupolas and belfries, the monastery has the appearance more of a castle than of a place of worship, study and contemplation. Inside, the crowding can be horrendous if only a single cruise liner has arrived; if two or three drop anchor at the same time, you will spend more time queuing than viewing. This was particularly true in 1988, when the monastery celebrated its nine hundredth anniversary, but permanently makes it preferable to visit Patmos independently.

The monastery's greatest treasures are the 3,000 rare volumes and more than 900 manuscripts in its library, which are not on view to tourists. Its archives also include 13,000 documents issued by Byzantine emperors, popes, patriarchs, Turkish sultans and their officials, written in Greek, Latin, Turkish and Slavic, that together make up the largest collection of its kind outside the Vatican and form an invaluable source of general, local, ecclesiastical, diplomatic and cultural history.

Among treasures that are on display to the casual visitor are examples of the monastery's 200 masterpieces of Byzantine iconography of the eleventh to fourteenth centuries, 600 vestments of the seventeenth and eighteenth centuries, and more than 300 articles and votive offerings of gold and silver, many of them encrusted with precious stones. Visitors can also admire the terraced roof and bell towers, and take a look at the refectory.

To facilitate the work of scholars, the monastery has now been supplied not only with electricity but also with microcomputers. In the last decade, meetings have been held there of Greek Orthodox, Roman Catholic and Protestant clergy to debate Christian unity.

The monastery is open daily, except Sundays, from 9 or 10 a.m. until around noon, and on some afternoons. With only thirty monks in permanent residence, it still needs to be a fortress, not so much because of the number of visitors as to protect the treasures. The Monastery of the Apocalypse on the lower slopes of the hill, with the grotto of St John, is closed only on Sunday afternoons. You will not be admitted to either if considered improperly dressed.

Around the island

Patmos is almost two islands, joined by a narrow neck of land less than a kilometre wide; the east-coast port of **Skala**, where ferries tie up and cruise liners drop anchor offshore, is in a bay at the island's narrowest point. It is a small, cosmopolitan settlement with most of the Patmos hotels and public services, built on the site of Ancient Foras. Visitors can take a look at the remains of a third-century BC acropolis and swim from nearby beaches, but more commonly set off at once for the monastery and Hora.

Hora, the capital, known also as Patmos, is only 4 km from Skala. A settlement of old mansions and small houses along the slopes of the hill between the monastery and the sea, it quickly becomes deserted once the monastery closes for the day. The village itself dates from the thirteenth century, and some of the larger 'captains' houses' (Kapetanospita) from the sixteenth. Life in Hora centres on its two squares and one market place.

Grikos, winter population 29 when the summer inhabitants move to Skala and Hora, is a seaside village 5 km from Hora, and **Kambos**, population 405, just under 12 km from Hora in the northern section of the island, is the current 'tourist discovery'; it offers swimming in a sheltered bay, profuse greenery, two monasteries for those whose appetite for the ecclesiastical has not been sated already, but as yet has no listed hotels.

Patmos shares with its neighbour, Leipsi, the offshore islets of Arki and Marathos (see p. 254); both can be reached equally easily from

Beaches either island.

The best beaches are along the east coast, and include Lambi, Kambos, Agriolivadi, Meli, Grikos and Psili Ammos. While all can be reached by road, it is easier to take a small boat to Psili Ammos.

Where to stay There are seventeen listed hotels at Skala and eight at Grikos, all in the second-to-fourth categories, with a combined total of 434 rooms, as well as approximately eighty beds in furnished apartments and more than 850 in private houses.

At Grikos, you could well try the second-class **Xenia** (thirty-five rooms, tel. 31 219), which is also the only one with a restaurant. At Skala there are the **Skala** itself (second class, forty-eight rooms, tel. 31 343) and **Chris** (third class, twenty-six rooms, tel. 31 001), among a cluster of perfectly adequate pension-style units.

Where to eat Patmos has thirty-six restaurants, tavernas and snack bars, fifteen of them in Skala, seven in Hora, four in Grikos, three in Kambos and the rest in Lambi, Meli and Agriolivadi.

In Hora, you can be sure of eating well at the **Patiniotiko Spiti** (Patmian House), **Galaxias** and **Pyrgos**; a 'critic's choice' in Skala would include the **Villa Zaharo**, **Toxotis**, **Astro tou Aigaiou** (Star of the Aegean) and **Skorpios**.

Getting there Apart from cruise-liner calls, there are eight ferries a week in summer from Piraeus (a ten-hour trip).

Transport Patmos has four bus services: between Skala and Hora for the monastery and grotto (nine departures daily in summer), Hora and Grikos (four departures), Grikos and Skala (six) and Skala and Kambos (three). Cars and mopeds can be rented in Skala, taxis are available, and there are motorboats for reaching the remoter villages in the northern part of the island.

From Patmos Ports of call on the Piraeus and inter-Dodecanese ferries, and connections to many of the Cyclades islands. In the summer, hydrofoil links with Rhodes, Kos, Leros and Samos. Local boats to the islets of Arki, Marathos and Hiliomodi: the last-named is a rock inhabited one day a year, 27 July, when its only building, the Church of Aghios Pandeleimon, celebrates its patronal festival, but it does have a beach of black volcanic sand.

Telephone Police 31 303
Coastguard 31 231
Clinic 31 577/31 211

Simi

Lying within the embrace of two Asia Minor peninsulas, and therefore with Turkey on three of its sides, Simi (also written Symi and Syme) is an island with a fairly lush interior, rocky coasts studded with small, sandy coves, and a port capital of varied neo-Classical styles. It lies 230 nautical miles from Piraeus, but a more practical 25 nautical miles from Rhodes to the south-east.

Area: 58 sq km. Length of coastline: 86 km.

Population: 2,273 (2,165 in the capital, Ano Simi, and 60 in Pedi, the next largest settlement).

Area telephone code: 0241.

Mythology and history

In mythology, Simi was named for a princess of Rhodes who eloped to the island with a seaman, Glafkos. In antiquity it was known sometimes as Aigli, nymph mother of the Three Graces. Homer refers to it in the context of the Trojan War, and subsequent occupiers included Romans, Byzantines, Knights of St John, Turks and Italians. The Turks gave the island tax and trade concessions to ensure the continued construction of the renowned Simian ships, but cancelled them after it involved itself in the 1821 Revolution. The German surrender of the Dodecanese to the Allies was signed in Ano Simi in March 1945, though not until considerable damage had been caused by bombardment and demolition.

Bearings

Ano Simi (Upper Simi), known also as **Hora**, is a fifteen-minute uphill walk from its harbour suburb of Yialos, known also as Aegialo.

With the principal exception of the Crusader castle overlooking it, Ano Simi dates mainly from the second half of the nineteenth century, when the island was flourishing on the proceeds of shipping and sponge-fishing and had a population of around 20,000.

Since much of the Second World War damage is still unrepaired, Ano Simi and Yialos have been declared protected settlements, as a precaution for when redevelopment eventually acquires greater momentum.

Simi caiques, regarded as Greece's finest, are still being built in the smaller of the two Yialos anchorages.

What to see

Before heading for the beaches, take a look at the Castle of the Knights, the Church of the Panaghia (the island's largest) and the small museum, in which exhibits range from sculptures and coins to handicrafts. If short of time, you could swim from the Yialos public beach.

A drive of 15 km would take you to **Panormitis**, population 35, and a monastery of the same name that dates in its present form from 1783; during the Second World War it was one of the stopovers on escape routes to the Middle East. This and another monastery in the same area, the Megalou Sotira (Great Saviour), have cells for the passing stranger. Though the road is adequate, both can be reached more easily by caique. (If you plan to stay at the Panormitis monastery you should telephone 71 354, but without expecting the monk who answers to speak English.)

The only other settlements are:

- **Pedi**, a small east-coast harbour that produces figs, pears, olives, almonds and grapes, has Hellenistic and Roman ruins, and in summer can accommodate up to fifty tourists in rented rooms and feed them in seasonal tavernas and cafés.

- **Emborios**, known also as Nimborios, the island's second harbour, with a restaurant in summer, good swimming, Byzantine ruins and a loyal winter population of 5.
- And **Marathounda**, which is less developed than Emborios even though its winter population of 7 is 40 per cent larger.

Beaches

You are unlikely to be crowded at the more remote beaches, which are reached on foot or by caique: Aghios Emilianos and Nanou are probably the best, though nudists seem to prefer Disalona and Aghios Isidoros. To be really alone, you could try the offshore islets, such as Nimos and Seskli; though uninhabited in winter, some of them acquire family cook-shops, technically tavernas, in the tourist season.

Where to stay

Surprisingly for so small an island, there are four listed hotels in Hora/Yialos – two of first class and two of second – with a total of forty-two rooms: twenty-four in the first-class **Aliki** and **Dorian** (tel. 71 665 and 71 181 respectively) and eighteen in the second-class **Grace** and **Metapontis** (tel. 71 415 and 71 491 respectively). There are an estimated 500 beds on offer in furnished apartments and private homes at Ano Simi and another fifty at Pedi, and cells at the **Monasteries of Panormitis**, **Megalou Sotira** and **Aghios Emilianos**.

For general information on Simi accommodation, tel. 71 304 or 71 077.

Where to eat

If you want something French, try **Les Caterinettes** in Yialos; still in the harbour area, you can find more mundane food, including fish, at **Madame Butterfly**, the **Simi** and the **International**. Up in the Old Town, **Georgios** is recommended for its owner's personality and **Panorama** for the view, though the eating at both is also good.

Getting there

Two ferries a week from Piraeus, for the very patient, cover the distance in twenty-six hours; from Rhodes it takes one and a half hours on the daily boat, and less on the occasional hydrofoil.

Transport

A bus runs from Yialos through Ano Simi to Pedi; otherwise, you use caique, motorboat or feet.

From Simi

Ports of call on the Piraeus ferries, boats to Rhodes or, by local means, to the offshore islets: Nimos, Seskli, Troumpeto, Kouloundros, Diavatis, Oxia, Pidima, Megalonisi, Karavalonisi, Marmara, Aghia Marina and Ghi.

Telephone

Police 71 238
Coastguard 71 205
Clinic 71 316

Tilos

If you find yourself sharing Tilos with more than fifty other holiday-makers, you should have avoided peak season. If you decide to swim from a beach where more than five strangers are ahead of you, then clearly you like crowds. Lying 190 nautical miles from Piraeus but reached more conveniently from Rhodes, Tilos is a place to be alone. With Nisyros to the north and Halki to the south, it is one of the three stepping-stone islands between Rhodes and Kos.

Area: 62.8 sq km. Length of coastline: 62.7 km.

Population: 301 (189 in Megalo Hori and 112 in Livadia), down from 349 in 1971.

Area telephone code: 0241.

History

Known as Agathousa in the days of the Dorians, Tilos was sufficiently important by the seventh century BC to participate with Rhodes in founding a colony in Sicily, and in the fifth century BC it appeared on the Athens tax rolls. After lengthy obscurity, it was taken by the Knights of St John, who knew it as Piskopi, and from then on shared the fate of the Dodecanese as a whole.

Around the island

The east-coast harbour of **Livadia** is a new village built in traditional style, with little to attract the tourist. A cement road links it with the capital, **Megalo Hori**, which has rather more (the 6 km drive offers a view of the island's third village, Mikro Hori, now totally abandoned).

Built on the slopes of Mount Kastro, Megalo Hori has ruins of an acropolis and a Knight's castle, a small museum where the exhibits include bones of a dwarf elephant found in a nearby cave, and the more accessible of the island's two monasteries, that of Aghios Antonios.

The more impressive of the monasteries, dedicated to the island's patron saint, Aghios Pandeleimonos, is 6 km away on a hill overlooking the west coast; it dates from the fourteenth century, and has a small guest-house.

Beaches

You can swim in the bay of Livadia, at Eristo some 3 km away, and at Aghios Antonios and Plaka; really private beaches can be reached by motorboat from Livadia.

Where to stay

There is only one listed hotel, the fifth-class **Livadia** at Livadia (twenty rooms, tel. 53 202). In the unlisted category, there are two beach pensions at Livadia, two at Megalo Hori and one at Aghios Antonios as well as probably some hundred beds in rentable rooms (the exact number varies according to how many dispersed Tiliotes are back for holidays themselves and how many of the local inhabitants are taking their annual break).

Where to eat

At the **Ekonomou** in Megalo Hori and, for fish, the **Georgara** on

	the coast 2 km away (it also offers rooms); at the **Tropicana** and **Nafsicaa** in Eristo (they too offer rooms); and at the **Irina**, **Stefanaki** and **Hatzifondas** at Livadia.
Getting there	Two ferries a week from Piraeus (twenty-three hours) and five boats a week from Rhodes (just under five hours); also, excursion boats from Rhodes.
Transport	A matter of farm vehicle, small boat, mule, donkey, bicycle, feet, and a single twelve-seater bus.
From Tilos	Port of call on the Piraeus and inter-Dodecanese ferries, a weekly connection with Crete and local boats to Halki.
Telephone	Police/Coastguard 53 222 Clinic 53 210

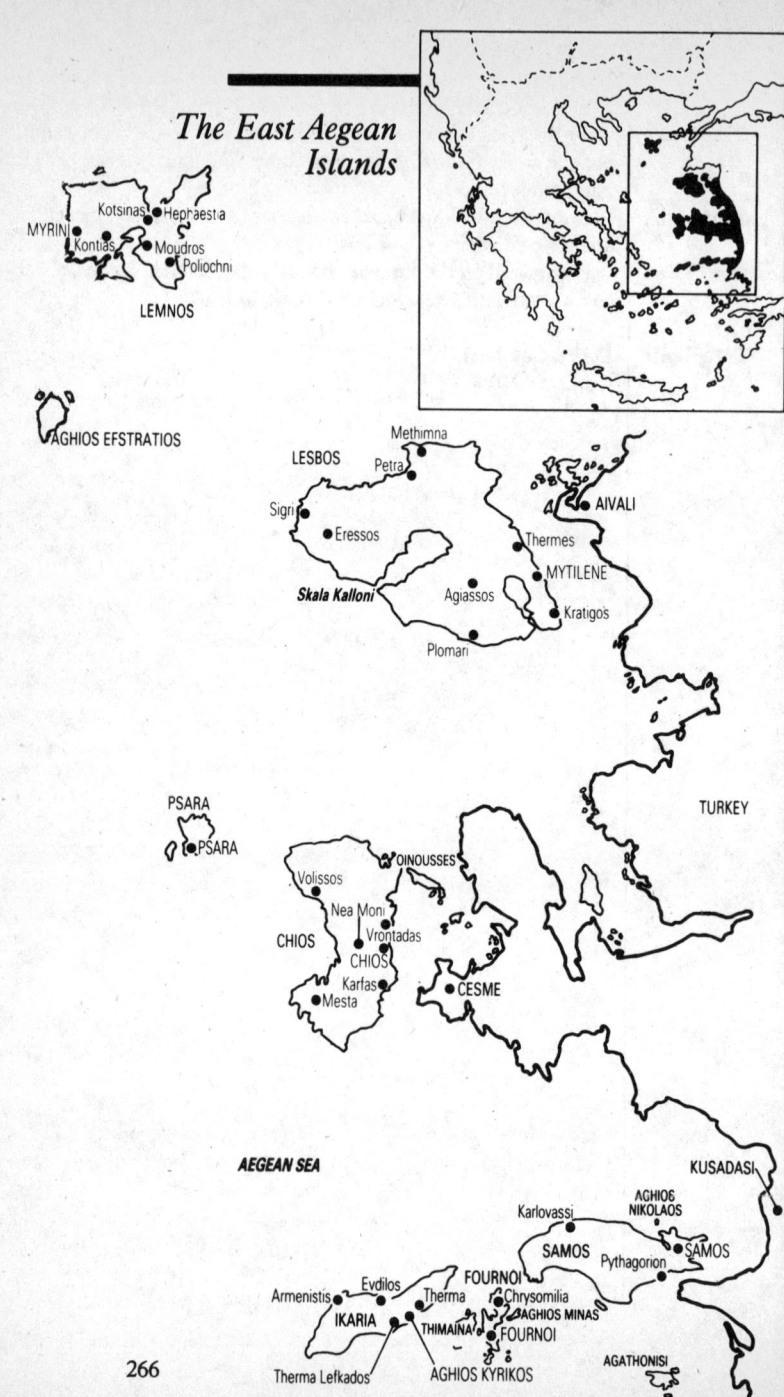

The East Aegean Islands

Introduction

Lying off the Turkish coast, at some points close enough for mainland roads and cultivations to be seen, these islands in a sense form the eastern frontier of Greece. If the Turks were ever to launch the invasion that many Greeks still believe possible, the first blows would logically fall on such islands as Lesbos, Chios and Samos; while they have been fortified accordingly, this need in no way deter the holiday visitor.

There are nine islands or clusters of islets in this group: from north to south, it comprises Lemnos, Aghios Efstratios, Lesbos, Psara, Chios, the Oinousses (or Oinoussai) islands, Samos, Ikaria and the Fournoi islands. The islands are home in total to rather more than 200,000 Greeks; Lesbos, the largest, has a population of 104,000 and is the seat of the Ministry of the Aegean. Chios and Samos are the next most populous.

They are islands that came late to Greece – only after the 1912 Balkan War – and late also to its tourist movement, to which some of them are now beginning to stake a resolute claim. Though none of them is anywhere close to qualifying for resort status, they offer the visitor adequate hotels, long beaches of yellow and white sand, tourist centres and unspoiled fishing villages, occasional archaeological sites, museums and monasteries, enchanting countryside and the unsurpassed Aegean light.

What they do not yet offer is the idea of easy accessibility, despite the airports on Lesbos, Chios, Samos and Lemnos. By sea, all of them are at the end of long and tedious journeys on ships that are not among Greece's most comfortable, some can be reached only by local boats from their larger neighbours, and cruise schedules ignore them.

If Greece is still largely unknown to you, a start could probably be made with Chios or Samos. Lesbos has its charms once you get past Mytilene, its port and capital, but the rest could well be regarded as perfect tidbits for those whose appetite for Greece has become perhaps a little jaded by indulgence in the more highly-developed islands. Hold them in reserve for the time when you need to be persuaded that

Greece as a holiday country can never be exhausted, never fully known and never stale.

Aghios Efstratios

Most of the Greeks with personal knowledge of Aghios Efstratios are now at least middle-aged and proud of their police files. This is because, since the restoration of democracy in 1974, Greek governments have ceased to equate political opposition with treachery and therefore Aghios Efstratios has become an island to be visited only voluntarily. Hopes of refurbishing its image as a former place of exile, however, were scarcely assisted by an earthquake in 1968 that destroyed almost half its houses. Twenty nautical miles south of Lemnos, its closest neighbour, and lying west of Lesbos and north of Skyros, it is one of only a handful of islands where you can feel really isolated, gazing out to sea at empty horizons. Difficult to reach, somewhat bleak and without hotels, it requires of its visitors the same kind if not the same degree of self-reliance now as when it was a place of enforced residence.

Area: 43 sq km. Length of coastline: 30 km.
Population: 296 – the drop from 422 in 1971 is attributed to the earthquake, not the jailing of the Colonels.
Area telephone code: 0254.

History Traces have been found of a Mycenaean settlement, and Greeks, Romans and Byzantines were also there. The island takes its present name from Aghios Efstratios, who lived and died in exile there in the ninth century and whose tomb can be visited.

Bearings You land at **Aï Strati**, a village on the north-west coast that is the island's port, capital and only settlement and that may once have been attractive, before the earthquake reconstruction. You can swim there or walk for an hour or so to more remote and rather pleasanter beaches. The best beaches of all are reached by fishing boat – they include Aghios Dimitrios, Lidario, Ftilio and Tripiti on the south coast and, in the north, the 2-km stretch of sand at Alonitsi.

Where to stay On the rare occasions when the twelve-bed **local authority guest-house** at **Aï Strati** is full (tel. 93 202), someone will offer a room in a house.

Where to eat Costas Makris and Antonios Tsikrikas have café-bars and will always rustle up some eggs: give them time and they will find fresh fish too.

Getting there Two boats a week from Lemnos and one a week from Kimi (Euboia), Aghios Constantinos (mainland coast) and Lesbos. Some of the Piraeus–Kavala ferries also call there.

Transport Small boats, and your own feet.

From Aghios Efstratios	By caique to two offshore islets, Roumbas and Aghii Apostoli (the Saints Apostolos).
Telephone	Police 93 201 Clinic 93 222

Chios

Chios, pronounced Hios, is known to the world outside mainly by reputation. The island of Homer and Columbus, chewing gum and sticky humour, a famous massacre and the greatest Byzantine monastery in the Aegean, it has yet to be adopted by European travel agents. Without their assistance, no island can develop into a real tourist centre when it takes almost twelve hours to reach it on the fastest ferry, it has at most four flights a day from Athens, and it is ignored by cruise liners. Its problem is distance: it is 147 nautical miles from Piraeus, 220 from Thessaloniki and 177 from Kavala. Lying within sight of the Asia Minor coast, north of Ikaria and Samos and south of Lesbos, Chios is pre-eminently a front-line island. Just conceivably, it is where the next Greek–Turkish war could begin.

Area: 841 sq km. Length of coastline: 213 km.
Population: 48,700 (Chios town 24,070).
Area telephone code: 0271.

Mythology and history	In mythology, Chios was first settled by Cretans under the leadership of Oinopionas (Wine-Drinker), who introduced the production of wine. Excavations in northern Chios, however, have produced evidence of habitation at least as far back as 4000 BC. The island is one of several claimants to the honour of being Homer's birthplace and has a large rock, Daskalopetra (Teaching Rock), where the bard is reputed to have lectured on whatever it was he taught when not at work on his epics. A flourishing maritime, commercial and artistic centre by the sixth century, Chios was occupied by the Athenians, Macedonians, Romans, Byzantines, Venetians, Genoese and Turks before finally rejoining Greece in 1912.
The story of mastic	There is a tradition that when Aghios Isidoros was being led to martyrdom by the Romans he wept tears of pain and sorrow, each of which became a lentisk tree. Thus he bequeathed to the island a tree which, though it grows elsewhere in the Mediterranean, seems to produce gum mastic only on Chios.

A more scientific explanation is that the volcanic soil of Chios is particularly suited to the terebinth lentisk (*Pistacia lentiscus*), a round, bushy tree with dark-green leaves that exudes mastic in the form of crystals.

The earliest known reference to gum mastic is by Theophrastus of Lesbos in 300 BC. While it was known to the Ancient Greeks and Byzantines, it appears to have become a crop of importance only during the Turkish occupation; then, for a time, the Chios lentisk groves were the collective property of the ladies of the Sultan's harem, who used the proceeds to finance purchase of the trinkets that made life endurable.

The mastic tree is 'milked' in the summer by incisions being made in the bark: like Aghios Isidoros, the trees then weep 'tears' that solidify and fall to the ground, where they are collected and graded according to colour, size and purity.

By all means sample a few crystals while in Chios, but do not expect to enjoy them. In its natural state, mastic is a scented gum of extreme adhesiveness but little real flavour. Its more common uses are as a raw material of chewing gum, the basis of the *masticha* aperitif sometimes drunk as an alternative to ouzo, and the principal ingredient of a sticky jam offered in a few coffee-shops as a dessert under the name *Ypovrichion* (Submarine) because a teaspoonful is always served submerged in a glass of iced water – having eaten the *Ypovrichion*, swishing the water around in your mouth eventually enables you to separate upper from lower teeth without the need to count them afterwards.

The Columbus connection

The Greeks themselves had forgotten about Columbus until stimulated by their natural reluctance to be left out of the celebrations of the 500th anniversary of his voyage of discovery. Scholars then consulted the forgotten texts, and suddenly all Greece became aware that as part of his preparations he had visited Chios to consult records and maps in the island's library (see also The Greeks and the Sea, p. 32). Incidentally, he too made mention in his letters of the mastic trade. To commemorate his eighteen-month stay on the island, Chios and Genoa in Italy have been proclaimed 'sister cities'.

The Nea Moni

The Nea Moni, or 'New Monastery', an eleventh-century Byzantine imperial structure, is one of the most important monuments to have survived from the Byzantine Empire. It was built 9 km from Chios town where, in about 1040, hermits said they had found a miraculous icon of the Virgin. According to the story, they learned that a likely successor to the Byzantine throne, Constantine Monomachos, was in exile on Lesbos; they sought and were granted an audience, at which they told him that they had seen in a vision that he would be emperor within the year. He replied that if they were right, he would build them a monastery. They were, and he did, sending the finest craftsmen from Constantinople to supervise construction.

Numerous manuscripts dating from the period 1044 to 1054 testify to the emperor's interest in the monastery; latest research dates its operation as a place of worship from about 1049 and its mosaics from the following decade.

The monastery was twice burned by the Turks and was badly damaged by earthquakes in 1881 and 1948, with the result that much of the present structure is the fruit of painstaking restoration. But the mosaics survived.

Lavishly illustrated books on the monastery and the mosaics are available in Athens and Chios, but what strikes the ordinary visitor most forcibly is something that is difficult to describe: the way in which the light inside the monastery church reflects from the gold ground and coloured chips of the mosaic, giving the impression that the building is slowly revolving around him.

The massacre
In the first flush of the 1821 Revolution, the exuberant Chiotes made one of those 'mistakes' repeated so often in Greek history: they rebelled without pausing first to consider whether they had the resources to confront the inevitable reprisals. As a result, the Turks landed an army which, after five days of fighting, overcame all resistance on the island. An estimated 22,000 inhabitants were massacred and 45,000 were sold into slavery; the Turks left on the island only sufficient people to continue the mastic production.

The massacre, one of several that helped to fire the determination of philhellenes, especially in Britain and the United States, to support the Greeks' struggle for freedom, was immortalised in a painting by Delacroix that now hangs in the Louvre: a reproduction is on display in the Chios Museum, a converted mosque in the main square.

Greece's Andorrans
The Chiotes are the butt of much Greek humour and endless untranslatable jokes because of their supposed thick-headedness. For example, it is said, in one of several versions of a classic anecdote, that they always go about in pairs, one riding on the shoulders of another. The explanation: a certain Turkish pasha was inordinately fond of the game of piggyback, and the Chiotes simply hated to have to carry him.

Port and capital
Chios town, on the east coast opposite Asia Minor, is a long, straggling neo-Classical city extending to the coastal village of Vrontados, 4 km away, the site of Homer's 'teaching stone' and of seaside villas built by shipowner families of Chios origin.

The capital is built on the site of the ancient city, of which only the remains of a theatre and traces of walls can now be seen. The port area has a dual character: the old waterfront, where fishermen spread their nets to dry, and the new quays of the commercial port fronting modern buildings, restaurants and souvenir shops.

Streets lead up from the waterfront to the castle, built by the Byzantines and enlarged by the Genoese; within its precincts are the old Turkish quarter and a cemetery where the tombs include that of Kara Ali, the admiral who ordered the Chios massacre and who was killed in a later engagement when his flagship was fired in Chios harbour by the Greek revolutionary hero, Admiral Constantine Kanaris.

What to see
Worth a visit are the archaeological museum, the Korai Library with its 130,000 volumes and manuscripts, and the Philippos Argentis

folk museum. The modern Cathedral of the Aghii Viktoroi (Saints Victor) is of less interest than the older Church of Aghios Isidoros, containing the relics of the island's patron saint and mastic-weeper: taken to Venice after the Fourth Crusade, they were returned to Chios only in 1965.

Pride of place in the archaeological museum is given to the Letter of Alexander the Great to the people of Chios, a square marble plaque on which the chiselled 'letter' advises the restoration of democracy and return of exiled democrats.

Around the island

The second largest island in the northern part of the Aegean after Lesbos, with 623 km of roads, Chios would require a week or more to be explored thoroughly even though the roads are for the most part in excellent condition. Few visitors have either the time or inclination for that kind of detail. But the quickest of swings should include the Nea Moni, barely a half-hour's drive from Chios town, and Mesta, 35 km to the south-west.

Mesta is one of the medieval villages of Greece that has survived the centuries with the least damage and fewest changes. NTOG has a 'traditional settlement' there, providing twenty-three beds in four houses (tel. 27 908).

Homeric students might venture the 40 km drive to **Volissos**, a village crowned by another Byzantine castle and claimed as Homer's birthplace. Volissos is a good starting point for beaches along the north and west coasts.

Beaches

Recommended beaches include Komi and Emborios on the south-east corner, Fana in the south-west, Limnia and Aghia Markella further up the west coast, and Nagos in the north. It is possible to swim close to Chios town, at Vrontada to the north and Kambos, Karfas and Kallimasia to the south, but these beaches tend to be crowded in the holiday season.

Where to stay

The twelve listed hotels (six second class, two third and four fourth) provide a total of 386 rooms, in addition to which there are the Mesta settlement houses and some 600 non-hotel beds on offer, about half of them in Chios town.

Easily the best of the hotels is the **Chios Chandris** (second class, 156 rooms, tel. 25 761), built by the powerful and greatly diversified Chandris shipping family now of Athens and London but originally of Chios. You should also be comfortable at the **Xenia** at Bella Vista (second class, twenty-eight rooms, tel. 23 507) or, in third class, at the **Diana** (fifty-one rooms, tel. 25 993) or **Kyma** (fifty-nine rooms, tel. 25 551) in Chios town.

Where to eat

Among restaurants, Chiotes are particularly fond of the **Naftikos Omilos** (marine club) and **Yannis**; their preferred tavernas include **Chrysso Vareli**, **Hodia**, **Dolomas** and **Perivoli**. When in Vrontada, they are likely to eat at the **Kyma** and **Ios**.

Getting there

Olympic Airways has three or four flights daily from Athens, and there are ferries daily from Piraeus (eleven hours) and weekly from Kavala (seventeen hours) and Thessaloniki (twenty-one hours).

Transport Regular bus services to all the main villages and beaches. Taxis, cars and mopeds for hire. Excursions arranged by Chios travel agents.

From Chios By air (two or three flights a week) to Myconos, Lesbos and Samos. Ferry ports of call, and local boats to the Oinousses islands and Psara, as well as to Cesme for a brief acquaintance with Turkey.

Telephone Police 22 581
Tourist police 23 211
Coastguard 22 837
Olympic Airways 22 414
Hospital 23 495/23 151

Fournoi

The Fournoi islands, pronounced Fourni, are where the traveller is sorted out from the tourist. They 'go with' Ikaria in the same way as Ikaria goes with Samos, but are a little too large, populous and independent to be regarded as simple satellites. In Ikaria you may feel you have left the beaten track; in the Fournoi islands you are really beating the bushes.

The three islands comprising the Fournoi group, which takes its name from the largest, are so close together that until minutes before landing you think you are approaching a single island. They lie between Ikaria and Samos and are most commonly visited as a day's excursion from the former. If you decide to stay, you should not expect much luxury: you will board with a family, walk or take a motorboat to beaches where you will swim in splendid isolation, and dine on fish that until a few hours before had been sharing the sea with you.

Area: 30 sq km. Length of coastline: 126 km.

Population: 1,326 (including the 121 on Thimaina and the two on Aghios Minas, the other two Fournoi islands).

Area telephone code: 0275.

Bearings You land at **Fournoi** town, population exactly 1,000 at the time of the 1981 census, and from there can walk to the other village of the main island, Chrysomilia, population 157, from where caiques leave for Thimaina. The other organised beach, by the definition of having tavernas, is at Kambi, where the winter population of 11 expands considerably in the summer. The beaches elsewhere consist only of fine sand or pebbles and blue sea.

Where to stay and eat There are no listed hotels, but between seventy and 100 beds are on offer in private homes, almost all of them at Fournoi town.

In Fournoi town, the two tavernas open year-round are **Miltos** and **Remenzo**; *souvlaki* and such on the grill can be found at **Isokratina**.

At Chrysomilia you would look for **Kondilos**, not caring whether you ended up in the one run by Vangeli Kondilos or that of Yanni Kondilos, and at Kambi, in the summer, your fish would be eaten at **Achladi** or **Klados**.

Getting there Effectively only from Ikaria; there is a daily caique in summer (a trip of one and a half hours), and a full ferry, carrying the groceries, once a week. The only island you can easily reach from Fournoi is when you travel back to Ikaria.

Transport Caiques and motorboats.

Telephone Police 51 222
Coastguard 51 207
Clinic 51 202

Ikaria

Ikaria has close links with Samos – the two have been likened to a dolphin leading a turtle westward – and is frequently visited as an overnight excursion by holiday-makers based on the larger island. Most Greeks know it better for its medicinal springs than as a holiday island, despite some excellent beaches. Lying in the Gulf of Ikaria, it is 143 nautical miles from Piraeus but can also be reached by flying to Samos and then taking the daily steamer. Ikaria is in every respect a quiet corner of the Aegean.

Area: 255 sq km. Length of coastline: 102 km.

Population: 7,559 (2,386 in Aghios Kyrikos, 656 in Evdilos and 865 in Rahes).

Area telephone code: 0275.

The first air crash Known in antiquity as Dolichni and also as Oinoe (pronounced Ee-noyee; meaning Wine Island) from its abundance of wine, it took its present name from the first recorded civil aviation fatality. Daedalos and his son Ikaros both escaped from Minoan Knossos in Crete using wings stuck to their bodies with wax. Ikaros, in an attack of 'rapture of the heights', ignored his father's advice and flew too near to the sun; the wax melted and he fell into the Gulf now named after him and was drowned. Today, the School of Ikaros is the Greek Air Force cadet college.

In other respects, Ikaria is not among the islands that have made history: the Ionians were there from the ninth century BC, in the Middle Ages it was a pirate stronghold even though nominally under Venetian and then Turkish rule, and it reunited with Greece after the 1912 Balkan War (in the meantime it had revolted, and secured a kind of independent status for four months).

Sea and waters Landing is usually made at **Aghios Kyrikos**, the present capital on the north-east coast, though some ferries call also at the second port, Evdilos, on the north coast. Aghios Kyrikos has an elegant Church of

Aghios Nikolaos built with subscriptions from Ikaria emigrants, a Church of Aghios Dimitrios with a large crypt that was used as a place of refuge during pirate raids, a small archaeological/folk museum and the island's main bus terminal.

Spas The two principal spas, **Therma** and **Therma Lefkados**, are 2 km in opposite directions along the coast from Aghios Kyrikos. Known also in antiquity, their waters are claimed to be helpful for rheumatism, arthritis, nervous exhaustion and some forms of dermatitis. Therma also offers visitors the ruins of an ancient acropolis, and Therma Lefkados strikes back with a Monastery of the Evangelismos.

Excursions Recommended excursions would include:

● **Evdilos**, 38 km from Aghios Kyrikos, once the capital and now the second port, with neo-Classical houses and some good beaches between there and **Kambos**, 2 km further along the same road, where there are the ruins of Ancient Oinoi and a small museum containing some of the finds.

● And **Armenistis**, 15 km after Kambos, a fishing harbour with some fine beaches in the immediate vicinity and in the secluded bay of Na 3 km away, where there are also the ruins of the ancient harbour of Na and a Temple of Artemis.

Beaches Apart from Armenistis and adjoining Yialiskari, Ikarians swear by the long beach of Faros on the south coast.

Where to stay Most of the island's seventeen listed hotels (total 395 rooms) are at Therma and Therma Lefkados. The biggest are the second-class **Anyfantis** (151 rooms, tel. 22 298) at Therma Lefkados and third-class **Apollon** (thirty-nine rooms, tel. 22 477) at Therma. In addition, there are approximately 1,200 beds on offer in rented rooms.

Where to eat While you cannot go seriously wrong at any of the seaside fish tavernas, local residents speak well of the **Klimataria** and **Ta Adelphia** at Aghios Kyrikos, the **Ilios** at Armenistis and the **Kamitsis** at Therma.

Getting there There is at least one ferry a day from Piraeus (ten hours), and a ferry from Kavala calls once a week.

Transport About a third of the island's 300-km road network is paved, and mopeds can be hired at Aghios Kyrikos, Evdilos and Armenistis. There are two or three buses a day from Aghios Kyrikos to Evdilos, Yialiskari and Armenistis and one a day to Xylosyrti/Playia and from Evdilos to Rahes. Other beaches can be reached by small boat.

From Ikaria There are boats every day to Samos and Fournoi, four times a week to Paros, three times a week to Patmos, and once a week to Tinos and Syros. 'Ferries of the line' connect Ikaria once a week with Chios, Lesbos, Crete and the Dodecanese islands.

Telephone Police 22 222
Coastguard 22 207
Clinic 22 330/22 236

Lemnos

Lemnos, the island sacred to the blacksmith god and scene of an appalling massacre attributable to body odour, is where *Ta Turkika* – the dispute between Greece and Turkey over general Aegean issues – reaches the NATO conference tables. Lying near the entrance to the Dardanelles, a strait known in Greece as the Hellespont, Lemnos is a natural landmark for ships headed for the Black Sea and, for privileged passengers on the growing fleet of Soviet cruise liners home-based in Odessa, the first promise of Aegean delights to come. In the First World War, Moudros Bay was where the Allied fleet assembled for the Gallipoli campaign.

A long way from Piraeus, Lemnos is a holiday island mainly for the north of Greece. It is pronounced Limnos and could just as well be written that way, since in transliteration the Greek *eeta* drifts between 'e' and 'i'; however, the Greek Foreign Ministry at least seems to prefer Lemnos. Capitalised in Greek, the island is LHMNOS.

Area: 475 sq km. Length of coastline: 259 km.
Population: 16,017 (Myrina 3,744, Moudros 973).
Area telephone code: 0254.

Gratitude of a god

According to mythology, during one of the periodic upheavals in the household of Zeus, young Hephaestos made the mistake of siding with his mother, Hera. The natural reaction of 'the thunderer', always an irritable immortal, was to seize him by the foot and fling him off Mount Olympos. At the end of a whole day's fall he crashed on Lemnos, breaking both legs. The inhabitants found him and nursed him back to health, and in return he adopted the island.

Since 'lame' Hephaestos – apparently at least one of his legs never set properly – was patron of volcanoes as well as of fire and metalworking, and Lemnos was a volcanic island, the landing may not have been entirely due to chance. He set up his forge in a volcanic cave on Mount Moschylos, and in his honour the Lemnians named their city Hephaestia, built a temple to him, and staged the Hephaestian Games every four years.

The fact that Athens is the only other city to have a temple to Hephaestos (the one in the Agora now more commonly known as the Theseion) is regarded as indicative of the close links even then between Lemnos and Athens.

Excavations at Hephaestia were begun by the Italian Archaeological School in 1926 and are still continuing. They have confirmed the size and splendour of the town as a major commercial, social and cultural centre for the North Aegean, with a harbour, fortification walls, market, theatre, arcades and extensive suburbs. Some of the finds from there are exhibited in the Myrina museum, and others are in the Athens Archaeological Museum.

The Lemnian Evil

Still in the borderland of myth and history, the Lemnians were known as daring seamen who were unfortunate in their choice of wives. Becoming careless in their worship of Aphrodite, goddess of love, the ladies had an unpleasant charm laid on them: the goddess sentenced them to stink in perpetuity.

Their husbands' response was to raid the mainland and carry off a sufficient number of nubile Thracian girls, on whom they relieved their frustrations. Rather more than simply jealous, the neglected wives seized the weapons of their exhausted husbands and slaughtered every man on the island.

The deed is commemorated on the island in the name of one of the villages, Androfoni, 'the place where the men were murdered'. It survives more widely in Greece as 'the Lemnian Evil', a phrase applied to anything excessively unpleasant, or even boring.

It would appear that either the spell had worn off or an effective deodorant had been discovered by the time Jason and the Argonauts made a stopover on Lemnos during their quest for the Golden Fleece. For if the widows had not been back to normal by then, it is unlikely that Jason would have married Queen Hypsepyle and that some of his crew members would have selected wives from among the court ladies.

Recorded times

Lemnos was first settled by pre-Greeks, including the Pelasgians and Sindians. One of the towns dating from this period, Poliochni, was older than Troy itself.

The Ionians, who arrived on Lemnos in the ninth century BC, took over and enlarged the existing towns. Occupied by the Persians and liberated by the Athenians, Lemnos was an ally of Athens during the Peloponnesian War, before succumbing first to the Macedonians and then to the Romans.

Hephaestia was one of the first cities of the North Aegean to accept Christianity, in the first century; the message is thought to have reached the island through converts made by St Paul when he preached at Philippi, near Kavala. Lemnos remained part of the Byzantine Empire for longer than most of the Aegean islands: though it, too, was taken by the Venetians at the time of the Fourth Crusade, the Byzantines recovered it quickly and, except for a brief period early in the fifteenth century, held it until it fell to the Turks in 1478. Reunification with Greece followed the 1912 Balkan War.

The Lemnos question

This arises routinely at NATO defence planning conferences, and is part of a wider skein of Aegean disputes between Greece and Turkey (see also pp. 50-2). Every year, as a matter of course, Greece and Turkey veto each other's estimates to NATO of their national forces, in the form of 'country chapters', because of Lemnos.

The argument centres on whether Greek troops should be on Lemnos at all, and arises out of conflicting treaties.

The 1923 Lausanne Convention, which formalised the cession to

Greece of the eastern Aegean islands other than the Dodecanese (which had already been taken by Italy) and to Turkey of the islands of Imbros and Tenedos, provided for the demilitarisation of Lemnos, Samothrace, Imbros and Tenedos because of their position close to the entrance to the Dardanelles.

However, the Greeks contend that is was superseded by the Montreux Convention of 1936, which contained no provision for demilitarisation, and cite in this connection a 1936 statement by the then Turkish Foreign Minister in the Ankara national assembly: 'The provisions concerning the islands of Lemnos and Samothrace, which belong to our friend and neighbour, Greece, and which had been demilitarised by the Convention of Lausanne of 1923, are abolished also by the Convention of Montreux – and we are particularly pleased about this.'

But it is not, of course, a matter only of treaties. After the Turkish invasion of Cyprus in 1974 (see also p. 52), the Greeks discovered that Turkey had set up an Army of the Aegean along the Anatolian coast, opposite the east Aegean islands, and equipped it with a fleet of landing craft. Greece maintains that it has never, through any treaty or agreement, resigned the right to protect its national territory, and that the defence measures it takes are proportional to the threat it faces. Also, it says, its forces on the islands have no means of assault but are there purely to thwart a possible invasion; therefore, to remove them would not eliminate a threat to peace but increase the risk of war.

Bearings Lemnos is an island of peculiar shape, almost bisected by the great Bay of Moudros. Apart from its Gallipoli connections, Moudros was used also by the Greek fleet in the 1912–13 Balkan War; a naval battle near Lemnos in early 1913 secured Greek control of Aegean waters. Moudros today is only the island's second port, as well as the site of its airport and of a Commonwealth war cemetery dating from the Gallipoli campaign.

Visitors arriving by sea land at the modern capital of **Myrina** (sometimes called Kastro), a pretty-enough town of red-roofed houses on the west coast, with the ruins of a Byzantine castle and a museum housing exhibits covering a period of 4,000 years, for the most part discovered during excavations at Ancient Myrina, Poliochni and Hephaestia.

What to see The archaeological sites of **Hephaestia** and **Poliochni** are worth visiting, though not particularly easy to get to: the former is 35 km from Myrina on the north-east tip of the island, and the latter 39 km away at the south-east tip though only 9 km from Moudros. Excursions to both are organised by Myrina travel agents.

Beaches There are good beaches at Myrina itself and, on either side of the town, at Platy, Thanos, Aghios Ioannis and Kaspakis. Possibly the best swimming of all is close to Kontias (population 549), a village of fine old houses and a splendid church 11 km from Myrina. Kotsinas,

25 km away on the north coast, is a fishing village with some good tavernas and the ruins of another castle but with a less attractive beach: Lemnos earth, used in antiquity for the treatment of wounds and poisoning, used to be mined nearby. The best beaches on the east coast are at Voroskopos and Aghia Irene. Real privacy can be obtained by hiring small boats at Myrina or Moudros, the latter a town with little to detain the casual visitor.

Where to stay

All but one of the ten listed hotels, with a total of 339 rooms, are at or close to Myrina, as are more than half of the estimated 250 non-hotel beds on offer. If in funds, you could try the deluxe **Myrina Beach** (125 rooms, tel. 22 681); otherwise, there are the second-class **Kastro Beach** (seventy-two rooms, tel. 22 725) or the third-class **Sevdalis** (thirty-six rooms, tel. 22 691). For those who have to stay in Moudros, the second-class **Kyma** (tel. 71 333) has twenty-two rooms.

Where to eat

The **Myrina Beach Hotel** (Akti Myrina) has reputedly the best restaurant in the North Aegean, but it is not cheap. Myrina residents prefer the **Yamarellos** and **Alatzis** restaurants and the **Katsikoyannis**, **Argotoyiorgos** or **Xanthopoulos** fish tavernas. Kind words have also been spoken of the waterfront **Lakis**. Treat Lemnos wine with deep caution, as the Greeks do; it is scarcely a wine you would offer a friend.

Getting there

Olympic has two flights a day from Athens and, by light aircraft, one a day from Thessaloniki and four a week from Lesbos. By sea, the ferries from Kavala (three or four a week) cover the 72 nautical miles in about six hours. There are also weekly boats (occasional extra sailings in summer) from Piraeus, Aghios Constantinos and Kimi, along tedious and time-consuming routes.

Transport

Bus services from Myrina to the larger villages and better beaches. Taxis, cars, mopeds, bicycles and small boats available for hire.

From Lemnos

To Kavala, and ports of call on the ferry lines noted above.

Telephone

Police 22 200
Coastguard 22 225
Olympic Airways 22 078
Hospital 22 345/22 203

Lesbos

It is a pity, though probably inevitable given its size and commercial importance, that an island with as much natural beauty as Lesbos should have for its capital a town such as Mytilene. However, you would do better to get out into the island immediately than to start inquiring about the next boat for Piraeus. Once the hurdle of Mytilene has been overcome, Lesbos soon redeems itself. In resort terms, though, it is still an island in waiting.

First, to clarify the nomenclature: Lesbos, pronounced Lesvos, is the island and Mytilene the capital and main port.

The third largest Greek island after Crete and Euboia, Lesbos lies just off the Turkish coast, with Chios to the south and Lemnos to the north-west. It is the seat of the Ministry of the Aegean, one of only three such government departments – the others are the Ministry of Macedonia/Thrace in Thessaloniki and the Merchant Marine Ministry in Piraeus – located outside Athens, and also shares responsibility for the burgeoning University of the Aegean.

The ancient poetess Sappho was born on Lesbos, and so was Odysseas Elytis, Greece's only living Nobel laureate, of whose poems the best known are those that have been set to music by Mikis Theodorakis. The island is indented by two of the most dramatic enclosed gulfs in the whole Aegean, those of Kallonis and Geras (pronounced Yeras), and among its more spectacular sights is a petrified forest at Sigri. The Greeks know it best for its olives, olive oil and ouzo. It can be reached easily by air or sea, but no cruise company would dream of scheduling a call there, in view of the time required to savour the beauty of the island's interior and the absence of any major archaeological attraction.

Area: 1,630 sq km. Length of coastline: 370 km.

Population: 104,620 (24,991 in Mytilene).

Area telephone codes: 0251 Mytilene, 0252 Agiassos, 0253 Eressos/Methimna.

Mythology and history

According to mythology, King Makara had two daughters, Mytilene and Methimna, who gave their names to the island's principal towns; Methimna married Lesbos, who gave his name to the island.

Demonstrably inhabited at least 5,000 years ago, by 1000 BC Lesbos already had six towns: Mytilene, Methimna, Arisvi, Antissa, Eressos and Pyra. It enjoyed a cultural flowering between the end of the eighth century BC and its capture by the Persians in the sixth – Terpandros, the 'father of music', the poet Alcaios and Sappho lived on the island in that period – and a second during the Roman occupation.

Under Byzantine rule from the fourth century AD, the island subsequently suffered invasions by Slavs, Saracens, Genoese and Venetians. It was ceded to the Genoese in the mid-fourteenth century and held by them until taken in 1462 by Mohammed II, the conqueror of Constantinople. Though it joined the 1821 Revolution, and experienced Turkish retaliations, it had to wait until the 1912 Balkan War to secure its freedom; Admiral Pavlos Kountouriotis arrived there with the Greek fleet and obtained the Turkish surrender after a naval battle. The island's population was swollen by an influx of refugees after the 1922 Asia Minor Disaster.

Sappho

Plato is on record as maintaining that there were ten muses, not nine, and the tenth was Sappho. Born on Lesbos in approximately 620 BC, she was 'burning Sappho' to Byron, who recognised a kindred spirit. The first great lyric poet, with outspoken views on physical love, she was also an original feminist and an educator ahead of her times.

In a sense, mythology had prepared the way for her. According to the story, Orpheus 'of the Underworld', poet and musician, was killed by the Maenads on the instigation of Dionysos and his body was dismembered and thrown into the sea. His head and lyre were washed ashore on Lesbos, where the former was given honourable burial and the latter placed in a Temple of Apollo. In return, the sun god gifted the island with lyric poetry.

Sappho also wrote political verse, for which she was exiled to Sicily, where her daughter, Cleis, was born and her husband died. Allowed to return to Lesbos in her thirties, she founded what today would be described as a finishing school for girls from all parts of Greece, with a curriculum that included household economy, the humanities, music and the social graces in general. Turning away from politics, she produced her finest poetry, including love verses that shocked even the Romans.

The relatively small number of Greeks familiar with the little that survives of her work appear to regard it as unimportant whether she was or was not a 'Lesbian' in the international and not simply the geographical sense; they believe her contemporaries probably would, or at least should, have displayed a comparable indifference, in view of the Ancient Greek attitude towards male homosexuality.

Though you may stay at the Sappho Hotel in Eressos, her claimed birthplace, and see a depiction of Sappho and the lyric poet Alcaios in the Theophilos Museum, Lesbos as an island neither honours nor remembers her. Her contemporary and friend, Alcaios, has fared even worse (her hotel is third class while his is only fifth), and Terpandros, to whom is attributed the invention of the seven-stringed lyre and foundation of a school of music, is quite inn-less.

The capital If you travel to Lesbos by sea you will almost certainly disembark at **Mytilene**, which contrives not to look too unprepossessing from a distance. You see a pine-covered hill on the right crowned by the fourteenth-century castle, a harbour with multi-coloured caiques and white yachts, the large Church of Aghia Therapounda, and shops and hotels along and back from the waterfront. You may believe you are approaching two different cities, one with low houses and narrow streets leading up to the castle and the other, part neo-Classical and part modern, in the area of the commercial port.

What to see Before leaving, you might take a look at the castle (Byzantine, restored by the Genoese), the archaeological museum near the quayside statue of Freedom, the Byzantine museum near Aghia Therapounda church, the folk museum at the new harbour, the seventeenth-century Cathedral of Aghios Athanassios with its relics of Aghios Theodoros of Byzantium, whom the Turks martyred, and the nineteenth-century Aghia Therapounda itself, where the icons are older than the church and the chief relics are the maniples of a martyred ecumenical patriarch.

Modern Mytilene has obliterated most of the ancient town over which it is built, though traces of a Hellenistic theatre can be seen at the western edge.

Museums of art Two museums, the likes of which cannot be seen elsewhere, but involving a 3 km drive to the village of **Varia**, are those of Theophylos and Eleftheriadis-Teriad. The former has a unique collection of eighty-six works by Greece's greatest contemporary primitive painter, while the latter displays paintings by Picasso, Matisse, Braque, Dali and Chagall.

You may think that you painted like Theophylos when you were five years old; if closer scrutiny fails to convince you to the contrary, you have to take the word of experts that you didn't.

Theophylos Hadzimichail, who was born in or around 1868, literally painted for bread, and died in 1934 with his talent still unrecognised. If alive today he would be a millionaire, able to afford a far better house than the cottage where he lived and where his works are now on show.

A social misfit, largely self-taught, who rejected the trade of building worker to which he was apprenticed, Theophylos would cover a taverna wall with murals to pay for his meals. He was discovered too late in life, by Parisian art-lover Teriad, to enjoy the financial rewards that now accrue to galleries fortunate enough to come into possession of one of his works, which range from land- and sea-scapes through portraiture to scenes of village life and representations of the ancient myths.

Together, the two museums are well worth the effort of getting to Varia.

Around the island You could devote at least a week to the island of Lesbos and its excellent beaches. A purely indicative list of places to be sought out would include **Methimna** (known also as Molyvos), for its Genoese castle, museum and beach; **Eressos**, to be where Sappho was, see the remains of Ancient Eressos and swim at Skala Eressos; and Sigri, for the petrified forest.

Sigri is an eerie place, and appeals mostly to those with a taste for lunar landscapes. The phenomenon – vast stone trunks of trees, some as much as 7 m tall – is attributed to the effects of volcanic ash from an eruption of Mount Ordymanos several million years ago.

Beaches Swimming is possible close to Mytilene, but is better at Vigla, Neapoli, Thermes and Kratigos, all within 10 km of the town. Elsewhere, since distances are considerable on Lesbos, you will be likely to swim where you lodge, which will probably mean at Skala Eressos,

Skala Kalloni, Methimna, Petra, Plomari or Aghios Isidoros.

Where to stay

Lesbos has forty-four listed hotels, with 1,176 rooms: eight of the hotels with 313 rooms are in Methimna and ten with 346 rooms are in Mytilene. There are also at least 3,700 beds on offer in private homes, some 500 of them in Mytilene. Of the listed hotels, two are first class, twenty-three second class, ten third class and nine fifth class.

Methimna, as the main resort, has the larger and better hotels, none of them below second class. The first-class **Molyvos** (tel. 71 386) is highly recommended but has only thirty rooms. Dropping to second, you could try the **Alkeos** (fifty-six rooms, tel. 71 002) or **Delfinia** (eighty-two rooms, tel. 71 373). In Mytilene there is the second-class **Blue Sea** (sixty-one rooms, tel. 23 994) and, just outside the town, the **Mytilene Village** and **Xenia**, both second class, the former with fifty-two rooms (tel. 20 653) and the latter with seventy-four (tel. 22 713).

The hotels outside Methimna and Mytilene are shared by seventeen beaches and beauty spots, leaving acres of unexploited magnificence still awaiting the developers.

Where to eat

Inhabitants of Mytilene, as of any large city, say they like to drive out on a summer night to some small fish taverna on a remote beach, but when eating in town would choose the **Arhivada**, **Arapis** or **Viktora**, all fairly central from the waterfront.

Getting there

Olympic has six flights a day from Athens in summer, one a day from Thessaloniki and from two to four a week from Chios, Lemnos, Rhodes and Samos.

There are daily ferries from Piraeus (187 nautical miles, fifteen hours), and weekly sailings from Thessaloniki, Kavala and Rhodes.

Transport

Though the bus service is adequate, the distances on so large an island make it worth taking or hiring a car. Taxis are plentiful, and so are mopeds. Coach and caique excursions are available.

From Lesbos

Ports of call on the ferries, the islands served by Olympic, and daily boat excursions to Aivali in Turkey (16 nautical miles, two hours).

Telephone

(telephone code 0251)
Police 22 021
Tourist police 22 776
Coastguard 28 827
Olympic Airways 28 660
Hospital 28 412

Oinousses

Oinousses, written also as Oinoussai but with the first syllable in either form pronounced to rhyme with 'eeny-meeny', is a remarkable little island of absentee seamen and shipowners who may spend an

GAZETTEER

occasional holiday there. For the casual visitor, there are two small hotels and a few rented rooms. The island, and another eight without permanent inhabitants, collectively comprise the Oinousses (or Oinoussai) islands, lying in the narrows between Chios and Asia Minor. Tourism is really a matter of day-trippers from Chios, only a mile from the main island for seagulls but 10 nautical miles as the caique wallows.

Area: 14 sq km. Length of coastline: 48 km.
Population: 705.
Area telephone code: 0272.

In general terms, whatever happened to Chios happened also to the Oinousses islands. They were fortified in turn by the Genoese, Venetians and Turks, and frequently served as pirate bases. But always, their inhabitants were seamen.

Town and island

Oinoussa, the port, capital and only settlement, is at the same time a picturesque fishing village and one of Greece's smallest municipalities, with the honoured status accorded in recognition of its shipowner connections. Apart from shipowner mansions in the 'town' and seaside villas just outside, occupied for a few weeks every summer, there is little to attract the sightseer except an old castle, a three-gallery naval museum housing a collection of paintings relating to the sea, a Monastery of the Evangelismos 3 km away and a Church of Zoodochos Pighis on the islet of Passas.

Mayor Dimitrios Methenitis acknowledges that the visitor is likely to be disappointed unless he has arrived in search of 'peace, spotless beaches and a family atmosphere'. The best of the beaches are at Apiganou, Bilali, Fasoli, Fokias and Aghios Ioannis.

Where to stay

There are two hotels, the second-class **Thalassoporos** (eleven rooms, tel. 51 475) and the fifth-class **Prasonisia** (nine rooms, tel. 51 513), plus about twenty beds for rent in private houses.

Where to eat

The choice may fairly be described as limited, since Oinousses has only one restaurant, the **Pateroniso**, and three fish tavernas. However, there is a waterfront nightclub, the **Remengo**, which helps the shipowners feel at home, and the **Marine Club** is open to non-members.

Getting there

Only from Chios, on a boat that sails daily in the summer; in winter it rests on Thursdays and whenever the sea is stormy.

Transport

Of the 24-km road network, only 6 km is paved. The island has no buses and, since a petrol station has received planning permission but has yet to be built, there are still no cars or mopeds for hire. There are motorboats, which pick up their fuel in Chios; otherwise, you use your legs.

The motorboats will take you to the coves and bays, and also to the islets of the group, where you can expect to be entirely undisturbed.

From Oinousses

Back to Chios only.

Telephone Police 51 222
Coastguard 51 209
Clinic 51 300
The Mayor 51 400

Psara

Psara – 'glorious', 'historic' Psara, immortalised by a famous Greek stanza – could easily be regarded as no more than an offshore islet of Chios, 12 nautical miles to the east, and indeed has regular communications with nowhere else. Its few visitors are for the most part day-trippers from Chios, and its only mention in NTOG brochures is in that context. Invited by letter to list the island's after-dark attractions, the Psara municipality replied tersely: 'Night life it doesn't have' (*nichterini zoi den ehei*). Not for Psara the wickedness of the city, or even the big island; after 9 p.m. you watch television or go to bed. And yet, if you find yourself on Chios with a day to spare for an excursion, or three days for a proper visit, Psara will reward you nicely.

Area: 39 sq km. Length of coastline: 35 km.
Population: 460 in 1981, a drop of 27 in the ten years since the previous census.
Area telephone code: 0272.

A magnificent disaster

Psara was always one of those islands that built ships and bred seamen. Its greatest son was Revolutionary hero Constantine Kanaris, said to have been a distant ancestor of the German Admiral von Canaris who was hanged by the Nazis in the last days of the Second World War for plotting against the Hitler regime, and a number of Greece's present shipowner families regard Psara as their home island.

When the 1821 Revolution broke out, Psara had a population of around 10,000 and a fleet of sixty ships of above 100 tonnes. Along with Hydra and Spetses, it was one of the first three islands to join the uprising. Led by Kanaris, its fleet harassed Turkish shipping and raided along the Asia Minor coast.

In the early summer of 1824, at a moment when the island's population had been temporarily swollen to more than 20,000 by refugees from Chios, Lesbos and Asia Minor, the Turks struck back. A fleet under the command of Hosref Pasha landed 14,000 Janissary 'shock troops' on the north-west coast, and the island's defences were quickly overcome. In the custom of the day, the men and boys who survived the fighting were beheaded and the more comely of the maidens carried off to the harems. Contemporary reports agree that only some 3,000 escaped, along with Kanaris, to found the settlement of New Psara on Euboia. As a naval and commercial power, Psara was finished. Nevertheless, as one of a chain of massacres, the Psara holocaust provided further inspiration and ammunition for the philhellene pressure for Great Power intervention in support of the Greek struggle for freedom – a pressure that helped to make possible the naval battle of Navarino (see p. 21). It also inspired Greece's national poet, Dionysios Solomos, to pen a heroic stanza that is required learning for every Greek high school pupil but that simply does not translate adequately into English.

On Psara itself, the massacre is commemorated by a simple white monument and a ceremony of remembrance each year on 22 June.

Rescue operation

The wave of migration after the Second World War, first to the mainland and from there to the Greek communities abroad, hit Psara as hard as most of the other small, remote islands: the difference was that it could less afford the loss of its youth. By the middle of the 1970s the population was down to 330, and well over half of it consisted of old people. Any child wanting more than a primary school education had to go elsewhere; usually his family went with him, and as a rule nobody came back.

In the spring of 1978, on the initiative of the late Greek President and Academician Constantine Tsatsos, a Committee for Abandoned Areas was set up – the name was intended as a reminder that underdevelopment is assured even more by the absence of people than by a dearth of resources. The objective of the committee was not repopulation through ambitious, costly and probably unviable industrial or tourist development, but creation of the circumstances – especially educational, medical and social services and means of entertainment – that would relieve young people of the sense that there was no real alternative to migration.

With funding in part from Greek banks and in part through an appeal to Psarians abroad, a secondary school was built, Psara acquired a paved road as well as a regulation restricting the number of vehicles on the island, abandoned buildings were restored and one of them was turned into a municipal guest-house, zoning laws were introduced, and assistance was provided for the development of fishing, livestock breeding, handicrafts and small factories.

Additional support came from an unlikely source: a group of Leicestershire educational institutions, among them the Classics Department of Leicester University, Longsdale Upper School, Birstall Community College and Brockington College at Enderby, founded a 'Friends of Psara' association in Britain to encourage joint educational projects and exchanges.

Today, Psarian youth can and increasingly does stay on the island, though obviously, given the population balance of ten years ago, this will take time to be fully reflected in the island's vital statistics.

For the visitor

Psara town, the only settlement, has an archaeological museum and a fifteenth-century castle. Two hours away on foot or twenty minutes on a farm truck, a Monastery of the Dormition of the Virgin on the slopes of Mount Prophet Elias is open to visitors.

Beaches There is good swimming from tiny beaches in rocky coves near the harbour and along the north, west and south coasts. The best beaches close to the town are at Kato Yialos and Katsouni; further away, but still within walking distance, are Lazoreta, Limnos and Lakka. The more distant beaches are best reached by motorboat.

Where to stay and eat You have a choice among the **Community** and **NTOG guest-houses** (tel. 61 293 and 61 116), the new twenty-room **Miramare** pension, and about fifteen beds on offer in rented rooms. The capacity of the NTOG guest-house is currently being expanded from seventeen to forty-five beds. The two guest-houses also have the island's best restaurants.

Transport Officially, only by motorboats. Unofficially, by hitching rides on farm vehicles (it is a courtesy to offer payment even if one is not demanded).

From Psara Back to Chios, on a boat that is daily in summer.

Telephone Police 61 222
Coastguard 61 252
Clinic 61 277

Samos

Samos is an island of famous men and exquisite beaches, the largest ancient temple in Greece and a tunnel that was an engineering wonder in the sixth century BC. Though well provided with hotels and relatively easy to get to, it is big enough never to seem crowded even in peak season. The most easterly and at the same time greenest of the East Aegean islands, it lies between Patmos and Chios and at one point is separated from the Turkish coast by a channel barely a mile wide. Nevertheless, it avoids giving the impression of a frontier outpost. Its most renowned product is a cloying red wine that inspired wrath in Lord Byron ('Dash down yon cup of Samian wine!') for reasons having nothing to do with its flavour, is generally regarded with contempt by serious drinkers, and helps promote the consumption of beer.

Area: 476 sq km. Length of coastline: 159 km.
Population: 31,634 (Samos town/Vathy 7,773, Karlovassi 4,843 and Pythagorion 1,406).
Area telephone code: 0273.

Mythology and history Excavations at Pythagorion have found indications that Samos was inhabited at least from the third millennium. By the time the Ionians arrived in approximately 1000 BC a cult of Hera, the virgin goddess, was already established on the island: they continued it, and built the great Temple of Hera near Pythagorion, on the ruins of a prehistoric temple to the same goddess.

Ancient Samos reached the peak of its power under Polycrates the tyrant in the sixth century, and established its own colonies. Naval architects of the period designed a new type of fast fifty-oared boat, the *Samaina*, and, with a fleet of 100 of them built in local shipyards, Samos ruled the nearby seas. Decline set in after the murder of Polycrates, with the island falling successively under the sway of the Persians, Athenians, Macedonians and Romans. Scourged by piracy during the Byzantine period, it was held at one time or another by the Franks, Genoese and Venetians, and finally by the Turks.

An earthquake in 1476 so devastated the island that it was almost deserted for close on a century. Incentives for resettlement provided by the Turks led to repopulation from other parts of Greece; echoes of these movements linger today in the names of some of the villages – Mytilenios for the settlers from Mytilene, Pyrgos for those from Pyrgos in the Peloponnese and Pagondas after a district of Euboia.

Samos succeeded in expelling the Turks during the 1821 Revolution, but in 1830 the island was handed back to the Ottoman Empire by the Protecting Powers, on condition that it should be granted a degree of autonomy. Reunion with Greece came in 1913.

Sons of Samos

● Pythagoras, the philosopher and mathematician, was born on Samos around 570 BC, though he moved to southern Italy while still a young man to establish a school that survived him for some eight centuries. As he reputedly demonstrated, the square on the hypotenuse of a right-angled triangle is equal to the sum of the squares on the other two sides. There is a Samos legend that on stormy nights fishermen used to steer to a safe landing with the help of a mysterious light on the top of Mount Circe, which they held to be the spirit of Pythagoras.

● Samos was also the birthplace of Aristarchos, the third-century astronomer, who was both revolutionary and right in concluding that the earth rotates on its own axis and travels around the sun, but was less successful in his attempts to calculate the relative sizes of the earth, sun and moon and the distances between them.

● Additionally, there were Roikos and Theodoros, the architects of the sixth and fifth centuries who designed the Temple of Hera; Mandrocles who built the bridge of boats across the Bosphoros for the Persian monarch Darius in 513 BC; and Efpalinos who, although hailing from Megara, constructed the aqueduct of Pythagorion by tunnelling into the mountain simultaneously from two sides – the feat, of course, was the meeting in the middle. Only the entrances to the tunnel are now open to visitors.

Port and capital

Samos town is built around the bay of Vathy, one of Greece's largest natural harbours. **Vathy** is the old quarter of the town, running up a gentle slope behind the mainly neo-Classical port city.

Before moving on, time should be found for a stroll through both Samos town and Vathy, a look at the church of Aghios Spyridon and the old Parliament building, now the town hall, and a visit to the archaeological museum beside the town hall. The two-storey museum houses exhibits from all eras of Samos history, with a natural emphasis on the sixth century. There is also a Byzantine museum in the Bishop's Palace, with a notable collection of seventeenth-century icons, and an art gallery.

The long esplanade is especially attractive at night, with the lights of Vathy in the distance. A peculiarity of Vathy lies in the construction of its houses, which for the most part are of two storeys; the second storey protrudes over the first and the roof protrudes over the second, giving some of the narrower lanes almost the sense of a tunnel. Though shaded, the breezes ensure that they are far from airless.

Pride of place in the archaeological museum is given to the Kouros of Samos, a 5-metre-tall statue discovered in 1980 during excavations at the Heraion archaeological site, and dating from around 575 BC. The torso was found first, and to accommodate it the floor of the museum had to be lowered; later, when the head turned up, the roof had to be raised.

Kouros (male) and kore (female) are ancient Greek statues dating from the ninth to the sixth centuries and, archaeologists explain, mark the beginning of the concept of man as an object of enquiry.

Around the island

With its rolling hills, vineyards and succession of beaches, and its well-developed road network, Samos is an island that cries out to be toured. This can be done by local buses from the capital, in your own or a hired car, and to some extent by fishing boat. Sound local advice offered to the first-time visitor is to use one of the full-day coach tours organised by Samos travel agents, which take in all the main sights: you then return later to what most attracted you.

One way or another, a point should be made of going at least to **Pythagorion**, an elegant little port built on the site of Ancient Samos, 12 km south of the present capital. There you can see the remains of the ancient Polycrateian walls, take a look at the Efpalinos tunnel, visit the small archaeological museum, swim from the long beach of Potokaki, then drive the 8 km to the Heraion where the goddess Hera was said to have been born and see the remains of a temple that Herodotus described as a bold and wonderful construction.

The temple was three times destroyed by natural causes, and the third reconstruction was made by Roikos and Theodoros.

There are also Hellenistic and Roman ruins and early Christian and Byzantine churches to see.

Karlovassi, the second port of Samos with its neo-Classical buildings, ruined castle beside the harbour, thirteenth-century Church of the Metamorphosis (Transfiguration) and eighteenth-century Monastery of the Prophet Elias on a nearby hillside, well repays the 33 km drive from Vathy.

If you are in Samos between the beginning of the year and July, you can hope to see flamingos on a seaside lake at **Alykes**, about 10 km from the capital. The flamingos, of which there are usually between twenty and forty but sometimes up to 200, share the lake – until it dries out in July – with other migratory birds, among them wild ducks, herons and storks.

Monasteries Samos is exceptionally well provided with monasteries that relied for their security on fortified walls rather than inaccessibility, and are therefore easy to reach during a swing round the island. The more impressive include: the Panaghia of Vrondiani, dating from 1566, outside the village of Vourliotis; the Megali Panaghia, 1586, near Koumaradaioi; Aghia Zoni, 1695, and Zoodochos Pighi, seventeenth century, both in the Vlamari plain just outside the city of Samos; the more modern Aghios Ioannis outside Karlovassi, dating from 1823, and, in the same general area, Profitis Ilias, 1625, with well-preserved frescoes; the deserted Panaghia Makrini, built in a cave only 15 m high above Kallithea and dating from the ninth century; the convent of the Panaghia in a wood close to Votsalakia, where the Gregorian calendar is still in use; and Aghios Ioannis the Almoner, in the Marathokambos area, which is under the ecclesiastical jurisdiction of the Church of the Holy Sepulchre in Jerusalem.

Beaches In general, the better beaches are along the north and south-west coasts. Specially recommended, and provided in summer with small restaurants or fish tavernas, are those of Gangou, Psili Ammos, Pythagorion, Potokaki, Heraion, Tsopela, Votsalakia, Potami and Avlakia.

Where to stay Samos has 128 listed hotels with a total of 2,430 rooms: they include two of first class, thirty-seven of second and forty of third. At Vathy you could try the second-class **Aeolis** (fifty-one rooms, tel. 28 904) or third-class **Samos** (105 rooms, tel. 28 377); at Pythagorion the first-class **Doryssa Bay** (176 rooms, tel. 61 360) or second-class **Phito** (eighty-one rooms, tel. 61 314); and at Karlovassi two of second class, the **Aegean** (fifty-seven rooms, tel. 33 466) and **Merope** (eighty rooms, tel. 32 650).

There are also at least 2,300 non-hotel beds on offer, about half of them in Samos/Vathy and Pythagorion.

Where to eat You can eat well at almost any Samos beach. Especially recommended in Samos/Vathy are the **Tasos**, **Samos**, **Souda** (for fish), **Steki**, **Manolis**, **Kouros**, **Kalami**, **Dionysos** and **Aeolis**. In Pythagorion you could look out for the **Delfini**, **Lito**, **Manolis**, **Samaina** or **Tria Adelphia**, and in Karlovassi for the **Samos Light**, **Hippokambos**, **Kima**, **Cavo Doro** and **Mikro Parisi** (Little Paris).

Getting there Olympic Airways has three flights a day from Athens, and there are from one to three ferries a day from Piraeus (about twelve hours for the 174 nautical miles). Samos can also be reached by sea from Kavala, Rhodes and Crete.

Transport A good local bus service, taxis, cars and mopeds for hire, and coach and caique excursions.

From Samos By air to Chios, Myconos and Lesbos (two or three flights a week), and by sea to almost any other Aegean or Dodecanese island provided you are prepared for long, round-about voyages. There are direct services in summer to Chios and Patmos, and daily excursions to Kusadasi in Turkey, from where buses run to Ephesus. You can also go by motorboat to the offshore islets of Samiopoula, Aghios Nikolaos, Prassonissi and Vareloudi.

Telephone (Samos/Vathy)
Police 27 404/27 980
Coastguard 27 318
Olympic Airways 28 491
Hospital 27 407/27 426

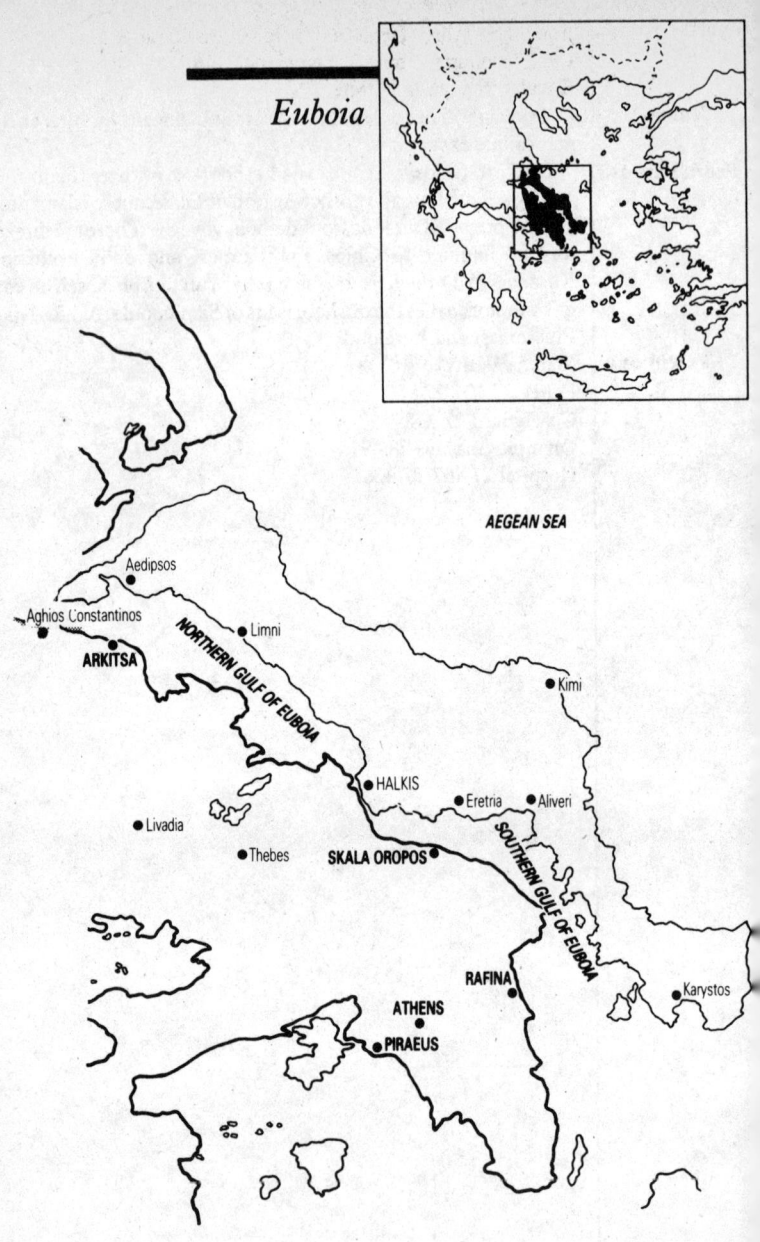

Euboia

Introduction

You do not need to be eighty years old to feel comfortable on Euboia, but it would probably help: regular holiday-makers do include many elderly Athenians, who find comfort in the thought that they are only ninety minutes by train from home and family doctor.

Written sometimes as Euboea and sometimes as Evia, which is the way it is pronounced, Euboia is the second largest Greek island after Crete but hugs the mainland so closely for most of its 180 km length that, when there, it is difficult to acquire the feeling of being on an island. Like Crete, it belongs to none of the island groups.

Very wet in winter, very hot in summer and very often windy, Euboia is where Athenians escape to on weekends when desperation drives them out of the capital but they cannot afford the risk of being marooned by a sudden storm. For this reason, hundreds of Athenians have their weekend homes in the southern part of the island – if it has only two rooms and an outhouse it is still a 'villa' in conversation, though a five-room spread with swimming pool would be depicted to the tax authorities as a shack. Weekend trade is the real mainstay of the island's hotels.

With apologies to those who cannot see why Greece's spas should be less famous than Baden Baden or Biarritz, a tourist would need to feel pretty sick before taking the waters at Aedipsos.

Personal advice would be to forget about Euboia except as a short detour, to see its capital, during a drive along the north–south motorway from Athens to Thessaloniki.

Area: 3,653 sq km. Length of coastline: 677 km.
Population: 138,410 (44,867 in Halkis).
Area telephone code: 0220 to 0228, depending on district.

History Inhabited since prehistoric times, by the eighth and seventh centuries BC Euboia had two main towns – Halkis and Eretria – which founded coastal colonies in Thrace, Sicily and Italy, as well as elsewhere in the Aegean. It passed from Athenians to Macedonians to Romans to Byzantines to Franks (1209) to Venetians (who named it Negreponte) to Turks (1470) and finally to Greece in 1830. The island has little to show from its ancient past, but rather more from Byzantium and the Middle Ages.

The capital **Halkis**, which you will see written also as Khalkis, Chalkis and

Halkida, is partly on Euboia and partly on the mainland: it spreads along both sides of the Evripos straits at a point where the island is only 40 m from eastern Greece, to which it is linked by a swing-bridge. Though attractively sited, with the old town on the island and new town (and railway station) on the mainland, it is for the most part a commercial city, with the inevitable concrete and glass. It offers the visitor little beyond a small Turkish quarter and an unusual Byzantine church with fourteenth-century Gothic overlays that serves as the Cathedral. It is best regarded as a base for excursions, where you can stay comfortably and eat well; swimming is possible from the Halkis beaches, but is better elsewhere.

If you see people standing on the bridge staring down into the water, they are probably waiting for the flow to change direction: it does so at approximately six-hour intervals, as you can test for yourself by dropping a piece of paper into the current at its moment of decision. The first movable bridge across the narrows was built in AD 540, and the latest dates from 1962.

Halkis has archaeological, Byzantine (in an old Turkish mosque) and folk museums, and is the main terminal for island bus services.

Around the island

Aedipsos, population 3,907, is 117 km from Halkis, in the north of the island. While it is less than certain that Hercules really built up his strength on its waters, like a parsimonious Popeye, it is more reliably recorded that the Roman Emperors Augustus and Hadrian drank there. The modern exploitation of its eighty hot springs dates from the 1880s, and you may gain the impression that so do most of its hotels. The water is said to be appropriate for rheumatic and urological conditions, and can be imbibed or soaked in at twenty-two private installations and one run by NTOG. Other Aedipsos attractions are remains of Roman baths and a nunnery. The easiest way to get to Aedipsos is not through Euboia but along the mainland motorway to the small port of Arkitsa, from where ferries make the forty-minute crossing up to fourteen times a day in the summer.

Eretria, population 2,501, 22 km south of Halkis, is similarly served by its own ferries from Skala Oropos on the Attica coast. The closest to a holiday resort, with some passable beaches, it is where the weekend 'villas' are thickest on the ground. Only a few traces remain of the ancient city.

Karystos, population 4,081, a holiday centre on the southern tip of the island 129 km from Halkis, can be reached more easily by ferry from Rafina than along the Euboia coast. It has a couple of thirteenth-century forts, a cluster of hotels and restaurants and a somewhat noisy nightlife. In Roman times, Karystos was known for its green marble.

Kimi, population 2,711, on the east coast of Euboia 91 km from Halkis, necessarily involves a drive through the island. The main point in going there would be to catch a ferry for the Sporades islands, for a shorter sea crossing than from either of the two more commonly used ports – Aghios Constantinos on the mainland near Kamena Vourla and Volos at the head of the Pagasitikos Gulf. If you are bound for Skyros you almost have to go to Kimi.

Aliveri, population 4,864, 47 km from Halkis, is economically an important little town, but one of little interest except to students of power stations and lignite mining.

Limni, population 2,300, 87 km north-west of Halkis, is beginning to catch on among the Greeks but has little to attract the tourist. Its ambitions are greater than its hotel capacity (sixty-two rooms in three listed hotels of third class and one of fifth), but the beaches have their admirers.

Where to stay

Euboia has 192 listed hotels, with 6,036 rooms; 102 of the hotels (2,238 rooms) are at Aedipsos, ten (405 rooms) in Halkis, and the other eighty (3,393 rooms) scattered around the island, as are the estimated 9,000 non-hotel beds. The hotels live essentially on Greek business and tend to be booked early.

However, the first-class, ninety-two-room **Lucy Hotel** in Halkis (tel. 0221 23 831) is one of Greece's real veterans, a showpiece in its own right, and can usually manage a bed for the unexpected arrival. Its restaurant is excellent, too.

Where to eat

At Halkis, apart from the **Lucy**, you could try the **Samaras** and **Vosporos** and, a little outside the town, the **Tzaki**.

Aedipsos residents wanting to eat in style at a hotel say they go to the **Aigli**, **Avra**, **Mytho**, **Iraklion**, **Galini** or **Thermae Sylla**. For non-hotel meals they speak well of the **Acapulco** and **Manolis**.

At Eretria you could look for the **Tzolias**, **Lakouvana**, **Mitsaleas**, **Ligouris** or **Nanakia**; at Karystos for the **Anemoni**, **Paralia** or **Evraïka**; and at Kimi for the **Alexiou** and **Xiros**, in town or, among fish tavernas by the sea, the **Spanos** and **Beis**.

Getting there

By road, turn off at the 55th km of the Athens–Lamia stretch of the north–south motorway, near Schimatari, and after another 25 km you are in Halkis.

By bus from Athens to Halkis (one and a half hours), Aedipsos via Arkitsa (three and a half hours), Eretria (one and a half hours), Kimi (four and a half hours) or Karystos (five and a half hours); departures every half hour for Halkis in the summer.

By rail from Athens to Halkis, from the Larissis station; seventeen trains a day, ninety minutes.

By ferry from Rafina to Karystos (22 nautical miles, two hours, two to four sailings a day) and from Skala Oropos to Eretria (4 nautical miles, thirty minutes, departures every half hour in summer).

Transport

Plentiful bus services from Halkis, and cars for hire. The roads can be dangerous in the mountainous regions, with blind corners.

Telephone

(Halkis – 0221): Coastguard 22 580
Police 24 572 Hospital 21 905

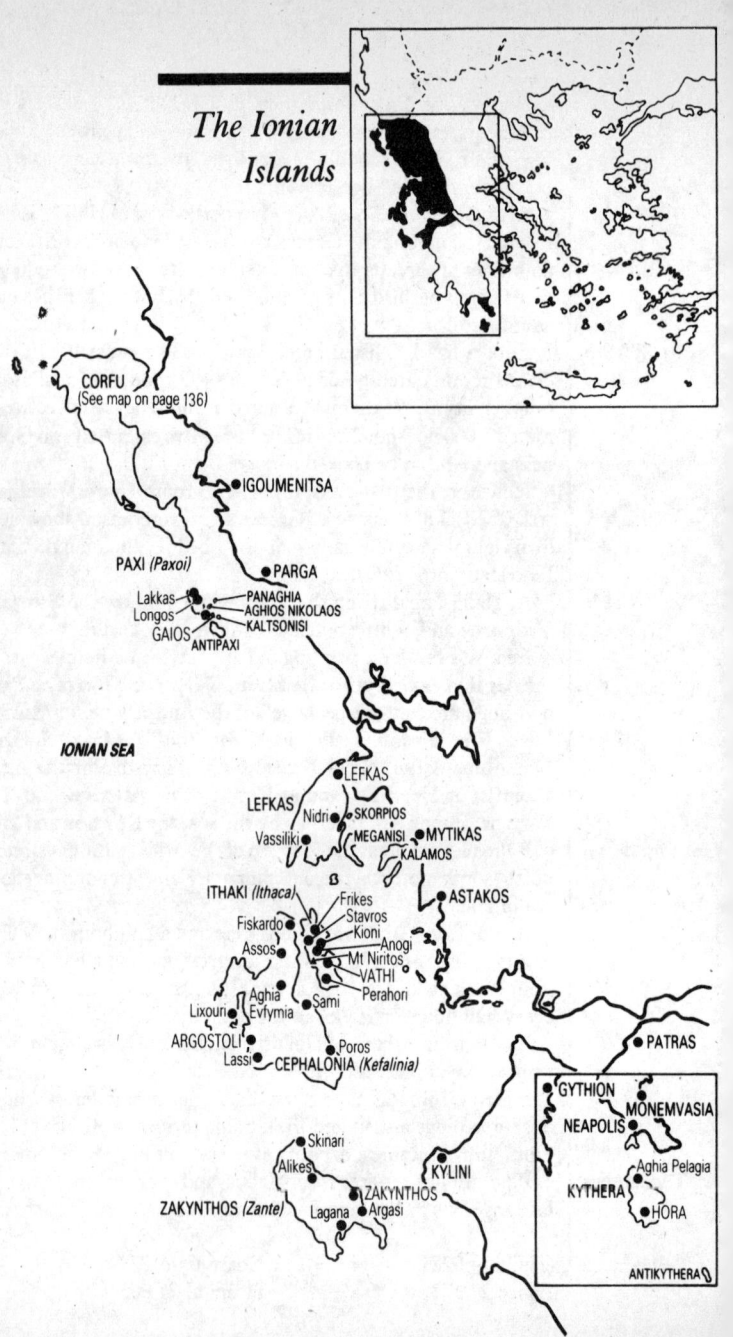

The Ionian Islands
See also Corfu, pp. 137-51.

Introduction

These are commonly known in Greek as the Eptanisa (Seven Islands). In contrast to the fourteen islands of the Dodecanese ('Twelve Islands') group, the designation this time is numerically correct, provided only the main islands are counted.

From north to south, the Ionians consist of Corfu, Paxi, Lefkas, Ithaki, Cephalonia, Zakynthos (Zante) and Kythera. The 'upper five' lie along the west coast of mainland Greece, as a kind of breakwater between the Ionian and Adriatic Seas; Zakynthos is off the Peloponnese, and Kythera is at the southern tip of the Peloponnese where the Aegean and Ionian meet.

As a group, they have a total population of just under 190,000, of which Corfu accounts for 97,000, Zakynthos 30,000, Cephalonia 27,000 and Lefkas 22,000. They are in many ways quite different from the islands of the Aegean: wetter, milder and less windy, they have a wealth of greenery unsurpassed anywhere else in Greece with the possible exception of Rhodes and parts of the Halkidiki peninsula in the northern mainland, and might at first glance appear to be dedicated to the olive tree. Their temperate climate ought to give them a longer tourist season: in fact it runs from Easter until the coming not of winter but of 'winter time' at the end of September, a ridiculously early date for so southern a country but one apparently forced on Greece by the need to conform with its European Community partners even at the cost of 7 p.m. autumn sunsets.

While the rest of Greece was subjected to the Turks, their proximity to Italy kept the Ionian islands under Venetian domination for most of the Middle Ages and until the destruction of the Venetian Republic by Napoleon. The older part of Corfu town is still architecturally a Venetian city, and intimations of Venice survive in Zakynthos and Cephalonia despite the rebuilding that followed the disastrous 1953 earthquakes.

The second dominant influence on Ionian architecture and tradition was supplied by the British, who held the group as a protectorate from the defeat of Napoleon until 1864 (see Corfu, pp. 139-40).

The Ionian islanders tend to regard themselves as more cultured than the Greeks as a whole: after all, in Ioannis Capodistrias they provided Free Greece with its first governor, and in Dionysios Solomos with its national poet. Though superseded by English as the second language, Italian is still widely spoken. There is a vigorous theatre movement, and more music in the streets and squares, from local brass bands, than anywhere else in Greece. With the possible exception of the Cephalonians, the Ionian islanders lay claim to keen rather than crafty minds, and tend to be more strongly represented in the liberal professions and diplomatic service than in the business world.

Touristically, only Corfu is of major importance: Zakynthos is developing fast, Cephalonia is trying to overcome its reputation of sulky indifference, Lefkas is ambitious but limited by what it has to offer, Ithaki is delightful but simply too small, and scarcely anyone ever goes to Kythera. Paxi relies mainly on day-trippers from Corfu.

It follows from their geographical configuration, in a long and curving line, that the islands can more easily be reached from Athens and mainland ports than from one another. Corfu, Cephalonia and Zakynthos have airports, and Lefkas can be driven to across a bridge. Otherwise, Igoumenitsa in Epirus is the mainland port for Corfu and, in the Peloponnese, ferries leave from Patras for Cephalonia and from Kylini for Zakynthos. For obvious economic reasons – the ease with which it is now possible to drive to Igoumenitsa and then take a ferry – you can no longer board a ship in Piraeus that will deliver you to Corfu twenty-four hours later, after a call at Cephalonia on the way.

Although Corfu is only a few hours from Brindisi on the ferries to Patras, the tourist movement is still largely British and German rather than Italian.

Cephalonia

Come back to Greece in fifteen or twenty years and you may find that Cephalonia (in Greek, Kefalinia) is a tourist resort equalling Zakynthos and possibly mounting a challenge even to Corfu. It has the potential, but is only slowly acquiring the will. For the moment, it is a little-visited island that is making a half-hearted attempt to live down its reputation as a good place to leave.

In contrast to its wines, the Cephalonians travel well; they also travel far, and often. If you happen to meet a Greek running a petrol station in a Chinese village, mining opals in Australia or guiding a safari in central Africa, there is an even chance that he will have been born on Cephalonia.

Also, while the Greeks say of themselves that they thrive best when they emigrate – they seize opportunities that lie waiting and create others, obey the laws and pay their taxes, becoming uncharacteristically 'good citizens' – the Cephalonians' rise begins from the moment they reach Athens. They are disproportionately well represented in business, politics, services, the arts and entertainment, as well as in the shipping industry both as owners and seamen.

Cephalonians, like Cretans, are fairly easy to recognise: their surnames for the most part end in 'atos' and their Christian name is likely to be Gherasimos, Dionysios or Eleftherios. They also stick together: Greeks from other parts of the country often regard them, not without a touch of envy, as clannish, crafty and parsimonious – sarcastic Corfiots like to pretend that a Cephalonian coffee is served with two saucers, to be split three ways!

One result of Cephalonian restlessness is the relative underdevelopment of an island of unexploited resources, for industry as well as tourism. Migrant money goes rather for holiday or retirement homes, or to help younger family members make their own escape, than for factory or hotel investment. For this among other reasons, the largest of the Ionian islands and sixth largest of all the Greek islands has only forty-two listed hotels, and a proportion of elderly among its population slightly above the national average.

As a visitor, you will not find the Cephalonians inhospitable: on the contrary, you will probably be impressed by the warmth of your welcome, and the way in which little gifts – for example, a flower or a glass of wine – will be continuously pressed on you. But you will find also that the island has not put itself about to cater to your needs in the way that Corfu and Zakynthos have. You take it as it is; if it doesn't suit you that way, try somewhere else!

Consider the 1953 earthquake, which measured 7.5 on the Richter scale and caused equal devastation on Cephalonia and Zakynthos. The Zakynthians, as if poets at heart, in effect said to themselves 'That's it, for another couple of centuries,' and reconstructed with delicate reverence for the past. The Cephalonians, saying 'Hah, so we're going to have earthquakes!', went for concrete and steel and now live for the most part in graceless settlements.

And yet, Cephalonia is pre-eminently Greece's island of song. They blow a better trumpet on Corfu, but you should not pass up an opportunity to attend a concert by a Cephalonian male voice choir.

Lying immediately opposite the entrance to the Gulf of Patras, south of Lefkas and north of Zakynthos, with Ithaki as its virtual dependency, Cephalonia is the most mountainous of the Ionian islands. It can be reached by air from Athens or by boat from the Peloponnese and mainland Greece.

Area: 781 sq km. Length of coastline: 253 km.

Population: 27,649 (Argostoli 6,788, Lixouri 2,842, Sami 935); a drop of 13 per cent in the ten years to 1981.

Area telephone code: 0671 for Argostoli and Lixouri, elsewhere 0674.

History The island's history is the same as for all the Ionian islands, with the distinction that the Turkish occupation lasted for only fifteen years, from 1485 until recovery of the island by the Venetians. Byron stayed there from 1823–4 on his way to Missolonghi. Much of the road network dates from the time of the British protectorate. In 1943, after the Italian Second World War surrender, the Germans moved in and massacred an entire Italian division there.

Around the island

Cephalonia has an unusual shape: a central portion with three mountain ranges, and two peninsulas. One peninsula, Paliki in the west, is separated from the main part of the island by the deep Gulf of Argostoli; the other, in the north, flanks Ithaki across a long and narrow channel.

Argostoli, the island's main port and its capital since 1715, is an uninteresting modern town on a headland at the entrance to the gulf of the same name; it is linked to the main part of the island by a causeway-bridge dating from the British protectorate. It is the main hub for bus services to the island's principal towns and villages and to some of the better beaches – in particular Lassi, Platys Yialos and Tourkopodaro – and departure point for a ferry service to Lixouri, half an hour away on the other side of the Argostoli gulf. For those who intend to miss nothing, there are archaeological and folk museums.

Some 9 km from Argostoli is the thirteenth-century castle of Aghios Georgios above a village, **Kastro**, that was the medieval capital of the island; the inhabitants moved to Argostoli after an earthquake in 1636.

Katavothres, just outside Argostoli, is a curious rock formation where the sea pours out of the land after an underground journey from the other side of the island. The island's other geological oddity is Kounepetro ('Moving Stone'), near Lixouri, which sways like a pendulum.

Lixouri, built in the 1530s and rebuilt after 1953, is a 31-km drive from Argostoli but only 3 nautical miles on the ferry; it offers the ruins of Ancient Pallis a few kilometres to the north and access to beaches some of which, though far from the best, do tolerate nudity.

Most visitors prefer the east coast, where they have a choice mainly between Sami and Fiskardo.

Sami, second in importance to Argostoli as a port but a rather more elegant town, is a 22-km drive from the capital along a good road. It is an area of archaeological remains, including those of Ancient Sami at Palaiokastro, and of interesting caves. There are good beaches in the immediate neighbourhood and at Aghia Evfymia about 10 km to the north. Best of the caves are those of Drongarati (stalactite and stalagmite formations) and Melissani, which has a lake in the centre that is open to the sunshine.

Poros is a picturesque harbour 41 km south-east of Argostoli, offering swimming at Skala and a visit to the island's oldest monastery.

Fiskardo is really the place to go; the only trouble is that the secret is out, and with a winter population of only 100 it can easily become crowded. One of the few villages that survived the earthquake almost unscathed, it can justifiably be described as traditional and unspoiled. Four of its houses have been converted by NTOG into 'traditional settlement' guest-houses, providing fifty-one beds in twenty rooms, and the entire village has been designated a protected site. Named for a Norman ruler who died there in 1085, it is now essentially a Venetian-style village of the eighteenth and nineteenth centuries, with excellent swimming and interesting opportunities for speleologists. All the same, it is a lengthy drive whether from Argostoli or Sami.

On the north-west coast of the same peninsula, **Assos** is a charming village with a fairly well preserved Venetian castle standing on a promontory; you can swim there and at nearby Myrtos, and admire the kind of sunsets that you add to your collection.

You can also drive to the summit of Mount Ainos, at 1,630 m the tallest peak in the Ionians, from which you have a magnificent view of the island's dark green woods of Cephalonian fir (*Abies cephalonensis*).

Where to stay

Of the forty-two listed hotels (1,237 rooms), two are first class, eight second and twenty third. In addition, there are the four NTOG guest-houses at Fiskardo (tel. 0674 139 78) and approximately 1,200 non-hotel beds.

The biggest of the hotels are the 227-room **Mediterranée** at Lassi just outside Argostoli (first class, tel. 0671 28.760) and 162-room **White Rocks** (first class, tel. 0671 23 167) at Platys Yialos.

Good reports are made of the **Summery** in Lixouri (second class, fifty-six rooms, tel. 0671 91 771) and the family-owned **Lassi** at Lassi (third class, tel. 0671 23 126, but only twenty rooms).

Where to eat

The whole island is exceptionally well provided with seaside fish tavernas, especially in summer, and there is no real need to look for any particular place.

However, in Argostoli you can eat well at the **Kefalos**, **Port of Kefalos** and **Thalasomilos** and, just outside the town, at the **Memory** at Fanariou, the **Apostolis** at Katavothres, and the **Il Posto**, **La Trata** and **Oscar** at Lassi.

Recommended tavernas and restaurants at or just outside Lixouri include the **Apolafsi**, **Akroyiali**, **Lotos**, **Mouries** and the municipality-owned **Touristiko Periptero** (Tourist Pavilion).

Fiskardo has the **Panormos**, **Dendrinos** and **Nikolaos**.

Wines

Cephalonian wines are among Greece's best; if they are also among the most expensive, this is partly because of their fancy bottles. Some, like Robola and Calliga, even reach Athens.

Getting there

Olympic Airways has from two to four flights a day from Athens. There are from one to three ferries a day from Patras to Sami (53 nautical miles, three and a half hours), two a day from Kylini in the Peloponnese to Poros (22 nautical miles, two hours) and two a day

Transport	from Astakos in Aitoloakarnania to Aghia Evfymia (28 nautical miles, two and a quarter hours). An adequate bus service (especially between Argostoli and Sami), plus plenty of taxis, coach and caique excursions, and cars and mopeds for hire.
From Cephalonia	There are four flights a week to Zakynthos, and boat services from Argostoli to Zakynthos (three hours), from Sami to Ithaki (one hour) and Nidri in Lefkas (two hours), and from Fiskardo to Vassiliki in Lefkas (one and a half hours) and Frikes in Ithaki (one and a quarter hours). Patras and Kylini are good launch-points for touring the Peloponnese, as is Astakos for western mainland Greece.
Telephone	(telephone code 0671) Police 22 200 Tourist police 22 222 Coastguard 22 224 Olympic Airways 28 808 NTOG 22 847 Hospital 22 434

Ithaki

Ithaki, or Ithaca, is the island that Odysseus spent ten years trying to get back to after the Trojan War. Today, it generally takes the sons of Ithaki rather longer than that!

The smallest of the 'Seven Islands' except for Paxi, Ithaki is the only one with a demographic problem severe enough to cause concern to the local authorities – though not so much to the central government in Athens, which reserves its anxieties for islands closer to the Turkish coast. The population drops steadily, census by census, in part because of the outward flow to Athens and the communities abroad and in part because of the merchant marine. Like their illustrious ancestor, the young men of Ithaki go to sea; unlike his, their war ends when they take their pensions. One result is that English is spoken more widely than would be expected on an island with so few visitors.

Ithaki provided some of the original Greek migrants to Australia, towards the end of the nineteenth century and early in the twentieth, and made a second contribution to the communities there after the Second World War.

A progressive local authority, waiting neither on Athens nor the European Community, has solved what used to be an acute water problem in dry summers, and has established local music and drama festivals of greater significance than the size of their audiences would suggest. Nevertheless, the average tourist still sees Ithaki on a one-day excursion from Cephalonia or Lefkas, or from the deck of a cruise liner which, after threading its way through the neck of the bottle into the astonishing pool of silence that is Vathi harbour, turns in the sharpest of circles and leaves without bothering to anchor. Vathi is a wonderful sight from a distance: exploration can be anticlimactic.

Area: 96 sq km. Length of coastline: 101 km.

Population: 3,648 (Vathi 2,037). The ten offshore islets – Arkoudi, Atokos, Vromonas, Drakonera, Karlonisi, Lazareto, Makri, Oxia, Pontikos and Provati – have a combined population of two.

Area telephone code: 0674.

According to Homer, the birthplace and kingdom of Odysseus was 'a rough land, but fitting nurse for a man.' Little is known of the island between the 'heroic' age of the Homeric epics and the ninth century AD, when it re-emerged as part of the Byzantine province of Cephalonia. Following the arrival of the Venetians in the late fifteenth century, its fate was standard Ionian.

Town and island

Ithaki is almost cut into two by the long and narrow Gulf of Molos on the east coast, from which another long and even narrower inlet leads to Vathi, the capital and port. The island is hilly in both sections, with Mount Niritos in the north and the Marathia plateau in the south. Apart from a couple of beaches near Vathi, the coast is indented with small coves offering swimming from rocks or short stretches of fine sand.

Extensively reconstructed after the 1953 Ionian earthquake, **Vathi** is too much dwarfed by its surroundings to be a 'comfortable' town, and the silence can easily become oppressive. However, it is the obvious base for exploration of the island by bus, taxi, caique or motorboat. You can take a look at the ruins of two forts at either side of the harbour entrance, pass an hour in the museum, and swim near the harbour or take a caique to Loutsa or Gidaki for some better beaches.

Anogi, population 93, 16 km from Vathi, is a hill village near the ancient town of Alkomenes; Schliemann dug among the ruins there in quest of Odysseus, without enjoying his customary good fortune.

Hani, at the narrowest point of the neck of land linking the two sections of the island, offers views of the Adriatic and Ionian Seas and the east coast of Cephalonia. The nearby Monastery of the Panaghia Kathariotissa dates from the sixteenth century, was restored in the late seventeenth, and has a small guest-house.

Kioni, population 265, 21 km from Vathi, is a traditional seaside village that has been designated a protected site, is becoming a tourist centre, but so far is without a listed hotel.

Perahori, a village 2 km inland from Vathi, with 470 inhabitants, is close to the ruins of what may have been the ancient capital, and a good beach.

Stavros, 16 km from Vathi on the north-west corner of the island, population 364, is the other contestant for the title of ancient capital, on the basis of more recent excavations, and also the main village in the northern section of the island.

Frikes, only 3 km from Stavros but on the opposite coast, is where you go for a really good swim. But with a population of only 55, it obviously offers little else.

Cave of the Nymphs

A 3-km walk along the coast from Vathi will bring you to the Cave of the Nymphs, known also as the Marmarospilia (Marble Cave); you are free to believe that this was where Odysseus concealed the treasures of the Phaeacians that he had carried with him from Corfu.

Where to stay

Ithaki has five listed hotels (two second class, two third and one fifth) with seventy-eight rooms in all, plus at least 200 non-hotel beds in Vathi and Kioni. Among the hotels, you could try the **Mendor** at Vathi (second class, thirty-six rooms, tel. 32 433) or the **Nostos** at Frikes (third class, twenty-seven rooms, tel. 31 644).

Where to eat

The two recommended Vathi restaurants are the **Thiaki** and that of the **Mendor Hotel**; tavernas include **Nikos**, **Athinaiki Gonia** (Athenian Corner), **Kantouni**, **Trehandiri**, **Dendrakia**, **Tsailis** and **Nea Ithaki**, while along the coast just outside the town are the **Palaio Karavo**, **Tsiribis** and **Vrahos**.

Getting there

The one or two ships a day from Patras cover the 53 nautical miles in four and a half hours, and there is a daily boat from Astakos in Aitoloakarnania (23 nautical miles, two hours).

Transport

Buses from Vathi to Stavros, Frikes and Kioni, and a Vathi–Kioni caique service. Taxis are available, and motorboats, mopeds and bicycles can be hired.

From Ithaki

Nidri (Lefkas) and Sami (Cephalonia) can be reached from Vathi, and Vassiliki (Lefkas) and Fiskardo (Cephalonia) from Frikes. By motorboat to the offshore islets.

Telephone

Police 32 205
Coastguard 32 909
Clinic 32 282

Kythera

Kythera, Kythira or Cythira, known also as Cirigo (Tsirigo) and once as Porfiroussa, is an island that scarcely seems to be sure where it belongs. Its inhabitants have proved equally restless.

Officially part of the Ionians but inaccessible even from its nearest 'Seven Islands' neighbour, Zakynthos, it lies between the southern tip of the Peloponnese and Crete and belongs administratively to the Department of Piraeus. It can be reached by ferry and hydrofoil from Piraeus and ports of the southern Peloponnese and, thanks to the Greeks of Australia, by air from Athens. Though few Greeks and even fewer tourists would consider it for a holiday, those who find their way to Kythera discover that it has more to offer than they had been led to believe, at least in terms of natural beauty; creature comforts will presumably be provided later.

Area: 278 sq km. Length of coastline: 51 km.
Population: 3,354 (Hora/Kapsali 588, Aghia Pelagia/Potamos 555).
Area telephone code: 0733.

The Australian connection

Kythera is one of the two Greek islands – the other is Samothrace – from which there was particularly heavy migration to Australia early in the present century and again after the Second World War, to the extent that there are now said to be more Kytherans in Melbourne, Sydney and Adelaide than on the island itself.

This proved useful when, in 1971, the inhabitants decided they could no longer be at the mercy of wind and weather – Kythera was always one of the first of the islands to be isolated by winter gales and among the easiest to be stranded on even during the summer. They took a collection locally and in Australia for the cost of an airstrip, contributed the land, built runway and apron with their own labour, and handed Kythera Airport to the Greek state as a going concern. Olympic Airways then did the gentlemanly thing.

Kythera lives to a greater extent than most islands on emigrant remittances, and would have still less of a holiday movement without the summer visits of Greek Australians.

Mythology and history

Once dedicated to Aphrodite and known as the island of love, Kythera was a colony of Minoan Crete, became a pirate stronghold in the Middle Ages, and was taken by the Venetians in 1717: its subsequent history followed that of the Ionian islands, including the British protectorate (when most of the roads were built) and union with Greece in 1864.

Around the island

Boats to Kythera disembark their passengers either at **Aghia Pelagia** on the north-east coast or **Kapsali**, the harbour for Hora, in the south. From Aghia Pelagia it is a 26-km drive to the capital.

Hora is built on a hill sufficiently far from the sea to provide, if not safety from pirates, at least sufficient warning of their approach; it has a castle dating from the early sixteenth century, now housing the island's archives, and a small archaeological museum.

Having travelled so far, it would be a pity to leave Kythera without going at least to **Palaiopoli** on the east coast, to see the ruins of Ancient Skandia. Said once to have had a population of 25,000, Skandia was destroyed by the effects of the same explosion of the Thera volcano that wrecked the Minoan empire (see also p. 224). The church of Aghios Kosmas there was built with material taken from a Temple of Aphrodite.

Beaches

For the visitor, Kythera is really an island waiting to be discovered, and therefore to be developed. Aghia Pelagia for the moment is the closest it has even to an embryonic resort: the best beaches are there and at Diakofti and Fryamos.

Where to stay

Kythera's six listed pension-sized hotels (one of first class, three of second and two of third) provide a total of fifty rooms, and there are also approximately 300 non-hotel beds on offer. The largest of the hotels is the third-class **Kythera Beach** at Diakofti (thirteen rooms, tel. 33 252); the **Kytheria** in Aghia Pelagia (second class, tel. 33 321) and **Keti** in Hora (second class, tel. 31 318) have ten and eight rooms respectively.

Where to eat

At Kapsali, the **Kalokairinou**, **Verzou** and **Kamares tou Mayeira** (The Cook's Chambers). At Hora, **Zorbas**. At Aghia Pelagia, the **Faros** (others open seasonally but only the Faros keeps going in winter).

Getting there

By air from Athens (one or two flights a day by light aircraft), or by boat or hydrofoil from Piraeus or such Peloponnese ports as Monemvasia, Neapolis and Gythion. The Piraeus boats, of which there are two a week, take about ten hours to cover the 150 nautical miles to Aghia Pelagia; the four hydrofoils a week take half the time. The shortest crossing is from Neapolis (daily in summer, 12 nautical miles, one hour) to Aghia Pelagia; from Gythion to Kapsali takes three hours.

Transport

The main bus route is between Aghia Pelagia and Kapsali, via Hora. Taxis are available, and cars and mopeds can be hired.

From Kythera

The ferry and hydrofoil ports of call mean that the Peloponnese is within easy reach. Otherwise, only to Antikythera and Crete. Antikythera, population 115, is almost exactly half-way between Kythera and Crete, in one of Greece's windiest corners. To go there would require a really pressing reason.

Telephone

Police 31 206
Coastguard 31 222/33 280
Olympic Airways 33 362
Clinic 31 243/33 325

Lefkas

Lefkas, which you will see written also as Lefkada, is an island you drive to – it is linked to the mainland province of Akarnania by a bridge – and one where you really need a car for comfortable exploration. Although as verdant as the Ionians in general, and with some splendid beaches, it has yet to build up much of a tourist movement: groups are relatively few, and usually Greek. The tourist movement, to the extent that it exists, is concentrated on Lefkas town and the east-coast village of Nidri, 17 km away, which the late Aristotle Onassis helped to put on the map by purchasing the offshore islet of Skorpios. The nearest airport is at Aktion on the mainland; this helps to deter European package tours and to preserve Lefkas for the independent traveller. The name means 'white', and derives from the

chalky cliffs at the southern tip of the island.
Area: 302 sq km. Length of coastline: 116 km.
Population: 21,863, including the offshore islets (Lefkas town 6,415).
Area telephone code: 0645.

History

Except that Lefkas, because of its proximity to the mainland, was occupied by the Turks on and off between the end of the fifteenth century and the beginning of the eighteenth, when it too was taken by the Venetian Republic, the island's history broadly followed that of the Ionians as a whole – including the period as a British protectorate.

Worth a stroll

Lefkas town, at the north-east tip of the island where the bridge to the mainland spans a canal only 25 m wide, is a picturesque place to walk through but scarcely holds the attention for more than a couple of hours. When you have covered the mile-long main street in each direction (and decided whether to buy jewellery, embroidery, lace or honey), and delved into the maze of alleys running off it, you have exhausted the immediate possibilities.

There remain an archaeological museum and equally modest folk museum and, a little outside the town but still within walking distance, the ruins of a theatre and fortifications that show where Ancient Lefkas once stood. The approaches to the canal are guarded by a fourteenth-century Frankish-Venetian castle with Turkish additions that is now in very poor condition. You will notice the long beach on the northern edge of the town, and equally that it is neither protected from wind and sun nor much used for swimming.

Some 3 km south-west of the town, the Monastery of the Panaghia Faneromeni, dating from the seventeenth century but largely rebuilt after a fire in 1886, has a guest-house with accommodation for twenty passing strangers.

Since Lefkas town has the island's larger and more comfortable hotels, it is best regarded as a base for exploration. It has been extensively reconstructed since the 1953 earthquake.

Nidri and the Onassis island

Only twenty years ago, **Nidri** (written also as Nydri) was a tiny fishing village in a setting of exquisite peace: holiday-makers were served by a couple of tavernas, perhaps a score of rooms in village homes, and small boats from which they could fish or swim. Then Onassis bought Skorpios and built a palatial villa on it, spent many a summer night in the Nidri tavernas, and made the whole place fashionable.

Onassis, his son Alexander and daughter Christina are now buried in the same chapel on Skorpios where the shipping magnate married Jacqueline Kennedy. The great white yacht, the *Christina*, with the old masters and the gold taps, on which Onassis hosted Winston Churchill and Maria Callas, among others, is seen no more at Nidri: it has passed to the Greek state, is officially the presidential yacht *Argo*, and rarely leaves the naval base on Salamis island. It has acquired the reputation of an unlucky ship, because of the regularity with which 'the late' has had to be prefixed to the names of those who once sailed in it; this, however, would seem to take insufficiently into allowance the consideration that Onassis, the poor boy from Smyrna who never got an education, felt a need to surround himself with the rich and famous, who by definition are rarely young.

Nidri ought by now to have recovered its peace. Unfortunately, it has not; to the contrary, it is the one uncomfortably crowded spot on Lefkas.

By all means take a look, have a swim, eat a meal at one of the fish tavernas, and hire a boat for a circumnavigation of Skorpios that will give you tantalising glimpses of the shuttered Kingdom of Ari. There are a couple of small hotels if you insist on staying in Nidri, and some 700 beds in village homes; then you may flee the sightseers by taking boats to islets on which you *can* land – Sparti, Madouri and Skorpidi.

(In the Second World War Count Ciano, the Italian Foreign Minister, took Skorpios for his wife Edda, Mussolini's daughter, but this proved a very temporary arrangement.)

Elsewhere on Lefkas

● **Vassiliki**, on the south coast 38 km from Lefkas town, is a developing resort with accommodation on offer in hotels and rented rooms, the ruins of a Temple of Apollo, and a Monastery of Aghios Nikolaos on a promontory. Caiques will take you from there to more remote beaches.

Close to the temple, there is a 70 m cliff from which, it is said, youths used to dive as a cure for unrequited love – if they survived, they then knew that life was still sweet. The cliff is also identified by some as the one from which Sappho committed suicide, and for that reason is known locally as the Cape of the Lady (Kavo tis Kyras).

● **Lygia**, 5 km from Lefkas town on the coastal road to Nidri, is a seaside village with a tree-shaded beach, a population of 430, hotel and rented-room accommodation, and a Valley of Erotas (Love) for a stroll in the moonlight while the emotion is still requited.

Beaches

Other good beaches are at Aghios Nikitas on the north-west coast, Periyiali (Passas Beach) on the east coast, Poros (Mikros Yialos) in the south-east, and Kalamitsi on the west coast.

Where to stay

Lefkas has fourteen listed hotels (seven second class, two third class and five fifth class) with a total of 411 rooms. Easily the most comfortable are two of the second-class hotels, the **Xenia** (sixty-four rooms, tel. 24 762 and 24 454) and **Lefkas** (ninety-three rooms, tel. 23 916) almost side-by-side in Lefkas town. The island as a whole offers some 2,500 beds in private homes.

Where to eat

Anywhere, in a fish taverna. In Lefkas town, local inhabitants with no time to drive to a beach will settle for the **Adriatika**, **Romantica** and **Pyrofani**.

Getting there

Normally by road from Athens (the three or four buses a day from the capital cover the distance in six hours) or by air to Aktion near

Transport

Preveza; the airport is 25 km from Lefkas, but the one or two daily flights connect with special buses.

Island bus services, from Aghios Minas Square, cover all the main villages; the longest journey, of 40 km, takes about an hour.

A trip along the east coast and back along the west involves a drive of about 75 km, for which cars and mopeds can be hired in Lefkas town. Taxis are also available.

There are ten buses a day to Nidri and beaches en route (a twenty-minute trip), four a day to Vassiliki (one hour) and two a day to Aghios Nikitas (twenty minutes).

From Lefkas

There are daily boat connections in summer from Nidri and Vassiliki to Ithaki and Cephalonia. The offshore islet of Meganisi is served by four boats a day from Nidri (4 nautical miles, thirty minutes), but the islets of Kalamos and Kastos are more easily reached from Mytikas on the mainland coast. Local travel agents offer day trips to Cephalonia, Ithaki, Meganisi and Kalamos.

Meganisi is the largest of the Lefkas satellites, with a population of 1,346 in three villages, a Cave of the Demons, good swimming and a few beds on offer in private homes. Kalamos, population 602 in two villages, has less to offer.

Telephone

Police 22 346
Tourist police 22 100
Coastguard 22 322
Hospital 22 336

Paxi

Paxi, to call it by that name, is the smallest of the Ionian islands as distinct from islets and, with the possible exception of Kythera, the least visited by holiday-makers planning to sleep there. But thousands cull a brief acquaintance with it every summer, on day trips from Corfu. The fewer than 600 tourists able to stay on Paxi at any one time with a roof over their heads are on to a good thing, but can hardly be unaware that the island's fame is spreading and its tranquillity is under threat.

Paxi, the phonetic transcription of the Greek Paxoi, is a plural noun and really means the Paxi Islands – Paxos, Antipaxos and half a dozen satellites. But the Greeks invariably speak of Paxi and Antipaxi, except for the islanders themselves who say they live on Paxous, which rhymes with 'loose'.

Paxi is 32 nautical miles south-east of Corfu town but considerably closer to Cavo on the southern tip of Corfu, from where excursions to Paxi are organised at least once a week. It can in addition be reached from Parga, an attractive little port on the Epiros coast.

Area: 25 sq km. Length of coastline: 45 km.

Population: 2,375 (including the 126 inhabitants of Antipaxi).
Area telephone code: 0662.

Guest appearances

Paxi is not the kind of island that makes history, but it has taken a number of bows on the world stage.

- According to Plutarch, it was from Paxi that the momentous announcement was made that 'the great god Pan is dead.'
- Antony and Cleopatra spent their last night together on Paxi before sailing off to Aktion (Actium) and total defeat at the hands of Octavian, subsequently Augustus.
- In 1537, Venice won a naval battle against the Turks off Paxi.
- Though she chose Corfu for her palace, the Empress Elizabeth of Austria was enchanted by Paxi and went there often (see Corfu, p. 146).
- James Morris, in *Heaven's Command*, paints a hilarious picture of a visit to Paxi in 1858 by W. E. Gladstone, on an inspection tour as Special Commissioner to the Ionian islands.

The incident involving Pan, as Plutarch tells it, occurred during the first century AD, when the captain of a ship becalmed off Paxi heard a voice instructing him to proclaim the death of the Ancient Greek god. He ignored it twice but obeyed it the third time, whereupon a 'great lamentation' arose from the sea. In other interpretations of the story, the voice spoke at the moment of the Crucifixion.

(The Greeks have another legend, referring to the Aegean as a whole, according to which a captain may hear a voice inquiring: 'Where is Alexander the Great?' His ship is doomed unless he responds at once: 'Alexander the Great lives and reigns' [*Megas Alexandros zei kai vassilevei*].)

Bearings

Boats from Corfu or Parga moor at **Gaios**, population 1,286, the capital and port, from where a bus runs to Lakkas, population 428, at the northern tip.

Lying in a bay on the sheltered east side of the island, and guarded by two offshore islets, Aghios Nikolaos and Panaghia, Gaios has the appearance almost of a fjord. It is a typical Ionian town in miniature, with tavernas and coffee-shops on the quay, a central square, some attractive churches, much greenery, a Venetian castle on Aghios Nikolaos and a monastery on Panaghia. It also has most of the available accommodation and is the place to book excursions and rent mopeds, bicycles or small boats.

Paxi is easy on the hiker – barely 10 km from one end to the other, with the tallest hill only 270 m high – which simplifies the quest for a remote and private beach if too many yachts have descended on Gaios and the caiques have already left for Lakkas or Longos (population 275); a short walkabout will produce sanded seclusion. Astonishingly green for so small an island, Paxi claims 300,000 olive trees.

A number of sea caves along the more rugged west coast, some of them occupied occasionally by families of seals, can be reached only by boat, which you can hire quite easily.

Where to stay There are five listed hotels (two second class, one fourth and two fifth) with a total of eighty-three rooms, as well as at least 300 non-hotel beds on offer in Gaios, another sixty in Lakkas and twenty or so in Longos. Your best hope of finding an unbooked hotel room is at the **Paxos Beach** at Gaios (second class, thirty-nine rooms, tel. 31 211). The few furnished villas, and the self-catering apartments, can generally be reserved only through London package tour agencies. It is on islands such as Paxi that the wisdom of the NTOG insistence on putting 'unlicensed' accommodation out of business becomes most questionable, since if islanders with rooms on offer chose to close them rather than pay tax it would be the tourists who suffered, while the Greek state would still gain nothing in direct tax and would lose something in VAT and foreign exchange. However, it would probably be asking too much of any government, anywhere, to accept that it is better that money should be made from which the state takes no direct cut than that it should not be made at all.

Where to eat At Gaios, the **Paxos Beach Hotel** has a good restaurant, and there are also the **Taka Taka** (Quickly Quickly), **Rex** and **To Grill**. At Lakkas, look out for **Souris**, **Sgarelios**, **Petalouda**, **Pantheon** or **Klinis**.

Getting there For the non-tripper, there are two boats a week from Patras (105 nautical miles, nine hours) and up to four a week from Mourto on the Epiros coast (12 nautical miles, one hour), as well as occasional connections with Igoumenitsa. The excursions from Corfu or Parga allow time for swimming, a meal and a walk around Gaios, but not for wider exploration.

Transport Buses from Gaios to Lakkas via Magazia and Longos, rented mopeds or bicycles, caiques and motorboats.

From Paxi By caique or fishing boat to the offshore islets (Aghios Nikolaos, Panaghia, Mongonisi and Kaltsonisi) as well as to Antipaxi, 3 nautical miles from Gaios. Antipaxi has no official accommodation for the visitor, but it is possible to get a meal and the swimming is good: the island can be reached also by small boat from Mongonisi.

Telephone Police 31 222
Coastguard 31 259
Clinic 31 466

Zakynthos

Zakynthos (Zakinthos), or Zante, the most southerly of the 'real' Ionian islands (Kythera is so far to the south as to be a kind of interloper), lies west of the Peloponnese coast and is reached most easily from the small port of Kylini. It is associated with Edgar Allan Poe and the Greek poet Dionysios Solomos, produces a few miniature bananas and a kind of giant garlic as well as an overpowering 'cologne' that leads the sensitive to stay upwind of you just as surely as the garlic does, was devastated even more completely than Cephalonia by the 1953 earthquake and accompanying fire, and attracts holiday-making Germans and loggerhead turtles in heat, the latter supported in their mating activities by the United Nations, European Parliament, Council of Europe, Worldwide Fund for Nature and, since the Greeks know when to toe the line, by the Athens government also. It is known as the 'island of flowers', and is remarkably beautiful in a soporific sort of way.

Area: 402 sq km. Length of coastline: 123 km.
Population: 30,014 (Zakynthos town 9,767).
Area telephone code: 0695.

Mythology and history

Once part of the kingdom of Odysseus and later under Roman domination, Zakynthos became a province of the Byzantine Empire, passed through a Frankish period, flourished as a commercial and cultural centre under the Venetians from 1483 to 1797, was taken by Napoleon and from him by the British, and joined Greece along with the rest of the Ionians in 1864. The Venetians called it Zante, and to Poe it was 'O purple Zante! *Fioro di Levante*!' (the flower of the east).

The national poet

The connection between Zakynthos and Dionysios Solomos is more firmly established than that between the island and Poe: Solomos was born there and, though he spent much of his life on Corfu, is buried in Zakynthos town.

There are paradoxes in the life of Solomos that are somehow typically Greek. He was educated in Italy, studied Italian, French and English literature, was deeply influenced by Dante, and wrote his first poems in Italian. The outbreak of the Independence Revolution in 1821, three years after his return to Zakynthos, led him to write the 'Hymn to Liberty', the first four stanzas of which were later set to music as Greece's national anthem. Publication of the poem in Paris brought him instant fame and the admiration of Goethe, Hugo, Lamartine and Chateaubriand.

But for a famous meeting at the end of 1822 with a Greek diplomat and historian, Spyridon Trikoupis, Solomos might never have made the switch from Italian to Greek. Recalling the meeting in a letter written many years later, Trikoupis noted that Solomos had read to him an ode in Italian and asked his opinion. '"Your poetical talent," I replied, "assures you a distinguished place on the Italian Parnassos, but the highest positions there are occupied already. The Greek Parnassos has not yet found its Dante."'

Adopting Greek, Solomos mined some of its richest veins – the language of the people, and its folk songs. But he never once visited independent Greece. He died and was buried on Corfu in 1857; ten years later his body was returned to Zakynthos and placed in a mausoleum that today is a place of pilgrimage for Greeks making their first acquaintance with the island.

Port and capital

The greatest achievement of **Zakynthos** town, and an object lesson to the rest of Greece, dates from the second half of the 1950s: it was rebuilt after the 1953 earthquake to anti-seismic specifications but in Venetian style, and therefore it is still a charming city. The Cephalonians, tremendous businessmen, made no such attempt.

Twin landmarks on the long Zakynthos waterfront are the eighteenth-century church of Aghios Dionysios, the island's patron saint, at one end and Solomos Square at the other; St Mark's Square, a block back, is the restaurant centre.

The Museum of the Celebrities has the tomb of Solomos on the ground floor and mementoes of the poet in the room above. Aghios Dionysios displays the relics of the saint in a silver casket, and the Byzantine Museum houses a rich collection of icons of the Ionian School – a blending of Byzantine and Renaissance hagiography. On the waterfront itself, there is a sixteenth-century Church of Aghios Nikolaos that survived the earthquake. Together, they invite the trite conclusion that earthquakes destroy mainly the inconsequential.

There is also an unusual Museum of the Occupation and National Resistance (the reference is to the Second World War) in the basement of the public library, while paintings in the Art Gallery will give you an idea of what Zakynthos was like before the earthquake.

Walking around Zakynthos town is scarcely exhausting – it is a matter really of the waterfront and the two squares – but provides you with an introduction to something that will strike you more forcibly as you penetrate further into the island: the profusion and variety of the flora. Every house has its window-box, and every balcony is draped with flowers. As if the whole island were one vast hothouse (on a steamy day, it almost is), onions grow to the size of small melons and garlic cloves acquire gherkin dimensions; like the climate, they are bland, and without bite.

Lagana and the loggerhead

The island's most concentrated holiday resort, with twenty-one of its eighty-nine listed hotels, is at **Lagana**, a long and splendid beach 7 km south of Zakynthos town where tourists are being forced into coexistence with *Caretta caretta*.

The Lagana problem has always been its attractiveness to this particular species of sea turtle, which a few years ago appeared to be doomed by the onslaught of developers and the priorities of paying guests.

But wildlife, as the Greek government found, has its friends in high places, and its charter in the form of the Berne Convention on the Conservation of European Wildlife and Natural Habitats.

Yielding to concentrated and diverse international pressures, the government established zoning regulations at Lagana that would probably have been sufficient had they been properly enforced – it was another example of the Greek ability to find contentment in enacting legislation without too close an examination of whether it was, or could be, implemented.

By the time you visit Lagana, the government will probably have been persuaded at least to apply the theoretical prohibition of the use of speedboats in Lagana bay, in face of protests by the Greek Sea Turtle Protection Society that 'half the loggerheads that came to Zakynthos last summer (1987) for their nesting' were found to have been injured by holiday-makers going nowhere fast.

What is indisputable is that Lagana is big enough for man and turtle, and there is no reason to shun the concentration of hotels and fish and lobster tavernas there; it is not a matter of expelling the tourist, but of devising a more successful apportionment of beach and water *lebensraum*, something that the resort's largely German clientele should appreciate.

Around the island

In general, the east and south coasts are the more developed, with the better beaches. However, although the west coast is rugged and hard of access, a number of self-contained resort hotels are under construction or planned there, some of them by German developers.

A non-swimming excursion to the north of the island, involving a round trip of about 60 km, would take you through the inland villages of **Volimes** and **Upper Volimes**, allow you to inspect a fourteenth-century Venetian tower and sixteenth-century Monastery of Aghios Georgios, and make your day with a visit to the Galazia Spilia (Blue Caves) on the coast at Skinari. Two connecting sea caves that together comprise one of Greece's finest grottoes, the Galazia Spilia can be reached along an asphalt road or on a caique excursion from Zakynthos town.

Close to Zakynthos town, you can follow the Greeks to the hill of Strani, where Solomos was supposedly inspired to write the 'Hymn to Liberty', or take a look at the Venetian castle, from where the views are magnificent and sweeping.

Beaches

The beach in Zakynthos town is inviting enough for a quick dip, but scarcely the place to spend a day. The swimming is better at Alikes and Alikanas, two adjoining fishing villages north of Zakynthos town; Argasi, a little to the south of the capital; and a string of villages around the south-eastern tip of the island, including Vassilikos, Porto Roma, Geraki and Keri.

Where to stay

Of the eighty-nine listed hotels (2,291 rooms), thirty-two are in Zakynthos town, twenty-seven in Lagana and the rest in the smaller resorts; they include two of first class, sixteen of second and fifty of third.

The biggest of the hotels is the second-class **Zante Beach** at Lagana (252 rooms, tel. 51 130); as an alternative there you could try the second-class **Galaxy** (eighty rooms, tel. 51 171).

Two reliable second-class hotels in Zakynthos town are the veteran

Strada Marina (112 rooms, tel. 22 761) and **Xenia** (thirty-nine rooms, tel. 22 232).

The island's 3,500 non-hotel beds are concentrated in Zakynthos town and Lagana.

Where to eat

In Zakynthos town you could seek out the **Arekia**, **Odysseus**, **Carissimo**, **Kalvianos** or **Voultsos** or, on the coast about a fifteen-minute drive away, the **Koukla**. At Lagana, certainly for fish and hopefully for lobster, you could look for the **Limanaki**, **Perivolaki**, **Manthos**, **Carmen** and **Porto Koukla**.

Getting there

Olympic Airways has two or three flights a day in summer from Athens, and three a week from Cephalonia. The ferries from Kylini in the Peloponnese (at least six to eight a day in summer) cover the 18 nautical miles in an hour and a half. Kylini can be reached direct by bus from Athens; by train, you have to change at Kavasila.

Transport

Regular bus services, coach excursions, caiques and motorboats, taxis, cars, mopeds and bicycles. There are eight buses a day to Lagana, four to Alikes and two to Keri, from a terminal in Filita Street, a block back from the waterfront of Zakynthos town. The Zakynthos roads are generally good, but need care on the sharp turns.

From Zakynthos

Really only to Cephalonia, by air or sea. But from Kylini, of course, the whole Peloponnese is open to you – Zakynthos could indeed be a diversion on a tour of the Peloponnese.

Caiques can be taken to the **Strofades islands**, 42 nautical miles south of Zakynthos. Only 10 m above sea level at their highest point, they were known in antiquity as the 'floating islands'. You should hazard the trip only if you have a good stomach, enjoy the ruggedness of open boats, have a moth-like attraction to lighthouses, or are desperate to see the fortress monastery of Aghios Dionysios.

Telephone
Police 22 100
Coastguard 22 417
Olympic Airways 28 611
Hospital 22 515

The North Aegean Islands

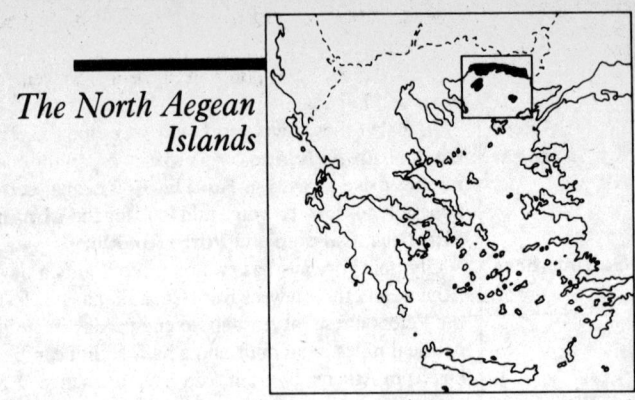

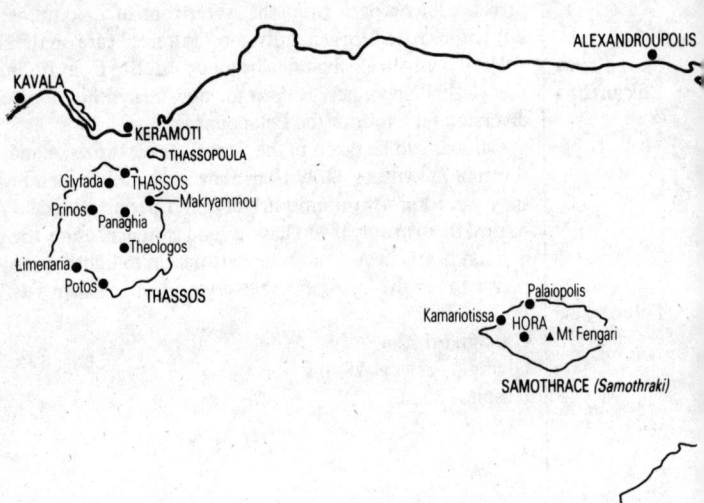

The North Aegean Islands

Introduction

There are only two of these, Thassos and Samothrace (Samothraki), lying off the coast of northern Greece between the Halkidiki peninsula and the entrance to the Dardanelles. The best way to reach them is by boat from Kavala and Alexandroupolis respectively, and the greater part of their holiday movement is made up of Greeks from Macedonia and Thrace.

Both islands have their beauties, and you would scarcely be bored if you visited them, but it has to be admitted that there are more interesting and rewarding Greek islands on which to spend a holiday. However, you would be missing an opportunity if you failed to allow a day or two for a quick look at one or both of them in the course of a leisurely drive between Thessaloniki and Istanbul.

Samothrace

Samothraki in Greek, the English variant of the name is preferred simply because Thrace, the part of mainland Greece between Macedonia and the Turkish border, is known to no one but the Greeks as Thraki. While consistency is an unattainable goal in the transliteration of Greek names, a gesture may sometimes be made in its direction. Also, the island is best known for the Winged Victory of Samothrace, scarcely of Samothraki, which the Greeks are perfectly content to see only when they visit Paris; with their own questionable consistency, they want the Elgin marbles back from the British Museum but have no desire to strip the Louvre of its Greek treasures.

Mountainous but green, Samothrace has the highest peak in the Aegean – Mount Fengari (Moon), 1,640 m – from the peak of which Poseidon is said by Homer to have watched the siege of Troy; though the island is close to the Dardanelles, you would need a god's vision to see the ruins of Troy itself. It was on Samothrace in 357 BC that

Philip II of Macedonia met Olympias, daughter of the King of the Molossians, while both were attending the Mysteries. They courted, married, and produced Alexander the Great.

Not many tourists find their way to Samothrace, and its few Greek holiday-makers are drawn mainly from the region of Alexandroupolis in Thrace, the only port from which the island can be reached easily. The beaches are second-rate by Aegean standards, and accommodation is limited. Samothrace is scarcely an island to visit in the winter: apart from rough seas, it receives a share of the rain and snowstorms that sweep the Thracian mainland.

Area: 177 sq km. Length of coastline: 58 km.
Population: 2,871 (Hora 941, Kamariotissa 546).
Area telephone code: 0551.

Mythology and history

Between visits by Hercules and the Argonauts and rejoining Greece after the 1912 Balkan War, the island attracted the attention of Romans, pirates, Crusaders, Venetians and Turks. In the Second World War it was occupied by the Bulgarians, as allies of Germany.

The Kabeiri Mysteries

These were a variation of the same fertility cult as that celebrated through the more famous Elefsinian Mysteries. Of pre-Greek origin, they survived until displaced by Christianity; the island then became a monastic centre, where clergy were trained before appointment to the Aghia Sofia church in Constantinople.

Almost as little is known of the details of the Kabeiri Mysteries as of the Elefsinian, even though initiation was open to anyone. A moral standard appears to have been required for the higher of the two degrees to which initiation could be obtained, and preparations involved fasting and possibly confession. But the records are meagre.

The sanctuary at which the Mysteries were held, and where the Winged Victory was found in 1863, is in the north of the island near Palaiopolis (Old Town), and has been excavated by French, Austrian, Swedish and American teams. The extensive site includes Cyclopian walls, the sanctuary of the Great Gods in whose honour the Mysteries were performed, remains of a stadium and theatre, and the largest circular building found anywhere in Greece, the Arsinoeion, built for Thracian-born Queen Arsinoe of Egypt in 280 BC with marble brought from Thassos. Portable discoveries, plus a replica of the Winged Victory, can be seen in the Palaiopolis Museum.

Bearings

The ferries from Alexandroupolis anchor at **Kamariotissa**, a fishing port at the north-west corner of the island, from where buses leave in two directions – along the north coast, and to the south coast through **Hora**, the capital, below the ruins of a Byzantine castle on the slopes of Mount Fengari. Hora offers splendid views and a chance to visit Palaiopolis, but there is little the visitor can actually do there.

Beaches

The better swimming is at Kamariotissa, below Palaiopolis, and along the south coast around Lakoma. The north coast thermal resort of Therma, also known as Psarotherma, has modern hydrotherapy

Where to stay

installations and a passable beach.

The five listed hotels have a total of 145 rooms. Best bets are the third-class **Niki Beach** at Kamariotissa (thirty-eight rooms, tel. 41 561) and second-class **Kaveiros** at Therma (thirty-five rooms, tel. 41 577). The second-class **Xenia** at Palaiopolis (tel. 41 230) may be the nicest, but with only seven rooms it fills easily. Some 500 non-hotel beds are on offer, mostly in Therma, Kamariotissa and Hora.

Where to eat

Samothracians say the best meals are found in Kamariotissa, at the **Oasis**, **Klimataria** and **Hatzikonstantis** restaurants, the **Lagada** taverna and the **Turkovrissi** fish taverna. There are also combination **taverna-bars** at **Hora**, **Therma** and **Lakoma**. The island is best known for its semi-wild goat, which is eaten grilled or stewed.

Getting there

The ferries from Alexandroupolis (two a day in summer) cover the 29 nautical miles in about three hours.

Transport

The two local bus services, and by fishing boat. Mopeds can be rented in Kamariotissa.

From Samothrace

To the mainland provinces of Thrace and Macedonia, through Alexandroupolis and less frequent connections with Kavala.

Telephone

Police 41 203
Coastguard 41 305
Clinic 41 376/41 217

Thassos

The principal resort island of northern Greece, Thassos is half expected to have a future as Greece's 'oil capital'; however, this question is not going to be resolved one way or another until Greece and Turkey come to an agreement on the whole Aegean continental shelf (see pp. 50–2). Even if new oilfields are eventually discovered, the experience from the first and so far only site located and exploited – the so-called 'Prinos' field just off the coast of Thassos – suggests that the island will be left unaffected: oil from Prinos is pumped to the mainland, so far without either mishap in the form of polluted beaches or benefit to the island from oil money. Oil is simply the conversational standby, on an island that is charming though difficult to reach except from Kavala.

The northernmost of the Aegean islands and almost circular in shape, Thassos lies off the coast of eastern Macedonia, with Samothrace to the east, Lemnos to the south-east and the Mount Athos peninsula to the south-west.

Area: 378 sq km. Length of coastline: 95 km.

Population: 13,111 (2,300 in Thassos town, 2,245 in Limenaria and 1,646 in Prinos).

Area telephone code: 0593.

History

Once on the borders of Greek civilisation and the barbarian world beyond, Thassos was settled at least as early as the neolithic period. Its first recorded inhabitants were Thracians, who knew it as Ydonis. It was a colony of Paros in the eighth and seventh centuries BC, repeatedly changed hands between Athens and Sparta in the Peloponnesian Wars, was occupied by Philip II of Macedonia, Alexander the Great's father, and flourished again under Roman rule. Several times ravaged by Slavs, Arabs and pirates in the Byzantine era, it fell to the Turks in 1455 and returned to Greece in 1913. In ancient times it was known for its gold and silver mines, now exhausted, and its marble quarries.

Confusion can be costly

The first thing to avoid on Thassos is confusion. The capital, Thassos town, is on the north coast and is known as Limena, while the second largest town, on the opposite side of the island, is Limenaria. Mixing them up can be wasteful both of time and money.

Limena is built on the ruins of an ancient city, and is an archaeologist's delight. An acropolis overlooks two ancient harbours, one commercial and the other military, and remains in the same area include Temples of Dionysos and Poseidon of the sixth and fourth centuries BC respectively, the gate of the ancient city with 4 km of fifth-century walls, and an ancient theatre in a pinewood, dating from the fourth century, which the Romans adapted for gladiatorial contests and which is still used in the summer for theatrical performances.

Limena itself is a picturesque little town and centre of the island's tourist movement, with twenty-four listed hotels, about 2,000 beds in rented rooms, and the first of the island's splendid beaches in the immediate vicinity. Its archaeological museum in the old harbour area is well worth a visit, as is the folk museum in the former Monastery of Aghios Nikolaos.

Around the island

As soon as you leave Limena you will appreciate how rich and green the island is, and why its viscous pine-flavoured honey, so dark as to be almost black, is regarded as Greece's finest by those who like sweetness to have a touch of the bitter. You should try to take in:

- **Theologos**, a beautiful old village roughly in the centre of the island, with a population of 918.
- **Limenaria**, the seaside town on the south coast, 40 km from Limena. With twelve listed hotels and 1,800 beds on offer in private homes, it is the second centre of Thassos tourism.
- **Panaghia** (population 902), overlooking the east-coast bay of Potamias, 7 km from Limena. Once the capital of Thassos, it still has a Macedonian flavour. A Cave of the Dragon there is named for one of its stalactites, not for a previous inhabitant. The village of **Potamias** (population 984) is 2 km further along the same road. Both Panaghia and Potamias are handy for nearby beaches, and are well provided with hotels and rentable rooms.
- **Potos**, a south-coast resort close to Limenaria with a population

of 505, has four listed hotels and about 500 household beds there and beside the adjacent beaches of Pefkari and Psili Ammos.

● **Prinos**, the inland village that gave its name to the oilfield, 22 km from Limenas, with thirteen listed hotels and 250 additional beds, is for those who prefer hillsides to beaches, and walking to swimming.

In general, the eastern part of the island has the wilder natural beauty, with deep valleys and small beaches that are reached more easily by motorboat than by road. The Archangelou Monastery on the south-east tip is an island showplace. The western part, including the west and south coasts, has the better road network.

Beaches Defining best beaches as those that are served by summer tavernas, you should be able to indulge magnificently in hedonism at Makryammou, Chryssi Ammoudia, Chryssi Akti, Alykes, Kinira, Psili Ammos, Pefkari, Skala Marion, Pachi, Papalimani and Glyfada; for this, you have the assurance of Thassos Mayor Eleftherios Meresis!

Where to stay Thassos has eighty-one listed hotels, with a total of 1,368 rooms: two are of first class, twelve of second, seventeen of third and the remaining fifty of fourth and fifth. There are also a suspected 6,000 beds on offer in private homes.

At Makryammou, you should be able to find a room at the first-class **Makryammos bungalow complex** (206 rooms, tel. 22 101), and at Glyfada the third-class **Glyfada Hotel** (fifty-four rooms, tel. 22 164). Best of the Potos hotels is the third-class **Olympion** (fifty-four rooms, tel. 51 930). At Limena and Limenaria the hotels are mostly small and of lower categories; at Limenaria you might try the third-class **Menel** (eighteen rooms, tel. 51 396) and at Limena the second-class **Galini** (sixteen rooms, tel. 22 195).

Where to eat Thassos really does abound in excellent restaurants and tavernas, and even the pizzerias are bearable. Among the Mayor's favourites are the **Zorba**, **Akroyiali**, **Papalimani**, **Glyfada**, **Syrtaki**, **Vournelis** and **Laimos**; you may spot them as you drive around the island, but have no need to fast until you do. At night, even the smaller tavernas generally run to a guitarist; there is also no lack of discos.

Getting there Effectively, only from Kavala (16 nautical miles) or Keramoti (3 nautical miles), the closest point on the mainland coast. The service from Keramoti is almost hourly in the summer.

Transport Thassos has 100 km of good quality roads, and cars, taxis, mopeds and bicycles for hire. There are thirteen buses a day between Limena and Limenaria, and almost as many on the other main routes.

From Thassos Via Kavala, you can reach Samothrace, Lemnos, Lesbos, Skiathos, Chios, Samos, Patmos, Kos, Rhodes, Simi, Euboia and even Piraeus if you enjoy long sea trips. From Thassos itself, there are caique trips to the desolate offshore islet of Thassopoula.

Telephone
Police 22 500 Clinic 22 190
Coastguard 22 106 The Mayor 22 118

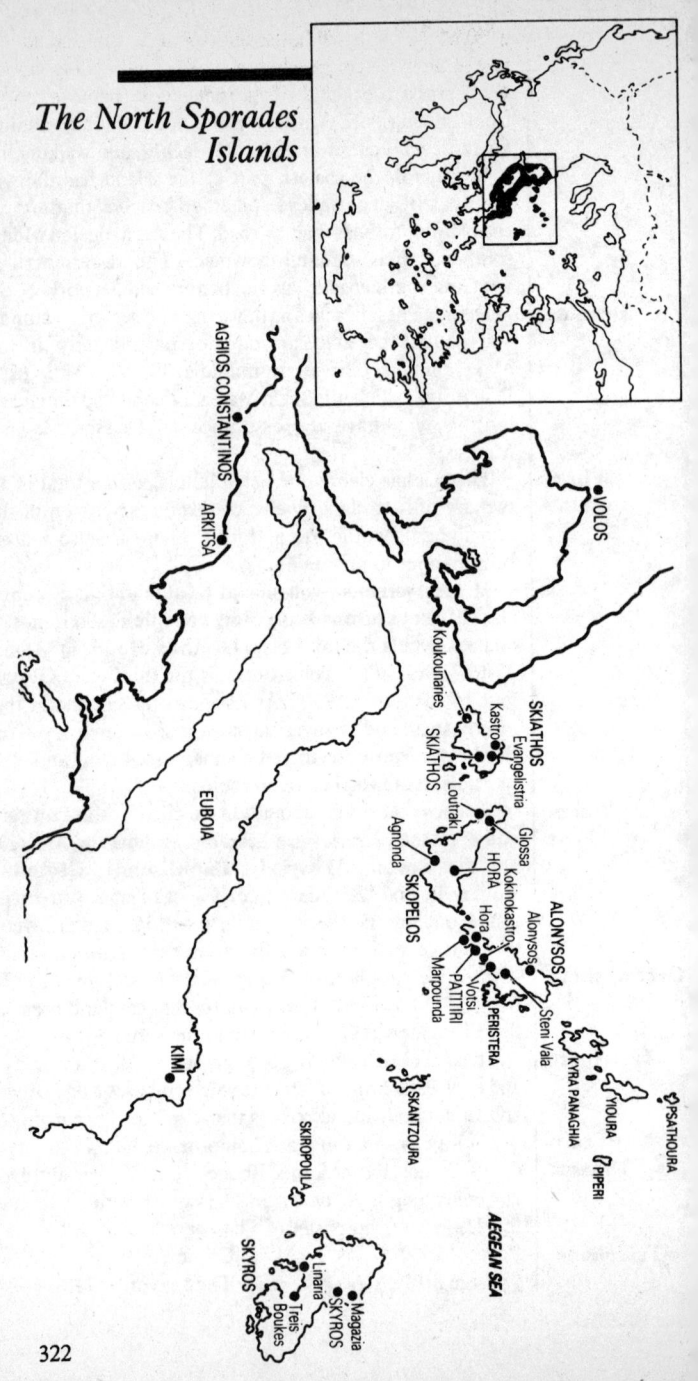

The North Sporades Islands

The North Sporades Islands

Introduction

Lying between the coast of Euboia and the Halkidiki peninsula, the North Sporades islands consist of Skiathos, Skopelos, Alonysos and Skyros and a host of uninhabited or sparsely populated islets – among them Aghios Georgios, Dasia, Dio Adelphia, Yioura, Kyra Panaghia, Peristera, Piperi, Skantzoura, Repi, Tsoungria, Psathoura and Skiropoula – that most Greeks have probably never heard of either.

The Sporades are reached most easily from the east-coast port of Volos (an overnight stay there would enable you to tour the delightful mountain villages of Pilion) or from the small harbour of Aghios Constantinos on the mainland coast near Kamena Vourla. The exception is Skyros, which is more accessible from Kimi, on the east coast of Euboia.

Relatively isolated until recent years, Skiathos in particular and Skopelos to a lesser extent have now acquired a faithful tourist movement. In addition, the absence of restrictions on land ownership by aliens (foreigners may not buy real estate in the 'border regions' of Greece, a definition that includes many of the islands) has led to widespread purchase of holiday homes in the North Sporades by British and Germans in particular; some of these homes are rented out for the 'unwanted' part of the season.

The Sporades are generally green, with excellent beaches. Though Skiathos tends to become overcrowded in peak season, modern comforts there can be exchanged for comparative isolation elsewhere in the group. The islands are unlikely to be your choice for a first holiday in Greece, but are useful reserves.

Alonysos

Alonysos is a tall, narrow island that lives in its basement: most of its roads, all of its major settlements and the bulk of its population are to be found in its southern corner, leaving four-fifths of the island virtually uninhabited. The 1971 census counted just eighty-six people living 'beyond the pale', and even they were in a village only half-way up the east coast. With a long history but in tourist terms no real present, it lies 68 nautical miles from Volos and 62 from Aghios Constantinos, is where the Sporades ferries turn back for their home ports, and cannot yet be reached by air. You would go there for the swimming, fishing and the possibility of watching Mediterranean monk seals, an international centre for the study and protection of which is under construction on the island.

Area: 64 sq km. Length of coastline: 63 km.

Population: 1,554, including the offshore islets. On Alonysos itself, Patitiri has 957 inhabitants, Votsi 455, Steni Vala 86, and the island's de jure capital, Hora, 26!

Area telephone code: 0424.

History

Alonysos took its present name on reuniting with Greece after the 1821 Revolution: it had been known in ancient times as Ikos, and in the Middle Ages sometimes as Hiliodromia and sometimes as Lianodromia. Inhabited well before the Mycenaeans took it in the fourteenth century BC, it had two towns in the Classical period that grew rich from their trade in wine. An Athenian naval base in the fourth century, it was subsequently seized by the Romans, destroyed by pirates and occupied by the Turks. Hora, known also as Palia Alonysos (Old Alonysos), owes its abandonment to an earthquake in 1965.

Around the island

Alonysos is a quiet, heavily wooded island that seems mountainous even though its tallest peak is only 470 m. The fertile valleys are cultivated and the slopes of the hills support flocks of sheep and goats, but the islanders' principal source of livelihood is the merchant marine and fishing.

You would land at **Patitiri** on the south-east corner, the largest town and *de facto* capital. Most of its inhabitants moved there after the earthquake, doubling its population in a little over ten years. Though too new and functional to be described as elegant, it is the obvious place to set up base, book an excursion and hire a boat.

Buses run to **Hora**, 5 km away, a town largely of roofless houses and the kind of vegetation associated with bomb-sites. Nevertheless, reconstruction is under way: it was started by foreigners, especially Germans, who bought and restored some of the ruined houses, sometimes settling there permanently, and now the Greeks are moving back, too. Accommodation is hard to find, but there is no real need to bother; it takes only an hour or so to see the remains of the Venetian fortifications and the old churches and monasteries, and the best beaches are elsewhere.

Beaches

There is especially good swimming at Kokinokastro (Red Castle), half an hour by caique from Patitiri. Excavations in the area found tools and animal bones of the Middle Paleolithic period, providing the earliest evidence yet discovered of Aegean habitation; some of the finds are on display in the Volos museum. The site of Ancient Ikos is nearby, with the remains of an acropolis and fortification walls.

Votsi, 1 km north of Patitiri, and Marpounda, 5 km to the south, are the likeliest candidates when Alonysos decides to create a tourist resort. Other excellent beaches are at Kalamaki, Tsoukalia and Yerakas.

Where to stay

Alonysos has ten listed hotels (one second class, three third and six fifth) with a total of 296 rooms, and some 1,100 beds in private homes. The second-class **Alkyon** at Patitiri (fourteen rooms, tel. 65 450) is nice if you can find a room, but more hopeful inquiries can be made at the three third-class hotels: the **Alonysos Beach** at Votsi (forty-five rooms, tel. 65 281), the **Galaxy** at Patitiri (fifty-two rooms, tel. 65 251) and the **Marpounda** at Marpounda (104 rooms, tel. 65 219).

Where to eat

The islanders insist that there is no reason to choose one taverna rather than another, pointing out that a cooperative of fishermen ensures fresh fish and lobster to all of them. However, you might keep your eyes open for the **Aloni** and **Paraporta** at Hora or, at Patitiri, three fish tavernas all in a row – the **Mourias**, **Akroyiali** and **Dichti** – as well as the **Alonisi**, **Metihos** and **Tzitzifia** for meat on the grill.

Getting there

By the Volos and Aghios Constantinos ferries (five hours) or the less regular service from Kimi (three and a half hours), or on the hydrofoils in the summer.

Transport

Mainly by bus, fishing boat or taxi; mopeds can be hired, but not cars.

From Alonysos

Ports of call on the ferries, and occasional connections with Lemnos, Kavala, Lesbos, Skyros and Halkidiki. The offshore islets, with their good beaches, can be reached on excursions or by fishing boats: they include Peristera (population 15), Kyra Panaghia (population 7), Yioura (population 2), Psathoura (population 2) and Piperi, Skantzoura and Dio Adelphia where the census-takers found nobody at home. On clear days, the remains of an ancient city, presumably sunk in an earthquake, can be seen at the bottom of the sea off Psathoura, and several Byzantine wrecks have been spotted off Kyra Panaghia. Yioura is an island of evil repute, since the Colonels reopened the concentration camp there during the 1967–74 military dictatorship, but for the voluntary visitor it offers a cave with stalactites and stalagmites.

Fishing among these offshore islets is said to be just about the best in Greece: you may use harpoons and masks, but not breathing apparatus (see p. 94).

Telephone

Police 65 205
Coastguard 65 595
Clinic 65 208

Skiathos

Anyone who doubts that success has its price should go to Skiathos. With a population of around 4,000, it receives rather than welcomes close on half a million tourists and Greek holiday-makers during its April to October season. The result is a profusion of fast-food outlets and discos, more than a score of tour offices to take bookings for local excursions, and occasional traffic jams on an island that in winter has only a few hundred cars. The problem is that tourism has been developed into big business *on* rather than *by* Skiathos. The ointment that eases the same ache on islands of comparable size, such as Myconos and Ios, in the form of money that stays where it was earned, is available to a far lesser extent on Skiathos: to the contrary, the inhabitants complain every year of 'carpet-baggers' who fly in from Athens with the swallows and leave them the crumbs of the holiday movement.

Only 38 nautical miles from Volos, Skiathos is the closest of the Sporades islands to the mainland; it can be reached also by air from Athens and charter flights from outside Greece.

Area: 48 sq km. Length of coastline: 44 km.
Population: 4,129 (3,838 in Skiathos town).
Area telephone code: 0427.

The island has borne the same name, which means 'shade' or 'shadow', since ancient times: it is assumed to derive from the number of trees, which are still among the principal Skiathos attractions.

The growth of tourism

Only thirty years ago, to visit Skiathos was to feel yourself a pioneer. With no Athens-Thessaloniki motorway, it took the better part of a day to drive to Volos; the train was faster but still tedious, involving a change and probable wait for connections at Pharsala in central Greece. After a night in Volos you embarked on the original *Kyknos*, a boat that could have rolled on a river and that bore no resemblance to its present namesake.

On Skiathos you found just two hotels, the Akti and Avra, and a few rentable rooms. To swim, you hired a boat or walked for a couple of hours along footpaths. To go to the Evangelistria monastery, a showplace then as now, you entrusted yourself to a mule that made a convincing pretence of suicidal tendencies – the mule-minder's explanation that he walked on the inside of the precipitous trails because mules prefer the edges had to be accepted, if not necessarily believed. You went to bed early because the electricity was cut off at 10 p.m., and you showered when the taps happened to produce water. But you did eat delicious fish, grilled over charcoal at simple waterside tavernas.

The outside world began its infiltration in the early 1960s when two Greeks from London sniffed the prospect of making a fortune, invested in a stretch of seaside land which they parcelled out into building sites, and advertised the opportunity to construct holiday villas. Within a few years, Skiathos had a British suburb. Hotels, blocks of furnished apartments, restaurants, tour offices, boutiques, jewellers, souvenir shops, discos and banks followed, while improved roads allowed the development to spread outwards, to the larger beaches. But the real mass movement, which today causes anxiety over its effects on the environment and anger over the flight of the profits, dates from the opening of Skiathos Airport in 1982 and the arrival of the first charter flights a couple of years later.

If it wished, Skiathos could lay claim to the dubious honour of having introduced a tolerance of nudism – ever so quietly, on Banana Beach – several years before Myconos did the same in its own, more exhibitionist manner.

Bearings **Skiathos** town, the port, present capital and only settlement of any importance, occupies the site of Ancient Skiathos but dates mainly from the 1830s, when the islanders found it safe to move back to the south coast. For the previous three centuries, fear of piracy had constrained them to live in **Kastro**, a now deserted medieval town that makes an interesting excursion.

The tides of the Second World War swept even over tiny, harmless, unfortified Skiathos, which was badly damaged by German bombing (one would like to believe that warlords today would show greater respect for their taxpayers' money). Subsequent reconstruction was in the style of the 1830s, as has been the greater part of more recent expansion, with the result that Skiathos is still a town of two- and three-storey white houses with red roofs, spreading uphill from the waterfront to the Cathedral. While there may have been an element of chance in the survival of the town's architectural harmony so far, islander vigilance should provide sufficient protection from now on.

Alexandros Papadiamantis Greek visitors make for the home, now a museum, of one of their country's best-known nineteenth-century writers, Alexandros Papadiamantis. The main street bears his name, and he is commemorated also by a marble bust near the causeway to Bourtzi, a pine-clad islet in the harbour where the Venetians built a fortress. The average tourist admires the views from the area near the Cathedral, but regards Skiathos town mainly as a place to hire a boat, book an excursion or look for an indifferent meal. The beauty and peace lie elsewhere.

Beaches Koukounaries, now linked by road with Skiathos and a budding resort area, is easily the best of the island's beaches, probably the best in Greece, and would possibly feature on any list of the world's ten finest. Unfortunately, to enjoy Koukounaries nowadays you have to like people; the same applies, to a lesser extent, at the other resort beach of Achladies.

Those who prefer solitude have from fifty to seventy beaches to choose among, some quite long and others not much bigger than a

What to see

tablecloth; the ones on the south and west coasts are mostly accessible by road, and those in the north are reached more easily by small boat. No other Aegean island can boast of so many beaches per kilometre of coastline, or so many with trees almost to the waterline.

As a change from soaking, you could take a look at Kastro and the Evangelistria monastery.

A walled settlement originally comprising 300 houses and twenty-two churches, entered during the pirate period only across a drawbridge but now reached by steps from the beach, **Kastro** has almost completely crumbled into ruin. The obvious reason for going – by caique, unless you prefer a three-hour walk – would be to imagine what it used to be like; very few of the buildings are still structurally sound enough to be entered.

During the Second World War Kastro was one of many links on the escape route from Greece to the Middle East, which ran across the Aegean to various points on the Asia Minor coast and from there to Egypt. In 1943 a Greek submarine was sunk off Kastro point.

The **Evangelistria** is a fortified monastery built in the early eighteenth century by monks from Mount Athos, with a small museum and library and some magnificent views. Of the numerous other Skiathos monasteries, most are now closed and in ruin.

Where to stay

The island has fifty-five listed hotels (one deluxe, two first class, five second class, twenty-nine third class and the rest of fourth and fifth class) with a total of 1,425 rooms. There are also fourteen furnished apartment complexes with more than 300 beds, and at least another 650 beds available in private homes.

If you are prepared to splurge, you could try the deluxe **Skiathos Palace** at Koukounaries (221 rooms, tel. 22 242). More modest accommodation on the same beach is provided by the **Xenia** (second class, thirty-two rooms, tel. 22 041). Other good beach hotels include the first-class **Esperides** (180 rooms, tel. 22 245) and the third-class **Belvedere** (sixty rooms, tel. 22 475), both at Achladies. The two veterans of pre-tourism still soldier on in Skiathos town: the third-class **Akti** (eleven rooms, tel. 22 024) and fourth-class **Avra** (six rooms, tel. 22 044).

Where to eat

Of the many restaurants, tavernas and cafés in Skiathos town, good reports have been made of the **Limanaria** on the waterfront and the **Stavros** in Evangelistrias Street. Any self-respecting beach, of course, has a fish taverna on it in summer.

Getting there

By air from Athens (three to seven flights a day in summer) and from Thessaloniki (three flights a week).

By ferry from Volos (two to five a day in summer) and Aghios Constantinos (one a day), involving about three hours on the water. The two boats a week from Kimi in Euboia take twice as long, and the hydrofoils from Volos and Aghios Constantinos about half as long.

Transport

Regular bus services run to Koukounaries and beaches en route,

THE NORTH SPORADES ISLANDS

and other beaches can be reached by caique or fishing boat. There are cars, taxis, mopeds and bicycles for hire.

From Skiathos To the other Sporades islands on the ferries or excursion boats, and to the nine offshore islets; the one most worth a visit is **Tsoungria**, which has two renowned beaches and a yacht anchorage.

Telephone
Police 22 005
Tourist police 21 111
Coastguard 22 017
Olympic Airways 22 200
Clinic 22 040

Skopelos

Tourism came late to Skopelos, but then grew swiftly: where a quarter of a century ago there were just two hotels, now there are thirty-six listed, with more under construction. However, Skopelos should not be regarded simply as an alternative if Skiathos happens to be 'full'; it has its own charms, and some Greek holiday-makers return year after year. Lying between Skiathos and Alonysos, 60 nautical miles from Volos, it is the second stop on most of the Sporades ferries whether from Volos or Aghios Constantinos. Those who appreciate its peacefulness are in no hurry to see an airport built there, though eventually one almost certainly will be.

Area: 96 sq km. Length of coastline: 66 km.
Population: 4,441 (2,668 in Hora and 1,171 in Glossa/Loutraki).
Area telephone code: 0424.

History Known first as Peparithos, Skopelos acquired its present name during the Hellenistic period. It was used by Byzantium as a place of exile, subsequently became part of the Duchy of Naxos, endured the usual Turkish period, and came back into the Greek fold after the 1821 Revolution.

Bearings Skopelos is a long and fairly narrow island with so inadequate a road network – only 28 km in total – that its inhabitants frequently prefer to travel by boat between the two main settlements, Hora in the south-east and Glossa in the north-west, although a bus service is available.

Most of the ferries touch at Loutraki, the port for Glossa, on their way to Hora, while a third, smaller harbour has been created at Agnonda on the south coast.

Hora, or **Skopelos** town, has a neo-Classical harmony, for which it has been declared an architecturally protected settlement, as well as most of the island's tourism infrastructure. Nevertheless, it lacks the basic requirement for a Greek holiday – a place to swim.

What to see Before making for the south- and west-coast beaches, you might take a look at the ruins of the fourth-century BC Temple of Asclipios at Ambeliki (partly excavated in 1965, when a large collection of coins from the Classical to Roman periods was found), the Venetian castle at the highest point above the capital, and the Church of Aghios Athanasios close to the castle walls; it dates in part from the ninth century, when it was built with material taken from a Temple of Athena, and has some interesting seventeenth-century frescoes. If this only whets your appetite for the ecclesiastical, Hora has more than a hundred churches; the island as a whole has some 350, plus forty monasteries. Those who prefer to ration themselves to just one monastery generally go to the Evangelistria, 4 km from Hora, which belongs to the Xyropotamon monastery on Mount Athos, has several fourteenth-century icons, and is open to visitors.

At **Loutraki/Glossa**, 24 km from Hora, there are ruins of the acropolis of the ancient town of Selinous as well as traces of ancient and Byzantine walls and a fifth-century Temple of Athena. For some of the older women there, local costume is still the normal dress.

Agnonda, 7 km from Hora on the south-west tip of the island, is used by ferries when the winds make Hora unsafe. You would pay a planned visit only for the exceptionally good swimming there and at nearby Limnonari.

Beaches

Other beaches accessible from the road along the west coast to Glossa include Panormou, Elios and Loutraki itself. The south coast has Stafilos and the east coast Glysteri, reached only by boat or on foot. Solitude can be sought on at least fifteen smaller and more remote beaches. The Tripitis grotto near Glysteri can be reached by motorboat from Skopelos town.

Where to stay

Of the thirty-six listed hotels, the four first-class units are small pensions that are likely to be fully booked from the beginning of the season. There would be a better chance of finding an unbooked room at the second-class **Amalia** (fifty rooms, tel. 22 688) or third-class **Aeolos** (forty-one rooms, tel. 22 233) at Hora, and the third-class **Prince Stafylos** at nearby Livadi (forty-nine rooms, tel. 22 775). The **Avra** at Loutraki (third class, twenty-eight rooms, tel. 33 550) is right beside the water and has a restaurant.

There are estimated to be some 1,500 beds on offer in private houses in Hora and another 500 elsewhere, mainly in Glossa.

Where to eat

Skopelos is well endowed with restaurants, tavernas and fish tavernas – **Selini**, **Rendezvous**, **Deilina**, **Xenia**, **Terpsi**, **Akteon**, **Spyros**, **Klimataria**, **Disti**, **Yannis**, **Kymata**, **Akroyiali** and **Pavlos** to mention just a few that you may come across in and around Hora. When pressed, local inhabitants will confess that they tend to prefer the **Selini** among the restaurants, the **Klimataria** and **Kymata** tavernas, **Spyros** for something simple over charcoal, and, when at Agnonda, **Pavlos** among a whole row of fish tavernas. You could end your meal with a dish of Skopelos prunes, and nibble on

Getting there some of the island's highly-prized almonds.

There are from two to four ferries a day from Volos (four hours to Loutraki/Glossa and five hours to Hora), and at least one a day from Aghios Constantinos (about half an hour less on the water). The island can also be reached from Kimi in Euboia, 47 nautical miles away. In the summer there are hydrofoil connections both with Volos and Aghios Constantinos.

Transport The Skopelos bus service, along the south and west coasts between Hora and Glossa, drops passengers within an easy walk of the main beaches. Cars and mopeds can be rented, as well as boats, and there are taxis at Hora.

From Skopelos The other Sporades islands on the Volos and Aghios Constantinos ferries, daily excursions to Skiathos and Alonysos and, by less frequent boats, some of the North Aegean islands and Kavala.

Telephone Police 22 235
Coastguard 22 180
Clinic 22 220

Skyros

The island of Rupert Brooke and the earliest recorded instance of draft-dodging, of tiny horses and miniature Byzantine furniture, Skyros is a two-in-one bargain for those who prefer, or can accept, non-hotel accommodation. In the approximate shape of a crouching dog, the upper part of the island is unmistakably part of the Sporades, with densely wooded slopes and green valleys. Below the waist, the vegetation dies out, the hills turn brown, and you could easily believe yourself in the Cyclades.

Skyros is the largest and least visited of the Sporades group, as well as the most difficult to get to; in a sense, although only 22 nautical miles from Euboia, it is among the most remote of the Aegean islands. There are numerous Greek islands where traditions so far have been largely unaffected by tourism, but few where they face less of a threat. Even the possibility of flights there has yet to make any real difference.

Area: 209 sq km. Length of coastline: 129 km.
Population: 2,757 (Skyros town 2,217).
Area telephone code: 0222.

Two reluctant warriors It is said that when King Menelaos of Mycenae called for war to recover his wife Helen, who had eloped with Paris and gone to Troy, both Achilles and Odysseus failed to show up. Odysseus had his arm twisted by threats to kill his son Telemachos, and did finally report for duty. On the principle that poachers make the best gamekeepers, he was ordered to go out and find Achilles, who was rumoured to be hiding out among the daughters of the King of Skyros.

It will be recalled that Achilles, rather like Strephon in *Iolanthe*, was an anatomical misfit: he was deathless only down to the heel by which he had been held when dipped in the waters of immortality. He or his mother, Thetis, had decided that the surest way to defy a prediction that he would not survive the war was to stay away from the fighting. The wily Odysseus disguised himself as a pedlar and presented himself in the women's quarters of the Skyros royal court carrying a tray of gifts – dolls, rings, bracelets and a single dagger. Achilles, unwilling to spoil a good story for Homer, plumped for the dagger and was whisked away to fight, and to die of an arrow in the heel.

Modern draft-dodgers (Greece is one of the few European countries to retain conscription) create no such difficulties for the Defence Ministry; unless they emigrate, computers get them every time.

When Troy finally fell, the message was flashed to Mycenae by fire signals across the Aegean; Skyros is said to have been one of the links in the chain.

Still in the shadowy areas of pre-history, Theseus, who slew the Minotaur, is said to have died and been buried on Skyros. In the Classical era his bones were transported to Athens and interred in the Theseon temple, making it a kind of early Les Invalides.

In recorded times, Skyros was an Athenian colony, a place of exile in the Byzantine era, went under the Turks in 1538 and was reunited with Greece after the 1821 Revolution.

Rupert Brooke: grave and statue

On the south-west tip of Skyros there is 'some corner of a foreign field that is for ever England' – the grave of Rupert Brooke, who died of blood-poisoning on 23 April, 1915 in a French hospital ship at the time of the Dardanelles campaign.

Brooke is commemorated by a bronze nude of 'Eternal Poetry' in Skyros town, erected in 1931 with the proceeds of a collection among poets around the world. When it was new, shocked islanders with linen to spare would sometimes drape it at night with a sheet, which police would confiscate in the morning. Vandalism has advanced since then, and in similar circumstances today the point would more likely be made with hammer and chisel; however, the question does not arise since even Skyros, remote from tourism though it may be, has come to terms with the human body to the extent of designating a beach for nudists.

A search for Rupert Brooke would take you to Treis Boukes, a natural harbour in the south-west protected by the uninhabited islets of Platia and Sarakiniko, where Brooke is buried in an olive grove on a hillside. Once a pirate stronghold, Treis Boukes was used by the British as a naval anchorage during the First World War. Nearby coves are home to some of the few remaining Mediterranean monk seals.

The Skyros miniatures

These are a matter of horses and chairs, the former not permitted to leave the island, but the latter definitely for export if you face no problem over weight and bulk.

The horses are about the size of Shetland ponies, have been there since ancient times, and are found nowhere else in Greece. They are wild in the sense of not owned and, for reasons not fully understood, are steadily diminishing in numbers although a protected breed.

While their precise origin is unknown, Skyros inhabitants like to connect them with the small horses of Ancient Greece immortalised on the Parthenon frieze in Athens. They are said to have existed on the island at least since the eighth century BC, and possibly earlier. Why they should have survived on Skyros and nowhere else is explained only in the general context of the island's isolation.

There appears to be general agreement that the period since the Second World War has seen a particularly rapid decline in their numbers, from probably around 2,000 to a present estimate of certainly fewer than 200, and that this has been a result of the mechanism of agriculture. In the days before there were tractors on Skyros, farmers would use them at least in the ploughing and harvest seasons, and therefore had a reason for helping them through the winter. Turned suddenly into useless mouths, they were left to fend for themselves in remote hill pastures – a hardship that proved too great for many of them. It would be pleasant to believe that this is only the obvious and not the actual explanation, but no other seems to be commonly on offer.

Despite occasional flurries of concern in the quality Athens newspaper and periodical Press, over whether the ponies could be headed for extinction, they have yet to find local or international champions comparable in influence to those who have obtained effective action to protect the even more elusive monk seals elsewhere in the North Sporades islands, or the turtles of Zakynthos. There has been an equal absence of response to suggestions that small groups of them, or even pairs, might be transplanted to other islands with a more developed tourist movement where, if they bred successfully, their role as an attraction for children could provide justification for the trouble and cost of trying to keep them alive.

What is quite certain is that you will be fortunate indeed if you catch sight of one by pure chance during a holiday on Skyros.

The elaborately-carved chairs, little more than 30 cm high and with cord-plaited seats, are of Byzantine origin and are also unique to Skyros. Somewhere among the cypress, mermaid or dolphin motifs you will see the double-headed Byzantine eagle. The chairs are designed to fit beneath low, round tables, and are decorative rather than comfortable. In the days when Athens had space for houses, they were almost standard hall furnishing; they are rarely to be found in the modern open-plan apartments.

Skyros craftsmen still make the chairs, always by hand, along with matching wooden 'dowry chests' (blanket boxes) carved with the same Byzantine motifs. With a couple of cushions on top, the chests make attractive emergency seating.

Ceramics and other souvenirs

The island is known also for its traditional unglazed ceramics, which are rather more portable but tend to be brittle. Bearing bird, fish and geometric designs, the pottery comes mainly in the form of large amphorae, jugs, pitchers, flower pots and vases, bowls and casseroles, with a small production of ashtrays for the tourist trade. If you feel nervous about entrusting your Skyros casserole to the oven, you can always use it for creamy desserts.

Hand-made Skyros embroidery tends to be expensive, and some of the finest examples are on display in the Athens Benaki Museum.

The unusual feature of the Skyros motifs is their whimsicality. One of the more delightful designs features a three-masted ship, with crew members lined up on deck or perched in the rigging and a couple of dolphins sharing the bridge with the captain. Like the furniture, the embroidery is a blend of Byzantine and Aegean elements, worked in a complex Byzantine stitch. Home-made vegetable dyes are still in common use, with the colours fixed by soaking both yarns and threads in flowing streams, in the same process as that used in parts of mainland Greece for the finest *flokati* rugs.

The most economical souvenir would be a half-kilo of the island's camomile, by which the Greeks swear: camomile tea is still regarded as the natural specific for any kind of bellyache.

Around the island

If you arrive by ferry you will land at Linaria, a sheltered harbour on the west coast of no particular interest. From there you can take a bus to **Skyros** town, 11 km away on the other side of the island, where there is much more to see.

Undiscernible from the sea, the capital spreads up a hillside crowned by a Byzantine castle with Venetian extensions that was built on the site of an ancient acropolis. Traces of neolithic settlement have been found there and also at Palamaria, at the northern tip of the island near the airport.

The fortified Monastery of Aghios Georgios of the Skyriani, close to the castle, was founded in 962 and belongs to the Megistis Lavra monastery on Mount Athos. Damage caused by an earth tremor in 1983 has since been restored.

Skyros town additionally has two museums: an archaeological museum housing finds from excavations in southern Skyros, and a folk museum for handicrafts and embroidery.

The island's tourist centre, to the extent that it has one, is at **Magazia** and **Molos**, two contiguous settlements back from a long beach a couple of kilometres north of Skyros town, served by buses but less than a half-hour's walk away. The island's sole listed hotel is there, and in summer about half of its estimated 700 beds in rented rooms as well as a taverna that spills out of a disused windmill.

Beaches

With the exception of Treis Boukes, the better and more accessible beaches are in the northern part of the island, and include Gyrismata, Votsala, Basale, Papa and the 'official' nudist beach at Houma. Dozens of small beaches can be reached most easily by boat.

Where to stay

The obvious first choice would be the second-class **Xenia** at Magazia (twenty-two rooms, tel. 91 209): apart from that, there are two fifth-class pensions, the **Aegaion** (five rooms, tel. 91 446) and **Elena** (ten rooms, tel. 91 738). If thirty-seven couples are ahead of you, reliance can be placed on islander hospitality.

Where to eat

On an average summer's day, about thirty tavernas, mainly offering fish and seafood, set out their tables in Skyros town, Linaria and along the Magazia/Molos beach. Islanders insist that there is no reason to choose one rather than another, but if you wish you can look out for the **Kabanera**, **Sisifos** and **Akti** in Skyros town and the **Marietta** in Molos.

Getting there

In summer, there are daily Olympic flights from Athens by light aircraft, three boats a day from Kimi in Euboia (a two-hour trip) and daily calls by the Sporades hydrofoils.

Transport

Skyros has an 80-km road network, about half of it asphalted. There is a bus service from Linaria to Molos via Skyros town, with extensions in the summer to other beaches. Mopeds and bicycles can be rented, and taxis and small boats are available.

From Skyros

To the other Sporades islands and Euboia, and by caique to the islets of Valaxa, Platia and Sarakiniko.

Telephone

Police 91 274
Coastguard 91 475
Olympic Airways 91 600
Clinic 91 707

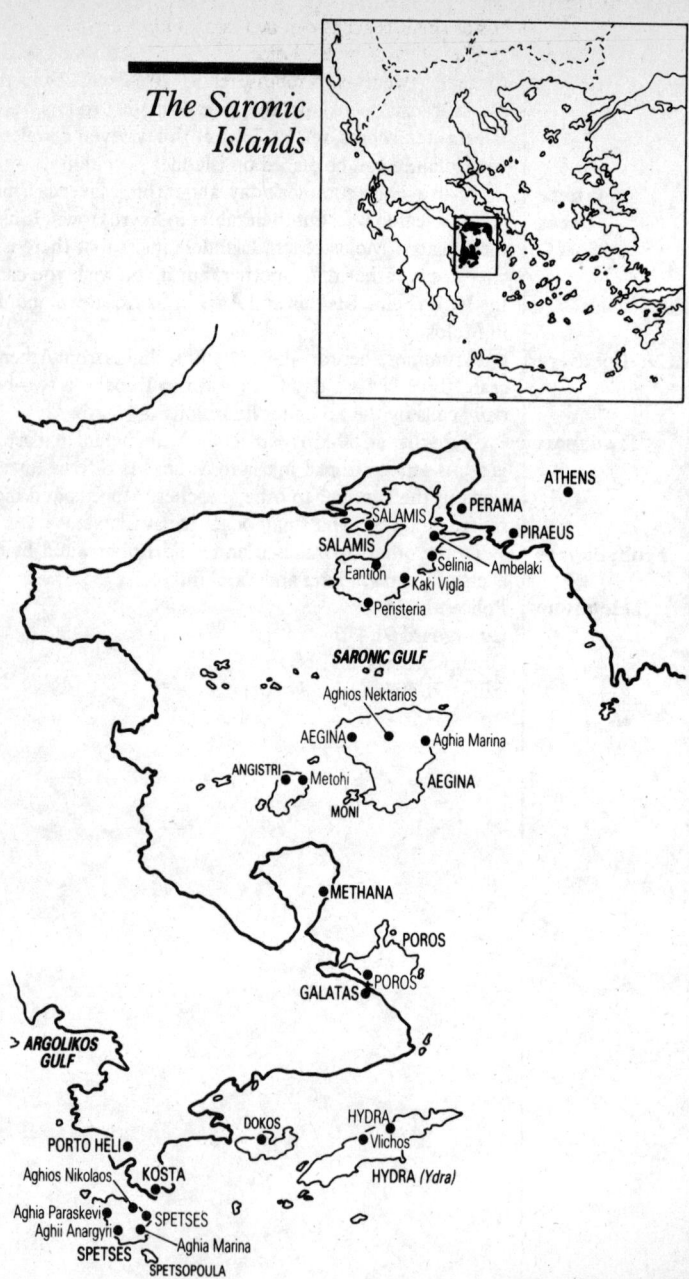

The Saronic Islands

Introduction

Known also as Argosaronic, these are the five offshore islands of Athens – Salamis, Aegina, Poros, Hydra and Spetses – familiarity with which can easily breed a casual attitude. They are simply too easy to reach, and too little evocative of the real thing, to constitute a reason for anyone to visit Greece.

Salamis is only twenty minutes from Piraeus by motorboat, and you could dart across for lunch if facing a long wait for ferry connections. Aegina, Poros and Hydra are from less than one to about two hours away by hydrofoil, and all three can be covered in twelve hours on one of the popular day cruises. Spetses is rather too distant for a day trip; also, it is the most popular of the five among Athenian holiday-makers in straitened circumstances, competing with whom can be a strain in July and August.

Any of the Saronic islands will give you the taste of island life, if the rest of your holiday is to be spent in Athens and the Peloponnese or mainland Greece.

Aegina

Roughly in the middle of the Saronic Gulf, 17 nautical miles from Piraeus, Aegina is the island of which the northern shore and central mountains are clearly visible from the Acropolis in Athens. It offers something for the Classical historian, the Byzantologist, the just-put-me-down-on-the-nearest-beach holiday-maker and even the numismatist. It is also likely to be the first real island ever visited by the children of the more than three million inhabitants of Greater Athens, and from that aspect a place of memory, and one for a weekend, rather than a regular holiday destination.

Area: 83 sq km. Length of coastline: 56 km.
Population: 6,730.

Area telephone code: 0297.

History

Aegina was settled and fortified in neolithic times, and was a shipping power active in the ceramics trade before the rise of Athens, when its population by some accounts may have neared a quarter of a million. Its coinage, most notably the Aegina turtle, was in circulation throughout the Mediterranean world, as was its system of weights and measures.

Aegina contributed thirty ships for the Battle of Salamis but subsequently allied itself on the wrong side in the struggle between Athens and Sparta. In what would today be considered an atrocity bordering on genocide, but was then a humanitarian alternative to massacre, the great Pericles ordered the amputation of all the men's thumbs, followed by the expulsion of the island's inhabitants and their replacement by colonists from Athens.

For the Classicist, Aegina offers the Temple of Aphaia, crowning a wooded hill above the bay of Aghia Marina on the east coast. Built in the fifth century BC of local limestone, it is one of the best preserved Doric temples in Greece, with twenty-two columns still standing. To see its sculptures, however, you have to visit Munich, where they were taken after their purchase in 1812 by the father of King Othon.

In more modern times, Aegina served briefly, in 1828, as the seat of the first free Greek government before the capital was established in Nafplion. Also, until capital punishment was effectively suspended (though not abolished) some fifteen years ago, Aegina was one of Greece's principal execution sites: the gendarmerie firing squad would line up at dawn on a hillside near the prison, and for the next few days the island would mourn its reputation. The prison is now unused, and the gendarmerie has been swallowed up by the Greek police.

Greece's last execution, for a particularly vicious murder, was carried out on Aegina in 1972. But the jail's most famous recent prisoner was Nikos Mountis, released in 1984 after commutation of his life sentence for the alleged murder of British journalist Ann Dorothy Chapman during the 1967–74 military dictatorship; Mountis never ceased to maintain his innocence, and few Greeks are convinced that the crime was ever properly solved. Miss Chapman's father, Edward, is among those who believe that Mountis was framed and that she died at the hands not of a 'Peeping Tom' but of a junta interrogator.

Town and island

You land at **Aegina** town, the island's capital and only large settlement, by tender from a liner but by the gangplank of a ferry. You can then do one or all of three things: wander through the narrow streets of the town for a little shopping, sit at a quayside café or restaurant, or take a bus to Aghia Marina for the Temple of Aphaia or to one of the island's two more interesting monasteries.

You can swim from a good sandy beach at **Aghia Marina**, provided you have no objection to fighting for space and are impervious to flies. This is where you would probably stay if you thought Aegina was a holiday resort. It is a trip of about half an hour by bus or taxi from the port.

Well worth a call for the beauty of the site, as well as for its Byzantine frescoes and wood carving, is a small monastery with a long name, Chryssoleontissa, dating from the early seventeenth century. Collectors can pair it up with the island's other main monastery, Aghios Nektarios, named for a bishop who died in the monastery in 1920 and was canonised in 1961.

Best buys on Aegina are pistachio nuts and, although weighty, the traditional clay jars that really do keep water remarkably cool.

Where to stay

Aegina has sixty-seven listed hotels (seven of them of second class and forty-two of third), with 1,595 rooms, and, at a conservative estimate, at least another 1,000 non-hotel beds. Thirty-eight of the hotels are at Aghia Marina.

Two second-class hotels in Aegina town with regular clients are the **Danae** (fifty-two rooms, tel. 22 424) and **Nausica** (Nafsika) (thirty-four rooms, tel. 22 333). Two hotels at Aghia Marina large enough to be likely to have a vacant room are the **Apollo** (second class, 107 rooms, tel. 32 271) and **Pantelaros** (third class, fifty-five rooms, tel. 32 431).

Where to eat

You can eat well in the **Vostitsanos** restaurant behind the Aiakion pastry-shop in Aegina town, especially if you are prepared to pay for good fish, or at the **Lalaounis** restaurant on the waterfront for local specialities. You might also try the **El Greco** and **Mourtzis** in the harbour, **Mihalatzikos** one street back behind the Agapi café and, just outside the town but known to every taxi-driver, **Baroutis** and **Vatzoulias**.

Getting there

While the one-day cruises are the commonest means for tourists, there are up to twenty ferries a day from Piraeus and almost as many calls by hydrofoil (trips of one and a half hours and about thirty minutes respectively). Though the terminal for the Flying Dolphins as a fleet is at Zea-Freattys, the hydrofoils for Aegina leave from the Piraeus central port at Karaiskaki Square, on the Akti Posidonos, close to the moorings for the conventional ferries to the Saronic islands.

Transport

Aegina has a good bus service, and taxis, cars, mopeds and bicycles can be hired. There are also still a few one-horse coaches in use.

From Aegina

The other Saronic islands, plus Methana, Ermioni, Porto Heli, Tolo and Nafplion in the Peloponnese.

You can also take a caique or small boat to the offshore islet of **Moni** and the larger island of **Angistri**.

With an area of 11 sq km and a population of 766, Angistri offers 278 rooms in twenty hotels (two third class and the rest fourth and fifth); apart from the sea-taxi service from Aegina, there are boats from Piraeus. You can swim close to where you land, at Skala, or take the island's only bus to the other main beach, at Metohi. Some of the more remote Angistri beaches are the closest of any to Athens where nudity is unofficially tolerated.

Telephone
Police 22 391
Tourist police 23 333
Coastguard 22 328
Hospital 22 251

Hydra

From only a few hundred metres away, you seem to be approaching a bare, treeless, uninhabited and totally inhospitable rock, then suddenly you turn into a tiny amphitheatrical harbour jammed with fishing boats and pleasure craft and backed by a hillside spread with white and grey red-roofed houses. For almost all visitors, Hydra *is* its town. Artists reach instinctively for pencils, and cameras acquire a momentum of their own.

Area: 49 sq km. Length of coastline: 56 km.
Population: 2,732.
Area telephone code: 0298.

Sometimes written as Ydra and pronounced 'ee-dra', the island is famed for its role in the 1821 Revolution (see also The Greeks and the Sea, p. 34). It was given a second lease of life, as a cosmopolitan tourist centre, after the film *Boy on a Dolphin* was shot there in 1957; in that respect, however, it now plays a muted second fiddle to Myconos. Of the thousands who visit Hydra every summer, few spend more than a couple of hours there for a meal and a little shopping (knitwear is a favourite purchase). There are some good beaches, but not in the immediate vicinity of the town.

Where to stay
Hydra has thirteen listed hotels (two of first class, six of second, two of third and three of fourth) with a total of 197 rooms, and an estimated 220 non-hotel beds on offer. The largest of the hotels has thirty-nine rooms and the smallest five, so obviously there is little to fear from groups.

Those who live on the island speak well of the air-conditioned **Greco Hotel** (second class, nineteen rooms, tel. 53 200), the **Hydroussa** (also second class, thirty-six rooms, tel. 52 217) and the **Leto** (third class, thirty-nine rooms, tel. 52 280).

Where to eat
You can eat well, with a choice among international and Greek dishes, in restaurants in the town; equally well, and with more to watch, you can snack on the quayside. Among recommended restaurants are the **Douskos** in a large courtyard some 300 m from the port, the almost adjacent **Tria Adelphia** (Three Brothers) and the **Kypos** (Garden) next to the cinema. The **Vlichos** taverna on Vlichos beach

can be well worth the half-hour's walk. If you feel in need of French cuisine, try the **Grenouille**.

Getting there By ferry or hydrofoil from Piraeus, or on a one-day Saronic cruise. There are two ferries a day (just over three hours) and up to twelve hydrofoils daily in summer (just under two hours).

Transport Hydra is one of those blessed islands without cars. So you either walk, or take a caique or motorboat.

From Hydra The other Saronic islands, or by caique to the offshore islet of Dokos.

Telephone
Police 52 205
Coastguard 52 279
Clinic 52 420

Poros

Poros, 36 nautical miles from Piraeus, is the island that Henry Miller, in *The Colossus of Maroussi*, predictably likened to 'the neck of the womb'. Separated from the Peloponnese by the narrowest of straits, the island's silence is palpable and its beauty overwhelming. Poros inevitably promises more than it could ever deliver, for after such an arrival, there could only be an anticlimax to follow.

Area: 23 sq km. Length of coastline: 43 km.
Population: 3,929.
Area telephone code: 0298.

Bearings You step out of your cruise liner, ferry or hydrofoil into the middle of the main street, lined with souvenir shops, restaurants and cafés. Across the water on the Peloponnese, the lemon groves of Galatas are lovely in all seasons, a cloud of blossom in spring, and only a ten-minute chug away in a fisherman's boat. If you have the time, you can take a taxi to the Temple of Poseidon where the Ancient Athenian orator Demosthenes, when words ran out, committed suicide in 322 BC; equally, you can try the Monastery of the Panaghia, which can be reached also by motorboat.

If you are on a one-day cruise, you will be allowed about an hour on Poros; you will therefore have time only for a walk through the town, and perhaps some refreshments. But a one-day excursion from Piraeus, especially by hydrofoil, will permit you to cross to Galatas and take a motorboat to one of the Poros beaches. It is mainly Athenian holiday-makers who actually stay on Poros.

Beaches While Poros is not really an island for swimming, the best beaches are at Megalo and Mikro Neorion. For a quick dip, you could try one of the three 'organised' beaches near the town.

Where to stay Poros has thirteen listed hotels (eight of second class and five of third), with a total of 597 rooms, and there are another four hotels (one second class, two third and one fourth) with 166 rooms at Galatas. Only four of the hotels can take more than 100 guests, and they rely mainly on Greek groups.

Costas Alexopoulos, who runs a travel agency on Poros, sends his friends to stay at the **Pavlou Hotel** (second class, thirty-six rooms, tel. 22 734) on the beach at Neorion, reached most easily by motorboat, or the **Sirène** (Sirina) at Monastiri, a few minutes outside the town by car or a half-hour's walk (second class, 120 rooms, tel. 22 741).

Across at Galatas, you could well try the **Stella Maris** (second class, ninety-three rooms, tel. 22 562).

In addition, there are an estimated 1,000 non-hotel beds on offer on Poros.

Where to eat	Mr Alexopoulos says his preferred tavernas are the **Dolphin**, on the steps near the Post Office, for fresh fish and Greek specialities, and the **Panorama**, a twenty-minute walk from where the ships tie up. Other popular places for a meal include the **Caravella** and **Lagoudera** on the waterfront, the **Adelphia** (Brothers) in the main square, **Dionysos** near the Lahtsi Hotel, **Paradissos** close to the Temple of Poseidon, **Nikolaos** on the monastery beach, the **Esperides** (in a Poros garden, for Greek dancing in the summer) and the **Iliovasilema** just outside the town for an especially good view.
Getting there	By ferry or hydrofoil from Piraeus (there are seven or eight of each daily, covering the distance in about two and a half hours and one hour respectively), or by road from Athens via Corinth to Galatas – the three buses a day via Nafplion take about three and a half hours. Small boats provide a taxi service between Galatas and Poros.
Transport	Taxis, cars, mopeds, bicycles and small boats are available. There is also a bus service to Askeli and the monastery.
From Poros	The other Saronic islands by ferry or hydrofoil, caique excursions to Ancient Troizen and Methana in the Peloponnese, and by road from Galatas to anywhere in the Peloponnese.
Telephone	Police 22 256/22 462 Coastguard 22 274 Clinic 22 596

Salamis

Salamis is easily the most populous of the Saronic five but, significantly, it has no hotel above third class, and none of any category with more than twenty-five rooms. At certain moments on the island you may feel you are in a semi-industrialised suburb of Piraeus, though one with the traditional blue-and-white island colouring.
Area: 95 sq km. Length of coastline: 103 km.

THE SARONIC ISLANDS

Population: 28,574 (20,807 in Salamis town).
Area telephone code: 01.

There are only two logical reasons for going to Salamis, except on business: to see the narrow strait in which the great Greek–Persian naval battle of 480 BC was fought, and the hill from which Xerxes is said to have watched the destruction of his fleet and ambitions, or to kill three or four hours while waiting for ferry connections in Piraeus. A meal on Salamis, plus the boat fare, will work out considerably cheaper than a fancier but not necessarily better meal in one of the snob fish restaurants of the Piraeus suburbs.

With a number of habitations too large to be villages but too small to be towns, and some rather pebbly swimming, as a beauty spot Salamis is definitely non-league. But even on the worst days, it is outside the Athenian smog belt.

Where to stay and eat

Salamis has four listed hotels with a total of sixty-four rooms. The best is probably the **Gabriel** at Eantion (third class, twenty-five rooms, tel. 466 2275).

For food, try the **Antzas** at Salamis town, the **Kanellos** at Kaki Vigla, the **Kapotsis** near Eantion and the **Votsalakis** at Ambelaki.

Getting there

Most easily (about a twenty-minute crossing) by motorboat from the Piraeus main port (Akti Posidonos). For vehicles, there is a ferry service from the Piraeus suburb of Perama, a crossing of about ten minutes.

Transport

The island has a sufficient population to support a fairly good bus service, mainly between Salamis town, where the industries are, and such more wholesome settlements as Eantion, Kaki Vigla, Ambelaki, Selinia and Peristeria.

From Salamis

Only back to Piraeus.

Telephone

Police 465 1100
Coastguard 465 1130
Clinic 465 3400

Spetses

Spetses, the most distant of the Saronic islands, 53 nautical miles from Piraeus at the entrance to the Argolikos Gulf, is too far away from Piraeus to be included on a one-day cruise but is a delightful place to visit if you have a full day, or preferably two, at your disposal.
Area: 22 sq km. Length of coastline: 29 km.
Population: 3,729.
Area telephone code: 0298.

Bearings

Easily the greenest of the five islands, Spetses could be mistaken at first sight for an Ionian transplant. It too has a Revolution history of note, and a picturesque harbour; it also offers good swimming, on the island itself or from Peloponnesian beaches half an hour away by caique, and comfortable hotels for an overnight stay. Offshore from Spetses, Stavros Niarchos occasionally holds summer court on his private islet of Spetsopoula, but for that you need an embossed invitation.

Spetses tends to be particularly crowded with Athenian holidaymakers in July and August, when there can be unseemly jostling for restaurant tables in the evening. But outside these peak months, it is a relaxing place in which to soak up sunshine and atmosphere, and take evening drives in horse-drawn cabs.

Beaches The numerous beaches outside the only town can be reached most easily by small boat. The two closest to the town are at Aghios Nikolaos and Aghia Marina; two better ones, on the other side of the island, are at Aghia Paraskevi and Aghii Anargyri.

Where to stay Of the twenty-three listed hotels (586 rooms), four are first class, five are second and four are third. There are also probably 1,000 beds on offer in private houses. Nevertheless, on a peak holiday weekend it can sometimes be necessary to sleep on a beach. Most of the hotels, particularly the larger ones, are of tourist-era creation – clean, new and unremarkable. However, there is one delightful survival from the turn of the century, the first-class **Possidonian** (fifty-five rooms but only eighty-three beds, tel. 72 208), which will give you a taste of accommodation as it used to be in the Edwardian age.

In first class you might also try the **Kasteli** (seventy-two rooms, tel. 72 311) or **Spetses** (seventy-seven rooms, tel. 72 602). A good bet in third class is the **Faros** (forty-seven rooms, tel. 72 613).

Where to eat In high season, you might be best advised to grab the first table you can find; you can scarcely go wrong. The locals speak well of **Lazaros** taverna close to the tourist police office, the **Psaropoulos** near the Possidonian Hotel and, further along the same seaside road, the **Patralis** near the Anargyrion School. In the opposite direction from the port, the **Trehandiri** in the Old Harbour offers 'baked fish Spetsiotika' – cooked in slices with tomato, onion and garlic.

Getting there By ferry or hydrofoil from Piraeus. There are two ferries a day (four to five hours) and up to ten hydrofoils (half that time). Spetses can also be reached by road through the Peloponnese – about 200 km from Athens, via Corinth – with the crossing to the island by caique from Kosta or hydrofoil from Porto Heli.

Transport There is a restricted bus service, and caiques and motorboats are available.

From Spetses Apart from the other Saronic islands by ferry and hydrofoil, you can cross easily to Kosta or Porto Heli to start, or continue, a tour of the Peloponnese. You can sail around Spetsopoula, but not land.

Telephone Police 73 100
Coastguard 72 245
Clinic 72 472

Useful Reading

There is no shortage of books and guidebooks on modern Greece. A highly personal choice would include:

Guidebooks

Blue Guide to Greece – Stuart Rossiter.
Fodor Guide to Greece – Editors: Peter Sheldon and Richard Moore.

Works of Literature

Lawrence Durrell's *Spirit of Place, Prospero's Cell, Reflections on a Marine Venus* and *Landscape of Rhodes*.
Nicholas Gage's *Hellas – A Portrait of Greece* for general information.
Nikos Kazantzakis' *Zorba the Greek* and *Report to Greco*.
Patrick Leigh Fermor's *Roumeli* and *Mani*.
The third volume of Olivia Manning's *Balkan Trilogy* is set against a background to Greece in the Second World War.
Henry Miller's *The Colossus of Maroussi* (for bubbling enthusiasm).
Mary Renault's novels provide an excellent feel for Ancient Greece.

Background Information

W. Stanley Moss's *Ill Met by Moonlight* for Second World War experiences in Crete.
Sir Steven Runciman's *Mistras* and *Byzantine Style and Civilisation* for more specialised information.

You will also find in the larger Athens bookshops well-translated and lavishly-printed editions of Greek publications on specific periods of ancient history, archaeological sites and museums.

Index

abortion 62-3
accommodation (*see also under* individual places) 95-102
Achilleion Palace (Corfu) 145-6
Achilles 146, 331-2
Achladies (Skiathos) 327
Achladiotou, Despina 247-8
Acrotiri (Thera) 16, 29, 225-6
Adamas (Milos) 201, 202
Aedipsos (Euboia) 294
Aegean Maritime Museum 29
Aegean Sea 27, 51-2
Aegina 33, 337-40
Aegina town 338
Aeolian Park (Kythnos) 197
Agathonisi 58, 254, 256
Agersani (Naxos) 211
Aghia Anna (Amorgos) 182
Aghia Marina (Aegina) 338-9
Aghia Marina (Kassos) 245
Aghia Marina (Leros) 255
Aghia Marina (off Simi) 263
Aghia Pelagia (Kythera) 305
Aghii Apostoli 269
Aghios Andreas 197
Aghios Efstratios 58, 268-9
Aghios Emilianos (Simi) 263
Aghios Fokas (Kos) 252
Aghios Georgios (Corfu) 147
Aghios Georgios (Heraklia) 199
Aghios Georgios (Naxos) 211
Aghios Georgios (North Sporades) 323
Aghios Gordis (Corfu) 149
Aghios Ioannis 200
Aghios Kyrikos (Ikaria) 274-5
Aghios Nikitas (Lefkas) 308
Aghios Nikolaos (Anafi) 183
Aghios Nikolaos (Crete) 170, 173, 175
Aghios Nikolaos (off Paxi) 310, 311
Aghios Nikolaos (off Samos) 290
Aghios Stefanos (Kythnos) 198
Aghios Stefanos (Myconos) 208, 209
Agnonda (Skopelos) 330
Agriolivadi (Patmos) 261
Aï Strati (Aghios Efstratios) 268

AIDS 75, 207
Aigialis (Amorgos) 182
Ainos, Mount 301
air conditioning 100
air travel 92
Alcaios 281
Alexander the Great 17, 272, 318
Alexis I Komninos 25, 26, 182, 259
Alikanas (Zakynthos) 314
Alikes (Zakynthos) 314
Aliki (Kimolos) 196
Aliki (Paros) 214, 215
Alimia 239
Alinta (Leros) 255
Aliveri (Euboia) 295
Alonysos 87, 323-5
Alopronia (Sikinos) 220-1
Alykes (Samos) 290
Ambelaki (Salamis) 343
Ambeliki (Skopelos) 330
Amorgos 58, 181-3
Anafi 58, 183-4
Analypsi (Astipalaia) 237
Anaximander 32
Androfoni (Lemnos) 277
Andros 26, 39, 58, 184-7
Andros (town) 184-5
Angali (Folegandros) 190
Angelicoussis, Antony 36-7
Angistri 339-40
Ano Mera (Myconos) 208
Ano Meria (Folegandros) 190
Ano Simi (Simi) 262
Ano Syros (Syros) 222
Anogi (Ithaki) 303
Anoyia (Crete) 176
Antikeros 200
Antikythera 306
Antimilos 202
Antiparos 216-17
Antipaxi 311
antiques, purchase of 73-4, 120
Anydro 183
Aperi (Karpathos) 242-3
Apikia (Andros) 186-7
Apirathos (Naxos) 211
Apollo 183
Apollona (Naxos) 211
Apollonia (Milos) 201-2
Apollonia (Sifnos) 219
Aprovato (Andros) 187
archaeological remains
on Alonysos 325
at Asclepion 250
on Cephalonia 300
on Crete 168, 171-2
on Delos 187-8

on Halki 238
on Kastellorizon 248
on Kythera 305
on Lemnos 278
on Leros 255
on Milos 201
on Rhodes 160
on Samos 289
on Samothrace 318
on Skopelos 330
on Syros 222-3
on Thera 229
at Zagora 185-6
Archangelos 255
architecture 25
on Corfu 143
on Crete 171, 172
of the Cyclades 180
on Leros 255
on Myconos 205
on Rhodes 159-60
on Skiathos 326
on Skopelos 329
Argonauts 29, 183, 277, 318
Argostoli (Cephalonia) 300
Ariadne 210
Aristarchos 288
Arkadi monastery (Crete) 173, 176
Arkassa (Karpathos) 242
Arkesini (Amorgos) 182
Arki 253, 254, 260
Arkouda 202
Arkoudi 303
Armenistis (Ikaria) 275
Artemonas (Sifnos) 220
Arvanitohoro (Kassos) 245
Asclepion (Kos) 250
Assos (Cephalonia) 301
Astipalaia 58, 236-8
Athens Archaeological Museum 16, 29, 226, 276
Athens, history of 22
Atlantis 224-5
Atokos 303
Australia, and Kythera 305
Avlaki (Nisyros) 257
Axos (Crete) 176

Balkan Wars 22, 278, 280
banks 123
Batsi (Andros) 185
beaches
on Corfu 147, 148
on the Cyclades 190, 191, 192, 198, 202, 208, 211, 214, 217, 223, 229
on the East Aegean Islands 272, 278-9, 282, 287, 290
on the Ionian Islands 314

INDEX

on the North Aegean Islands 321
on the Sporades 327-8
Benitses (Corfu) 146
Boecklin, Arnold 145
bouzouki music 118-19
Boy on a Dolphin (film) 340
Britannic 193-4
British, in Corfu 139-40, 297
Brooke, Rupert 332
bus services 84
Byron, Lord George 21-2, 210, 300
Byzantium 19-20, 32, 140, 270

caiques 33, 263
camp-sites 101-2
Cape Kefalas (Kythnos) 197
car hire 9
casinos 9, 157
Cassius, Gaius 155
catacombs 201
caves 190, 196, 198, 201, 216, 241, 244, 300, 304, 314
Cavo (Corfu) 147-8
Cephalonia 40, 298-302
  accommodation on 101, 301
  travel to 92, 301-2
Chanea (Crete) 170, 173, 175
characteristics
  of Cephalonians 299
  of Cretans 166-7
  of Greeks 67-9
Chios 39, 51, 267, 269-73
  accommodation on 101, 272
  history of 32, 34, 269-70
  travel to 57, 92, 272-3
  where to eat on 272
Chios (town) 271-2
Christianity (*see also* Greek Orthodox Church) 19, 277
Christodoulos 258, 259
Chrysomilia (Fournoi) 273
city states 17-18
climate 81-3
  of Corfu 82, 83, 141
  of the Cyclades 180
  of Euboia 293
clothing 123
coastguards 135
coffee 111-12
Colossus of Maroussi (Henry Miller) 149, 341
Colossus of Rhodes 154-5
Columbus, Christopher 32, 270
communications (*see also under* individual islands)
  between islands 57-8, 85-9
  on the islands 84

Communist Party 45, 48
Constantine I, King of Greece 23
Constantine II, King of Greece 48
consulates 125-6
Corfu 137-51
  accommodation on 149-50
  beaches on 147, 148
  climate of 82, 83, 141
  history of 137, 139-41
  museums in 144
  travel to 92, 151
  where to eat on 150
Corfu (town) 141-5
  Church of Aghios Spyridon 144
Corinth Canal 13, 19
Cousteau, Jacques-Yves 193-4, 226-7
credit cards 124
Crete 164-77
  accommodation on 174-5
  beaches on 173, 174
  folk dancing on 118
  history of 15-16, 20, 22, 167-9
  travel to 57, 92, 175-6
  where to eat on 175
cricket, on Corfu 143
crime 71-2
cruises 90-1
Crusades 20, 25-6
currency regulations 124
Cyclades Islands 179-233
  climate of 180
  history of 180-1
  travel to 181
Cyprus 52

Dandolo, Doge Henry 25
Dasia (Sporades) 323
Daskalio 197, 200
Delos 28, 32, 181, 187-9
Demosthenes 341
Despotiko 217
Dia (Crete) 176
Diafani (Karpathos) 242
Diavatis 263
Dio Adelphia (Sporades) 323, 325
Dionysos 184, 203, 210, 233, 281
Dodecanese Islands (*see also* Rhodes) 51, 235-65
  folk dancing on 118
  history of 24, 26
  travel to 236
Dokos 341

Donousa 58, 199
dovecotes, on Tinos 231, 232-3
Drakonera 303
Drima 200
drink (*see also* wine) 66, 112-15
Driopis (Kythnos) 198
drugs 73

Eantion (Salamis) 343
earthquakes 213, 249, 268, 288, 299
East Aegean Islands 267-91
economy 53-6
electrical current 125
El Greco 166
Elias (Myconos) 208
Elizabeth, Empress of Austria 146, 310
Elli 232
Ellinika (Kimolos) 196
Elytis, Odysseas 280
embassies 125-6
Emborio (Kassos) 244, 245
Emborio (Nisyros) 257
Emborio (Thera) 229
Emborios (Simi) 263
Engares (Naxos) 211
Epirotiki Lines 64, 90
Eratosthenes 32
Eressos (Lemnos) 282
Eretria (Euboia) 294
Ermoupolis (Syros) 34, 221, 222, 223
  Apollon State Theatre 222
Euboia 13, 293-5
European Economic Community 53, 70, 138
Evangelistria monastery 328
Evdilos (Ikaria) 275
exile 18
  on Folegandros 189

Faliraki (Rhodes) 161
family 59-61
  on Crete 166
Farmakonisi 256
Faros (Amorgos) 182
Faros (Sifnos) 220
Feast of the Assumption 232
Fengari, Mount 317
ferries 84, 85, 88
Filakopi (Milos) 201
Filoti (Naxos) 211
Finikas (Syros) 223
Finiki (Karpathos) 242
Fira (Thera) 228, 230
Fiskardo (Cephalonia) 301
flamingos 290
flora 126, 313

347

INDEX

Folegandros 58, 189-91
folk dancing 116-18
  on Crete 167
food 103, 107-10, 219
  in Corfu 150
  risks from 127-8
Foster Parents Plan 42-3
Fournoi 58, 273-4
frescoes 29, 226, 330, 339
Fri (Kassos) 244
Frikes (Ithaki) 304

Gaios (Paxi) 310
Galazia Spilia 314
Gallipoli 222, 278
Gavdos (Crete) 176
Gavrion (Andros) 185
Genoese 26, 280
Geraki (Zakynthos) 314
Ghi 263
Gladstone, W. E. 139, 310
Glaronisia 202
Glossa (Skopelos) 330
glossary of useful words 78-80
Glyfada (Corfu) 149
Glysteri (Skopelos) 330
gold 218
Gortys (Crete) 176
Greek Islands, history of 25-6, 28
Greek Orthodox Church 61-3
Greek Revolution, 1821 21-2, 271, 285
Greek Revolution, 1909 22
Greek-Turkish War 23
Grikos (Patmos) 260, 261
guest houses 100-1

Hadzimichail, Theophylos 282
Halepas, Yannoulis 233
Halki 58, 118, 238-9
Halkis (Euboia) 293-4
Hani (Ithaki) 303
health 126-8
Heaven's Command (James Morris) 310
Helice 227
Helios 154
Hephaestia (Lemnos) 276, 278
Heraklia 58, 199
Hercules 203
Herodotus 32, 218
Hiliomodi 261
Hippocrates 249-50
Hippodamos 154
Homer 17, 29
  and Chios 269, 272
  and Ios 191
homosexuality 75-6, 207

Hora (Alonysos) 324
Hora (Amorgos) 182
Hora (Anafi) 183
Hora (Andros) 184-5
Hora (Antiparos) 216
Hora (Astipalaia) 237
Hora (Folegandros) 190
Hora (Heraklia) 199
Hora (Ios) 191, 192
Hora (Kea) 194-5
Hora (Kimolos) 196
Hora (Kythera) 305
Hora (Kythnos) 197, 198
Hora (Naxos) 211
Hora (Patmos) 260
Hora (Samothrace) 318
Hora (Serifos) 217
Hora (Sikinos) 221
Hora (Skopelos) 329
Horio (Kalymnos) 241
hospitality 68
hotels 96-100
Hozoviotissa monastery 182
Hydra 34, 340-1
hydrofoils 87

Ida, Mount 164, 172
Ierapetra (Crete) 170, 174, 176
Ikaria 58, 273, 274-5
Ikaros 274
Iliki *see* Helice
Imbros 278
Imerovigli (Thera) 229
Integrated Mediterranean Programmes 57
Ioannidis, Dimitrios 46
Ionian Islands (*see also* Corfu) 297-315
  folk dancing on 118
  history of 20, 22, 139-40
  shipping in 39-40
Ios 58, 181, 191-3
Iraklion (Crete) 170-1
Iraklion disaster 169-70
Isidore of Miletus 213
islands
  communications between 57-8, 85-9
  government programmes for 57-8
Isternia (Tinos) 233
Ithaki 40, 298, 302-4

jewellery 122, 161, 204
John, Saint, the Evangelist 258, 259
Julius Caesar 155, 256

Kabeiri mysteries 318

Kaki Vigla (Salamis) 343
Kalafati (Myconos) 208
Kalamos 309
Kallithea (Rhodes) 161
Kalotaritissa (Amorgos) 182
Kaltsonisi 311
Kalymnos 58, 118, 239-42
Kalymnos (town) 240-1
Kamares (Sifnos) 219
Kamari (Kos) 252
Kamariotissa (Samothrace) 318
Kambi (Fournoi) 273
Kambos (Ikaria) 275
Kambos (Patmos) 260, 261
Kameiros (Rhodes) 160
Kanala (Kythnos) 198
Kanaris, Constantine 285
Kanoni (Corfu) 145
Kapsali (Kythera) 305
Karamanlis, Constantine 18, 46, 47-8, 68
Karavalonisi 265
Karavostasis (Folegandros) 189, 190
Kardamena (Kos) 252
Karlonisi 303
Karlovassi (Samos) 289
Karpathos 242-3
  folk dancing on 118
  travel to 92, 243
Karthaia (Kea) 195
Karystos (Euboia) 294
Kassiopi (Corfu) 148
Kassos 39, 92, 244-5
Kastellorizon 92, 245-8
Kastos 309
Kastro (Cephalonia) 300
Kastro (Sifnos) 219
Kastro (Skiathos) 327, 328
Katapola (Amorgos) 182
Kato Zakros (Crete) 174
Kavos 138
Kazantzakis, Nikos 166, 211
Kea 58, 193-5
Keri (Zakynthos) 314
Keros 200
Kimi (Euboia) 294-5
Kimolos 58, 196-7
Kini (Syros) 223
Kioni (Ithaki) 303
Kionia (Tinos) 233
Kleftiko (Milos) 201
Knights of St John 26, 156, 246, 251, 262
Knossos (Crete) 29, 171-2
Koftou (Kimolos) 196
Kolimbithres (Paros) 214
Kontias (Lemnos) 278
Korissia (Kea) 194

348

INDEX

Korthion (Andros) 187
Kos 57, 92, 249-53
Kos (town) 251-2
Kotsinas (Lemnos) 278-9
Koufonisia 58, 199
Koukounaries (Skiathos) 327
Kouloundros 263
Kouloura (Corfu) 148
Kountouros (Kea) 195
Kouros of Samos 289
Kynouros 183
Kypriaka, Ta 52
Kyra Panaghia (Sporades) 323, 325
Kyrenia II 31
Kythera 33, 87, 92, 304-6
Kythnos 58, 197-8

Lagana (Zakynthos) 313-14
Lakkas (Paxi) 310
Lakki (Leros) 255
Lambi (Kos) 252
Lambi (Patmos) 261
language 9, 11, 70, 77-8
Laskari, Bouboulina 204
Lassi (Cephalonia) 300, 301
Lassithion prefecture (Crete) 173-4
laundry 128
Lausanne, Conference of 277-8
law 70-1
Lazareto 303
Lefka Mountains 164
Lefkas 13, 298, 306-9
Lefkas (town) 307
Lefkimi (Corfu) 147
Lefkos (Karpathos) 242
Leipsi 58, 253-4
Leipsi (town) 254
Lemnos 51, 267, 276-9
  travel to 57, 92, 279
Leros 92, 254-6
Lesbos 267, 279-83
  travel to 57, 92, 283
Levitha 183
licensing hours 115
Limena (Thassos) 320
Limenaria (Thassos) 320
Limni (Euboia) 295
Lindos (Rhodes) 159-60
Little Cyclades 198-200
Livadaki (Kythnos) 198
Livadi (Astipalaia) 237
Livadi (Serifos) 217
Livadia (Tilos) 264
Livanos, Stavros 37-8
Lixouri (Cephalonia) 300
loggerhead turtles 313-14
Loutra (Kythnos) 197, 198

Loutra (Nisyros) 257
Loutraki (Skopelos) 330
Lygia (Lefkas) 308

Magazia (Skyros) 335
Makri 303
Makryammou (Thassos) 321
Mallia (Crete) 176
Mandraki (Nisyros) 257
Mandrakia (Milos) 202
maps, history of 32
Marathos 253, 260
Marathounda (Simi) 263
marble 180, 210, 213
Marinatos, Spyridon 16, 225-6, 227
Marmara 263
Marmari (Kos) 252
marriage 62
massacres 285-6
Massouri (Kalymnos) 241
mastic gum 269-70
Mastihari (Kos) 252
Matala (Crete) 174, 176
Mavrogenous, Mando 204
medical advice 127
Megalo Hori (Tilos) 264
Megalonisi 263
Meganisi 309
Megas Yialos (Syros) 223
Megisti (Kastellorizon) 248
Meli (Patmos) 261
meltemi 82-3, 207-8
Menuhin, Yehudi 206
Merihas (Kythnos) 197
Mesaria (Thera) 229
Messaria (Andros) 187
Mesta (Chios) 272
Metaxas, Ioannis 23
Methimna (Lesbos) 282, 283
military dictatorship 46-7
Milopotamos (Ios) 192
Milos 15, 92, 200-2
Miltiades 213
Ministry of the Aegean 57, 280
Minoans 15-16, 29
  in Crete 168, 171-2
  in Paros 213
  in Thera 225-6
Minos 168
miracles 232
Mitsotakis, Constantine 49, 166
Molos (Skyros) 335
monasteries 194, 195, 201, 208, 211, 217, 219, 222, 237, 240-1, 244, 255, 257, 287, 290
  on Aegina 339
  on Anafi 183
  on Chios 270-1

  on Corfu 144
  on Crete 173, 176
  of Hozoviotissa 182
  of Kalamiotissa 183
  on Lefkas 307
  on Patmos 259-60
  on Skiathos 328
  on Skyros 333
  on Simi 264
  on Thassos 320, 321
  on Thera 229
  on Tilos 264
Mongonisi 311
Moni (off Aegina) 339
Montreux Convention 278
mosques 156, 159, 252
mosquitoes 100
Moudros (Lemnos) 278
mules 228, 326
museums 194, 196, 201, 219, 222, 233, 248, 255, 262, 280, 305, 307, 333
  Aegean Maritime Museum 29
  Archaeological museum, Corfu 144
  Archaeological museum, Crete 170
  Archaeological museum, Samos 289
  Athens Archaeological museum 16, 29, 226, 276
  Byzantine museum, Paros 214
  Byzantine museum, Zakynthos 313
  Chios museum 271
  Goulandris art museum 185
  Kos museum 252
  Museum of Art, Varia 282
  Museum of Asiatic Art, Corfu 144
  Museum of the Celebrities, Zakynthos 313
  Museum of the Occupation and National Resistance, Zakynthos 313
  Myconos Folk museum 203
  Myrina museum, Lemnos 278
  Naval museum, Oinoussa 284
  Philoppis Argentis folk museum 271
  Thassos archaeological museum 320
Mycenaeans 16-17, 211
Myconos 202-10
  gay bars on 75
  history of 203
  shopping on 122, 204

INDEX

travel to 92, 181, 209
where to eat on 209
where to stay on 208-9
Myconos (town) 203-5
Myrina (Lemnos) 278
Myrties (Kalymnos) 241
Mytilene (Lesbos) 51, 279, 280, 281-2

Nafplion 87
Naoussa (Paros) 214, 215
Napoleon I 174, 312
Napoleonic Wars 33
national costume, of Crete 166-7
National Tourist Organisation of Greece 95, 97, 99
Navarino, battle of 21, 286
Naxos 58, 180, 210-12
Nea Kameni (Thera) 227, 228-9
Nea Moni (Chios) 270-1
Nero, Emperor 19, 140
Neropida (Kos) 252
Niarchos, Stavros 344
Nidri (Lefkas) 307-8
Nikia (Nisyros) 257
Nikouria 183
Nimborio (Halki) 238
Nimos (Simi) 263
Nissaki (Corfu) 148
Nisyros 28, 31, 58, 256-8
North Aegean Islands 317-21
North Sporades Islands 323-35
nudist beaches 128-9, 161, 182, 192, 207, 232, 254, 334

Odysseus 29, 140, 302, 331
Oia (Thera) 229
oil exploration 50-1, 319
Oinoussa (town) 284
Oinousses islands 39, 58, 283-5
Olympic Airways 84, 87, 92
Onassis, Aristotle 40, 92, 307
Ormos (Ios) 191, 192
Ornos (Myconos) 208, 209
Othon, King of Greece 22, 139
ouzo 112
Oxia 263, 303

Palaiokastritsa (Corfu) 148-9
Palaiopoli (Andros) 187
Palaiopoli (Kythera) 305
Palea Kameni (Thera) 227, 229
Pali (Nisyros) 257, 258
Pan 310
Panaghia (off Paxi) 310, 311
Panaghia (Thassos) 320
Panaghia Kastraki (Kea) 195
Panormitis (Simi) 262

Panormos (Kalymnos) 241
Panteli (Leros) 255
Pantokrator, Mount 148
Papadiamantis, Alexandros 327
Papadopoulos, George 46, 47
Papandreou, Andreas 48
Papandreou, George 48
Paradisia (Amorgos) 182
Parikia (Paros) 213-14
Paros 180, 212-15
 accommodation on 214-15
 Church of Panaghia Ekatondapiliani 213-14
 travel to 92, 215
Paschos, Basil 225
Passas 284
passport requirements 125
Patitiri (Alonysos) 324
Patmos 57, 58, 258-61
Paul, Saint 19, 277
Paxi 309-11
Pedi (Simi) 263
Pelekas (Corfu) 149
Perahori (Ithaki) 303
Peraticos, Michael 37, 38
Pericles 18, 338
Peristera (Sporades) 323, 325
Peristeria (Salamis) 343
Perseus 217
Petaloudes (Rhodes) 160-1
Phaestos (Crete) 174, 176
pharmacies 127
Philerimos (Rhodes) 160
Philip II of Macedon 17, 318, 320
photography 129
Pidima 263
Pigadia (Karpathos) 242, 243
Piperi (Sporades) 323, 325
piracy 33-4, 201, 211
Piraeus 41
 ferries from 181
 history of 30, 34
Pisses (Kea) 195
Plaka (Milos) 201, 202
Platanos (Leros) 255
Platia 334
Plato 224
Platy Yialos (Myconos) 208
Platy Yialos (Sifnos) 219-20
Pnevmaticos, Michael 37
police 72-3
Poliochni (Lemnos) 277, 278
Poliorcetes, Dimitrios 154, 155
political parties 48-9
Polyaigos 197
Pondikonisi (Corfu) 145
Pontikos 303
population 14

population drift 59, 179-80, 245, 246, 286, 302
Poros 341-2
Poros (Cephalonia) 300
Porto Roma (Zakynthos) 314
Poseidon 257, 317
Posidonia (Syros) 223
post offices 129-30
Potamias (Thassos) 320
Potos (Thassos) 320-1
potteries 122, 219
Pounda (Paros) 214
Prassa (Kimolos) 196
Prassonissi 290
Prinos (Thassos) 321
Provati 303
Psara 58, 101, 285-7
Psara (town) 286-7
Psarrou (Myconos) 208
Psathi (Kimolos) 196
Psathoura (Sporades) 323, 325
Pserimos 243
Psili Ammos (Patmos) 261
Ptolemy 32
pubs 114-15
pumice stone 229-30
Pyrgos (Thera) 229
Pyrgos (Tinos) 233
Pythagoras 288
Pythagorian (Samos) 289

Rallis, George 49
religion 61-3
Renaissance 21
Repi (Sporades) 323
restaurants 106-7
Rethymnon (Crete) 170, 172-3, 175
retsina 113
Rhodes 141, 152-63
 accommodation on 162
 beaches on 161
 Byzantine Cathedral 157-8
 Colossus of 154-5
 folk dancing on 118, 163
 history of 20, 26, 154-6
 shopping on 121, 161-2
 travel to 57, 92, 163
 where to eat on 162-3
Rhodes Town 156-9
Ro (Kastellorizon) 247, 248
Roda (Corfu) 148
Romans, in Greece 19, 32, 140, 155
Roman remains 201, 237, 252, 294
Roumbas 269
Roussos, Fotis 147
rugs 121, 162
Russians, in the Cyclades 180

INDEX

Salamis, 33, 342–3
Salamis, battle of 30, 338
Saliangos 217
Samaria Gorge (Crete) 173, 176
Sami (Cephalonia) 300
Samiopoula 290
Samos 31, 51, 57, 92, 267, 287–90
Samos (town) 288–9
Samothrace 51, 58, 278, 317–19
Santorini *see* Thera
Sappho 280–1, 308
Sarakiniko 332, 334
Saria (Karpathos) 242
Saronic Islands 90, 337–44
Sartzetakis, Christos 166
Schinousa 58, 199
Schliemann, Heinrich 16, 205, 303
Selinia (Salamis) 343
Serifos 58, 217–18
Seskli (Simi) 263
Severin, Tim 29
shipping industry 35–9, 40–2
ships
  history of 28, 29, 31, 34–5
  on Kassos 244
shopping 120–2, 123
Sidari (Corfu) 148
siesta 130
Sifnos 58, 218–20
Sigri (Lesbos) 282
Sikia (Milos) 201
Sikinos 58, 220–1
Simi 58, 261–3
Sitia (Crete) 170, 173–4, 175, 176
Skala (Patmos) 260
Skalkotas, Nikos 232
Skandia (Kythera) 305
Skantzoura (Sporades) 323, 325
Skiathos 33, 323, 326–9
  travel to 87, 92, 328
Skiathos (town) 327
Skiropoula (Sporades) 323
Skopelos 33, 87, 323, 329–31
Skorpios 307–8
Skyros 33, 87, 92, 331–6
Skyros (town) 333
smoking 130–1
social conditions, post-war 44–6
Solomos, Dionysios 286, 298, 312
souvenirs (*see also* jewellery; rugs) 120–2, 332, 339
Sparta 17
Spetses 343–4
Spetsopoula 344
Spinalonga (Crete) 176

sponges 239–40
springs 198, 241, 250–1, 257, 274, 275, 294
Spyridon, Bishop of Cyprus
Stavros (Ithaki) 303–4
Steni Vala (Alonysos) 324
Stenies (Andros) 186–7
Stratou, Dora 116, 117
Strofades Islands 315
Strongili 248
Suleiman the Magnificent 15
swimming 83
Syros 39, 58, 181, 221–3
  history of 34–5

tavernas 104–6
Telendos 243
telephones 131
Tenedos 278
terrorism 76
Thassopoula 321
Thassos 319–21
Themistocles 30
Theologos (Thassos) 320
Theotokopoulos, Domenico *see* El Greco
Thera (Santorini) 224–31
  accommodation on 101, 230
  history of 16, 224
  travel to 92, 181, 230
Therasia (Thera) 228–9
Therma (Ikaria) 275
Therma (Samothrace) 318–19
Theseus 168, 210, 332
Tilos 58, 264–5
time differences 131–2
time-shares 102
Tingaki (Kos) 252
Tinos 180, 181, 231–3
Tinos (town) 231–2
tipping 132–3
toilets 133
Tombras, Michael 185
tourism
  development of 64–5
  impact of 65–6, 71, 326
Tourlos (Myconos) 208
travel 84–90
travellers' cheques 124
Treis Boukes 332
triremes 30
Troumpeto 263
Tselemendes, Nikos 219
Tsoungria (Sporades) 323
Turkey, relations with 51–2
Turkika, Ta 50–2, 276, 277–8
Turkish occupation 20–1, 156, 168, 213, 235, 244, 263, 288

Valaxa 334
Valley of the Butterflies (Paros) 214
Valley of the Butterflies (Rhodes) 160–1
Vareloudi 290
Vari (Syros) 223
Varia (Lesbos) 282
Vassiliki (Lefkas) 308
Vassilikos (Zakynthos) 314
Vathi (Ithaki) 303
Vathi (Kalymnos) 241
Vathy (Astipalaia) 237
Vathy (Samos) 288–9
Vathy (Sifnos) 220
Venetians
  in Corfu 140
  in Crete 170, 173
  in the Cyclades 180, 211, 222, 231
  in Greece 20, 25–6, 297
  in the Ionian Islands 297
Venizelos, Eleftherios 18, 22, 166, 173
Venus de Milo 201
Vlachernai (Corfu) 145
Vlachou, Helen 46
volcanoes 228–9, 256–7, 276
Volimes (Zakynthos) 314
Volissos (Chios) 272
Vothonas (Thera) 229
voting systems 49–50
Votsi (Alonysos) 325
Vourkari (Kea) 195
Vromonas 303
Vrontada (Chios) 272

water 112, 250–1
welfare state 60
wildlife 133
Wilhelm II, Kaiser 146
wine 112–14
  from Cephalonia 301
  from Corfu 150–1
  from Thera 229
women
  rights of 60–1
  travelling alone 74–5
World War II 23–4, 232, 235–6, 327, 328
  Corfu in 140–1
  Crete in 169
  Kos in 249
  Simi in 262

yachting 93–4
Yiali 257, 258
Yialos (Simi) 262

INDEX

Yialyssas (Syros) 223
Yioura (Sporades) 323, 325
youth hostels 101

Zagora (Andros) 185–6
Zakynthos 92, 298, 311–15
Zakynthos (town) 313

Zeus 168, 188
Zia, Mount (Naxos) 211
Zorba the Greek 118, 173